AF531093

# Wildlife Photographer of the Year

## PORTFOLIO FIVE

*Designer*
GRANT BRADFORD

*Editor*
CATHY WRIGHT

*Project Co-ordinator*
SHEELAGH COGHLAN

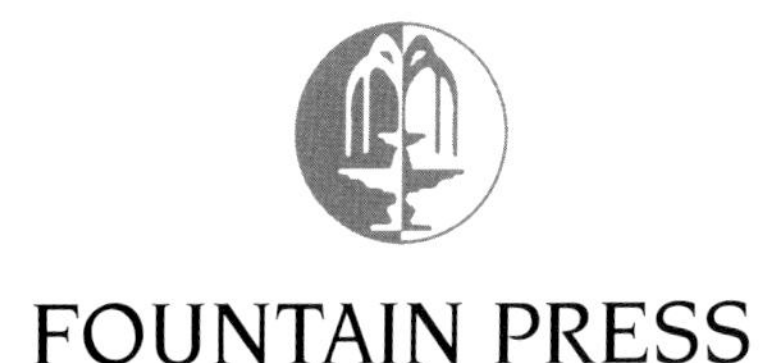

FOUNTAIN PRESS

*Published by*
FOUNTAIN PRESS LIMITED
*Fountain House*
*2 Gladstone Road*
*Kingston-upon-Thames*
*Surrey* KT1 3HD
*England*

---



*Picture Editor*
*Design & Layout*
*Grant Bradford*

*Editor*
*Cathy Wright*

*Captions*
*Helen Gilks, Cathy Wright, and Stephen Young*

*Project Co-ordinator*
*Sheelagh Coghlan*

*Editorial Consultant*
*Joseph Meehan*

*Print Consultant*
*Roger Multon*

*Colour Origination*
*Eray Scan - Singapore*

*Printing & Binding*
*Star Standard*
*Singapore*

ISBN 0 86343 396 0

# Contents

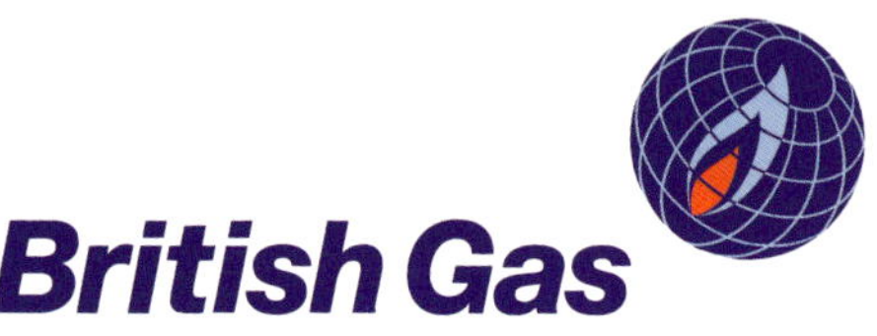


# Wildlife Photographer of the Year

## 1995

"There can be few competitions which, after 12 highly successful years, manage to break all records and attract an increase in entries of 46 per cent on the previous year. Such is the esteem in which the Wildlife Photographer of the Year Competition is held.

In this, the sixth year of our association with the competition, it has been especially pleasing to witness the participation of photographers from countries - such as the Czech Republic and Trinidad - where we have an increasing presence as a global company.

The photographs in this year's collection beautifully illustrate their creators' commitment to quality and to the environment, aspirations which British Gas is proud to share. As an energy industry with operations world-wide, we too are committed to excellence and have a long tradition of environmental responsibility.

It has been a privilege to be involved again."

*Cedric H Brown*
*Chief Executive, British Gas*

# Foreword

*Alauda arvensis* and *Turdus ericetorum*, the skylark and the song thrush, two common birds, essence of the English countryside, are getting rarer. Their British populations slashed in half by changing land-use practice. The Siberian tiger is heading for extinction thanks to poaching. All 17 of the world's so-called 'fish boxes' are now being over-fished and nine are in collapse. Wherever we care to look, habitat destruction and species extinction stare us in the camera lens.

However the saddest news of the year was the death of Gerry Durrell, the man whose untiring work has steered the overcrowded ark across the seas of destruction, and given hope to so many species and inspiration to so many workers in the world of conservation.

Thanks in part to his books, the zoo in Jersey and to all the wildlife photographers of the world, the eyes of more and more people are being opened to the wonders of creation. The tide of destruction is being turned. Great international corporations are putting their houses in green order, and more and more local governments and groups are responding to the challenges of Agenda 21, the agreement reached at Rio to fully integrate conservation principles at a grass roots level, involving local people. There is much good news in the world.

Bright lights are at the end of countless tunnels, and many have been captured on film by this year's winners. It is therefore fitting that a new award, 'The Gerald Durrell Award for Endangered Wildlife', has been included in the prize list, named after who else but our own modern Noah. I am glad the Bible tells us there are animals in heaven and I hope, for St Peter's sake, that none of them, not even the cockatrice or the asp, are in danger.

**David Bellamy**
*Bedburn* 1995

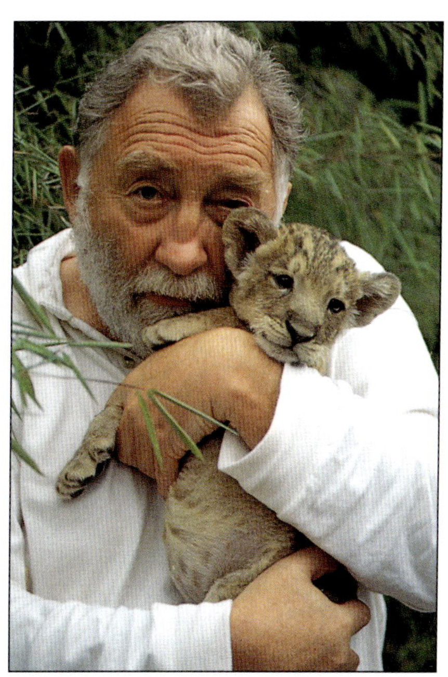

*Photograph: London Zoo*

# Introduction

This book displays the winning and commended images from the 1995 Wildlife Photographer of the Year Competition, which has been organised for the twelfth year by BBC WILDLIFE Magazine and The Natural History Museum, London, and sponsored for the sixth year by British Gas.

The competition aims to find the best wildlife pictures taken by photographers worldwide, and through these images to emphasise the beauty, wonder and importance of the natural world. This year the number of entries received by the competition increased from 12,000 to an amazing 17,500 slides from photographers in 57 different countries - demonstrating the worldwide passion for wildlife.

Photographs, which had to be colour slides, were entered in 14 different categories which each carried a first prize of £1,000 and a runner-up prize of £500. Where competition was particularly fierce, the judges awarded a specially commended, or third prize. Some of the photos that reached the final stages of the judging were highly commended. In addition, the Eric Hosking Award was given for the best portfolio of pictures by a photographer aged under 27 years. The Gerald Durrell Award for Endangered Wildlife was introduced this year to commemorate Gerald Durrell's long-standing involvement with the competition and his work with endangered species. There was also a special competition for photographers aged 17 years and under.

The winners gathered at The Natural History Museum in October for an awards ceremony compèred by Barry Paine, with prizes presented by a cast of celebrities from the fields of natural history, conservation and wildlife photography. They included David Bellamy, Julian Pettifer, Tony Soper, Bill Oddie, Chris Baines, Philippa Scott, Simon King, Nick Davies and Chris Packham. This awards ceremony marked the opening of the exhibition of winning and commended images at The Natural History Museum where it is on display for four months. Two further exhibitions tour the UK visiting some 24 different galleries, museums and nature centres. Additional exhibitions go on display in Australia, France, Germany, Holland, Japan and the USA.

## THE JUDGES

**Bruce Pearson**
Wildlife artist
and photographer

**Heather Angel**
Wildlife photographer

**Dr Giles Clarke**
Head of Exhibitions and
Education at The Natural
History Museum

**Rosamund Kidman Cox**
Editor, BBC Wildlife
Magazine

**Pedro Silmon**
Art Director, The Sunday
Times Magazine

**Jonathan Scott**
Wildlife expert
and photographer

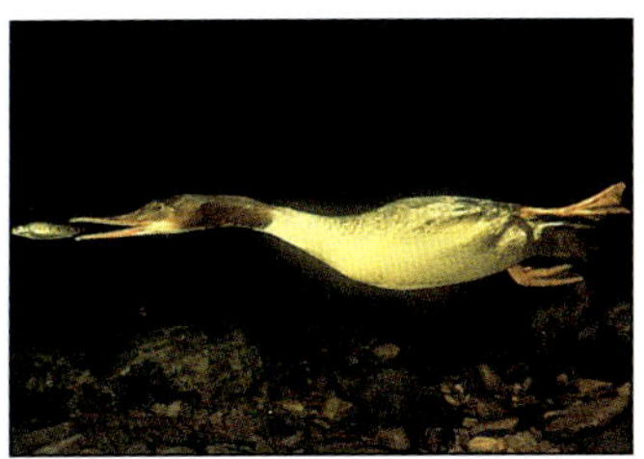

**1984**
**Richard & Julia Kemp**
United Kingdom

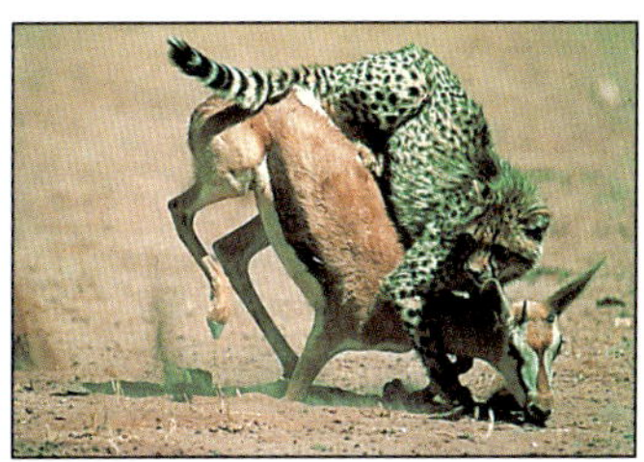

**1985**
**Charles G Summers Jnr.**
United States of America

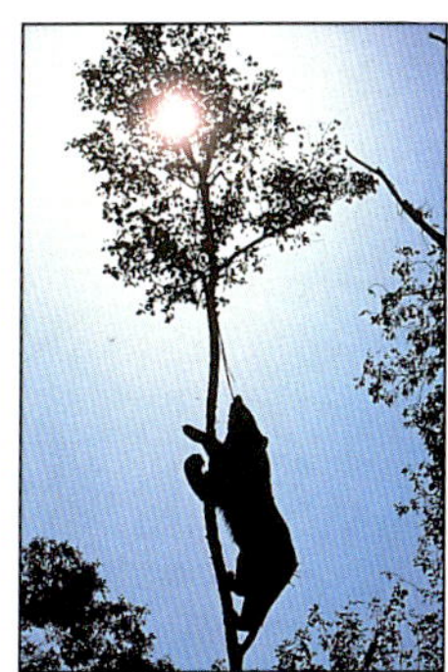

**1986**
**Rajesh Bedi**
India

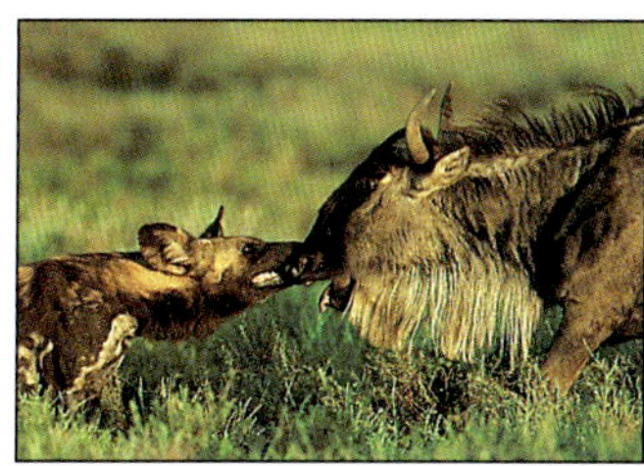

**1987**
**Jonathan Scott**
United Kingdom

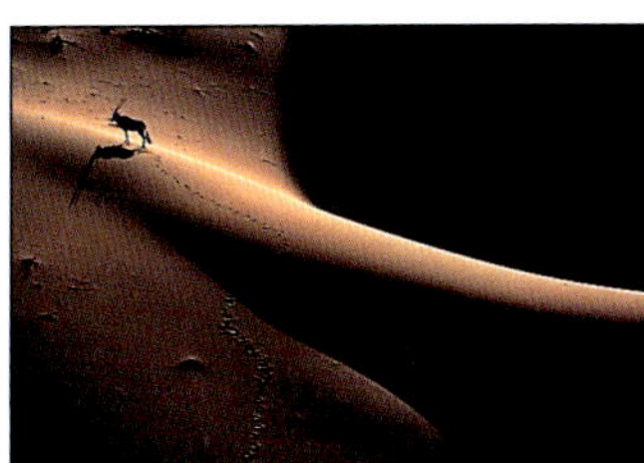

**1988**
**Jim Brandenburg**
United States of America

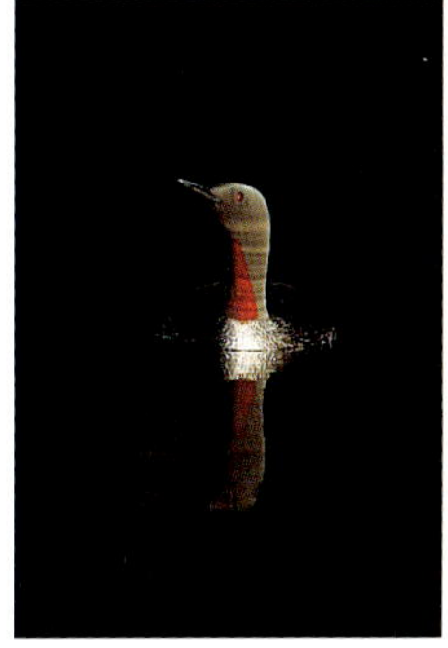

**1989**
**Jouni Ruuskanen**
Finland

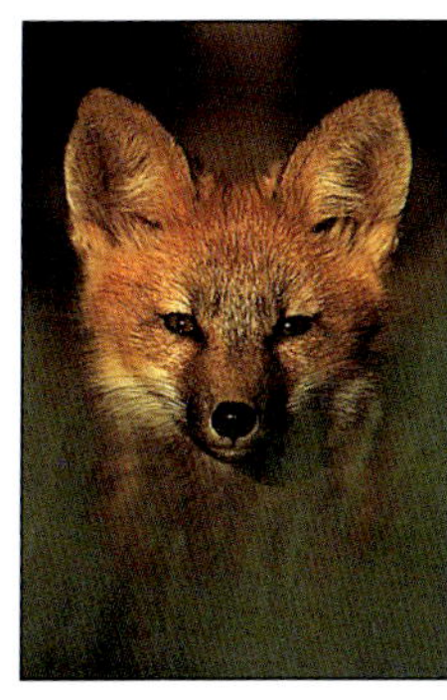

**1990**
**Wendy Shattil**
United States of America

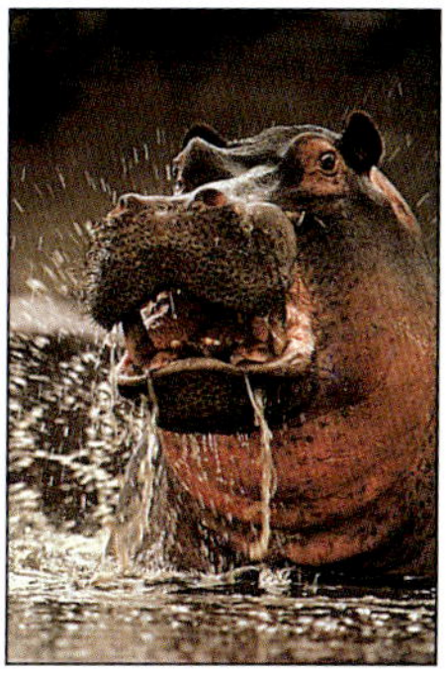

**1991**
**Frans Lanting**
The Netherlands

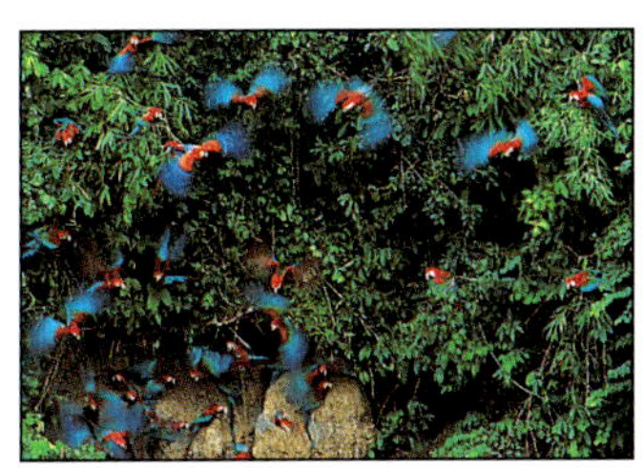

**1992**
**André Bärtschi**
Liechtenstein

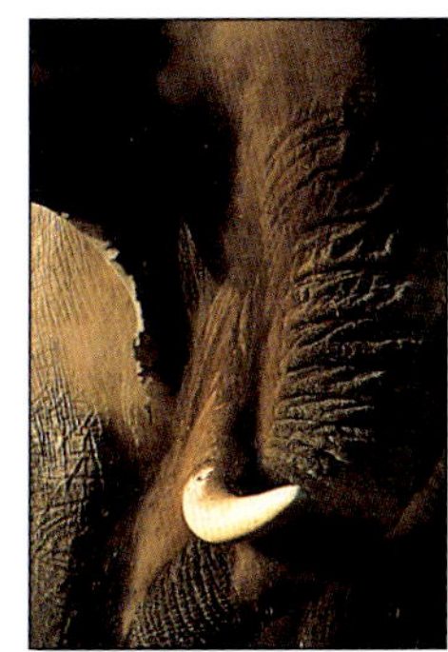

**1993**
**Martyn Colbeck**
United Kingdom

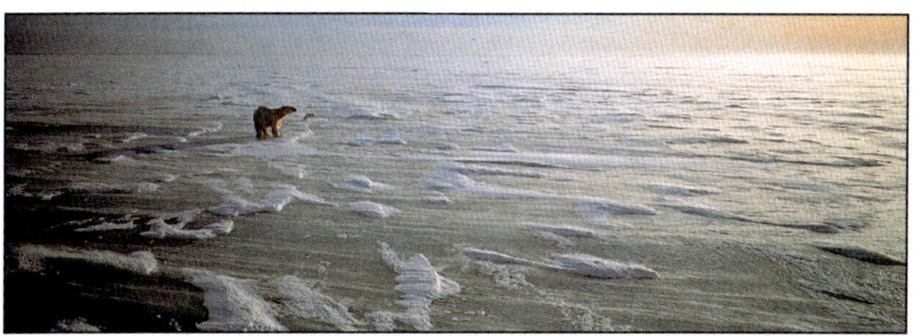

**1994**
**Thomas D Mangelsen**
United States of America

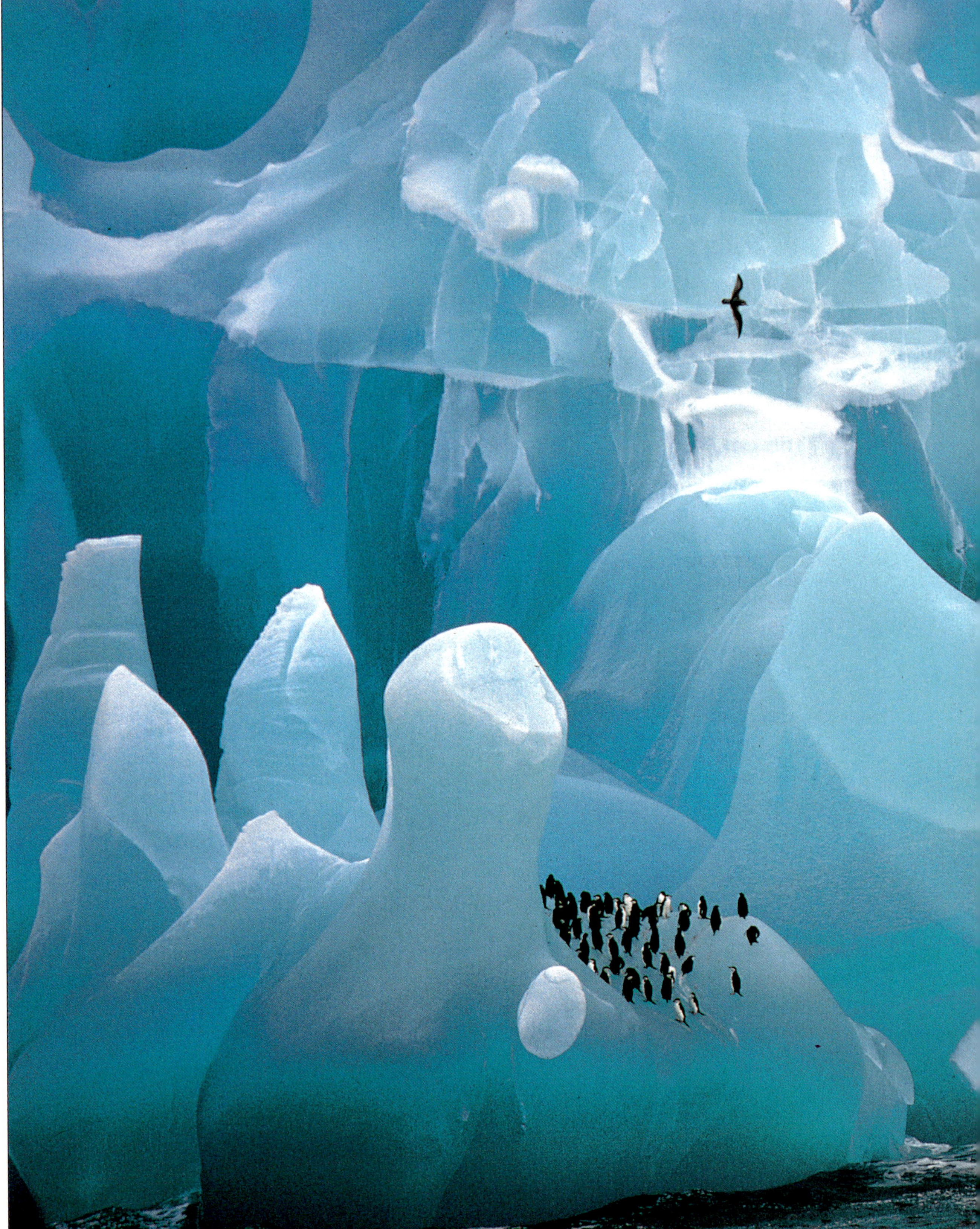

**Cherry Alexander**
United Kingdom
WILDLIFE PHOTOGRAPHER OF THE YEAR 1995

**Blue iceberg, Antarctica**

*"Blue icebergs are thought to consist of ancient, compressed ice that absorbs all light except the blue, and they are very rare. I was off the coast of Zovodovski Island, one of the South Sandwich Islands, when this particularly sculptural one came into view. We had seen a blue iceberg the day before and another photographer, while exposing miles of film, had commented that it wasn't quite perfect because there were no penguins on it. When we found this bigger one less than 12 hours later, none of us could believe our luck."*

Canon T90 with 80-200mm lens; Kodachrome 64

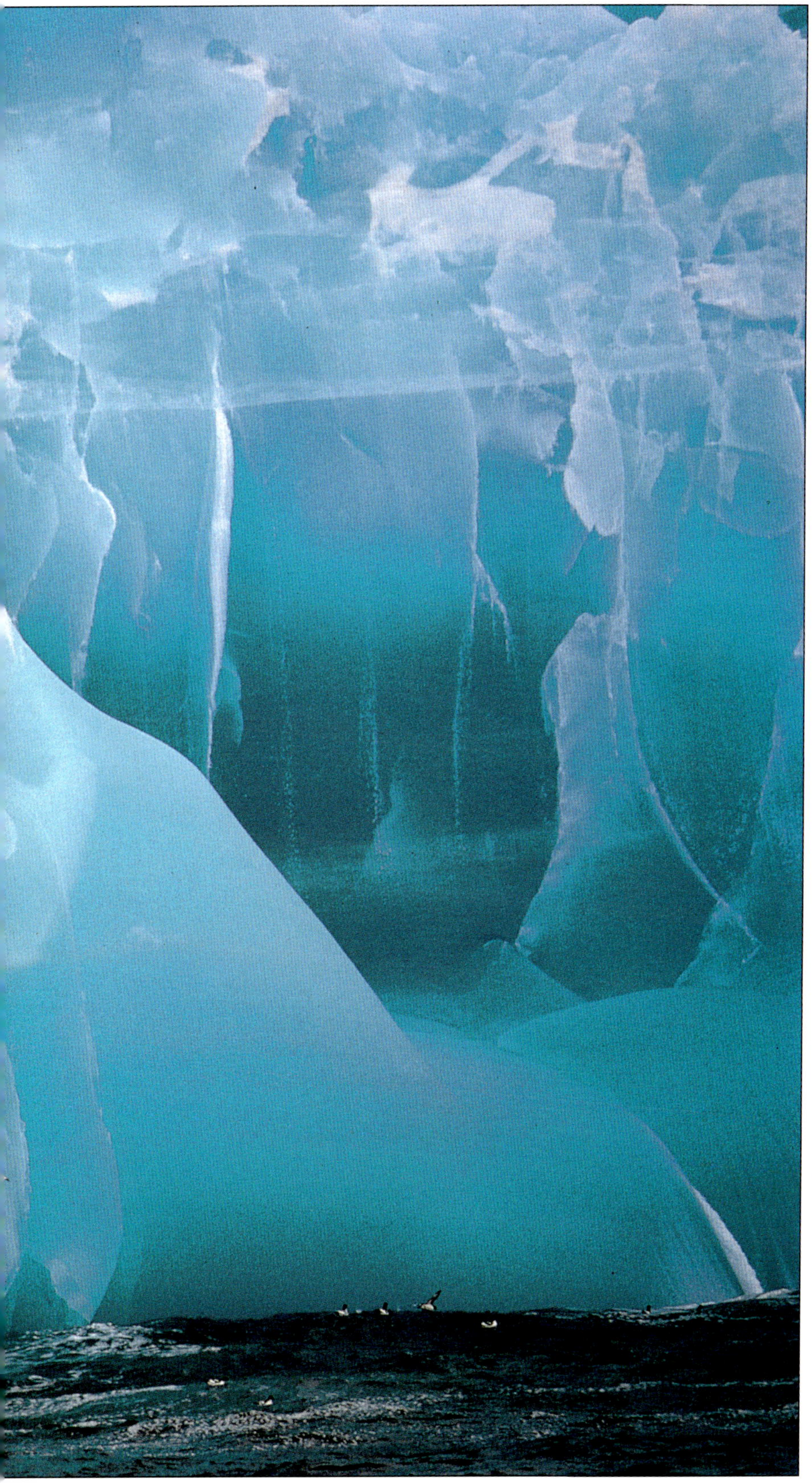

# Wildlife Photographer of the Year

The 'Wildlife Photographer of the Year' title was awarded for the single image judged to be the most striking and memorable of all the photographs entered for the competition. The 1995 winner, Cherry Alexander, received the British Gas award – a bronze trophy of an ibis and a cheque for £2,000.

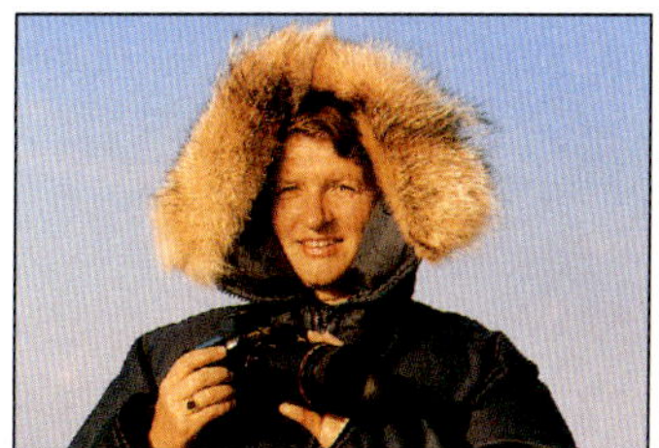

**Cherry Alexander**

By the time she was 12, Cherry Alexander was processing colour films in her father's darkroom, and the three-year photography course at the London College of Printing seemed the logical step when she left school. In 1974 she got hooked on the Arctic during a three-month stint photographing the Saami people in Northern Norway with husband Bryan, and a joint trip to North Greenland to photograph the Inuit followed. In recent years, she has tended to undertake the polar bear and wildlife shoots while Bryan concentrates on working with indigenous peoples, though they have also worked on many joint shoots for Smithsonian Magazine. Cherry Alexander now spends most of the year running their photo library, but still fits in trips to Iceland, Norway and, in 1994, when her winning shot was taken, to Antarctica, "which was even more extraordinary than I had anticipated."

# Animal Behaviour

## - MAMMALS -

The photographs entered in this category should show the subject actively doing something. Pictures are judged on their interest value as well as their aesthetic appeal.

**Richard du Toit**
South Africa
WINNER

***Female leopards fighting***

*"It only lasted a few seconds. The dominant female (the one on top) suddenly attacked, raking with her hind legs and ripping out pieces of white fur. Her opponent assumed a submissive pose, lying on her back. The fight was extremely fast moving, with savage snarls and growls. We watched them for another hour as darkness fell over the Mala Mala Game Reserve, but they stayed at least 10 metres apart."*

Nikon F-801s with 300mm lens; beanbag; 1/125 sec at f4; Fujichrome Velvia

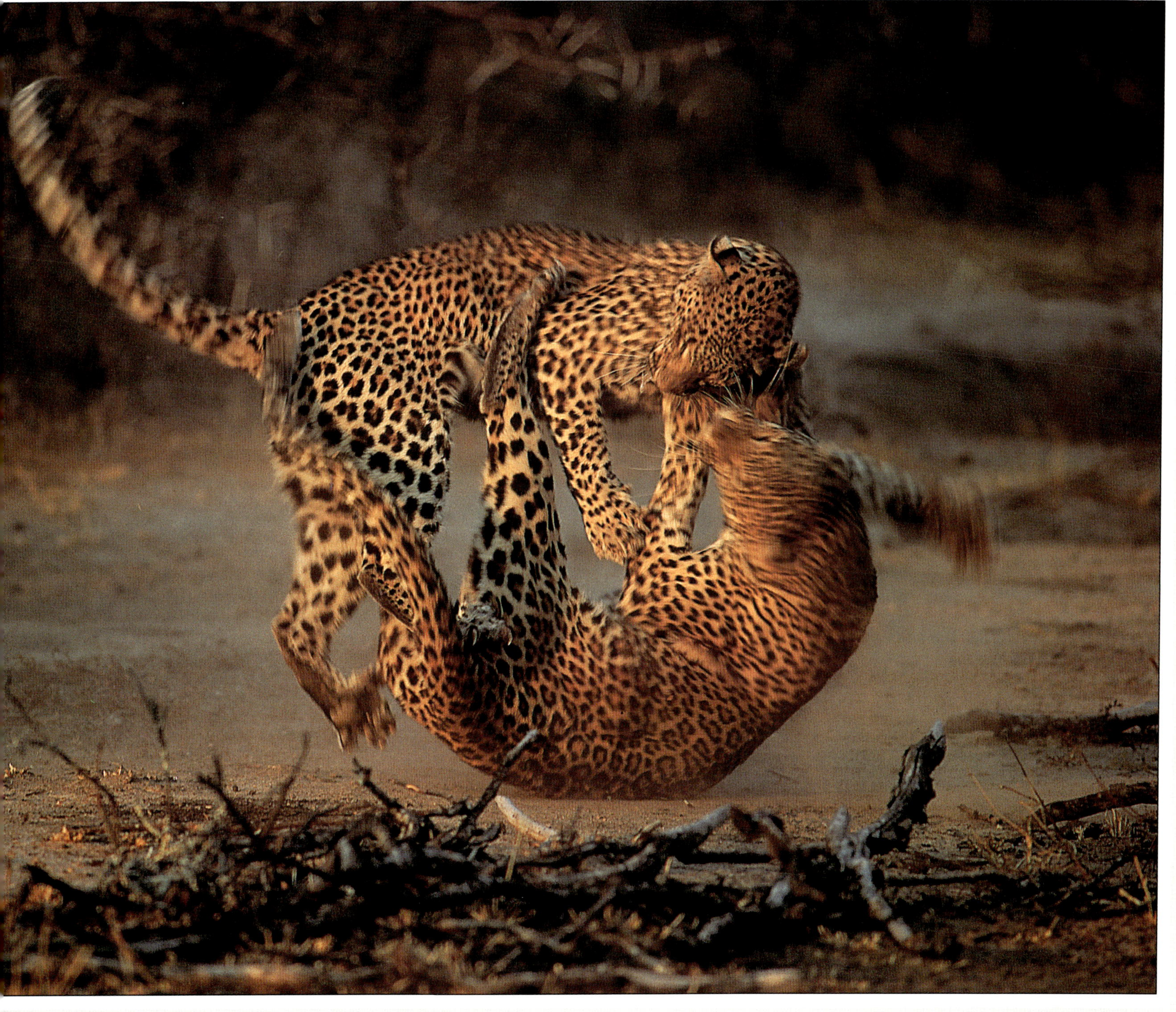

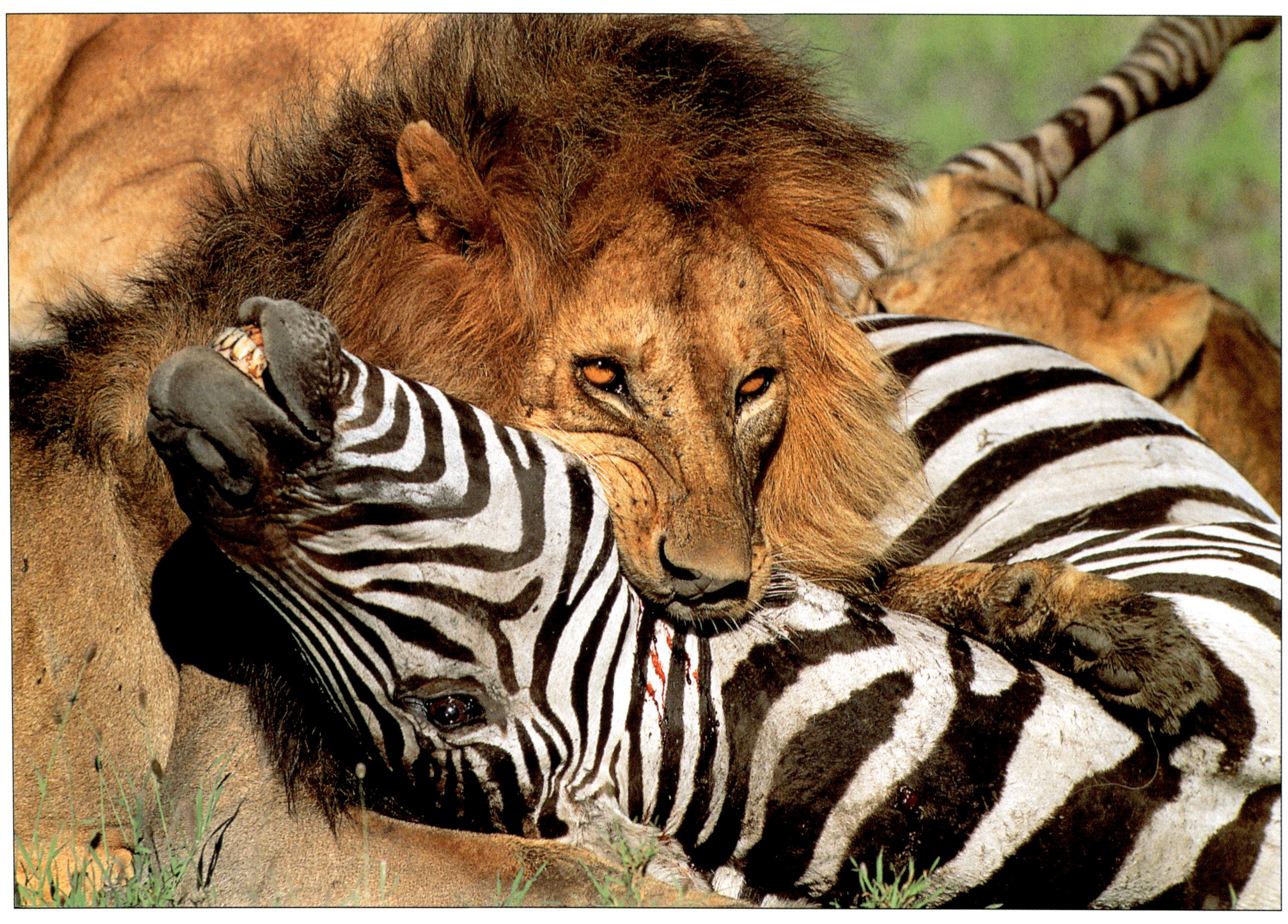

**Kevin Schafer**
United States of America
RUNNER-UP

***Male lion killing zebra***

*"I watched as a pack of Serengeti lions stalked a pair of zebras, who were feeding calmly. Suddenly the lions broke into a run and the male brought down one of the zebras. When I took the picture the zebra was still alive, but the female lions had already started to feed."*

Nikon F4 with 500mm lens; 1/250 sec at f5.6; Fujichrome Velvia

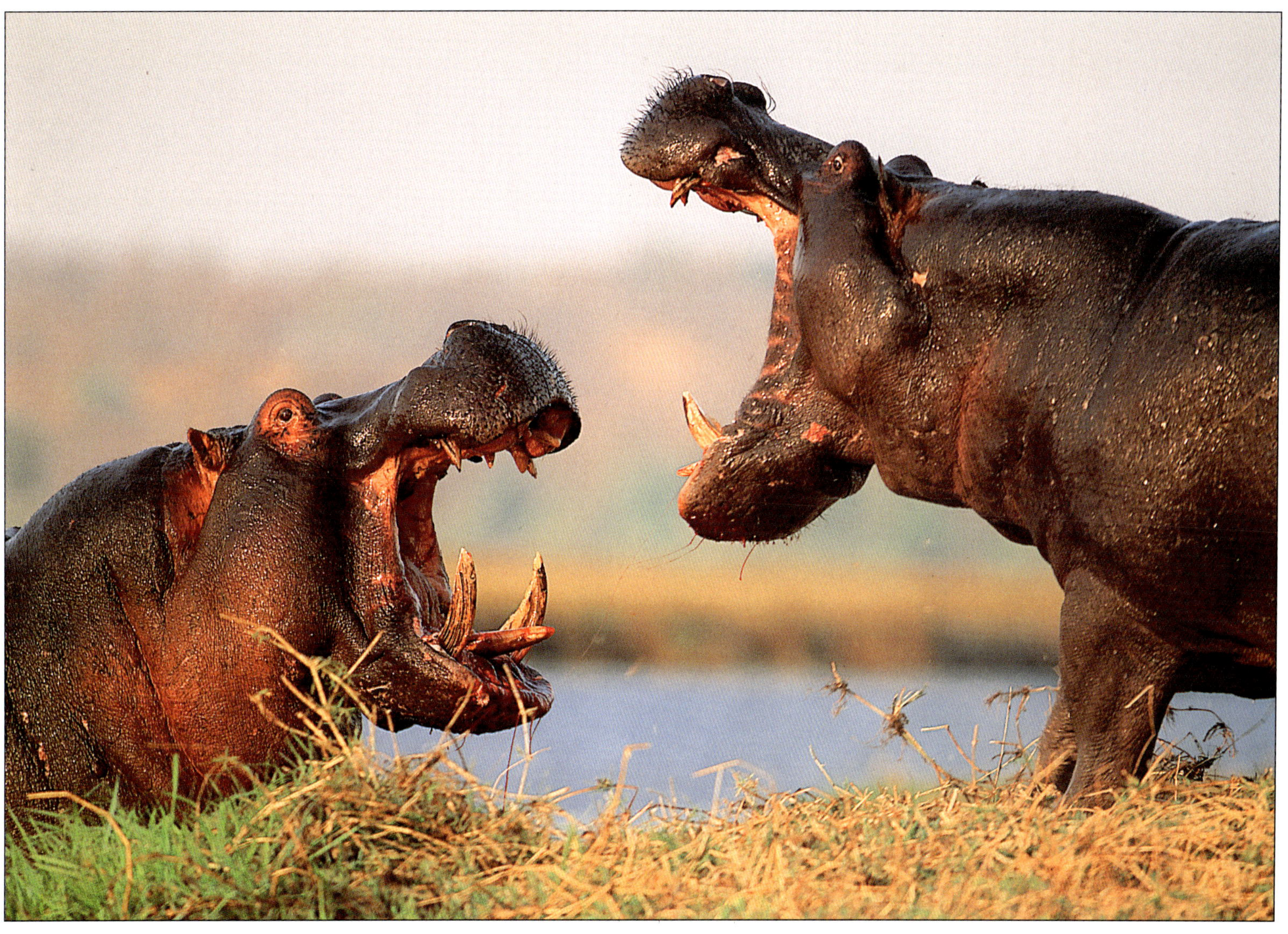

**Warren K Corning**
United States of America
HIGHLY COMMENDED

---

**_Hippopotamus fighting_**

*"We were in a small boat on the Chobe River, Botswana, when we saw two hippopotamus on the river bank squaring up for a fight. They reared high on their hind legs as they attacked, then they moved into the water. My camera was mounted on a tripod in the front of the boat, but the boat was rocking and only a couple of shots were perfectly sharp. The animal on the right was the eventual winner of the battle."*

---

Nikon F4 with 500mm lens; tripod; 1/125 sec at f4; Fujichrome Velvia

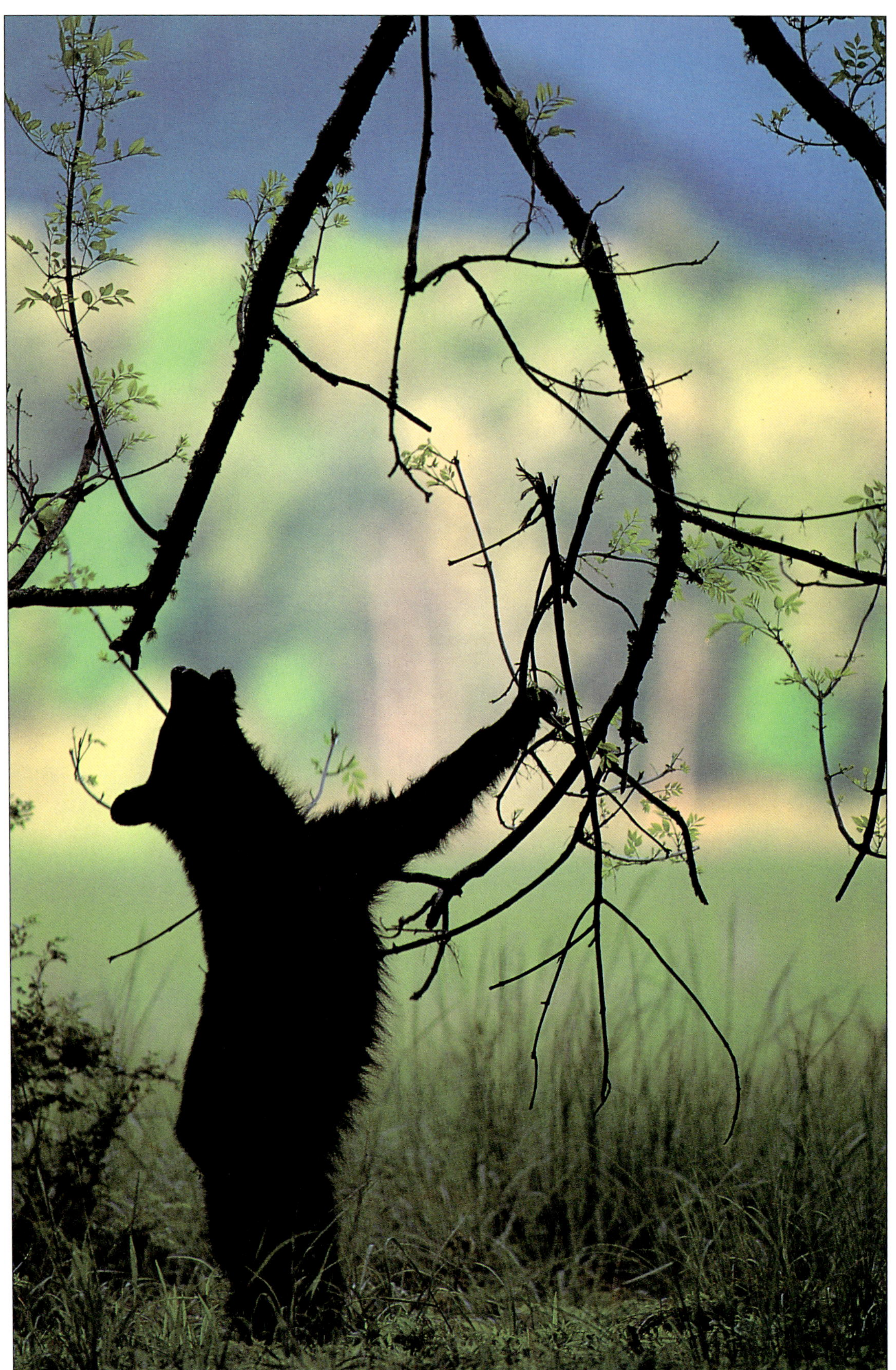

**Stephen Kirkpatrick**

United States of America

HIGHLY COMMENDED

### *Black bear cub feeding*

*"I had been following a black bear sow and her three cubs for several days in the Great Smoky Mountains National Park, Tennessee. One afternoon, this cub stayed on the ground while the others climbed the tree to feed. As he stood to reach for a branch, he was silhouetted against the rich colours of late evening. I knew then that, if it came out, it would be a great shot."*

Nikon F4 with 400mm lens; 1/60 sec at f3.5; Fujichrome Velvia

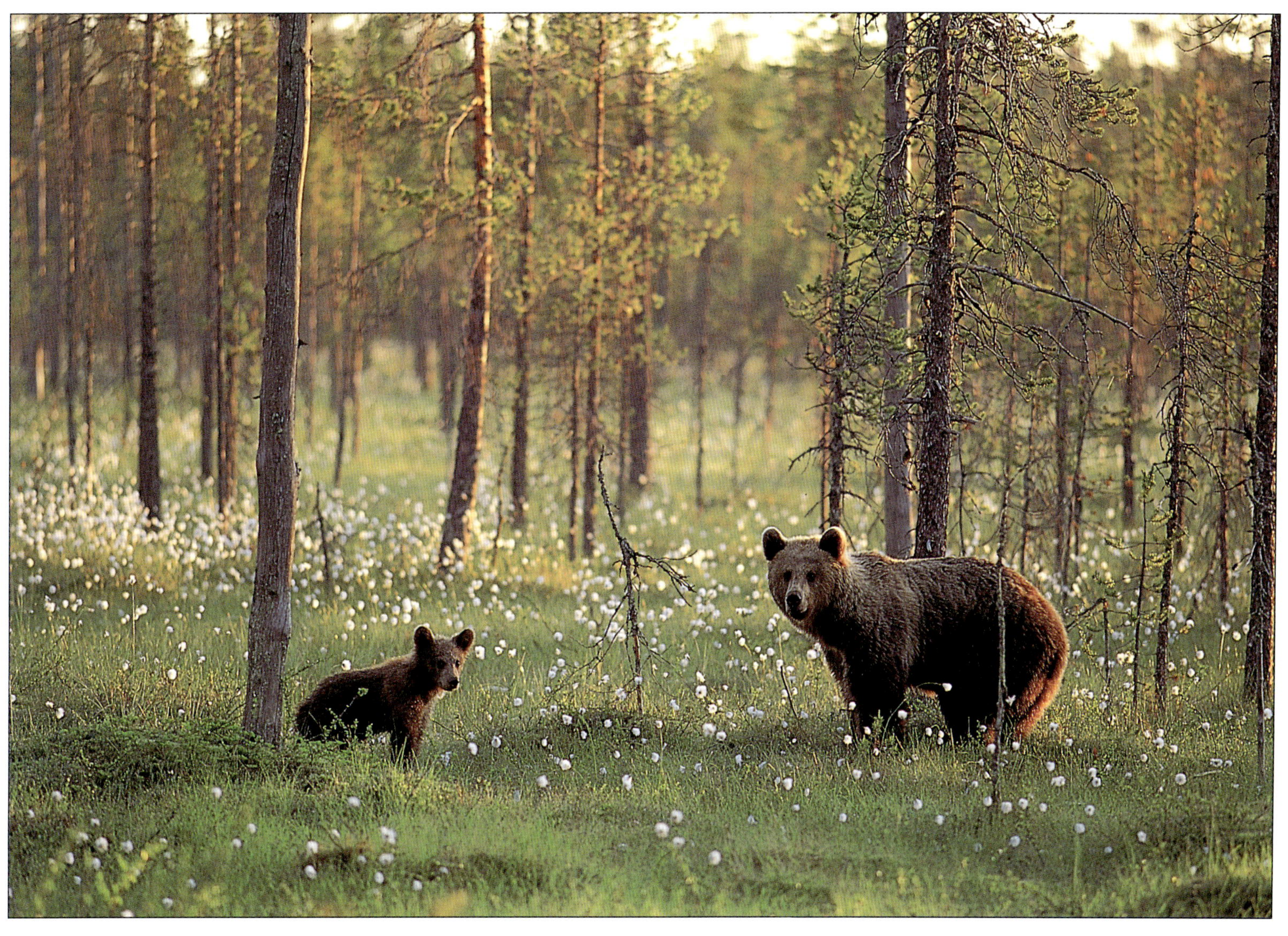

**Antti Leinonen**
Finland
HIGHLY COMMENDED

***Brown bear and cub***

*"In Finland, mother bears are very cautious when they are raising their cubs. If they suspect human presence, they keep well away. But early one morning, I was lucky enough to get the mother and her cub to approach my hide. It was the first time I had seen the cub."*

Canon EOS 100 with 200mm lens; hide; 1/125 sec at f2.8; Fujichrome Velvia

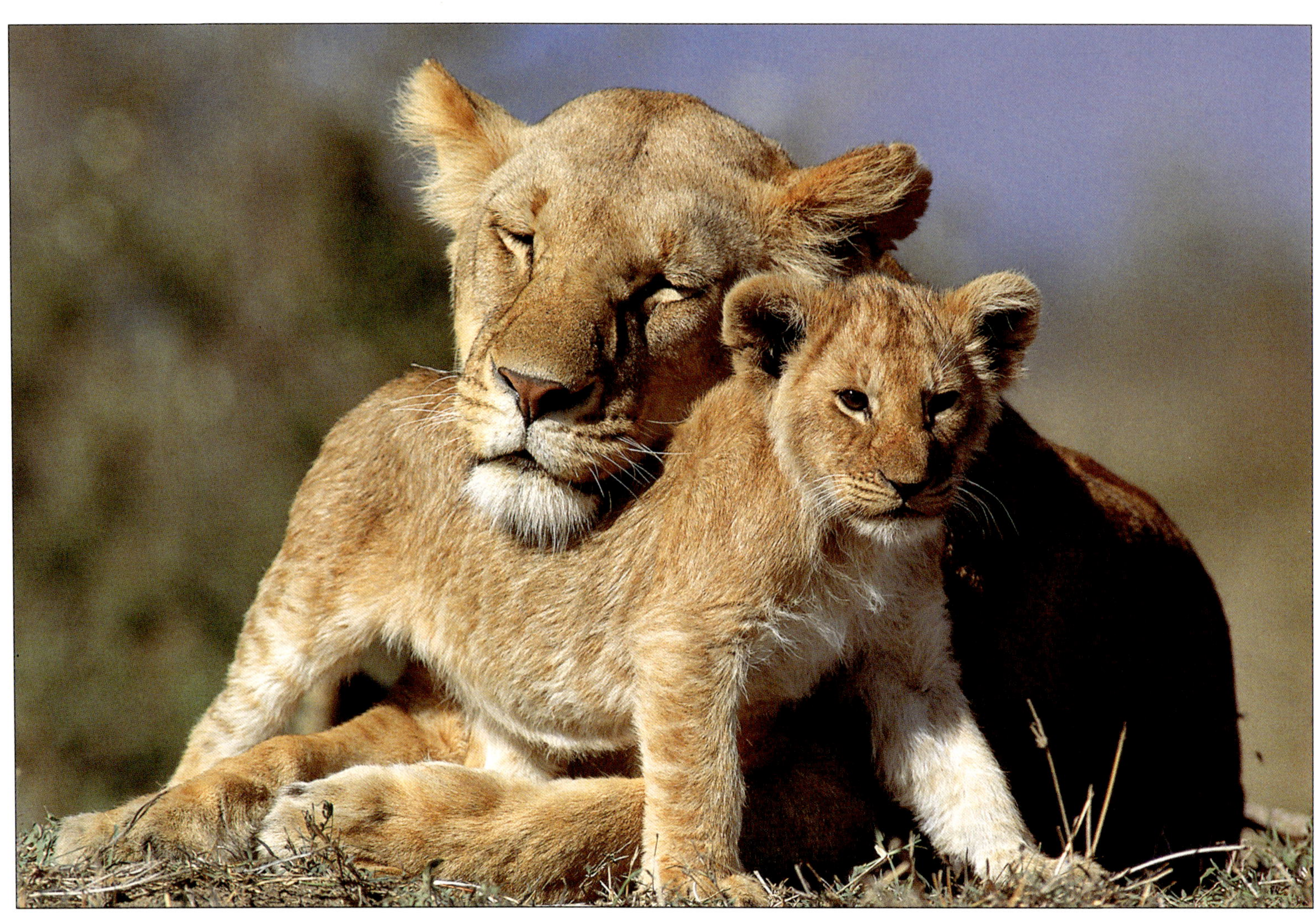

**Fritz Pölking**
Germany
HIGHLY COMMENDED

***Lioness and cub***

*"I took this photograph to show a very emotional interaction between mother and cub. It was taken in the Maasai Mara, Kenya."*

Nikon F4 with 600mm lens; auto-exposure at f4; Fujichrome 50

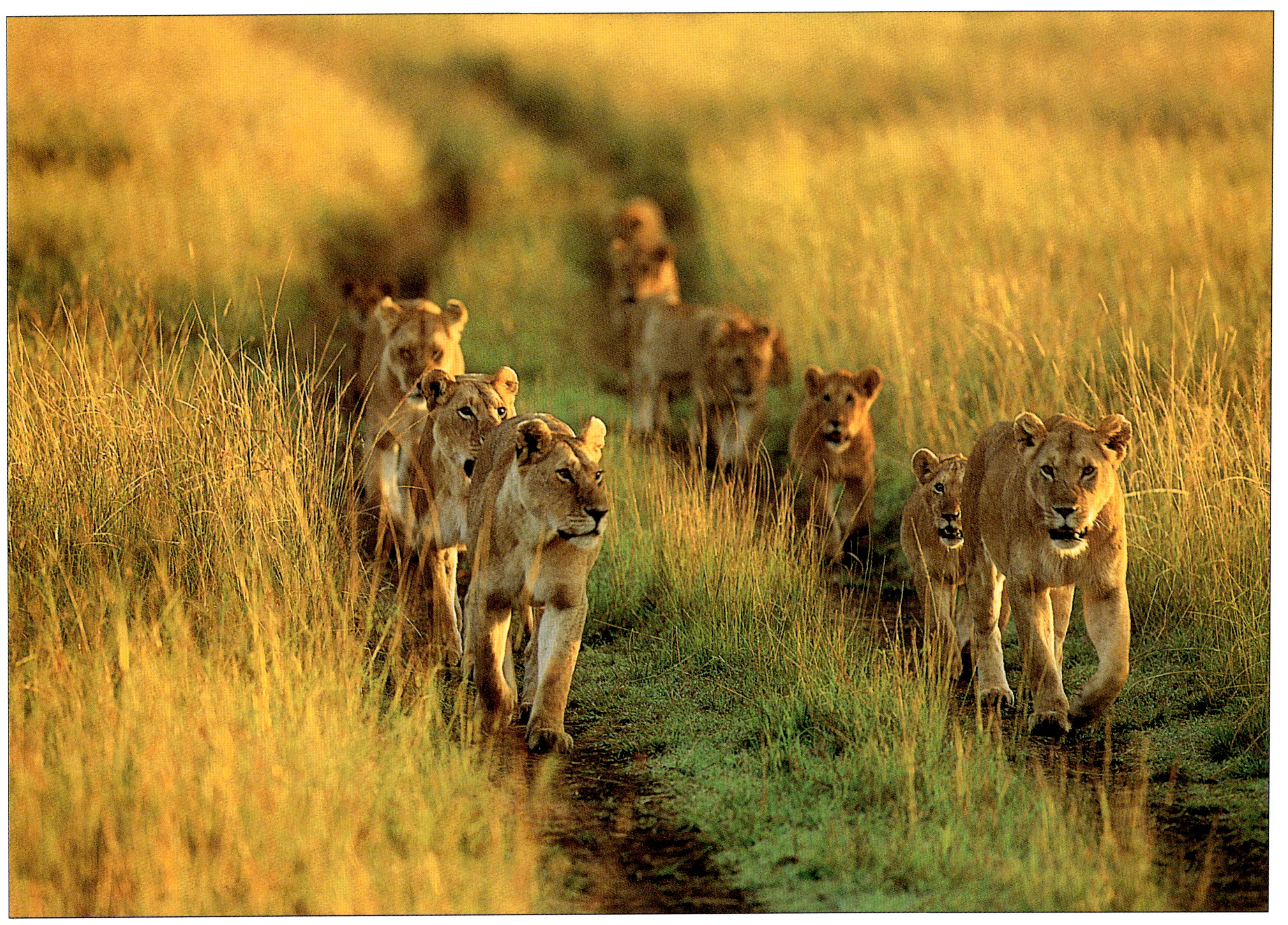

**Gabriela Staebler**
Germany
HIGHLY COMMENDED

***Lion pride on track***

*"We had been watching this pride - four adult females and seven cubs - for three weeks in the Maasai Mara, Kenya. One morning, the light turned the dew-wet grass into glittering gold as the pride walked fast towards a big desert date tree to spend the hot day in the shade."*

Canon EOS1 with 300mm lens; clamp-table tripod; beanbag; 1/125 sec at f4.5; Fujichrome Velvia

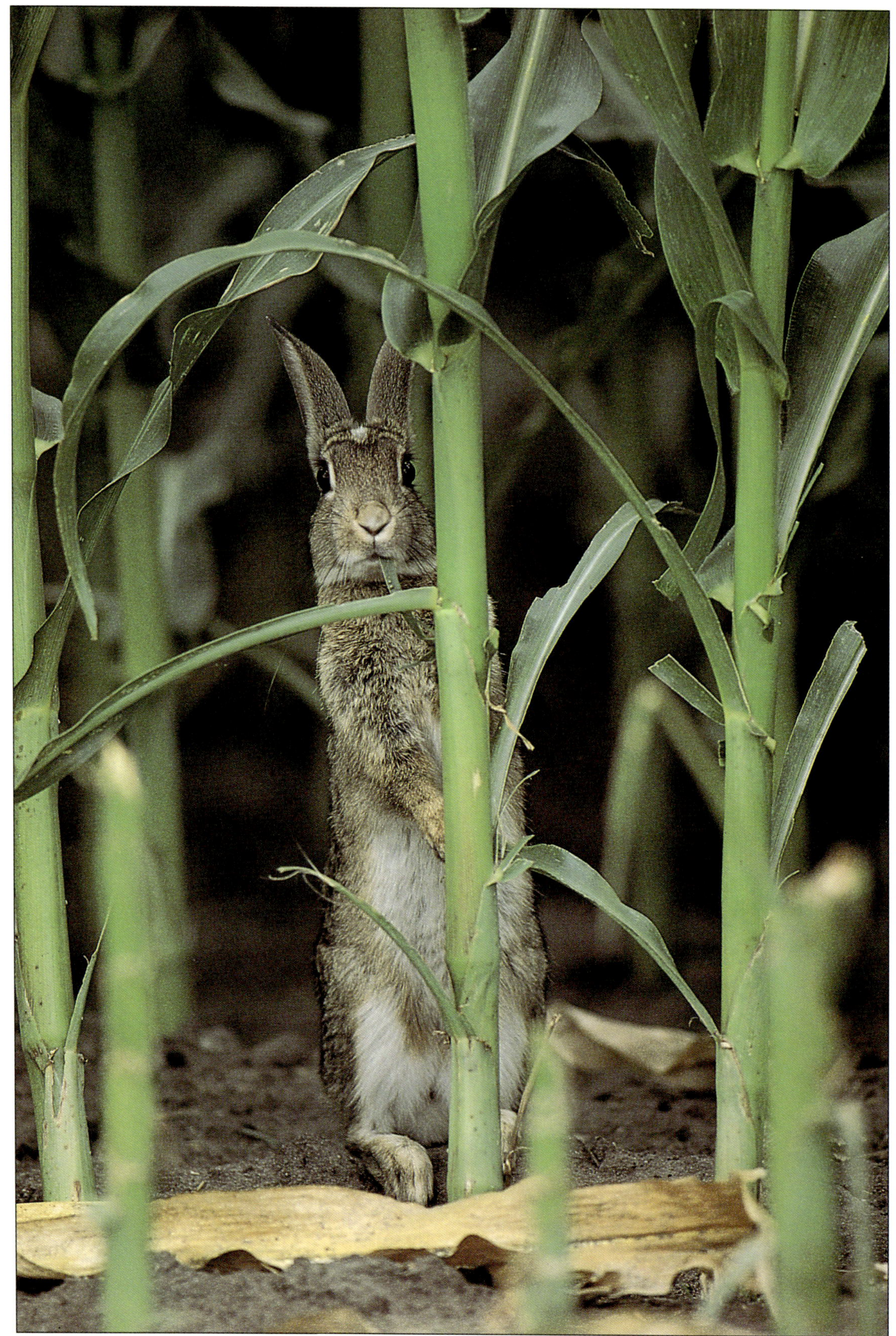

**Heidi & Hans-Jürgen Koch**
Germany
HIGHLY COMMENDED

**_Wild rabbit in cornfield_**

*"We were photographing wild rabbits for a German magazine, not an easy task, because although common, rabbits are extremely shy and always on the alert. Rabbits eating corn was one idea we hoped to realise. It took several days in a hide at the edge of a cornfield near our hometown of Cuxhaven, in northern Germany, to get the shot we wanted."*

Nikon F4s with 500mm lens; tripod; Kodachrome Professional 64

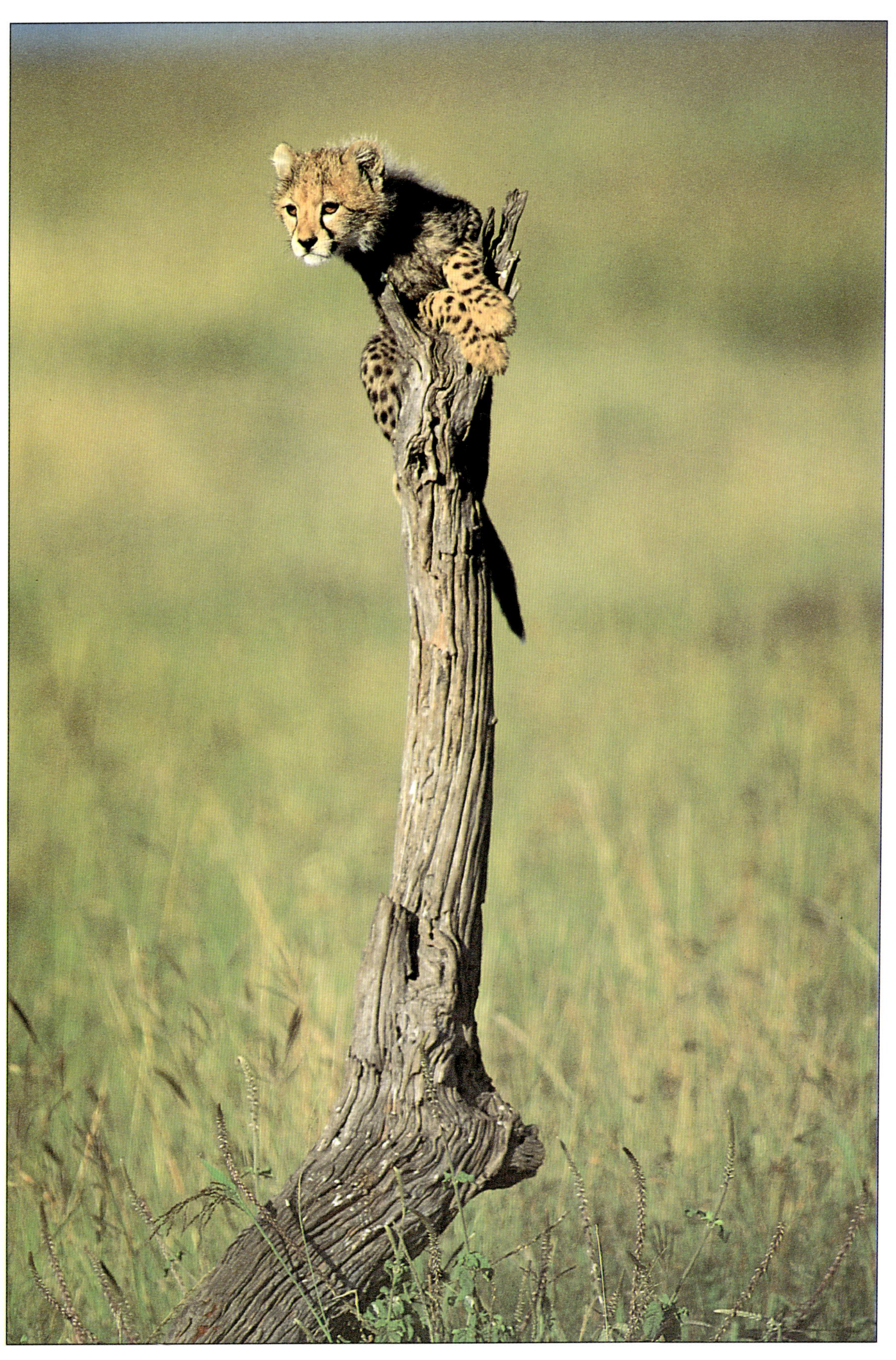

**Mike Hill**
United Kingdom
HIGHLY COMMENDED

### *Cheetah cub*

*"During a family photographic trip to the Maasai Mara, we spent a lot of time observing four cheetah cubs reputed to have a particularly good mother. We had been trying to get shots of interactions within the family, but the long grass made such shots difficult. So I grabbed the chance when one of the cubs climbed a dead tree to survey the scene."*

Nikon F4 with 600mm lens and x1.4 teleconverter; beanbag from vehicle window

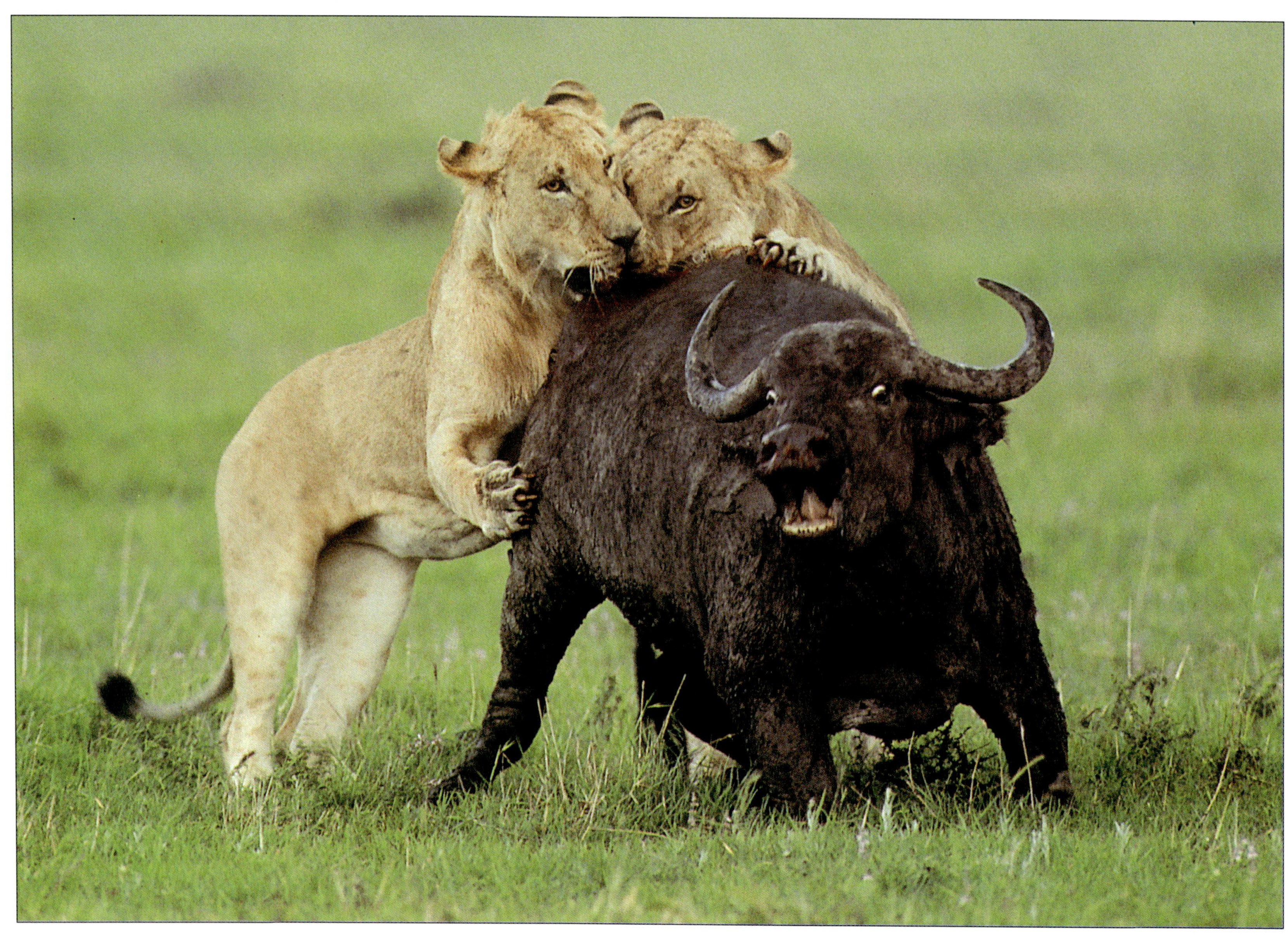

**Fritz Pölking**

Germany

HIGHLY COMMENDED

***Lions killing buffalo***

*"I took this photograph in the Maasai Mara, Kenya, to show the very dramatic situation as two lions killed a buffalo in the rain."*

Nikon F4 with 300mm lens; auto-exposure at f4; Fujichrome 100

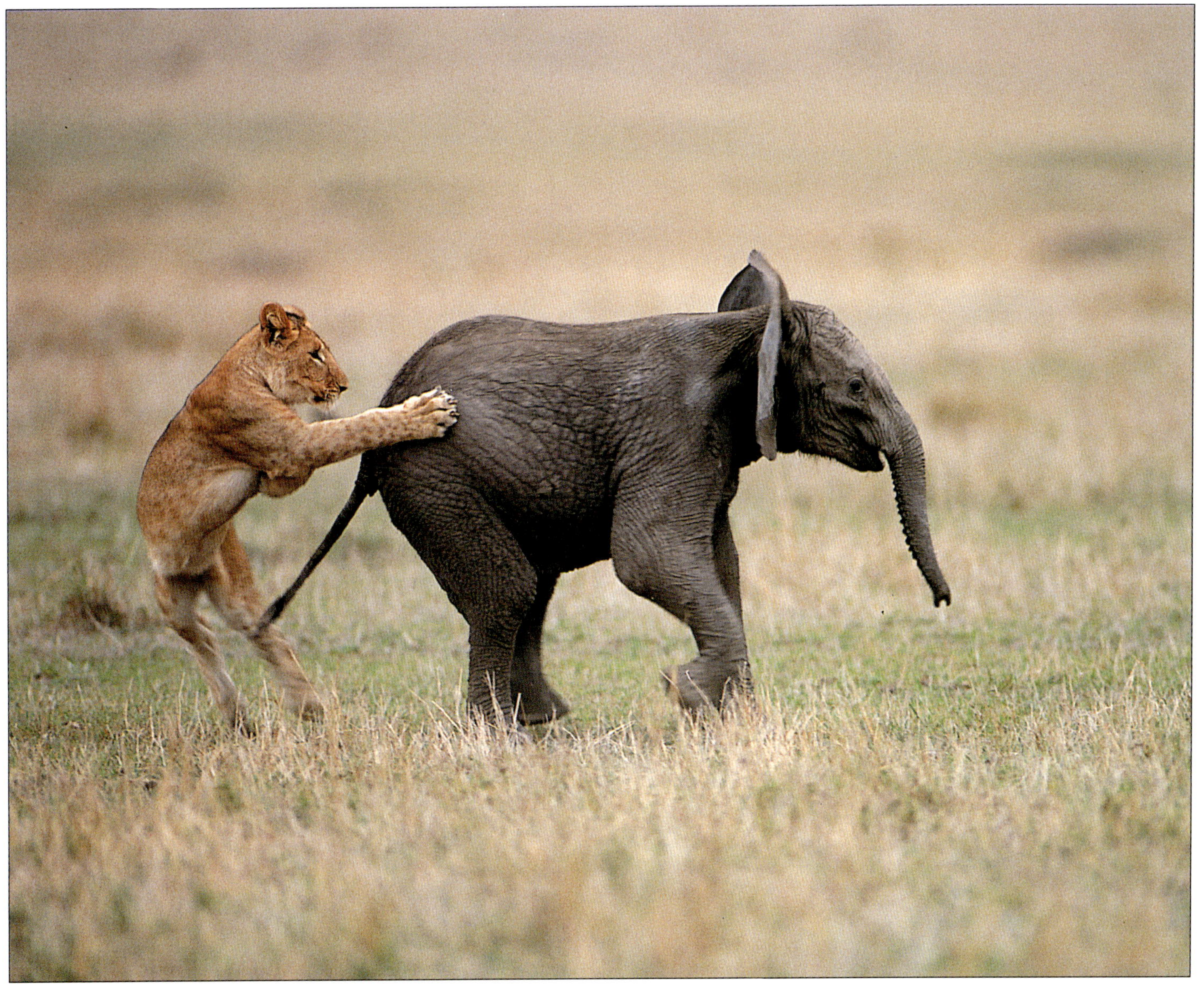

**Anup Shah**
United Kingdom
HIGHLY COMMENDED

***Lion cub attacking elephant calf***

*"The Bilashaka pride was resting, out in the open, when a baby elephant blundered along. Too late it realised its predicament. A female cub edged closer, sizing up her quarry. As the elephant tried to walk away, the cub reared up and slapped it with a forepaw in an unsuccessful bid to knock it over."*

Canon EOS 600 with 400mm lens; f2.8; Fujichrome 100

## Jill Sneesby & Barrie Wilkins

South Africa

HIGHLY COMMENDED

### *Wildcat and jackals catching sandgrouse*

*"The wildcat and jackals were waiting at the waterhole, in the Kalahari Gemsbok Park, for the sandgrouse to appear. The jackals know that the wildcat is better at catching sandgrouse, and so wait for it to catch a bird. They then mob the wildcat until it releases its prey and fight among themselves for the spoils."*

Canon EOS 1 with 400mm lens; car cambrac; f8; Fujichrome Provia 100

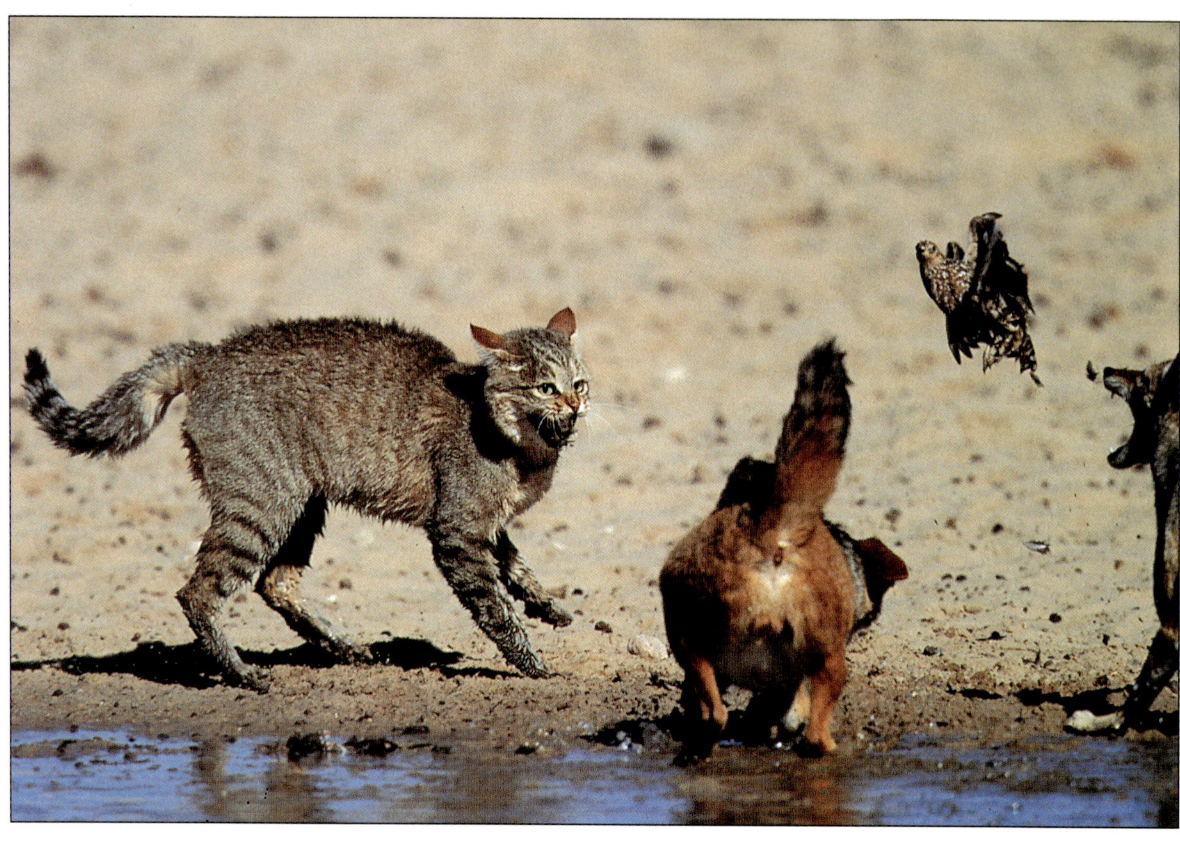

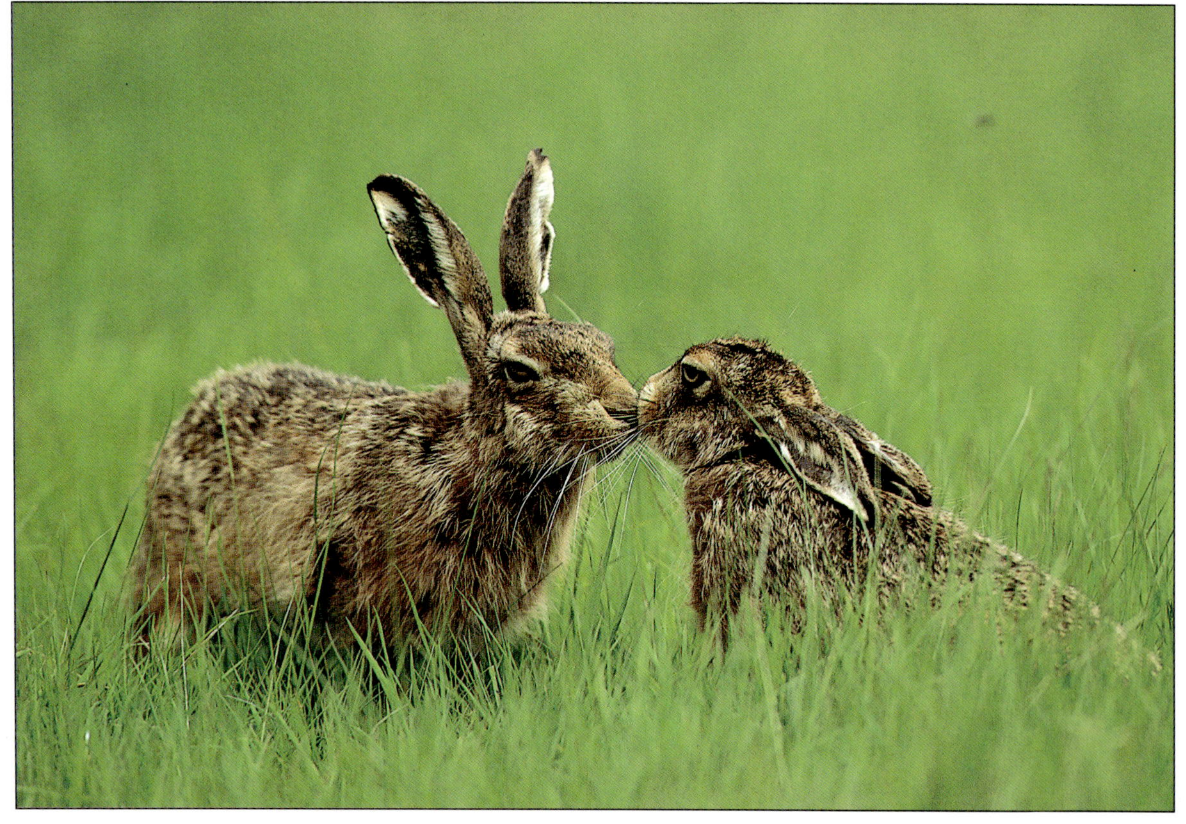

## Ernie Janes

United Kingdom

HIGHLY COMMENDED

### *Brown hares greeting*

*"The male hare (on the left) is approaching the female to smell her face. Apparently a gland indicates whether she is in season; if not, she will fend him off with her fore paws, hence the wary approach. I have specialised in taking hare photographs for the past four years, invariably from a four-wheel-drive, which I am sure my subjects in Bedfordshire now recognise."*

Canon EOS 1 with 500mm lens; beanbag; 1/250 sec at f4.5; Kodachrome 64

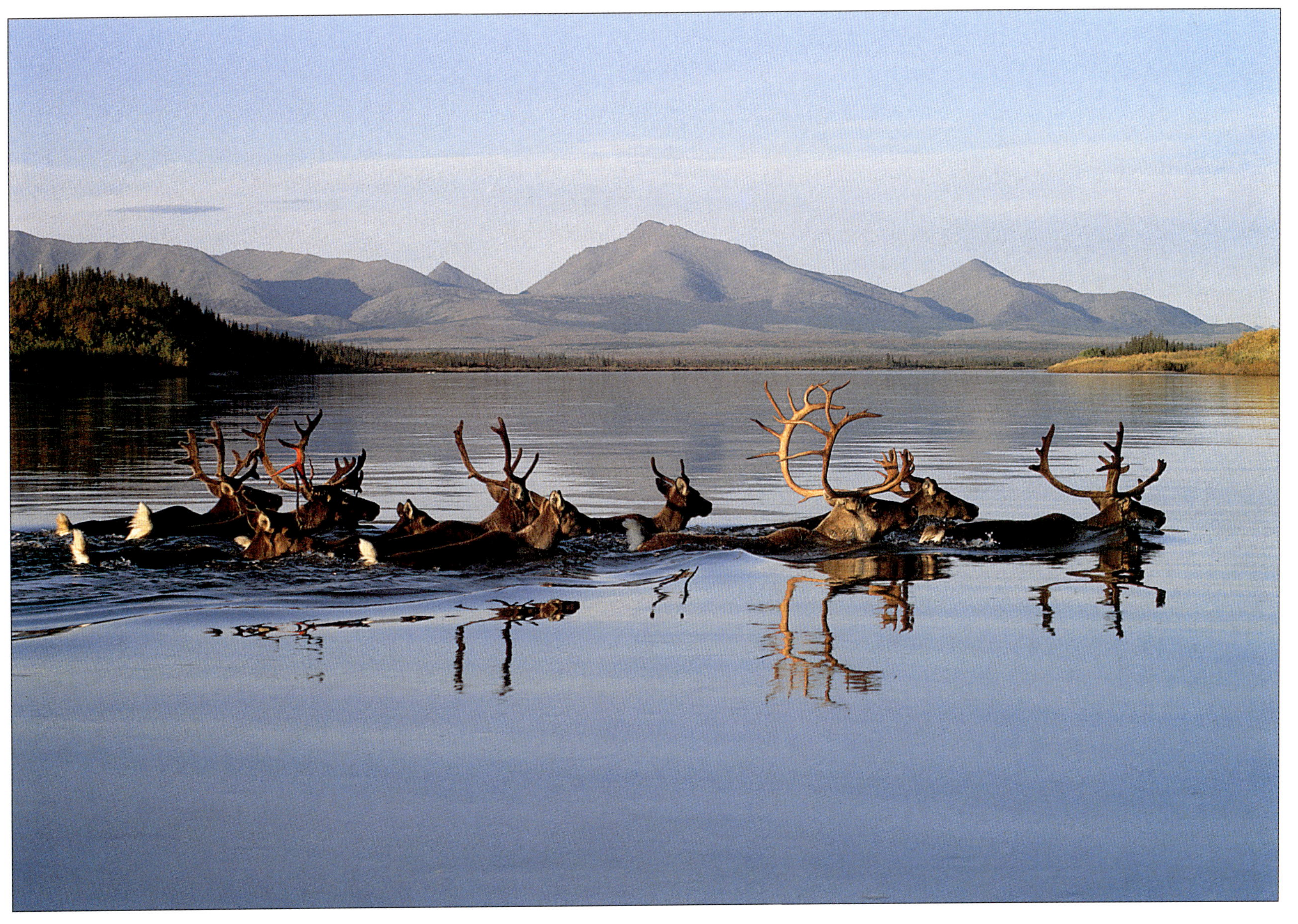

**Tom Walker**
United States of America
HIGHLY COMMENDED

***Caribou migration***

*"Caribou migrate to breeding grounds on the tundra in summer and then return to the shelter of the forests in winter. The picture was taken as they crossed the Kobuk River, Alaska."*

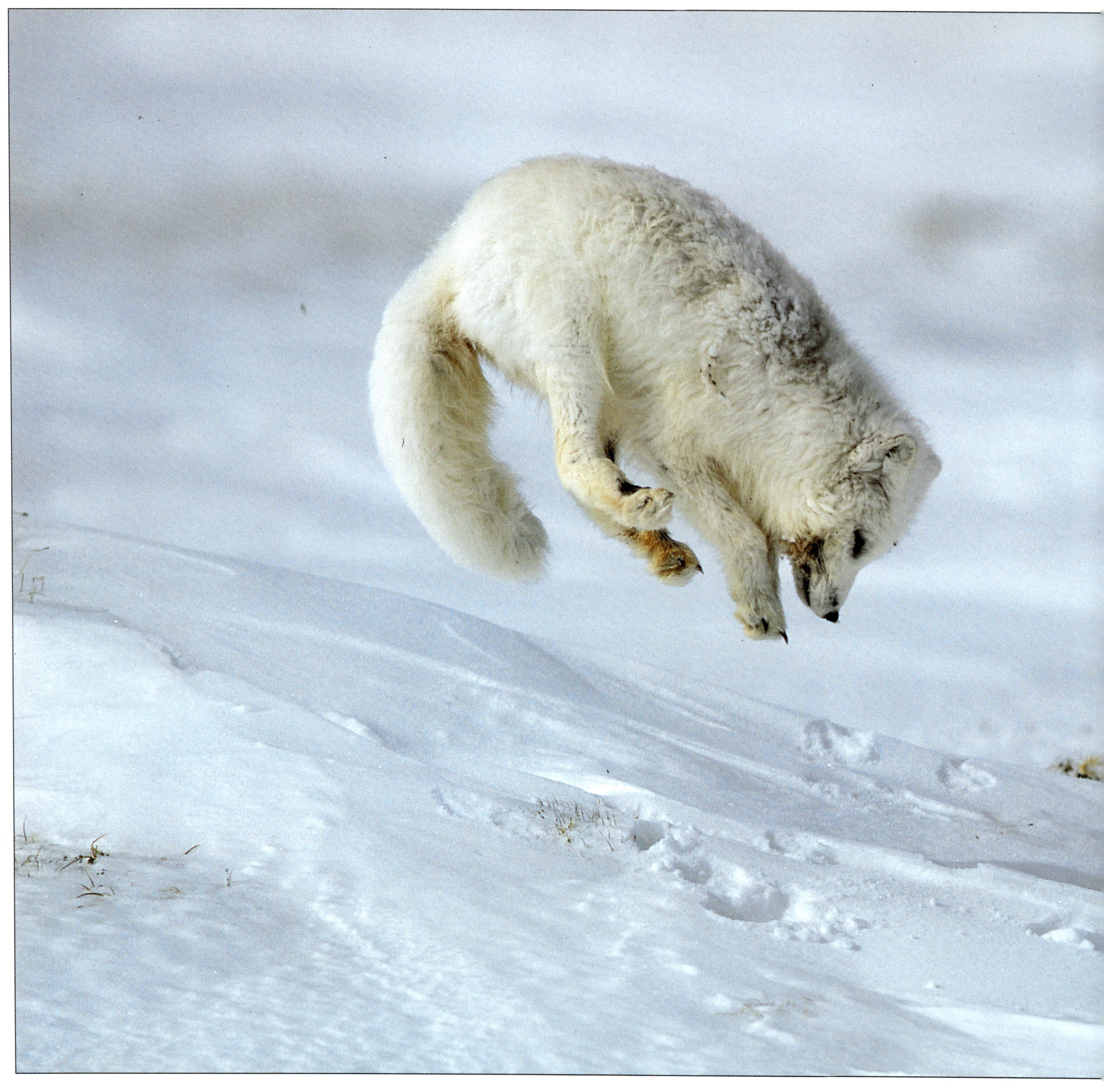

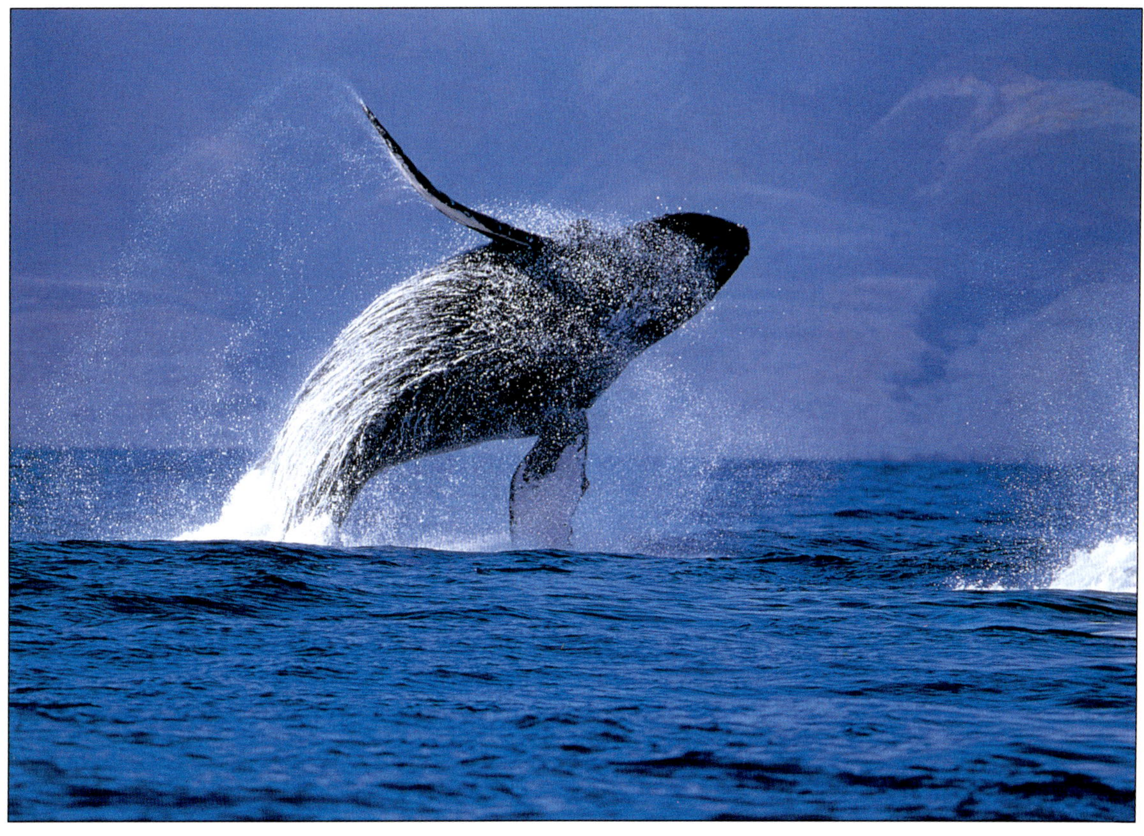

**Gary Schultz**
United States of America
HIGHLY COMMENDED

***Arctic fox hunting***

*"When I first spotted this fox, he was hunting voles on Alaska's North Slope. His technique intrigued me. First he would sniff the snow, then dig down with his nose. Every 30 seconds or so, he would spring up and then pounce down on the snow's surface, hoping to startle the voles from their snow tunnels."*

Nikon F4s with 500mm lens; 1/500 sec at f4; Fujichrome 100

**Doug Perrine**
United States of America
HIGHLY COMMENDED

***Humpback whale breaching***

*"This photo was taken during research off Hawaii. Breaching is a spectacular but poorly understood behaviour, which may serve various social purposes, as well as helping to rid the whales of remoras, barnacles and other parasites."*

(Photo taken under research permit 882 issued by US National Marine Fisheries Service)

Nikon F4s with 300mm lens; 1/500 sec at f4.5; Fujichrome Velvia

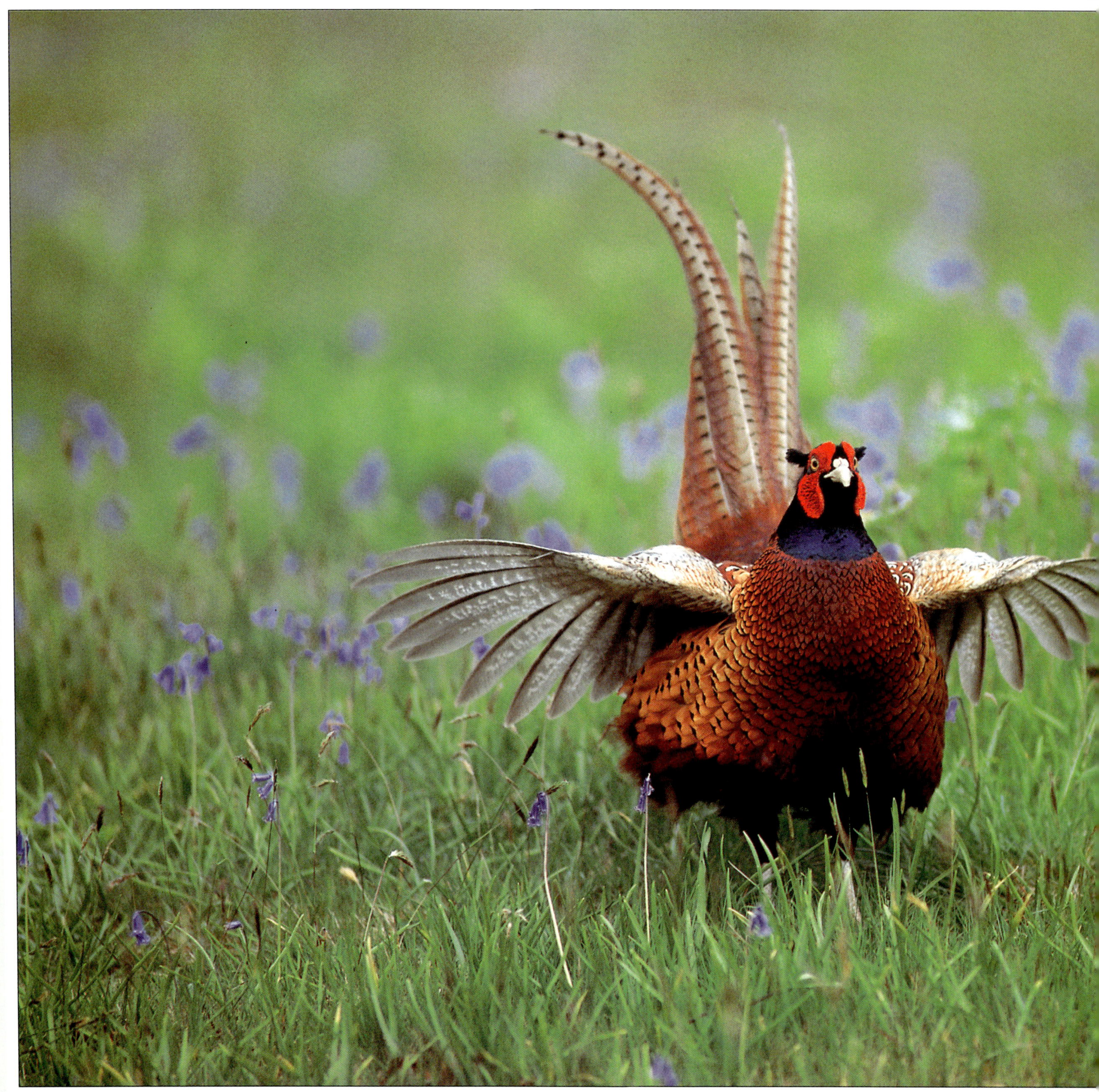

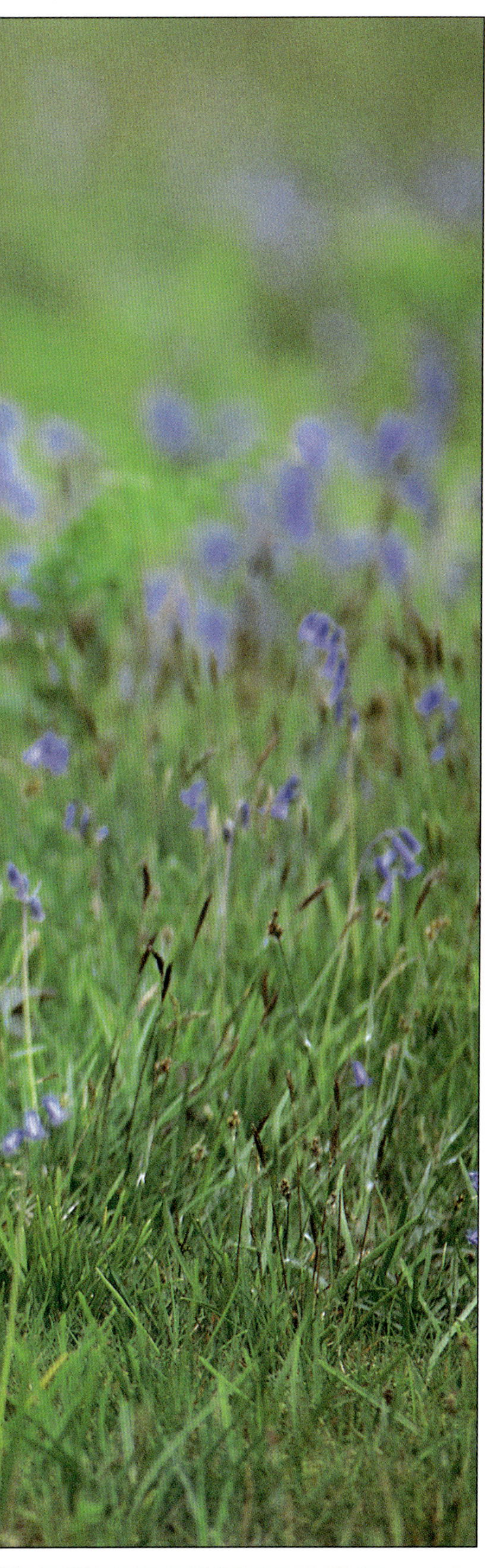

# Animal Behaviour

## - BIRDS -

The birds should be actively doing something. Pictures are judged on their interest value as well as their aesthetic appeal.

**Roger Wilmshurst**
United Kingdom
WINNER

***Cock pheasant crowing***

*"When pheasants crow, they lift their heads and necks very slowly and then call with their necks raised. This is followed by a loud whirr of the wings. I took the picture in open woodland near Ardingly, Sussex, in May. I particularly wanted to set it among the bluebells."*

Minolta 700SI with 300mm lens; 1/2,000 sec at f2.8; Fujichrome Provia 100 rated at 200

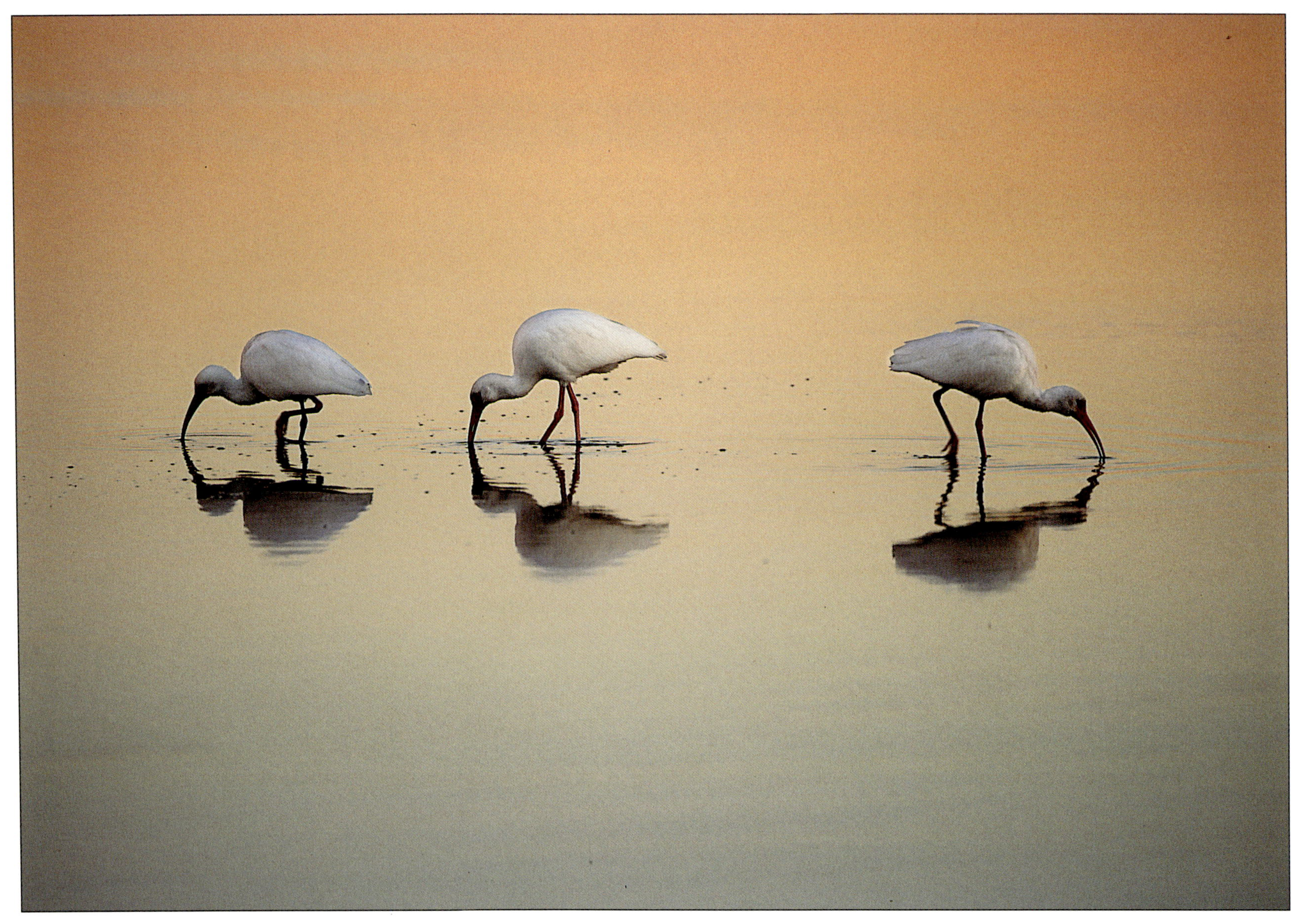

**Thomas D Mangelsen**
United States of America
RUNNER-UP

***White ibis group feeding***

*"It was late evening, and the tide was receding at Estero beach, near Sanibel Island, Florida, when I noticed these wintering ibis feeding in the shallows. I took the picture because I liked the sunset reflections on the calm surface."*

Nikon F4 with 200-400mm lens; tripod; 1/250 sec at f5.6; Fujichrome Velvia

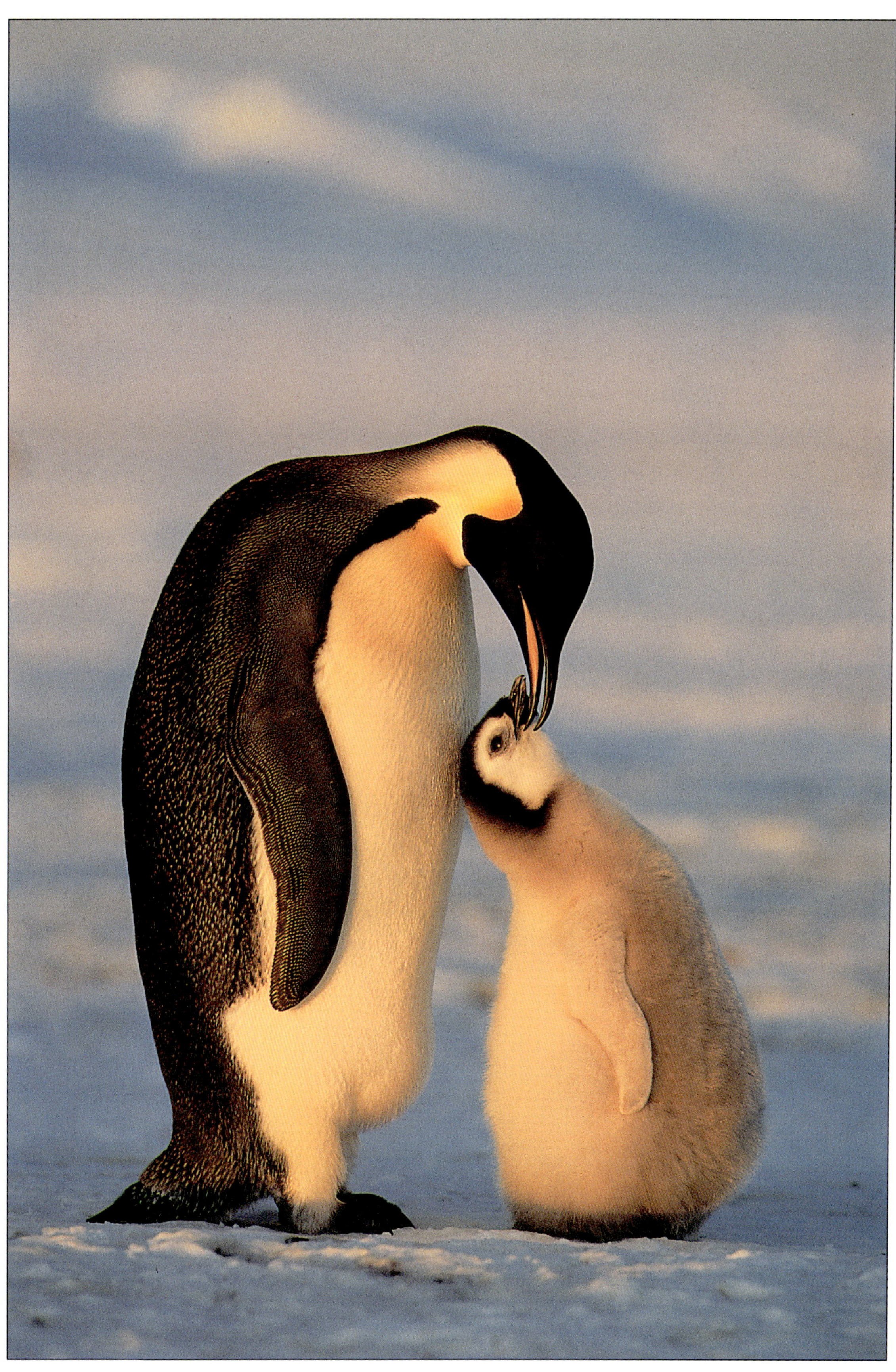

**Konrad Wothe**
Germany
SPECIALLY COMMENDED

***Emperor penguin with hungry chick***

*"I took this picture at 11pm, as an emperor penguin chick begged for food from one of its parents at Atka Bay, Antarctica. Emperor chicks always seem to be hungry. They are fed with a meal of predigested fish and squid by a parent who may have to walk as far as 100km across the ice to reach the sea."*

Canon EOS 1N with 300mm lens; tripod; 1/180 sec at f2.8; Fujichrome Sensia 100

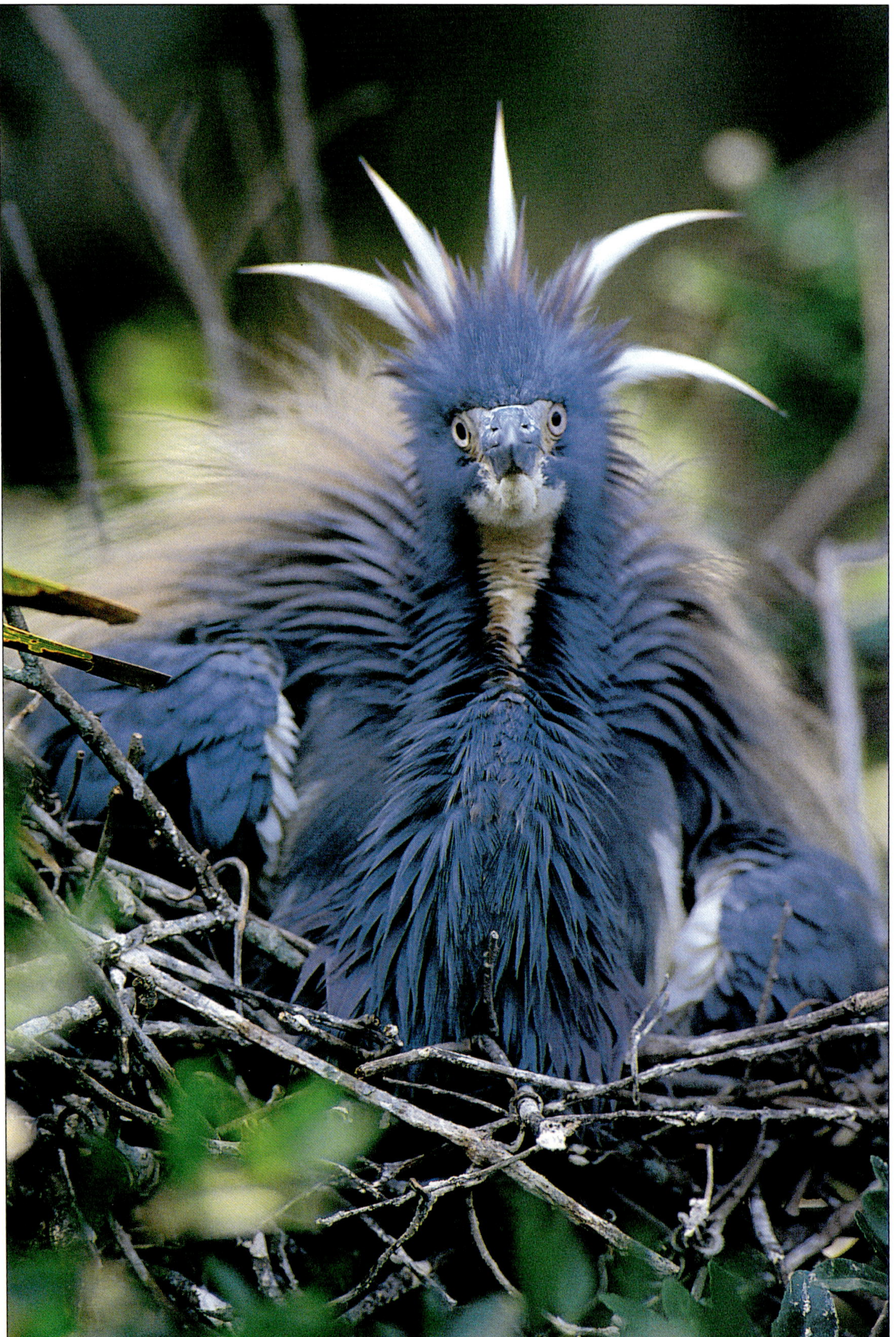

**Brian Kenney**
United States of America
HIGHLY COMMENDED

### *Tricolored heron threat display*

*"Fluffing up its feathers and raising its crest, this tricolored heron at a North Florida rookery is attempting to scare off a large fish crow that's after its eggs. I had photographed this threat display many times, but wanted a fresh perspective. When I noticed the crow always approached from the same direction, I set up my hide for this head-on view. The cloudy-bright day provided soft light at a fairly high speed - necessary to stop the action - even at pretty much wide-open apertures."*

Nikon F4s with 400mm lens and x1.4 teleconverter; tripod; 1/350 sec at f5.6; Fujichrome 100

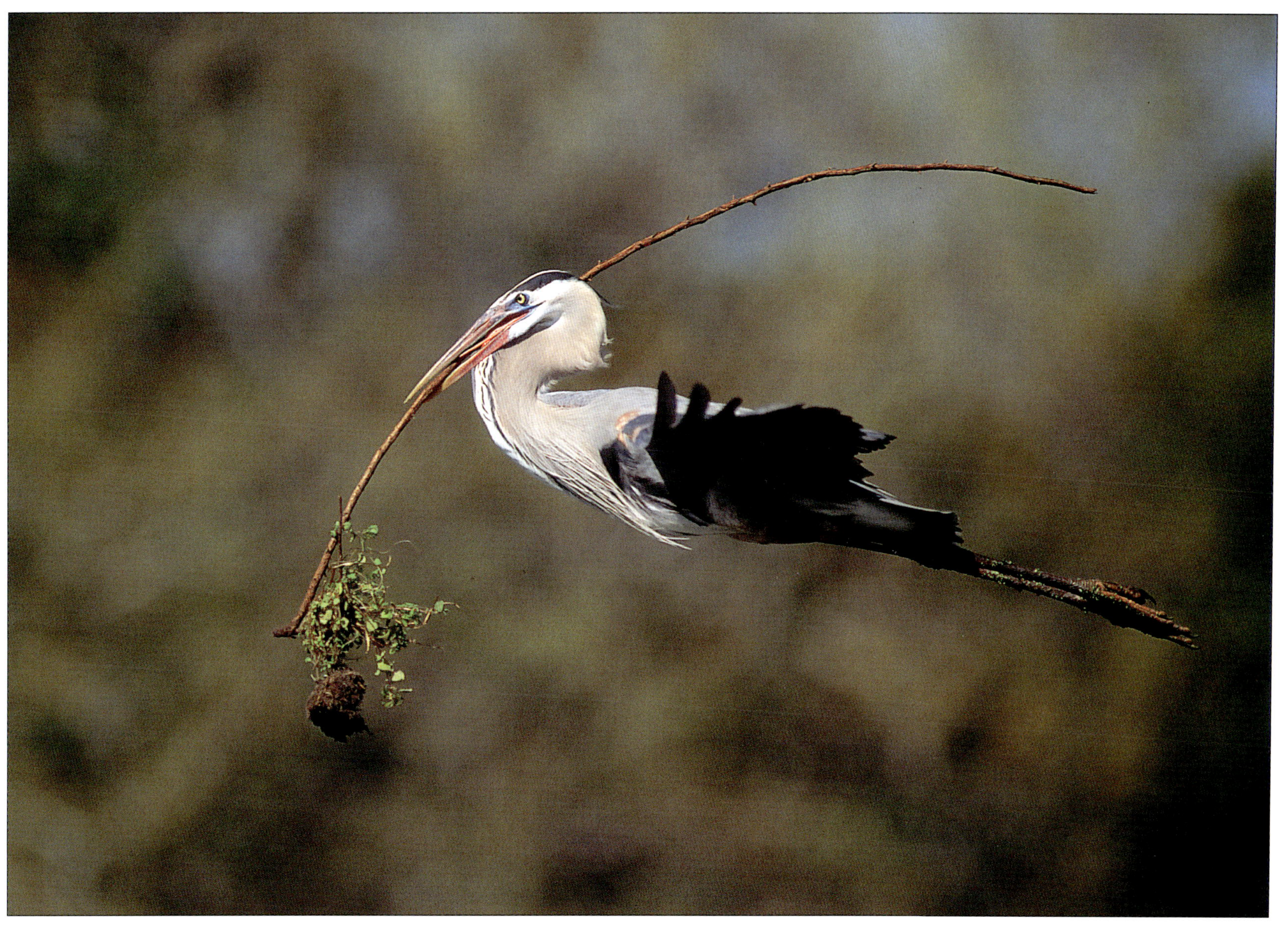

**James H Robinson**
United States of America
HIGHLY COMMENDED

***Great blue heron building nest***

*"I took this photograph at a rookery in southern Florida. Herons and egrets from the rookery often gather twigs and sticks from nearby areas for nest-building purposes. This particular item was obviously extracted 'roots and all', attesting to the heron's great strength."*

Minolta 9xi with 600mm lens; 1/1,000 sec at f4.5; Fujichrome 100

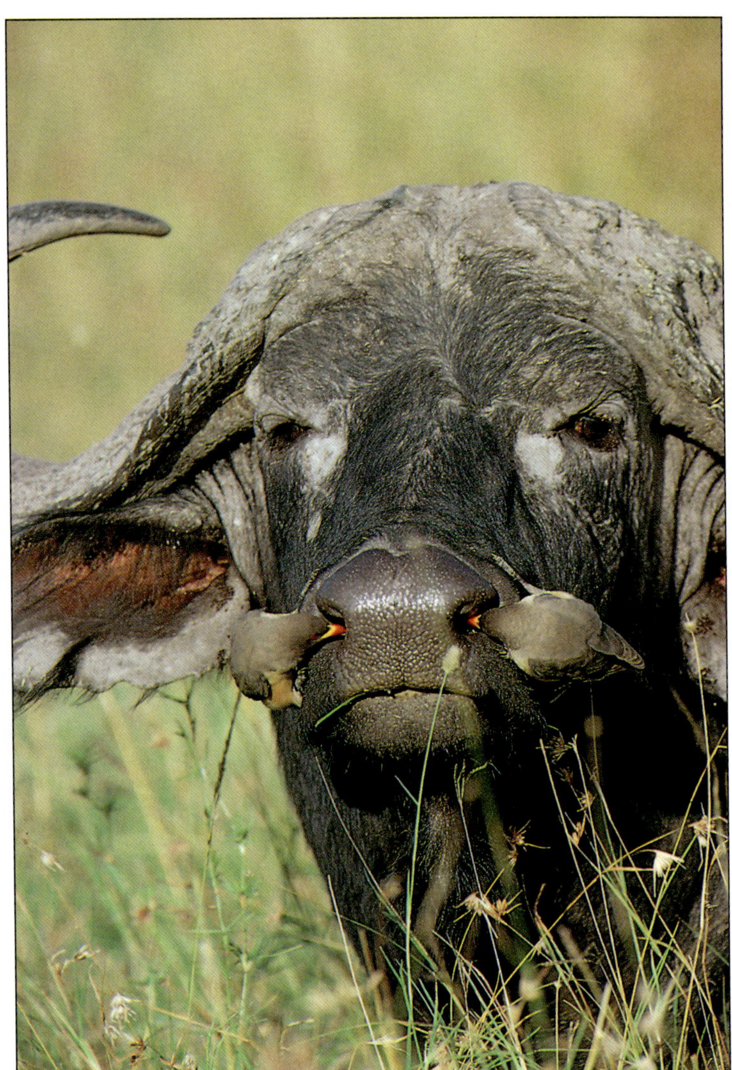

## Wolfgang Braunstein

Germany

HIGHLY COMMENDED

### *Hen party in the nose of a buffalo*

*"We left our camp in the Maasai Mara in late evening to catch some evening light impressions. I watched two oxpeckers moving all over the face of an old bull buffalo. They worked quite systematically, starting with the ears, then the eyes and finally the big nostrils. As I released the button, I knew it would be a good shot."*

Canon T90 with 500mm lens; sandbag; 1/250 sec at f4.5; Kodachrome 64

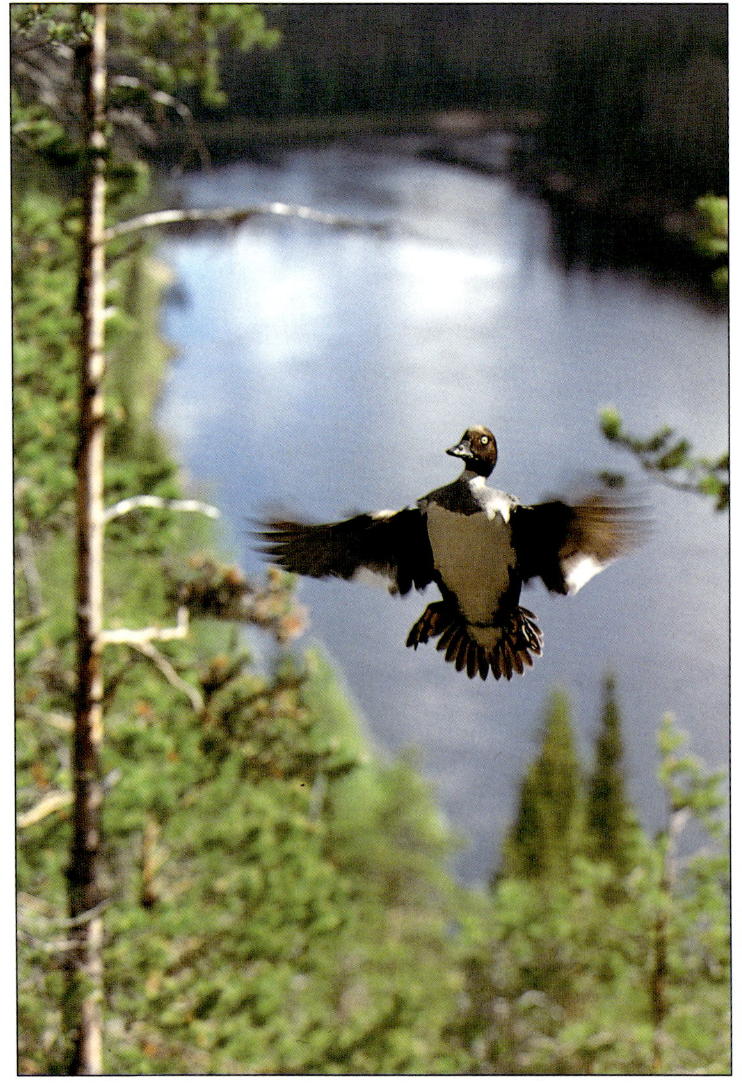

## Hannu Hautala

Finland

HIGHLY COMMENDED

### *Goldeneye duck coming to the nest*

*"This goldeneye duck has been nesting in the same hole of an old tree on the bank of the river Oulanka, in Oulanka National Park, for several years. Once a day it would go down to the river to feed, always flying back along the same route. With only one opportunity a day to photograph the bird, it took two weeks to get a good shot."*

Canon EOS 1 with 86mm lens; tripod; hide; Fujichrome RDP 100

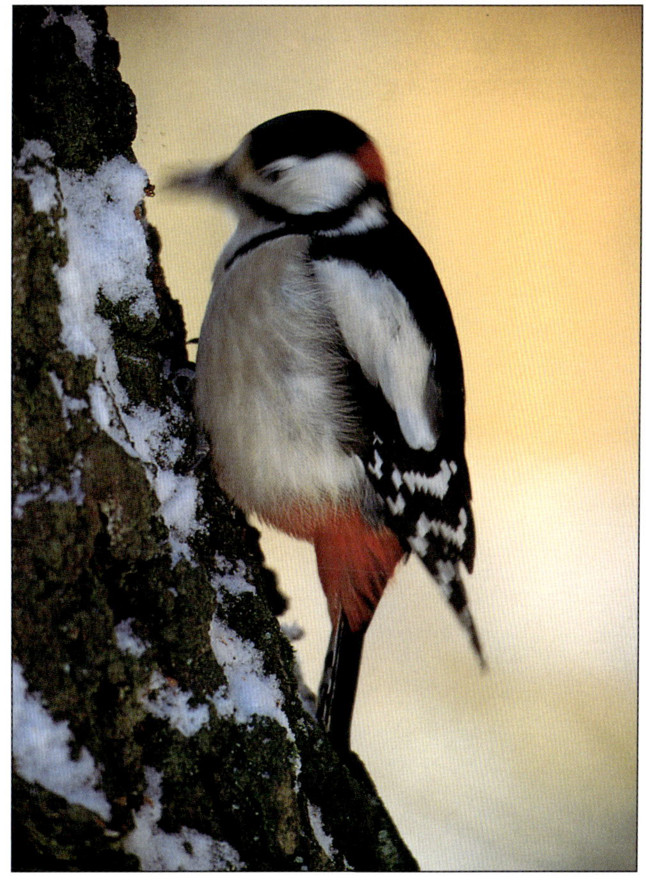

**Klaus Honal**
Germany
HIGHLY COMMENDED

***Great spotted woodpecker in action***

*"I photographed this woodpecker on a birch tree in Bavaria one January morning, about an hour after sunrise. The morning light was ideal, but I had to use a hide to get the shot."*

Canon EOS with 500mm lens; hide; tripod; 1/250 sec at f4.5; Fujichrome 100

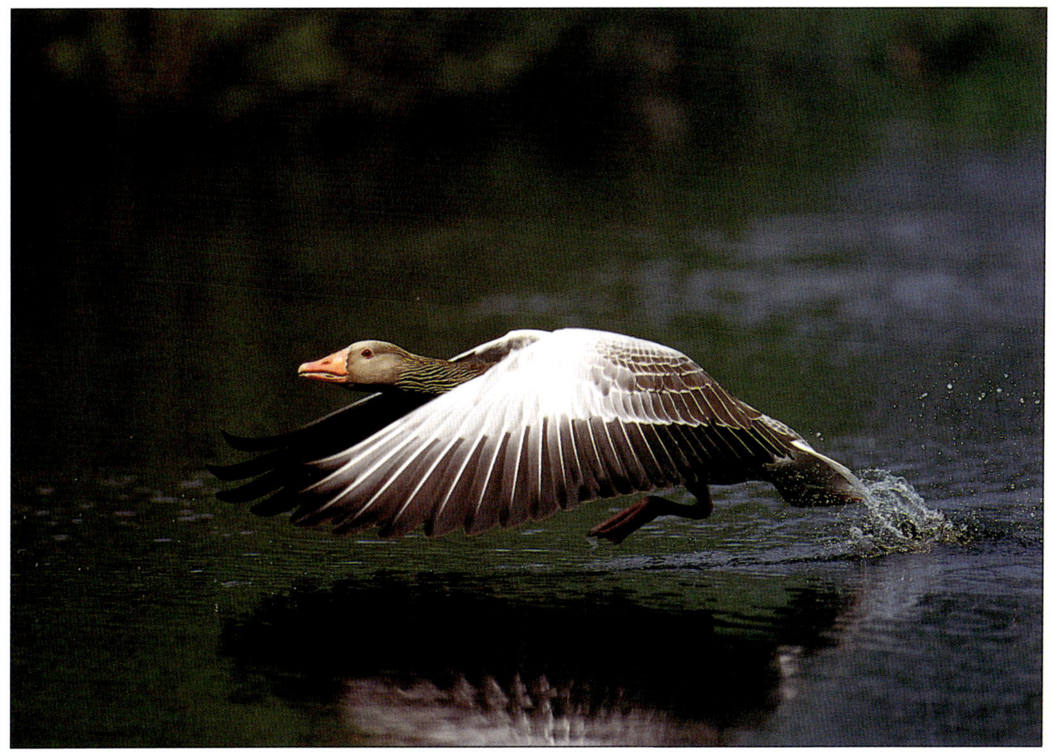

**Uwe Walz**
Germany
HIGHLY COMMENDED

***Greylag goose taking off***

*"I took this picture in Hamburg in spring. It is difficult to photograph a greylag with its wings in this position. I had to react very quickly. For me it was important that the background was dark and neutral."*

Canon EOS 1 with 300mm lens; tripod; 1/1,500 sec at f2.8; Kodak Ektachrome Panther 100

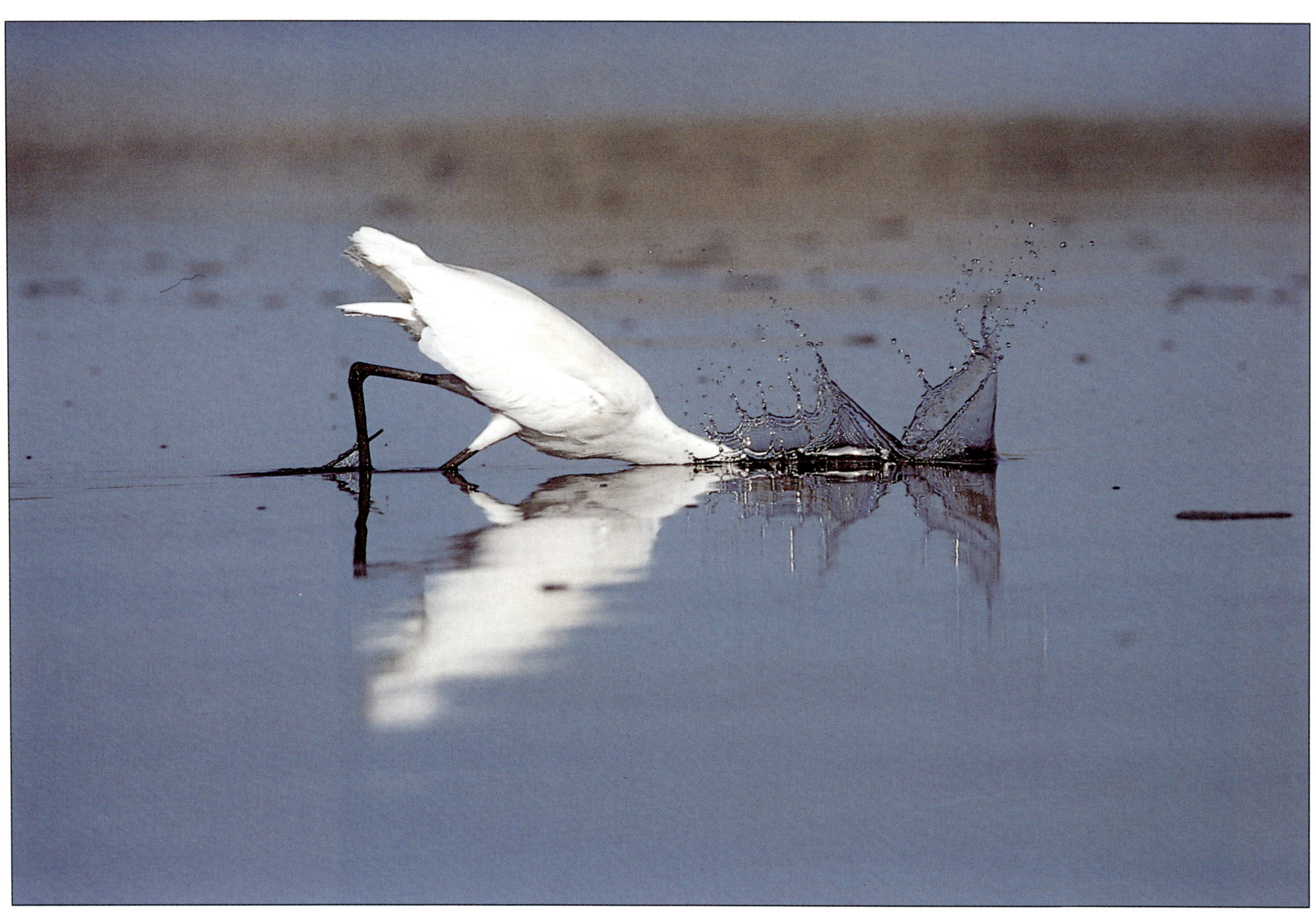

**Richard R Hansen**
United States of America
HIGHLY COMMENDED

***Great egret feeding***

*"I have seen these beautiful white birds hold themselves still for anything from 30 seconds to 30 minutes before delivering the final strike. Likewise, sitting in my kayak in Morro Bay, California, I was locked motionless, waiting to record this moment of action."*

Canon 630 with 400mm lens; 1/750 sec at f5.6; Kodak Lumiere 100

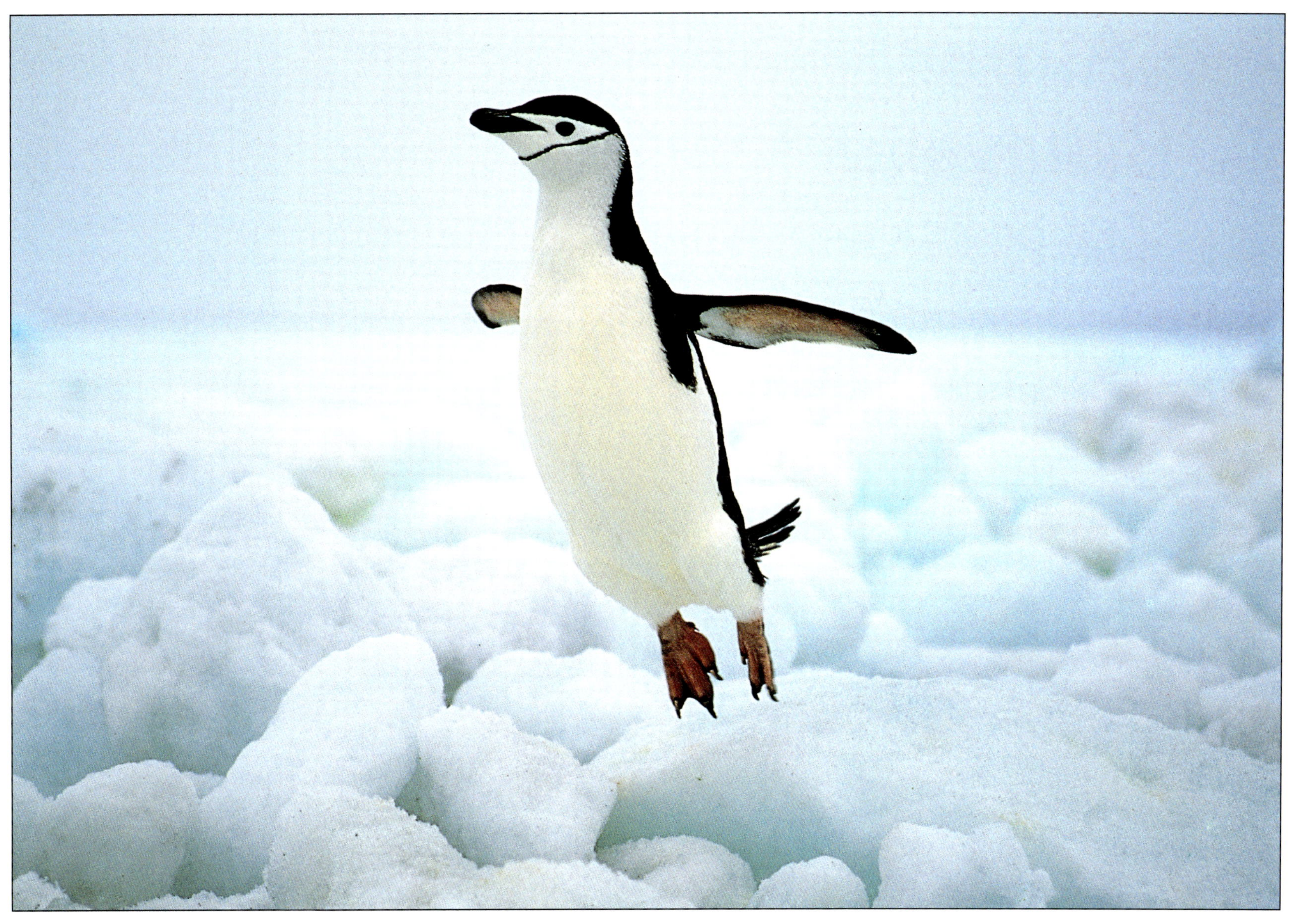

**Konrad Wothe**
Germany
HIGHLY COMMENDED

***Chinstrap penguin 'flying'***

*"When I visited Saunders Island in the South Sandwich Islands, I noticed that the chinstrap penguins were having to jump from ice floe to ice floe as they came ashore. I photographed one of these jumps from a very low position to make it look as if the penguin was flying."*

Canon EOS 1N with 28-70mm lens; 1/500 sec at f2.8; Fujichrome Velvia

# Animal Behaviour

## - ALL OTHERS -

The photographs entered in this category should show the subject actively doing something. Pictures are judged on their interest value as well as their aesthetic appeal.

**Doug Perrine**
United States of America
WINNER

***Seastar spawning***

*"I was diving near Baltra Island, in the Galapagos. It was late on an overcast and dreary day, and a fairly heavy sea was running. On the way back to the surface, I noticed this pyramid seastar releasing a milky fluid in short puffs. Since the cloud was visible only for an instant, it was difficult to get into position in the strong surge and focus. The brilliant colours of the seastar were a pleasant surprise, as they only became visible during the split second that artificial light was applied."*

Nikon F4s with 60mm macro lens and underwater housing; strobes; 1/125 sec at f22; Fujichrome Velvia

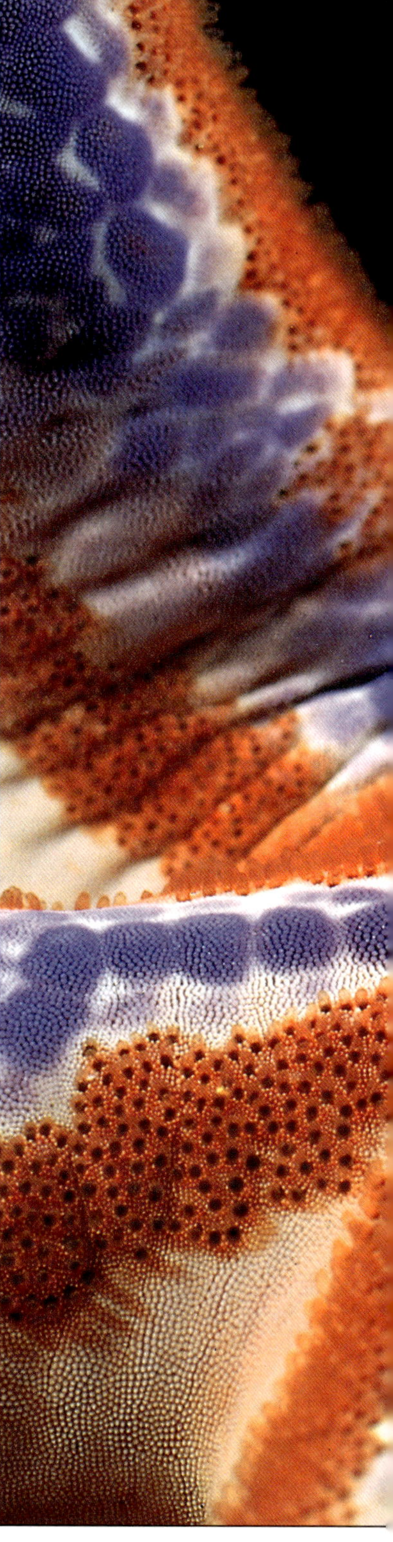

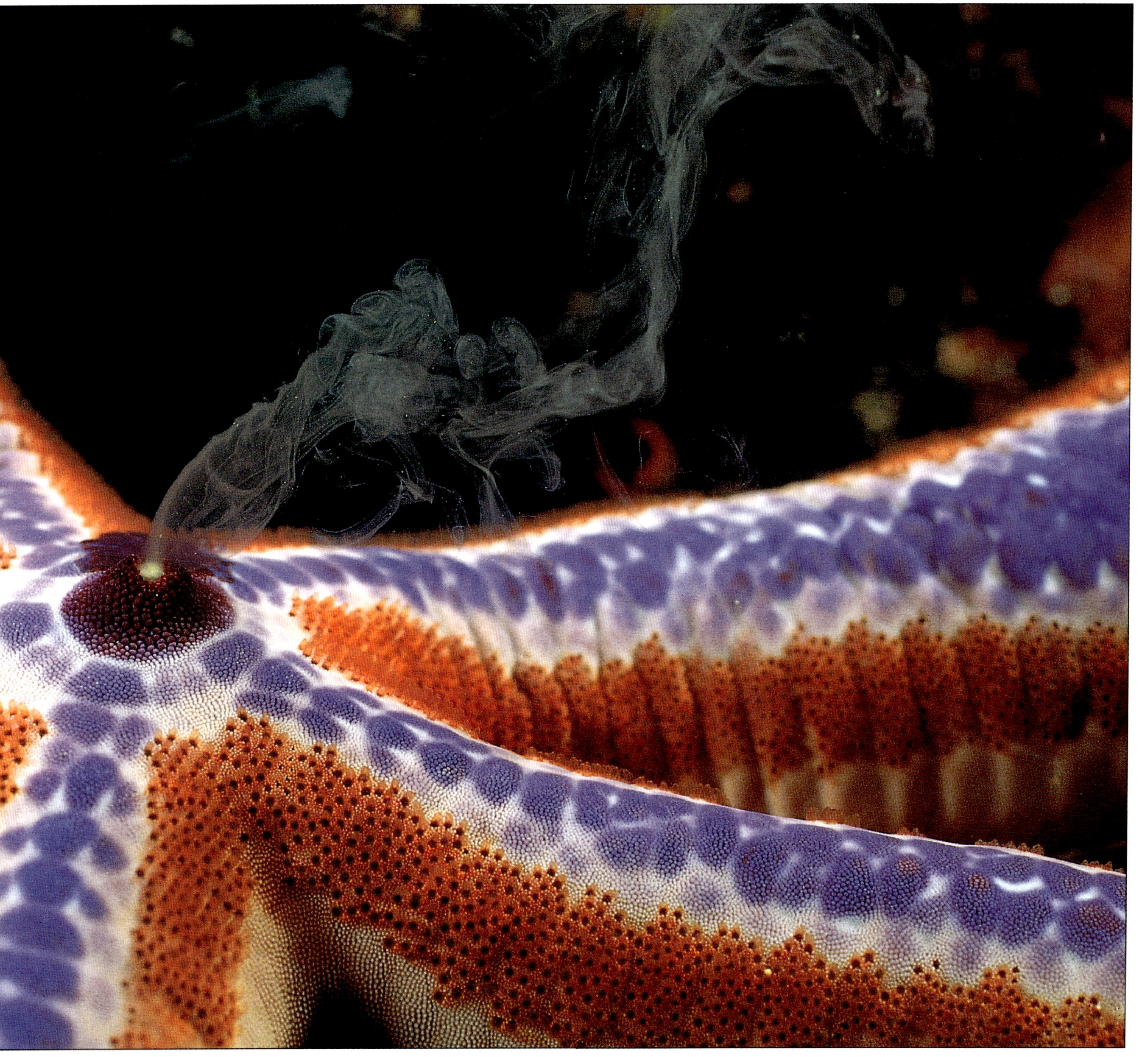

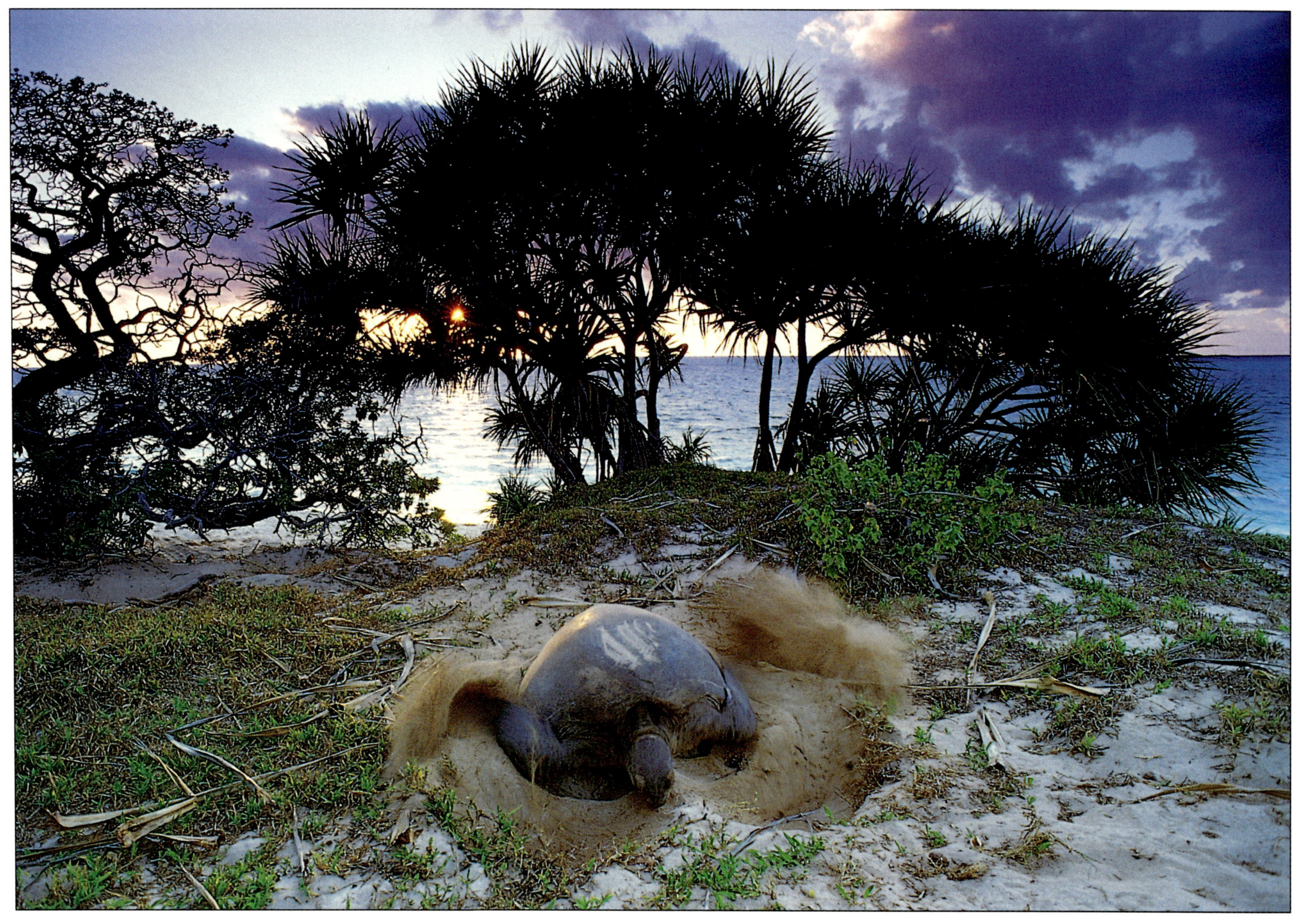

**Darryl Torckler**
New Zealand
RUNNER-UP

***Turtle digging***

*"I went to Heron Island, Australia, to photograph green turtles during their laying season. I spent many hours in the early morning searching for suitable subjects. Alas the island was full of tourists also looking for turtles, and only rarely did I get the chance to take some images before a crowd arrived."*

Nikon F90 with 20mm lens; tripod; 1/8 sec at f11; Fujichrome Velvia

**Frants Hartmann**
Kenya
HIGHLY COMMENDED

***Egg-laying chameleon***

*"During the dry season, the flap-necked chameleon digs a hole in soft soil in which to lay her eggs. This nest was in my garden at Karamaini, near Thika in Kenya. The chameleon's slow movements and well-known ability to blend in with the surroundings made it difficult to spot."*

Hasselblad 500C/M with 150mm lens; 21mm ext. tube; unipod; 1/250 sec at f8; Fujichrome 100

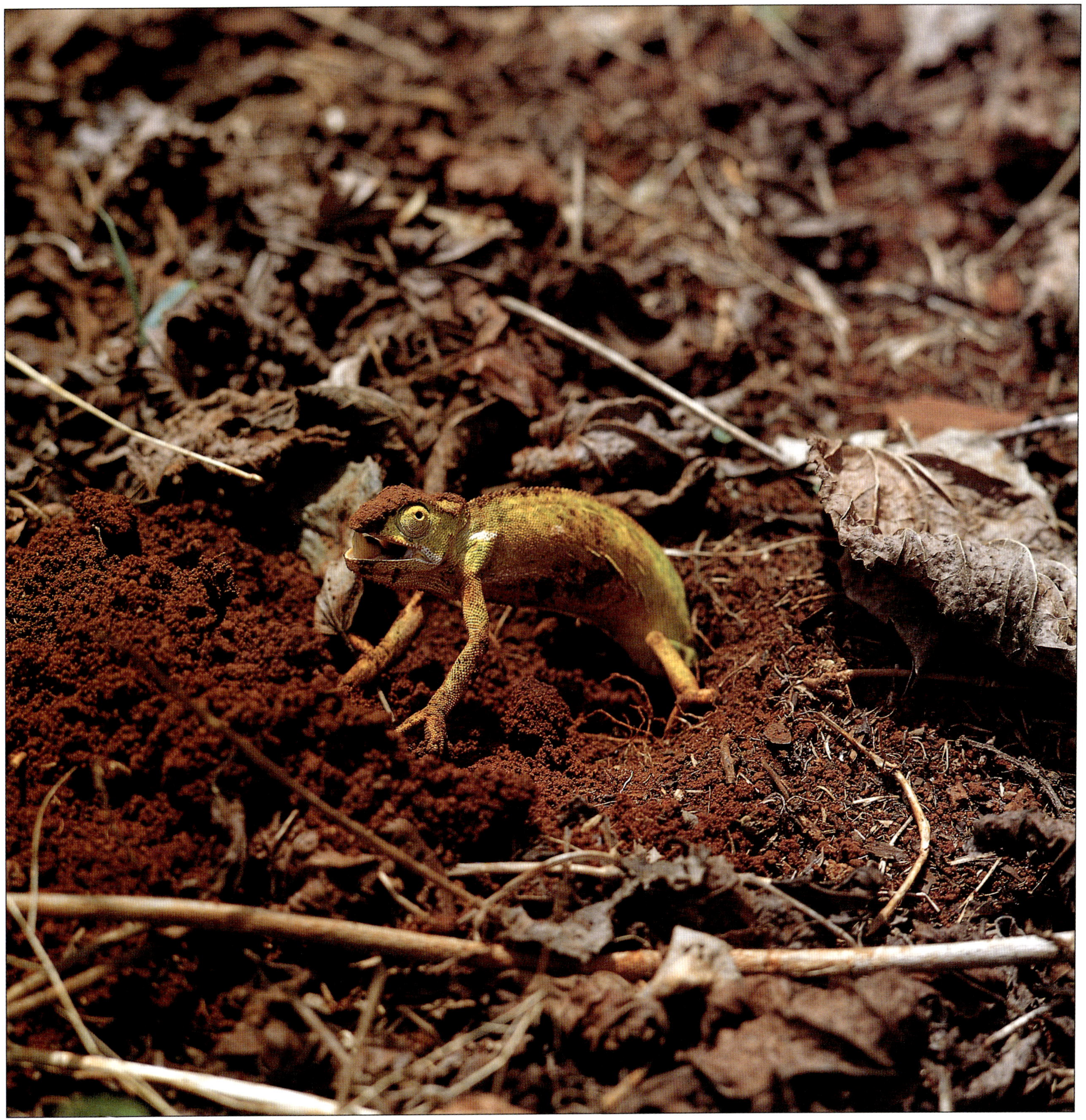

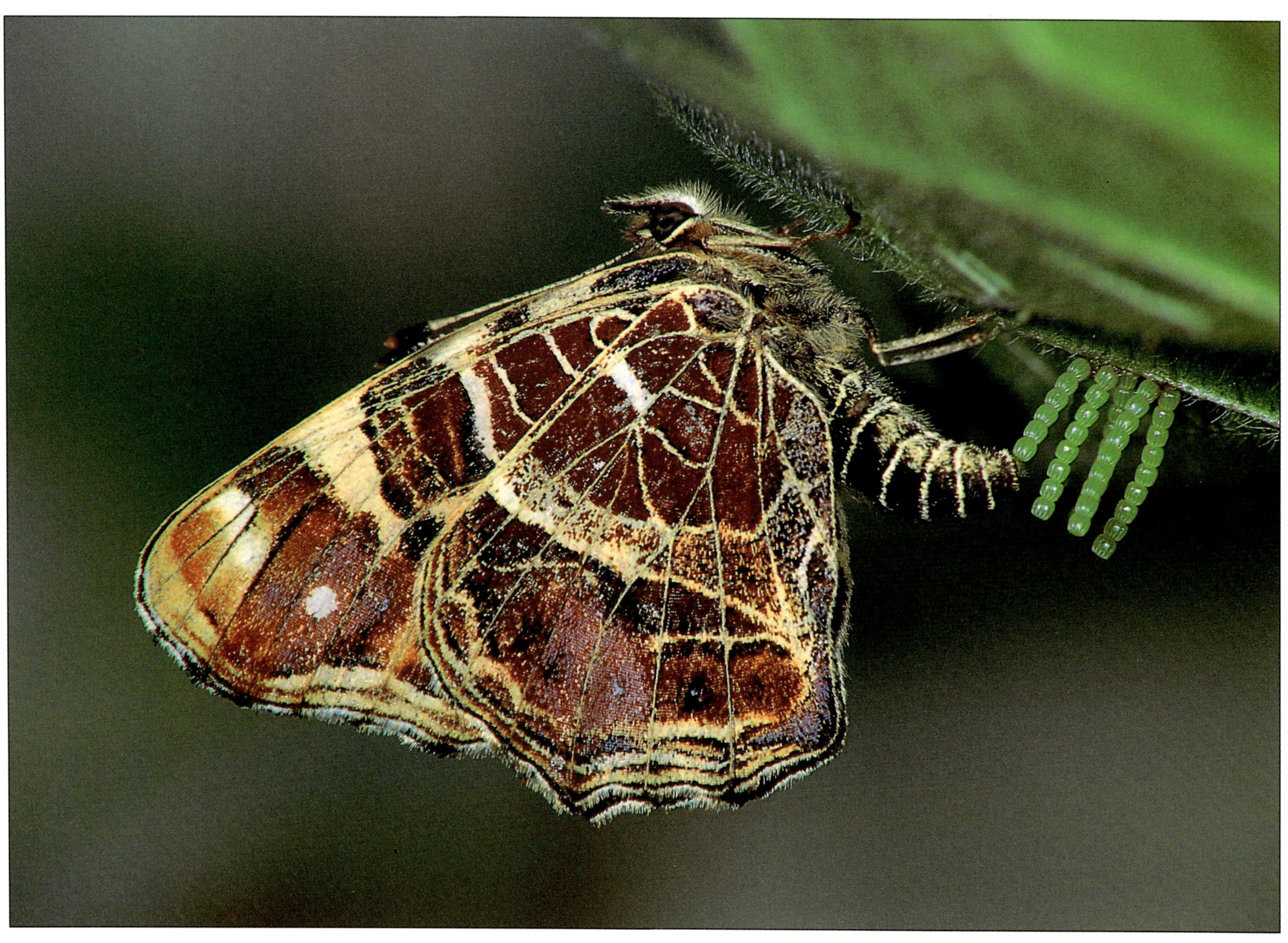

**Hans Christoph Kappel**

Germany

HIGHLY COMMENDED

**_Butterfly laying eggs_**

*"I discovered this map butterfly Araschnia levana purely by chance in our garden in mid-June. The female's 'tower-block' egg structures, here on the underside of a stinging nettle leaf, are thought to be unique among the butterflies."*

Canon T90 with 200mm macro lens; 1/90 sec at f16; Fujichrome Velvia

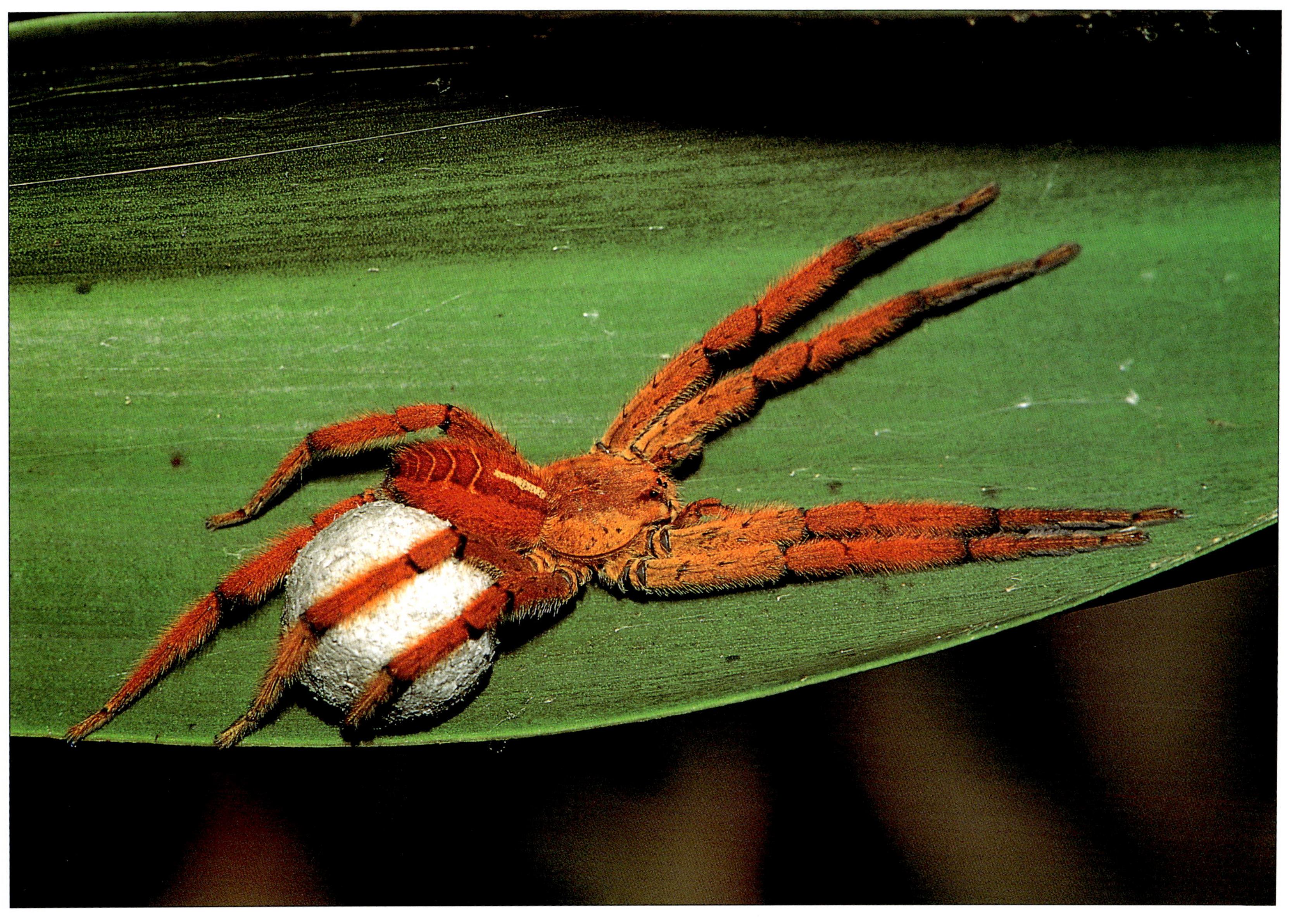

**Doug Locke**
United States of America
HIGHLY COMMENDED

***Hunting spider with egg sac***

*"I photographed this 10-centimetre-long hunting spider as it basked in the sun in Costa Rica. It had just emerged from its web in a rolled area of the leaf, and returned there soon after, still carrying the egg sac."*

Nikon 8008s with 200mm micro lens; tripod; flash; Fujichrome Velvia

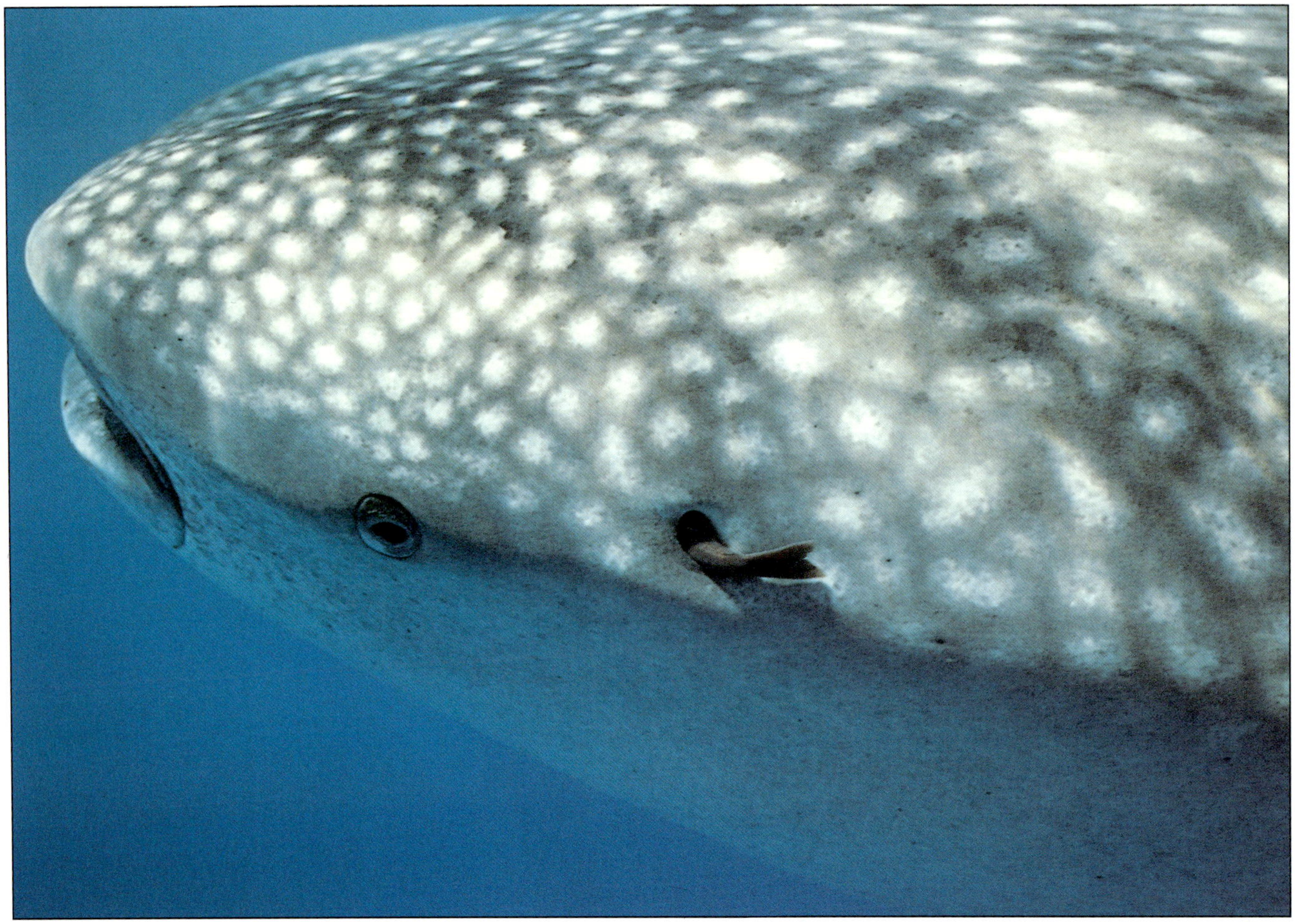

**Douglas David Seifert**
United States of America
HIGHLY COMMENDED

***Remora in whale shark***

*"Remoras often hide from predators by seeking the company of large pelagic animals, in this case a 10-metre whale shark on* Ningaloo Reef, *in* Western Australia.
*The remora inserted its head into the whale's spiracle chamber, giving a focus for a close-up shot of an animal usually portrayed by wide angle."*

Nikon RSAF with 20-35mm lens; 1/125 sec at f4.8; Kodak Lumiere 100X

**Linda Pitkin**
United Kingdom
HIGHLY COMMENDED

***Coral grouper with cleaner shrimp***

*"The shallower coral reefs of the* Maldive Islands *abound with cleaner stations. Every small outcrop has its resident cleaner fish and cleaner shrimps waiting for customers, who line up to have parasites removed and minor wounds cleaned. Everyone is so engrossed in what they are doing that it is possible to get very close."*

Pentax LX with 50mm lens in underwater housing; flash; 1/15 sec at f11- 16; Fujichrome Velvia

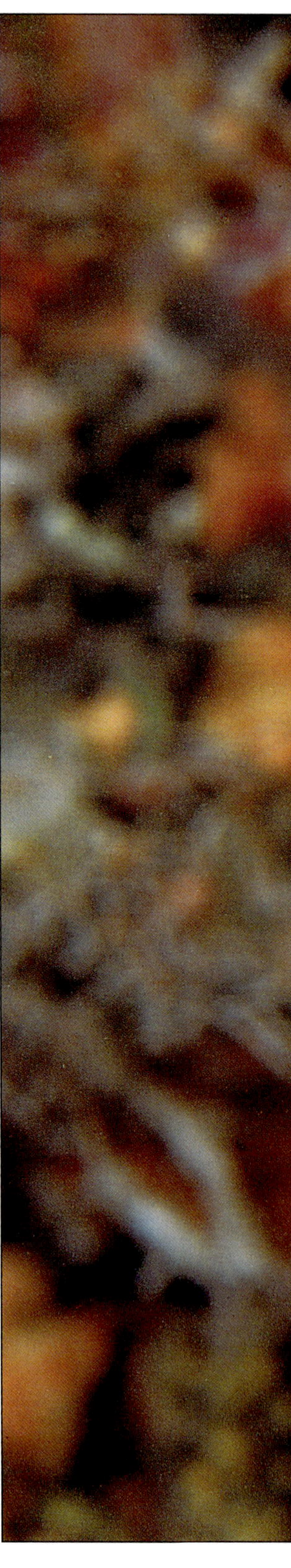

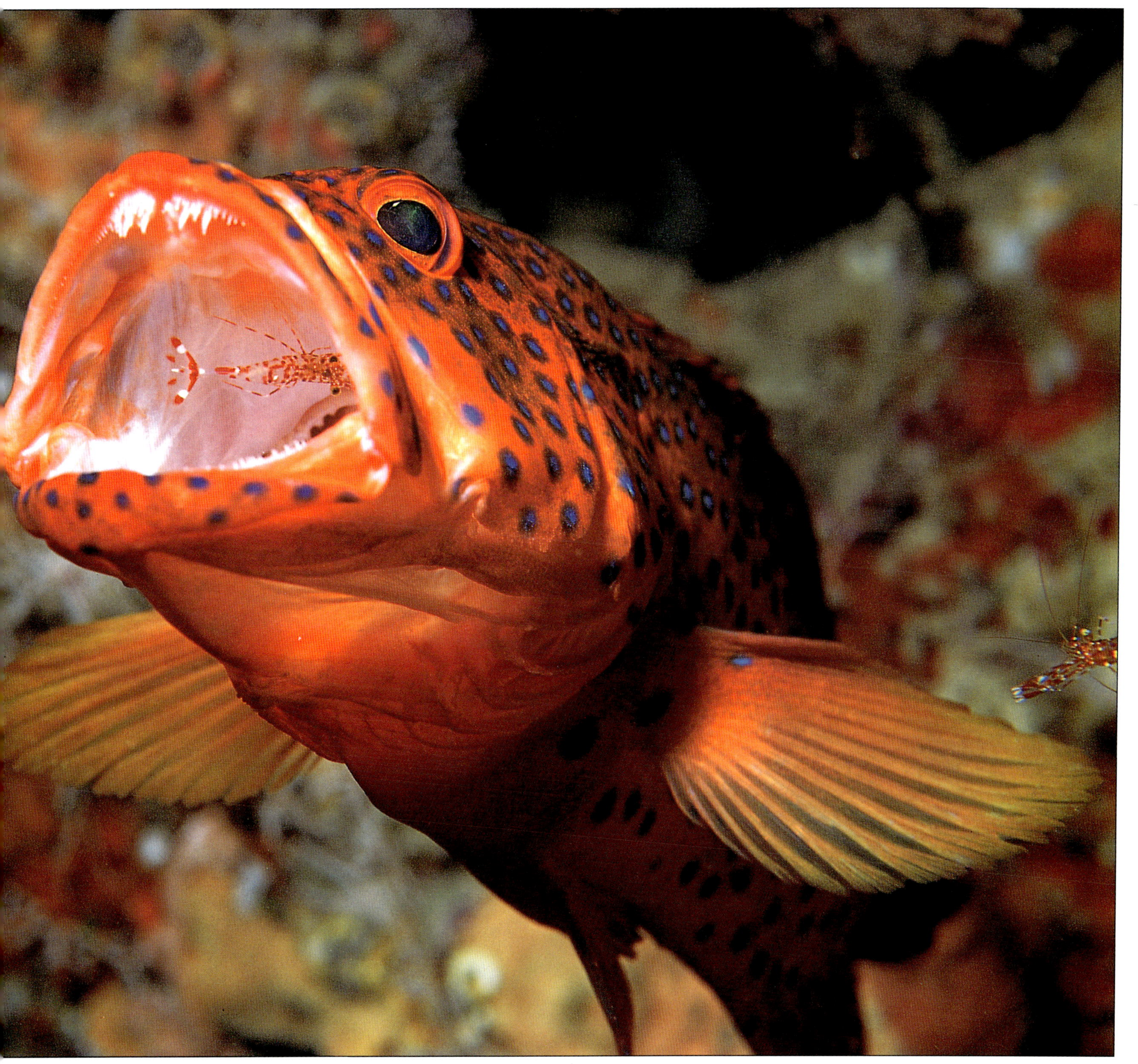

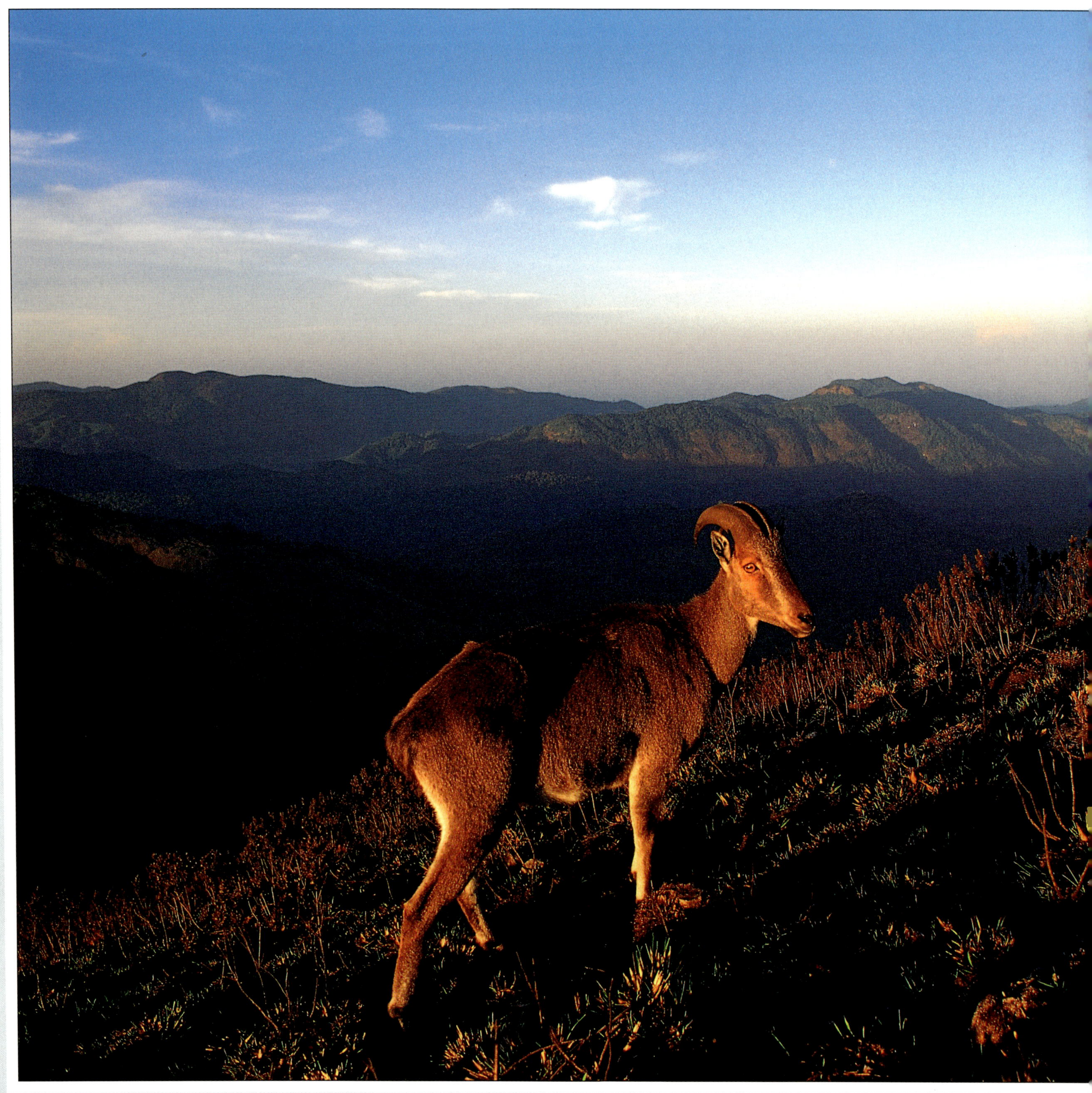

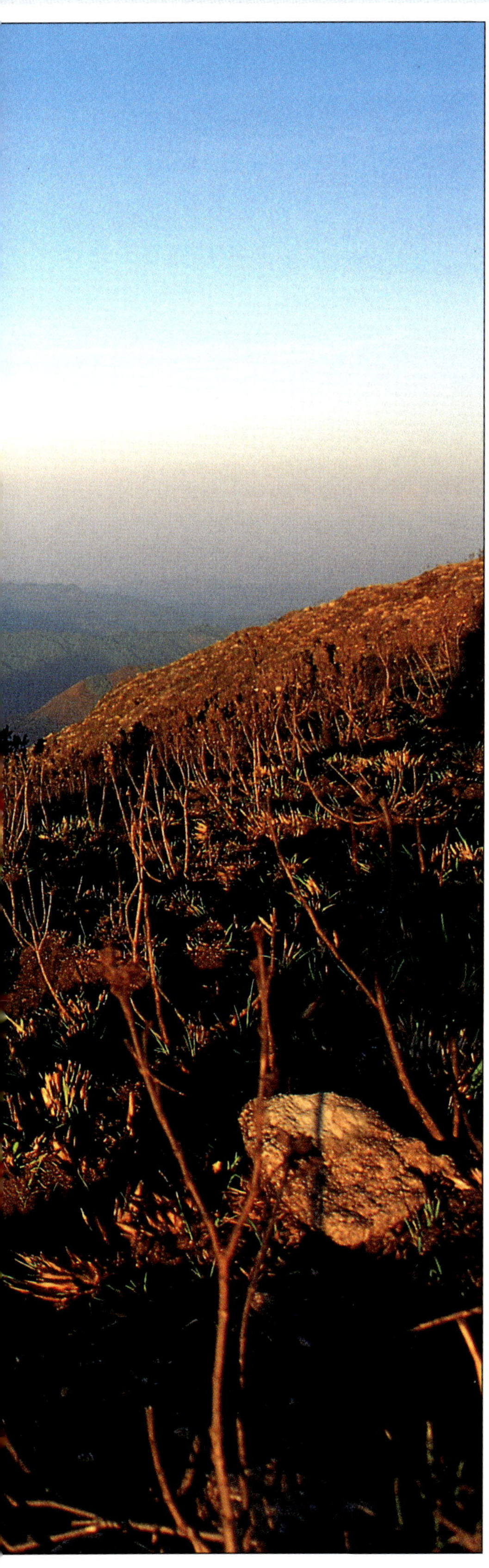

# The Gerald Durrell Award for Endangered Wildlife

This award was introduced in 1995 to commemorate Gerald Durrell's long-standing involvement with The Wildlife Photographer of the Year Competition and his work with endangered species. The subjects illustrated must be officially listed as endangered at an international or national level.

**Jean-Pierre Zwaenepoel**
Belgium
WINNER

***Nilgiri tahr***

*"I spent three weeks in the Eravikulam National Park in Kerala, South India, photographing Nilgiri tahr. This area supports about 700 of the total estimated population of 2,000 animals that live in scattered isolated groups above 1,200 metres along the high tablelands and rolling hills of the Western Ghats. As with other goats, it is sometimes possible to creep close to Nilgiri tahr if you approach them from above. One morning, I was lucky enough to get close to this young male just as the sun was coming up."*

Nikon F-801 with 24mm lens; 1/30 sec at f5.6; Fujichrome Velvia

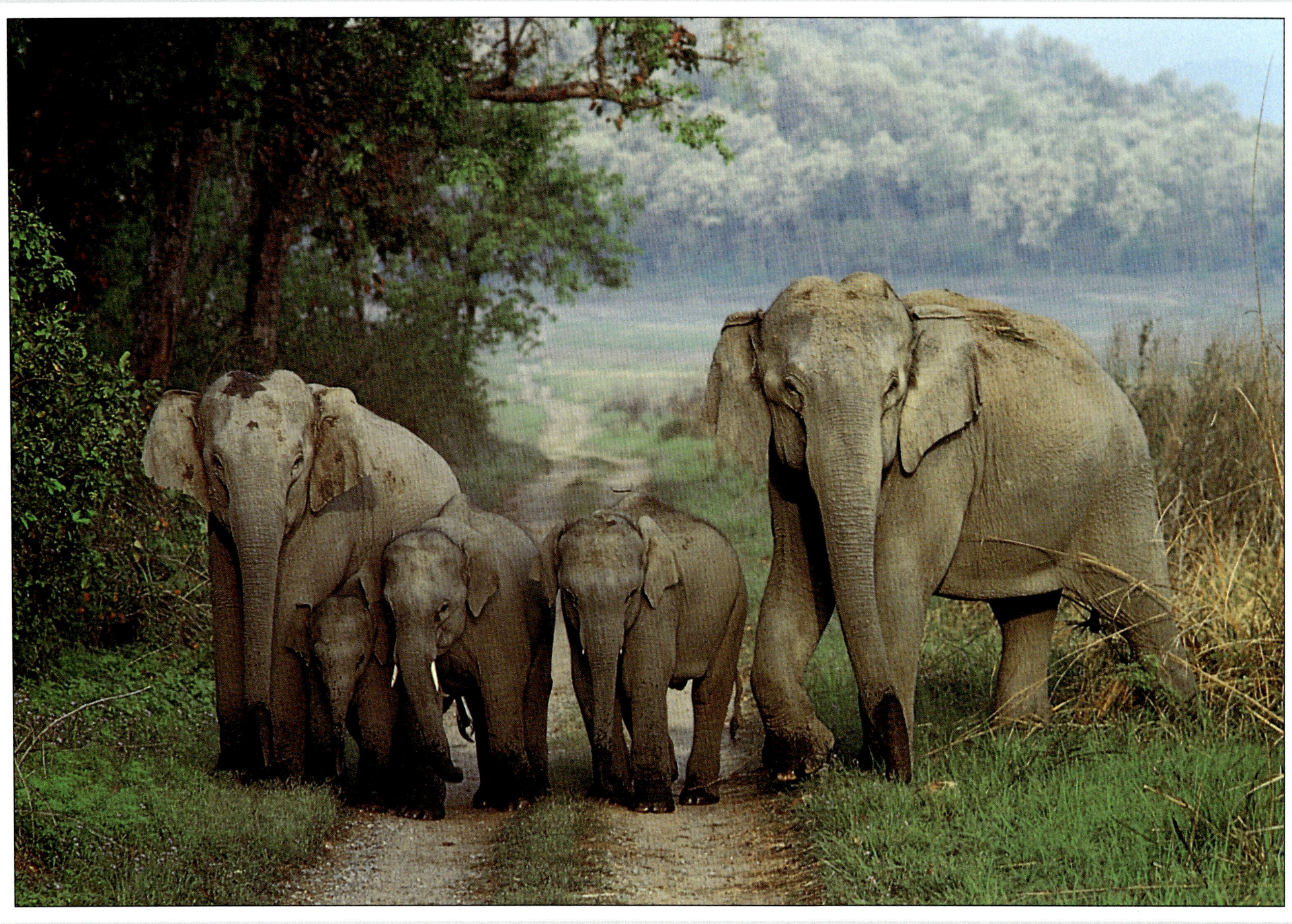

**Jagdeep Rajput**
India
RUNNER-UP

### *Indian elephant family*

*"I photographed this family group in the Corbett National Park as they were making their way into the forest. Elephants live in groups of related females and young. The females all help care for the young. I like this picture because it shows the elephants at every stage of growth, from very young to fully developed."*

Pentax Super A with 200mm lens; 1/125 sec at f5.6; Ektachrome Elite 100

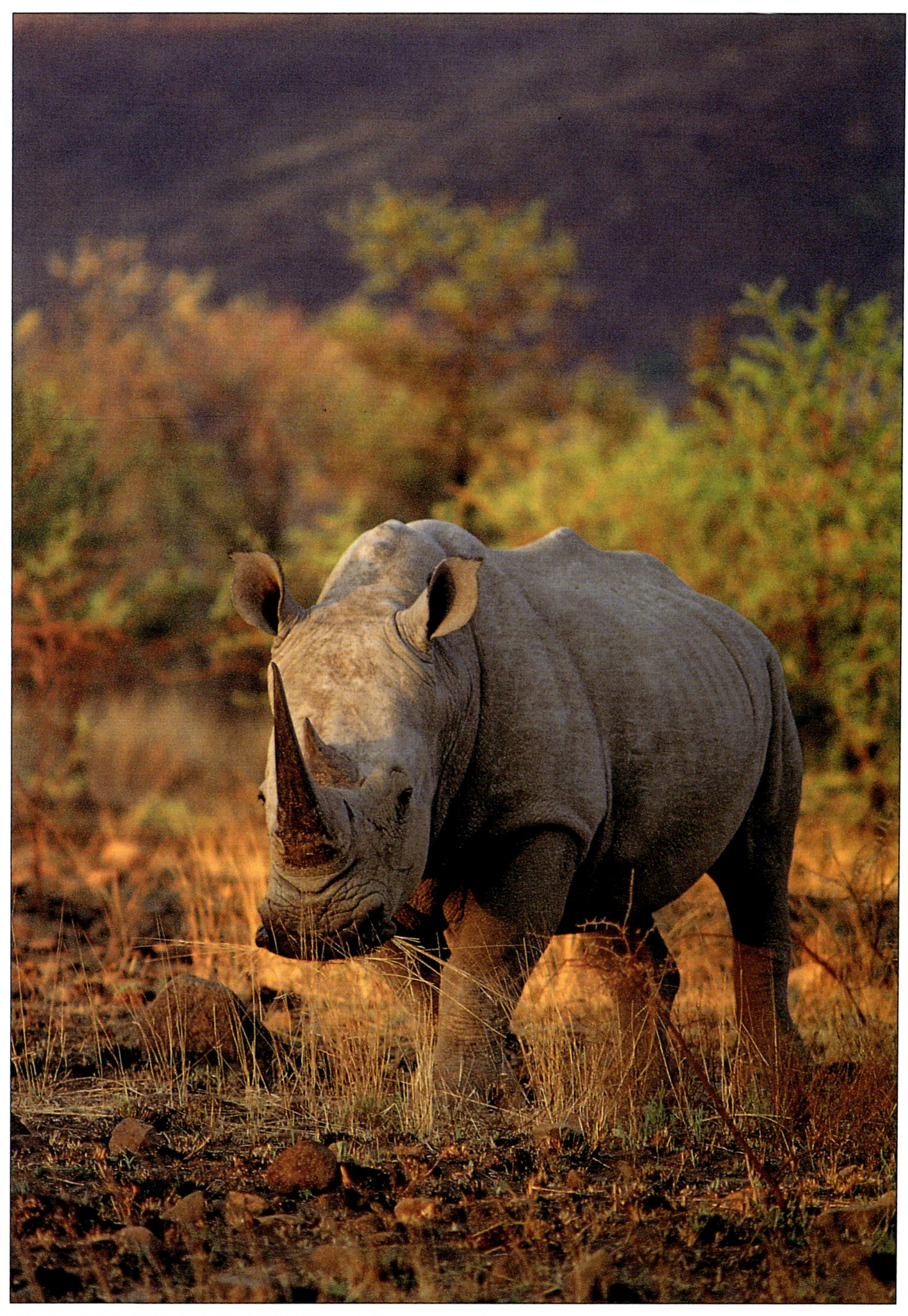

**Gus van Dyk**
South Africa
HIGHLY COMMENDED

---

### *White rhino*

*"The white rhino was almost driven to the brink of extinction by poaching for its horn, and, although numbers have since increased, it is still a target for poachers. South Africa is now the last sanctuary for these noble animals. This individual is walking along the edge of its well-defined territory in the Pilanesberg National Park. I knew its route, and so was able to position myself to get this head-on view."*

---

Nikon 801s with 180mm lens;
Fujichrome 100 rated at 125

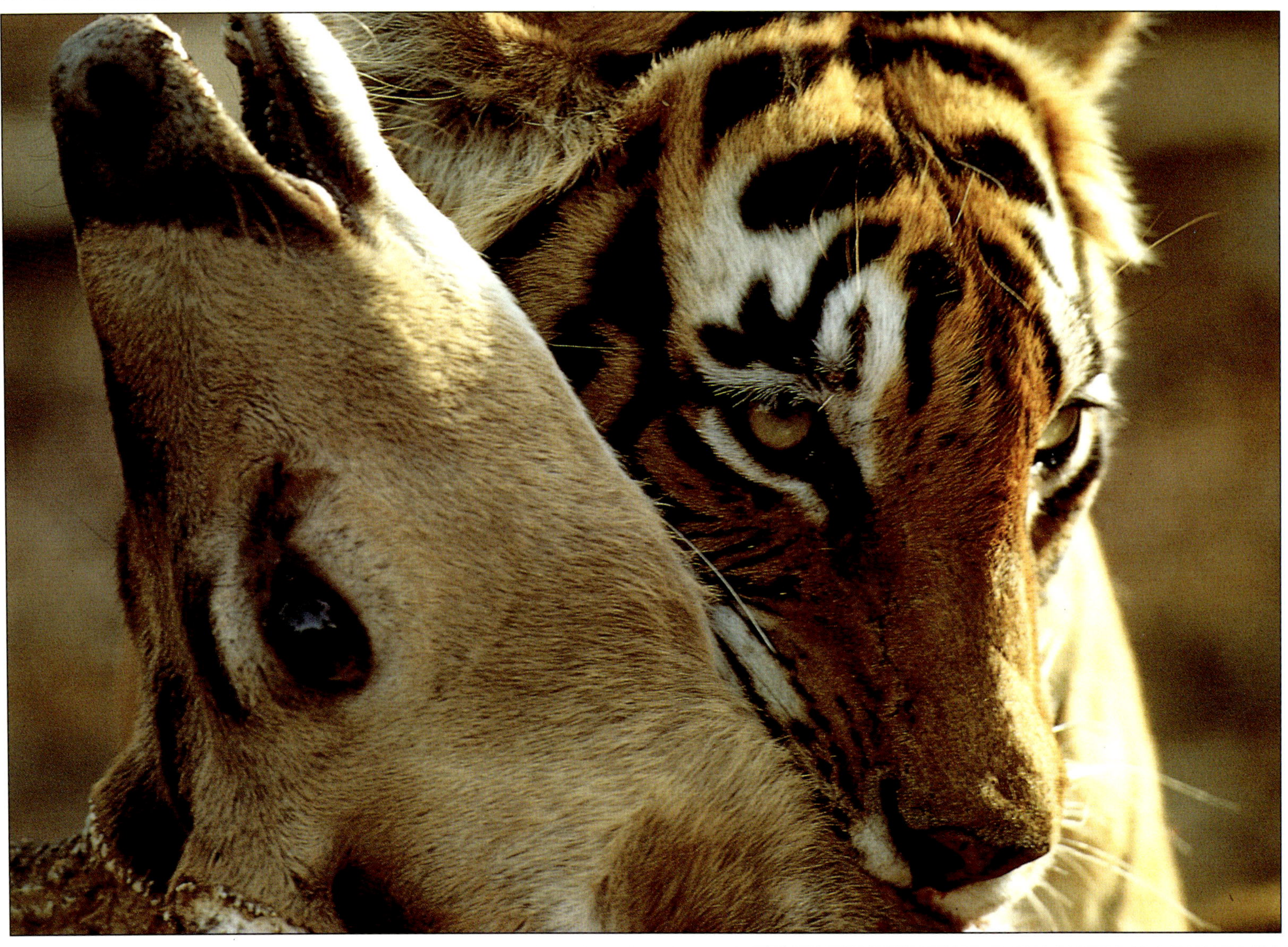

**Anup Shah**
United Kingdom
HIGHLY COMMENDED

---

***Tiger killing chital***

*"This is Noorjahan, a tigress living in Ranthambore National Park, India, suffocating a chital that she has caught. Once sure the chital was dead, she dragged it into the long grass to her waiting cubs."*

---

Canon EOS 600 with 600mm lens; f4;
Kodachrome 64

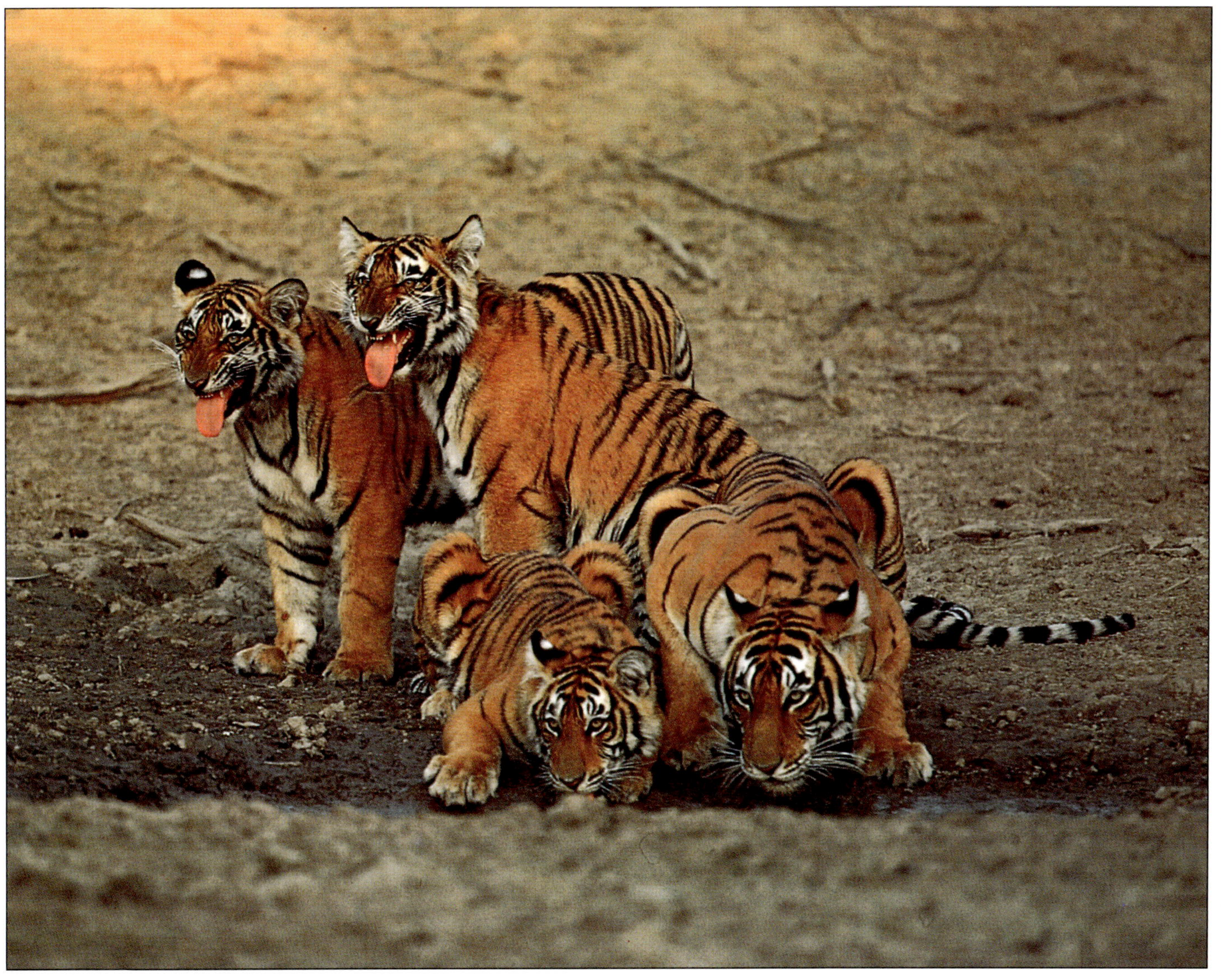

**Anup Shah**
United Kingdom
HIGHLY COMMENDED

***Tiger family***

*"This is Noorjahan, with her three nine-month-old cubs, drinking at a pool of water in a dried up lake bed. Two of the cubs have their tongues out in what is called the Flehmen gesture, to better inhale scents in the air."*

Canon EOS 600 with 600mm lens; f4; Kodachrome 64

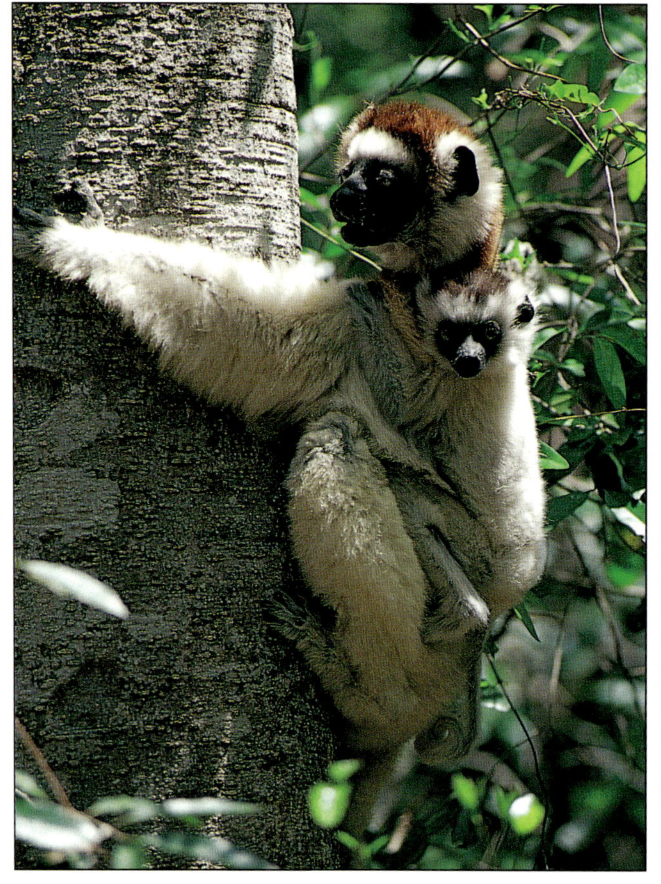

**Margaret Welby**
United Kingdom
HIGHLY COMMENDED

***Verreaux's sifaka with baby***

*"Walking along a forest track in Madagascar, I saw this female feeding on leaves up in the trees. Soon, she climbed down with her baby on her back to within a few feet of me.*
*With Madagascar's expanding population and increasing pressure on the forests, reserves such as Berenty, where this picture was taken, may soon be the last strongholds for the sifaka."*

Nikon F4 with 80-200mm lens; Kodachrome 200

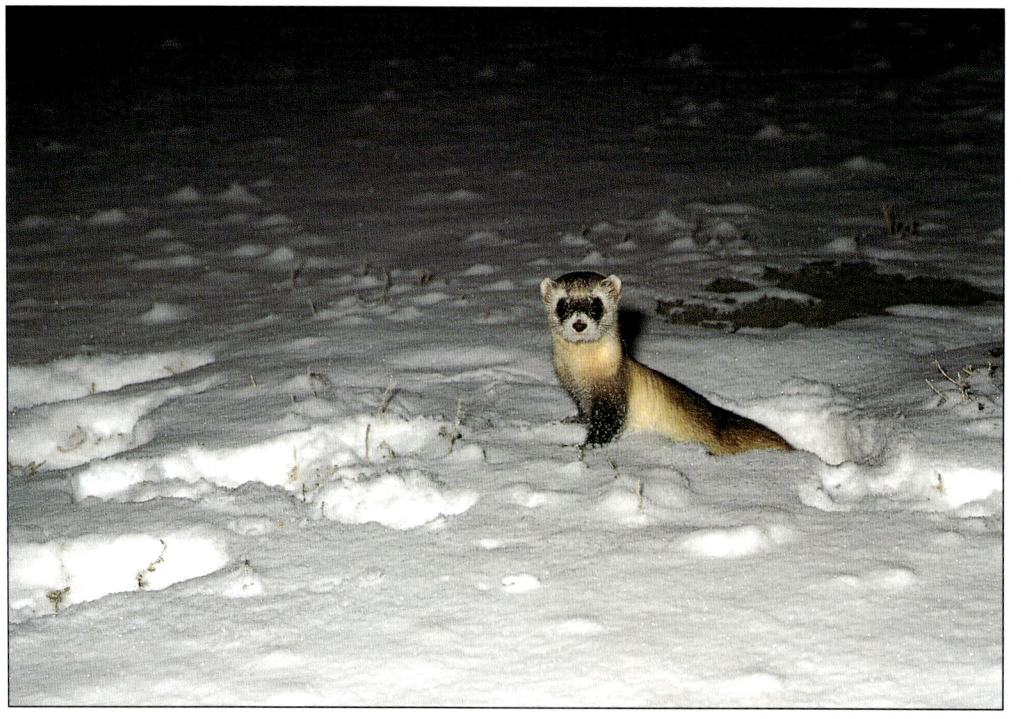

**William A Munoz**
United States of America
HIGHLY COMMENDED

***Black-footed ferret***

*"This individual was released into the U L Bend National Wildlife Refuge, Montana, at the end of 1994, as part of a programme to re-establish black-footed ferrets in the wild. Several months later, in freezing conditions, I photographed him as he went from one prairie dog hole to another."*

Pentax MX with 85mm lens; flash; 1/60 sec at f8; Fujichrome 100

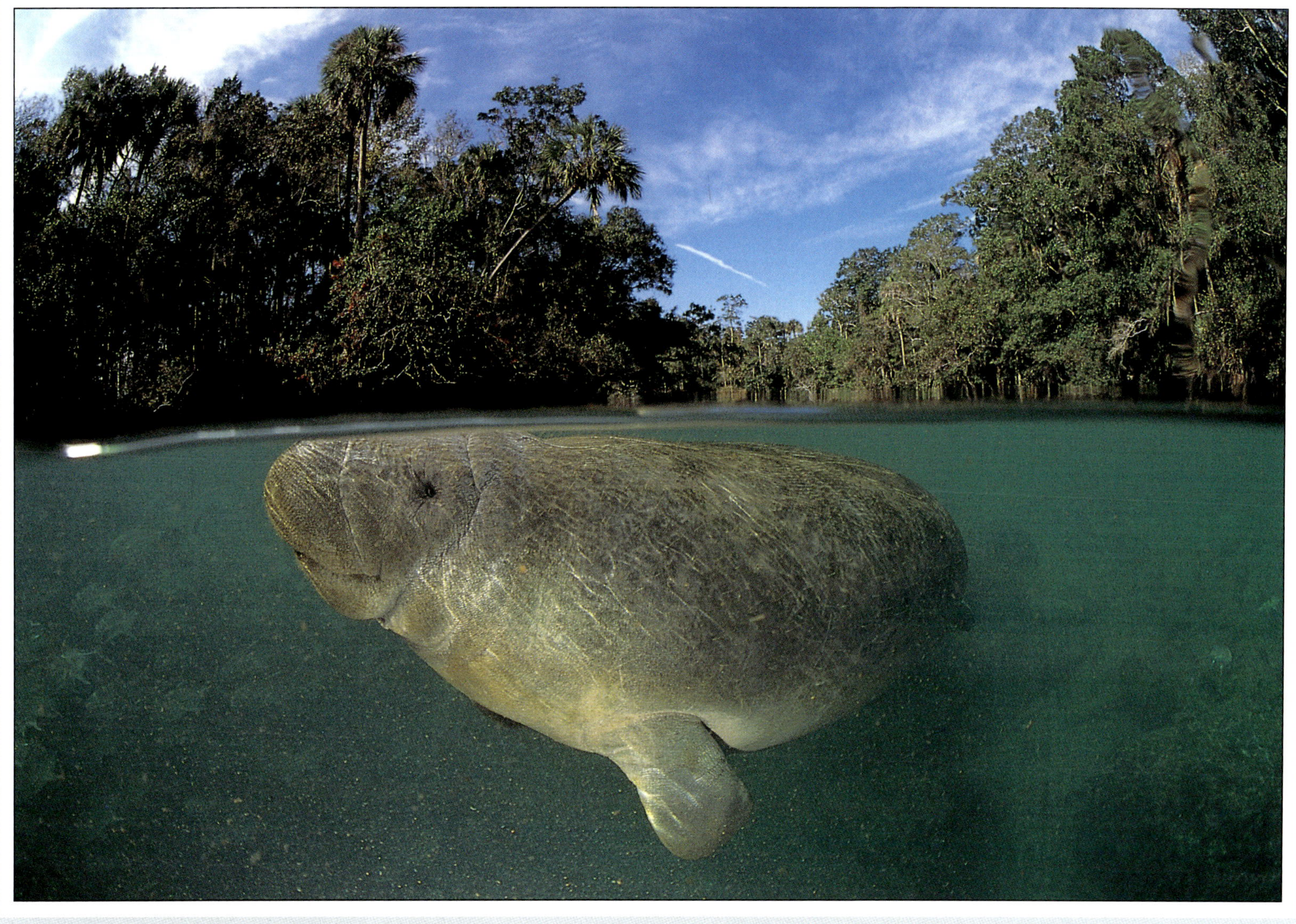

**Jürgen Freund**
Germany
HIGHLY COMMENDED

**West Indian manatee**

*"West Indian manatees are threatened with extinction - only some 1,800 remain in Florida. This gentle individual was rescued and treated for severe injuries caused by powerboat propellers. I photographed it in Homosassa Springs State Park before it was released back into the wild."*

Nikon F4 with 16mm lens in underwater housing; flash; 1/60 sec at f16; Fujichrome Sensia 100

# British Wildlife

Entries must feature wild plants or animals, which can be in wild or urban settings.

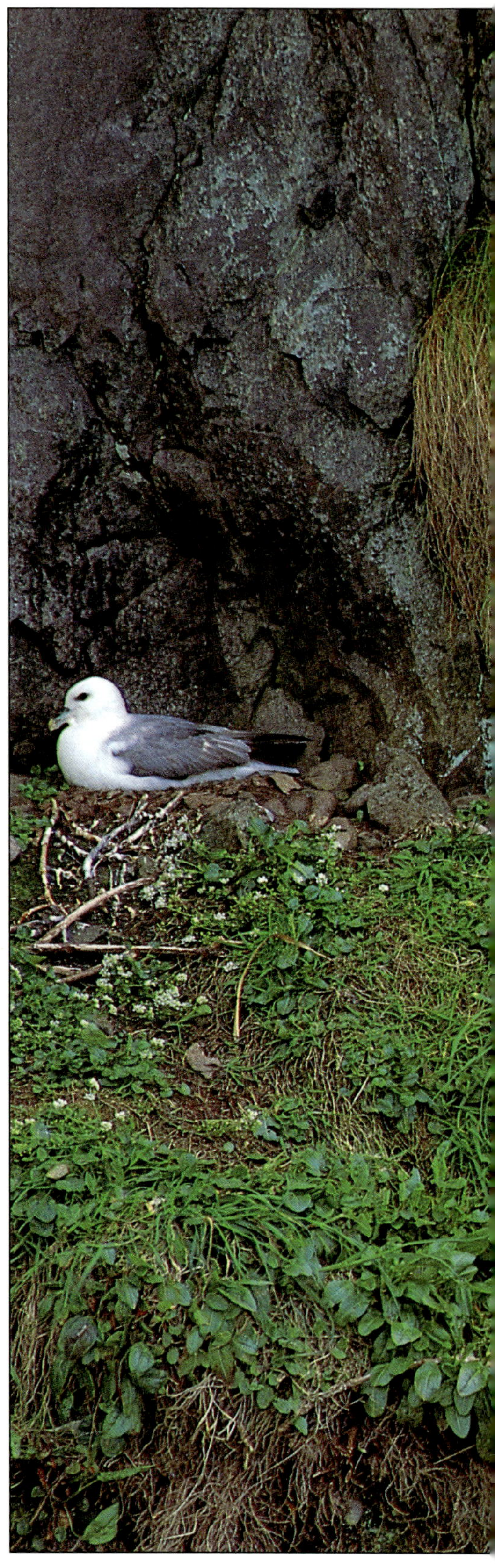

**Paul Hicks**
United Kingdom
WINNER

***Fulmar colony***

*"Every spring, fulmars return to this cliff on the Isle of Islay to breed. I was struck by the profusion of grasses and flowers growing all over the cliff and decided to capture the courtship behaviour of the birds in their beautiful setting. I isolated a section of the cliff, and as I was shooting into deep shadow with the sun in my face, I used my hat to shield the lens and prevent flare."*

Nikon F4s with 300mm lens; tripod; 1/30 sec at f5.6; Fujichrome Velvia

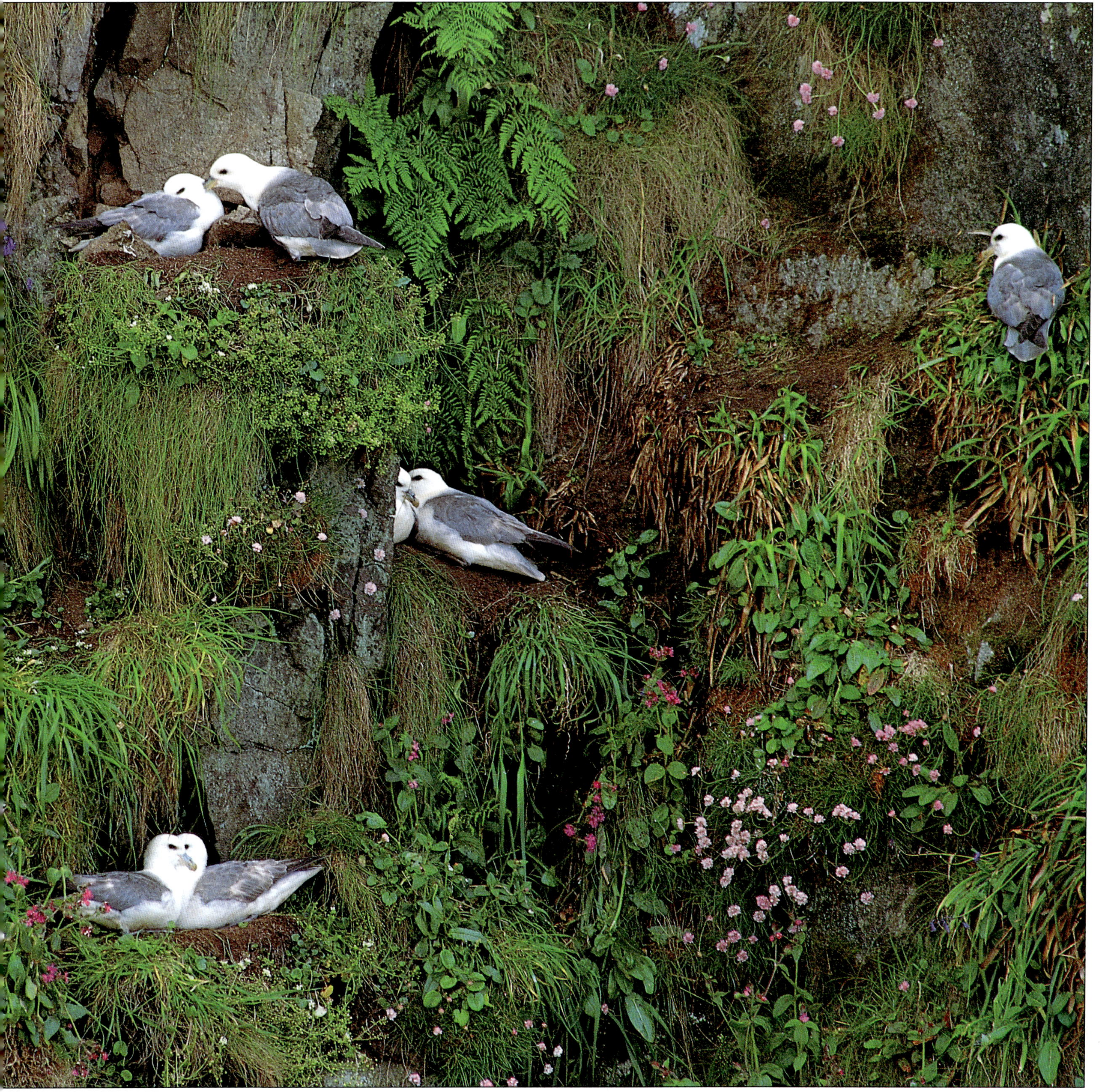

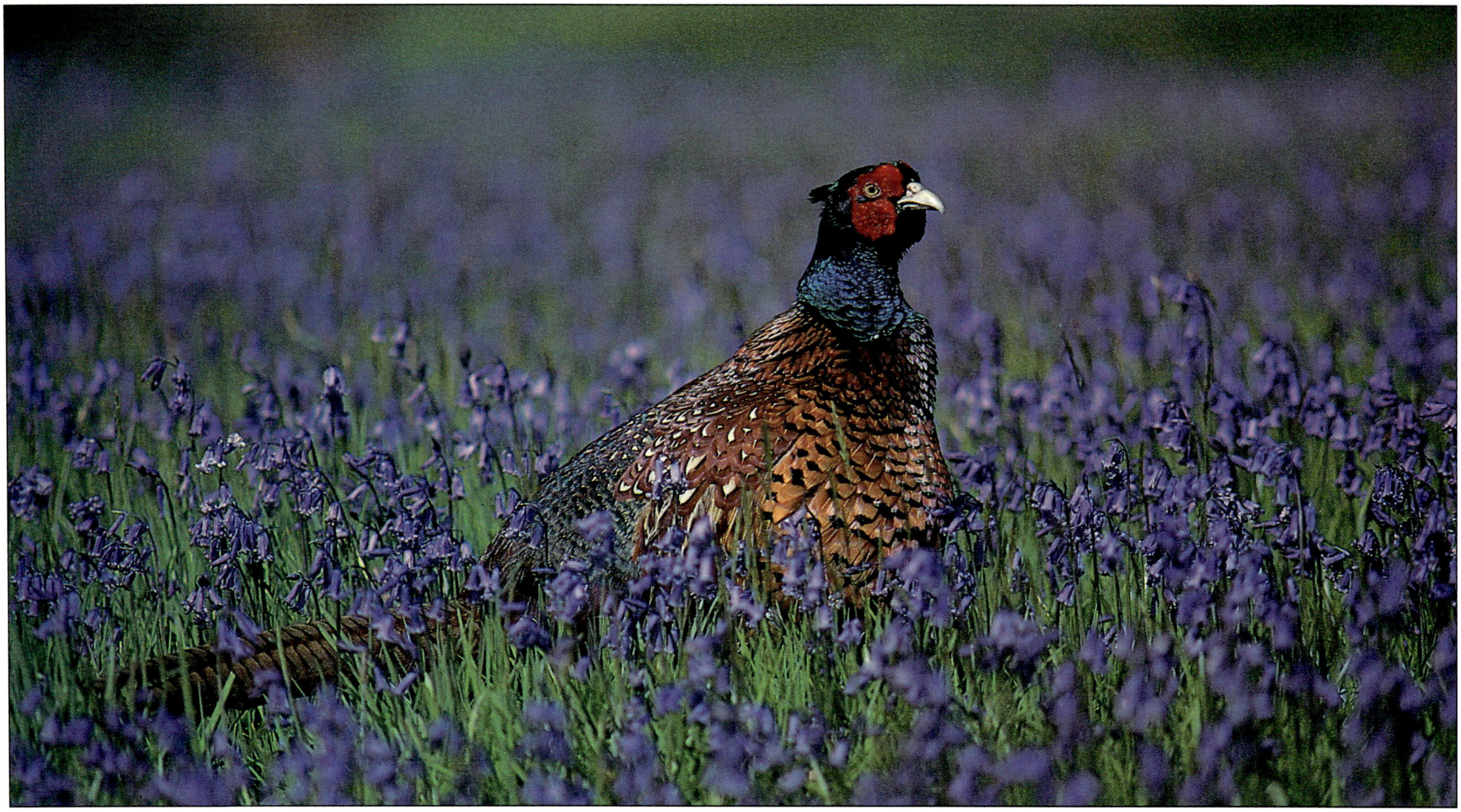

**Andrew Bailey**
United Kingdom
RUNNER-UP

***Cock pheasant and bluebells***

*"Among the bluebells at Wakehurst Place one spring day, I was lucky to find a hen pheasant with a male in close attendance."*

Minolta X700 with 300mm lens; 1/250 sec at f4.5; Kodachrome 64

**Laurie Campbell**
United Kingdom
SPECIALLY COMMENDED

***Capercaillie displaying***

*"I photographed this 'bold' capercaillie in native pinewood in Strathspey. Not having to use a hide, I could experiment with different viewpoints."*

Nikon F4s with 500mm lens; 1/500 sec at f4; Fujichrome Provia 100

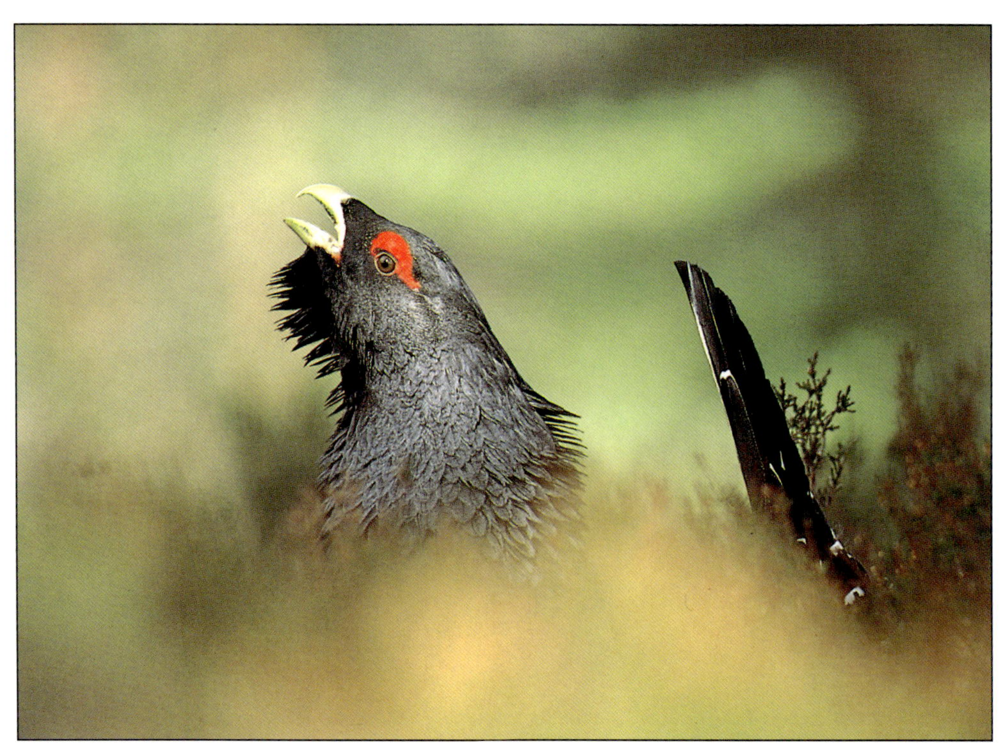

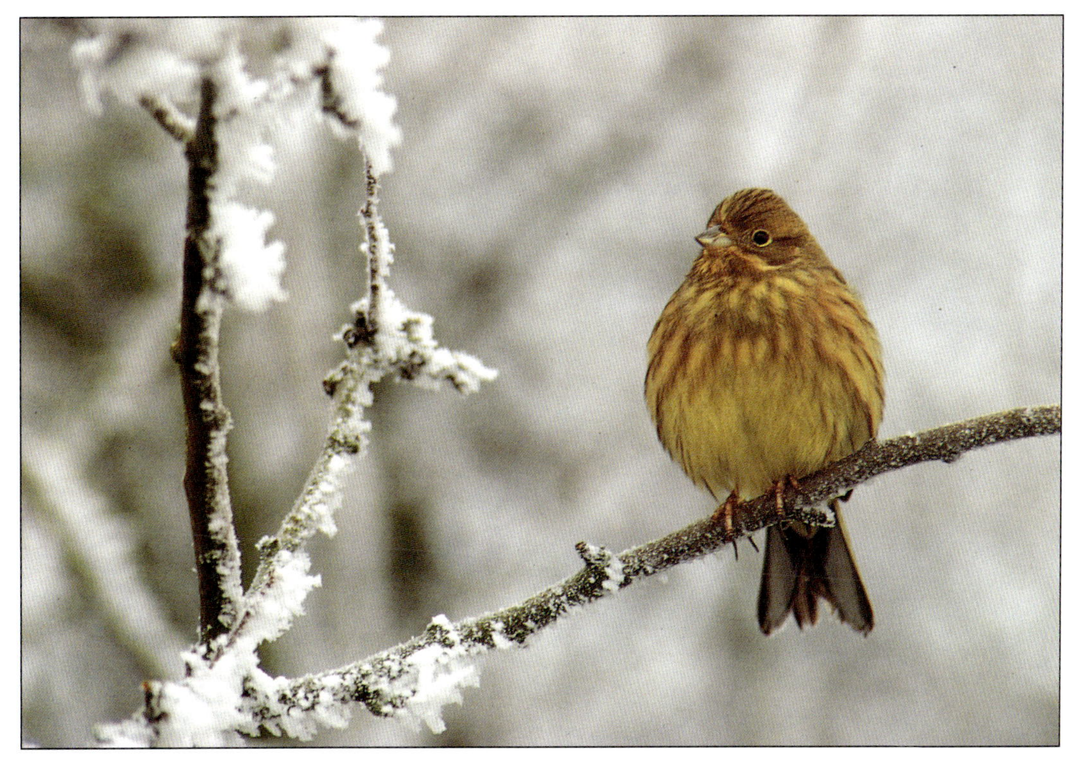

**Malcolm Freeman**
United Kingdom
HIGHLY COMMENDED

---

***Yellowhammer in hoar frost***

*"I set up a hide opposite a hawthorn bush on a local farm specially to photograph yellowhammers. I captured this female fluffing her feathers to keep warm early on a frosty Christmas eve."*

---

Nikon F4s with 300mm lens and x1.6 teleconverter; 1/30 sec at f8; Kodak Panther 100

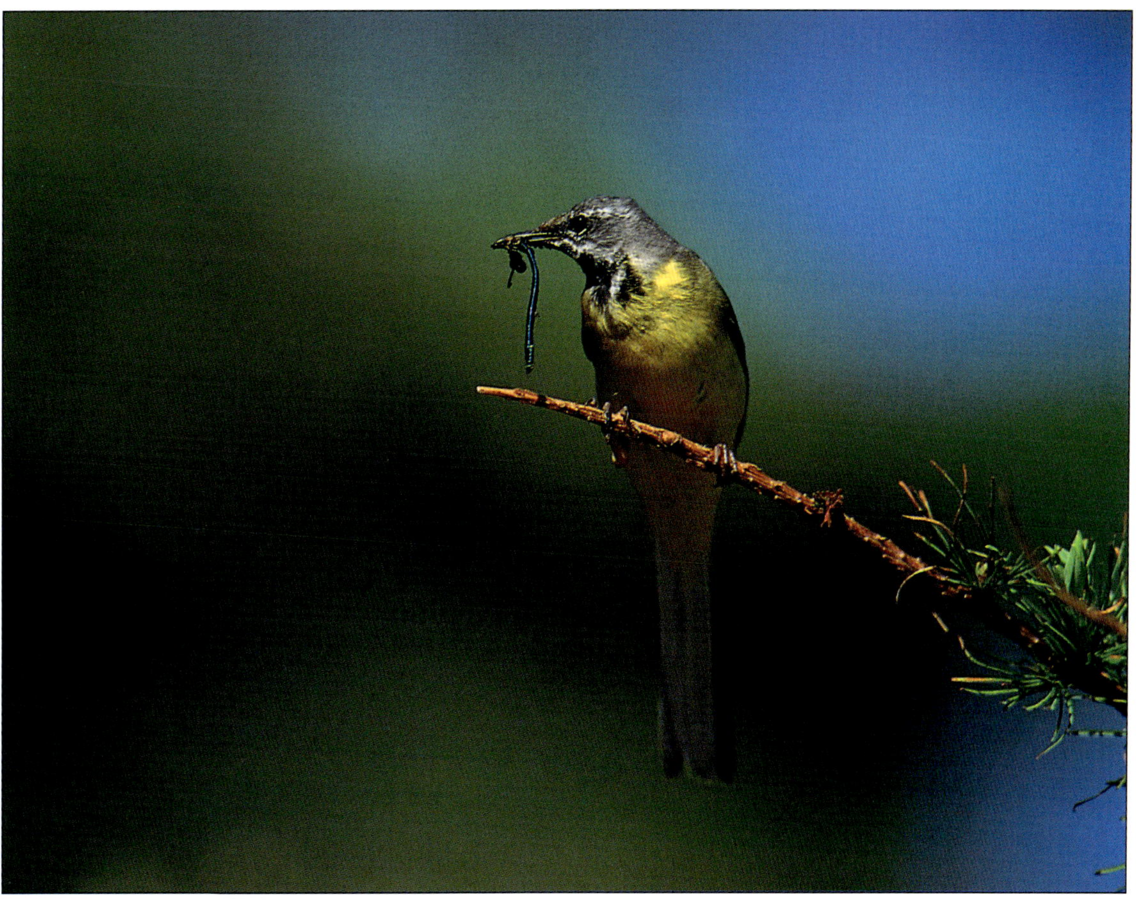

**Colin Varndell**
United Kingdom
HIGHLY COMMENDED

---

***Grey wagtail with damselfly***

*"The grey wagtail was feeding young in a nest in a stone wall of a mill house near the River Brit in Dorset. I am not interested in 'at the nest' photography, and so I positioned a camouflage screen where I could photograph the bird as it paused en route to feed its young. I wanted to record the range of insects it caught."*

---

Nikon FM with 500mm lens; tripod; 1/125 sec at f8; Fujichrome 100 rated at 125

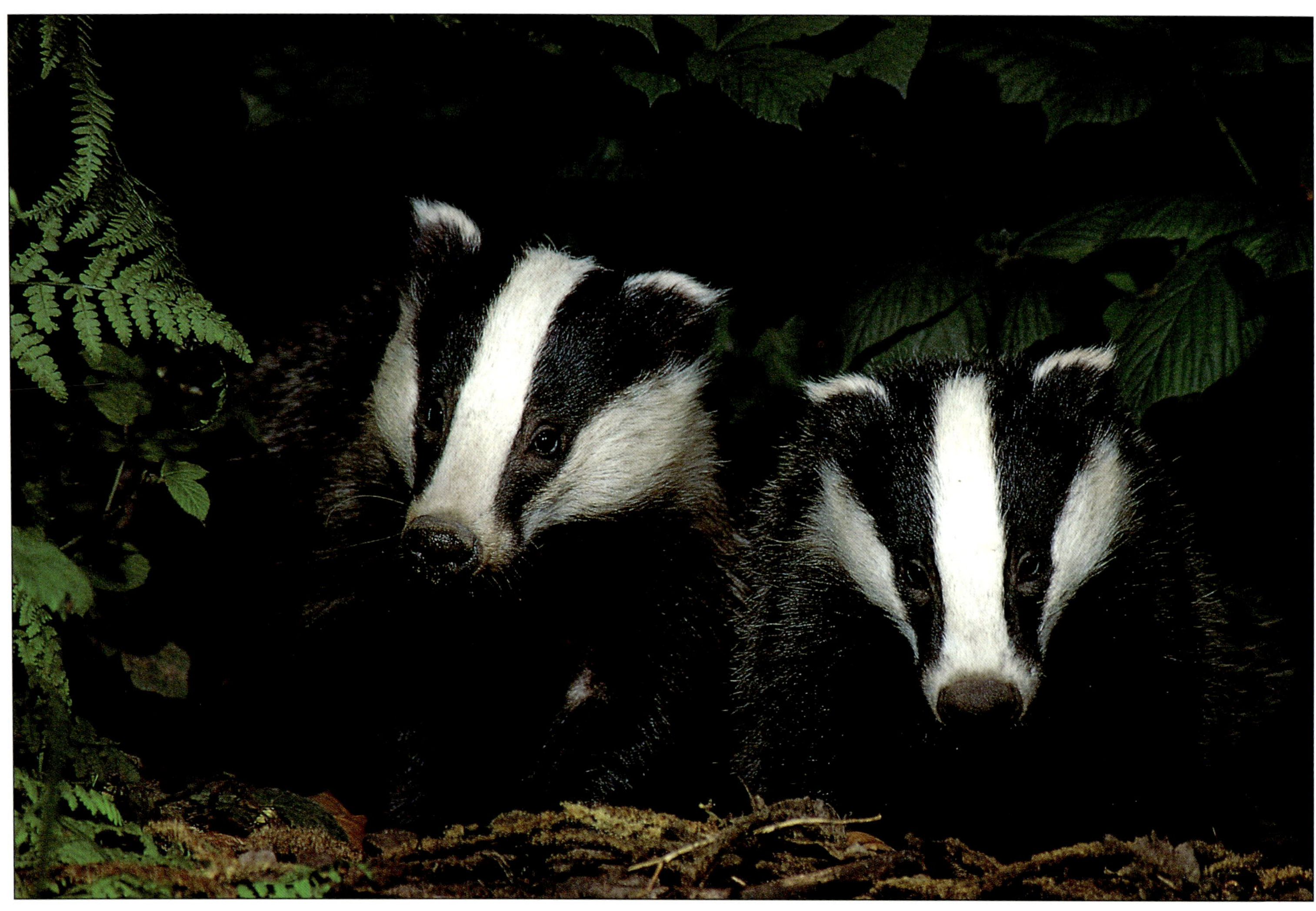

**Andrew Hadley**
United Kingdom
HIGHLY COMMENDED

***Badger siblings***

*"I visit a particular badger set five evenings a week throughout the year. The badgers - about 15 in all - have come to accept me, and I am able to photograph and film them about my feet. These are two-year-old male and female siblings photographed in 1993. Although the female has now had cubs, they still spend time together."*

Pentax ME Super with 75-300mm lens; two flashes; tripod; 1/120 sec at f11; Kodachrome 64

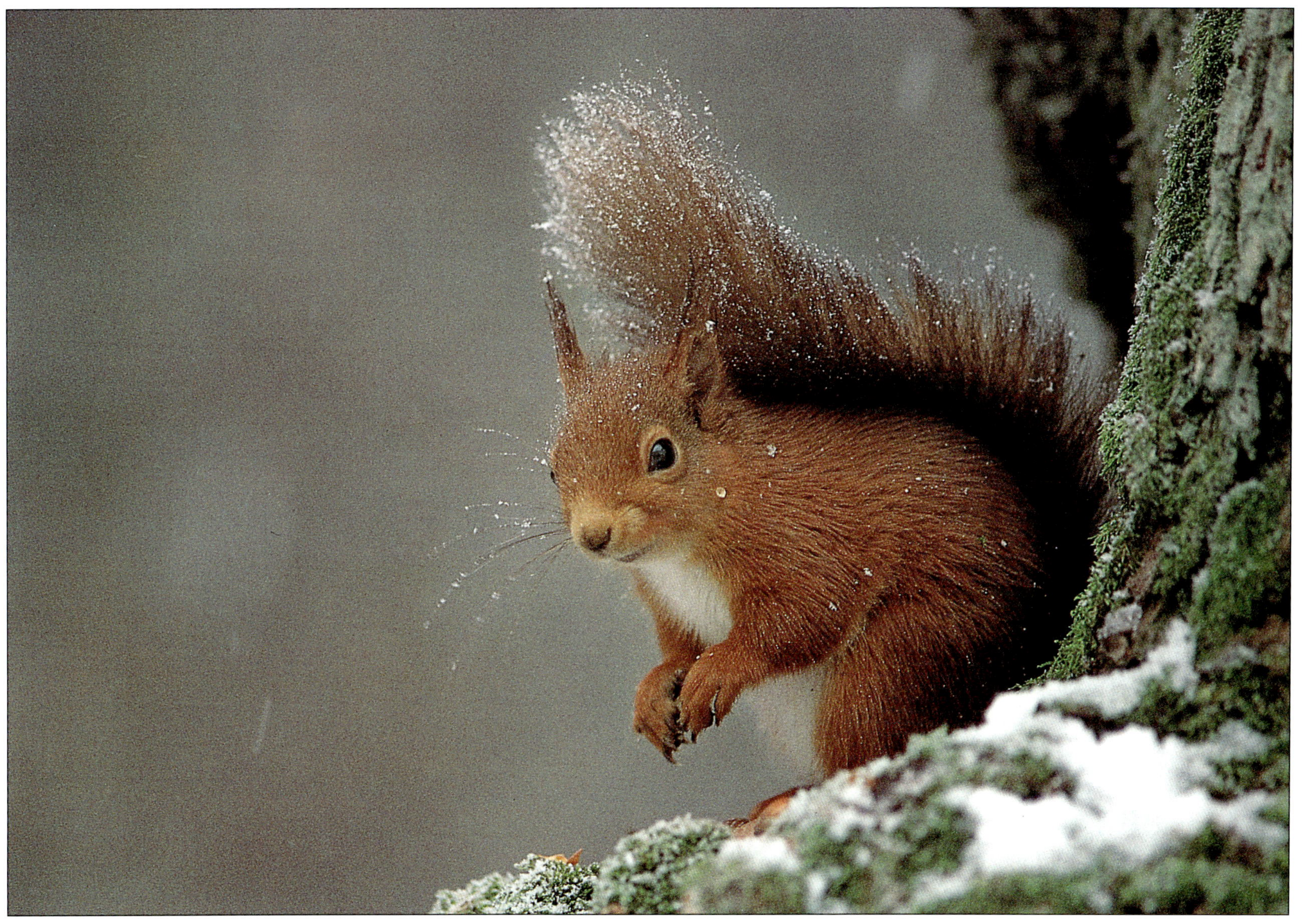

**Rob Jordan**
United Kingdom
HIGHLY COMMENDED

***Red squirrel in snow***

*"I built a hide and a feeding station in woodland close to my home in* Northumberland *specially to photograph red squirrels. I had virtually given up hope of snow when, one* April *morning, I woke to find it falling heavily. I was in the hide within minutes. Here the squirrel appears to use its tail as protection against the weather."*

Nikon F4s with 300mm lens; tripod; hide; 1/30 sec at f5.6; Kodachrome 200

# In Praise of Plants

Pictures can illustrate flowering and non-flowering plants in close-up or en masse, and should highlight their beauty and importance.

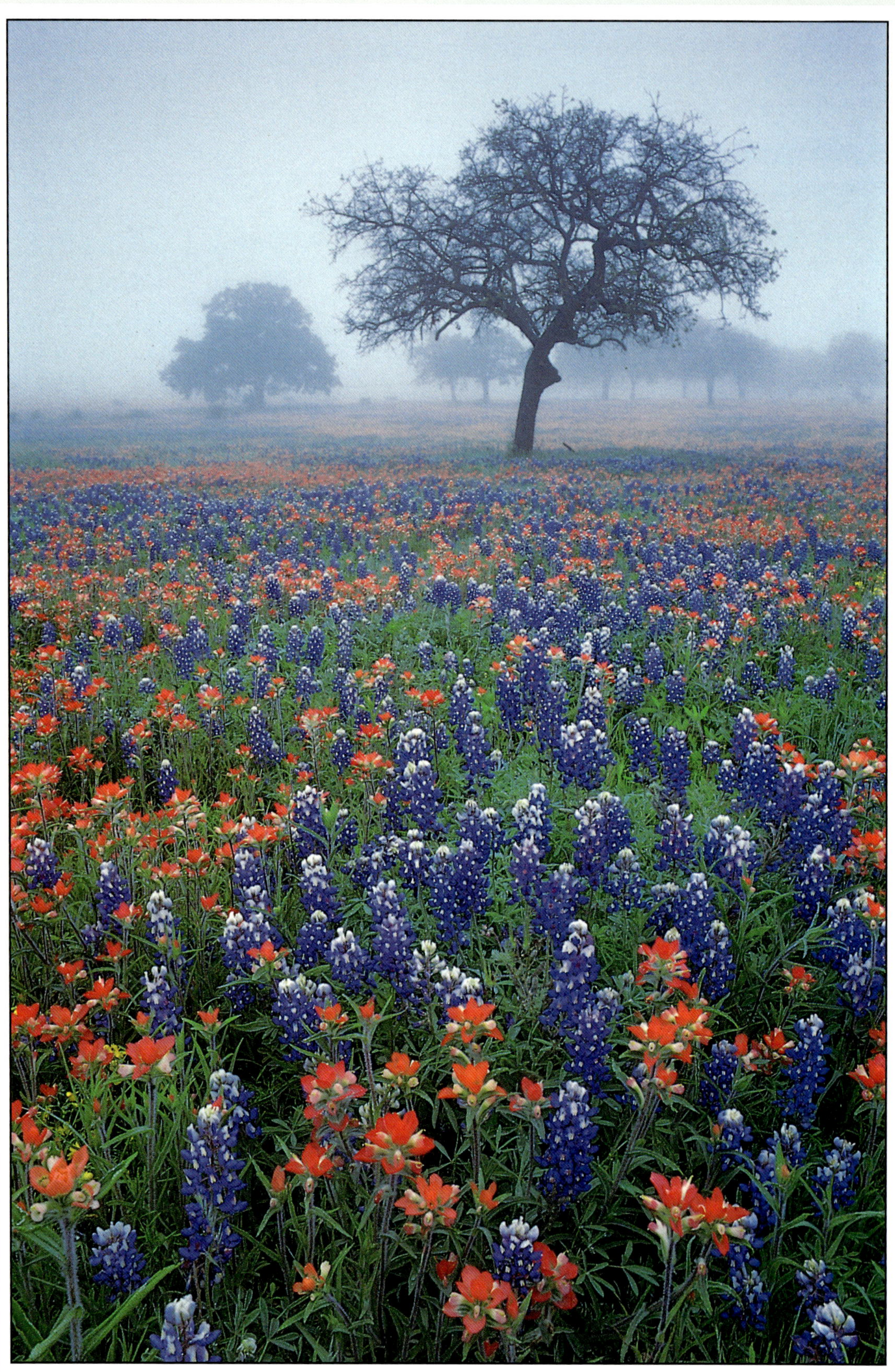

**Adam Jones**
United States of America
WINNER

***Texas paintbrush and bluebonnets on foggy morning***

*"It is somewhat unusual to encounter fog and calm winds in Texas. Calm was critical because of the four-second exposure needed to capture the flowers in the foggy predawn light of an April morning."*

Pentax PZ-1 with 28mm lens; tripod; 4 secs at f22; Fujichrome Velvia

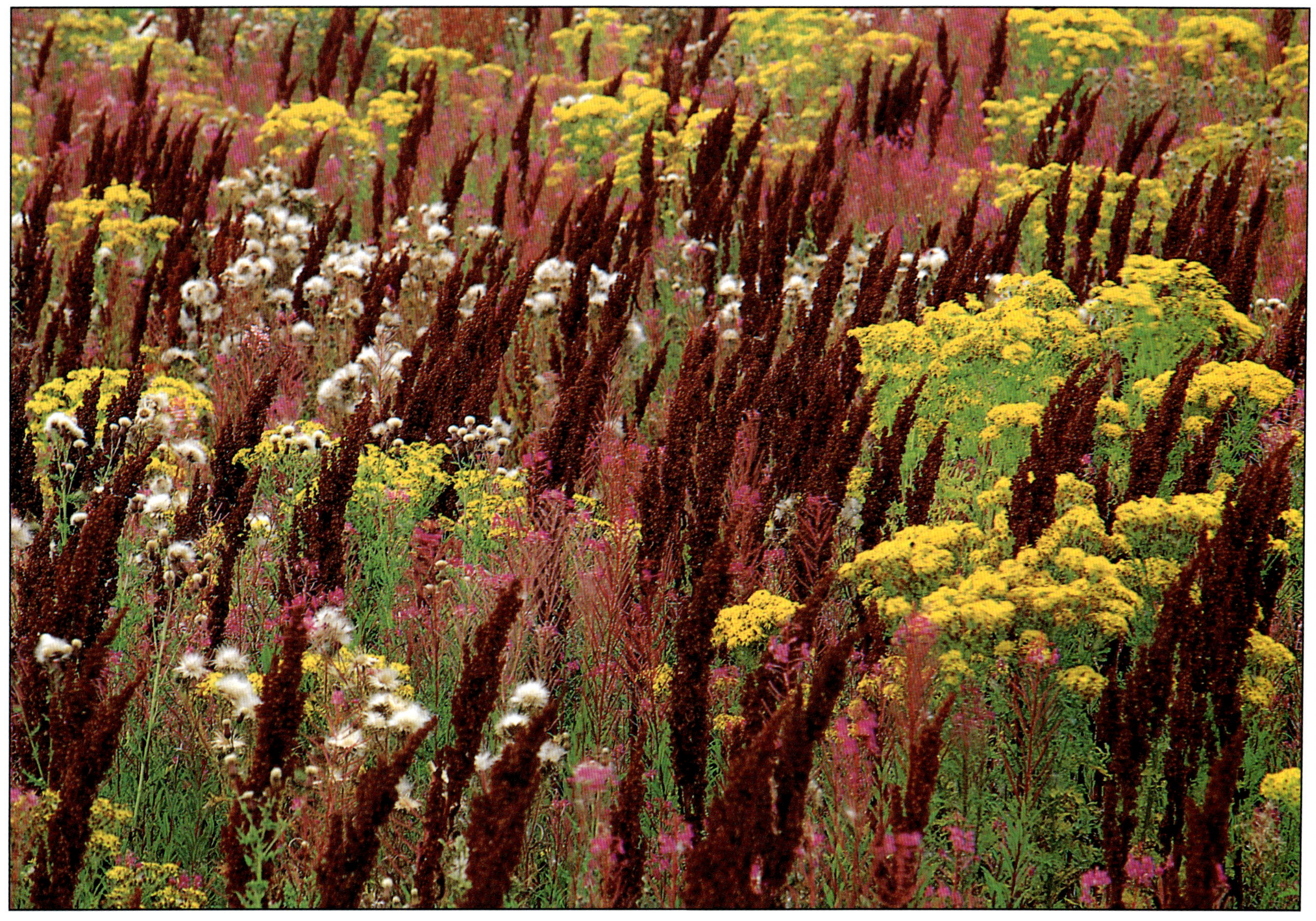

**Brian Lightfoot**
United Kingdom
RUNNER-UP

***Wild flowers on set-aside land***

*"I came across this special field of wild flowers on the outskirts of Forfar in Scotland. As soon as I saw the vibrant colours of the ragwort, rosebay willowherb, docks and thistles, I knew there was bound to be a good photograph."*

Nikon F4s with 28-85mm lens; tripod; Fujichrome Velvia

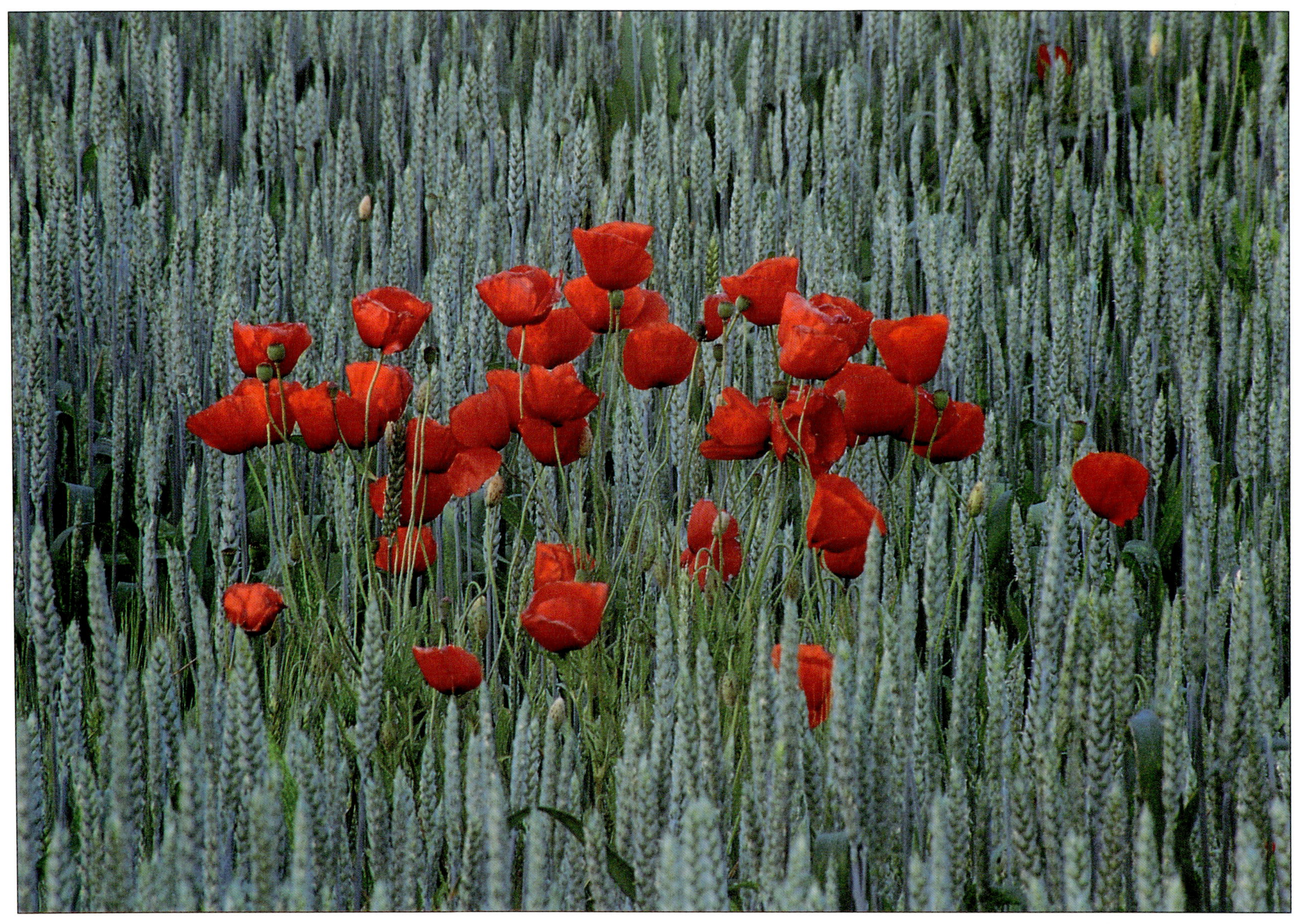

**Csaba Forràsy**

Hungary

SPECIALLY COMMENDED

***Poppies***

*"One afternoon in May I was walking in the countryside in western Hungary, when I noticed there were quite a lot of weeds growing in the cornfields. Suddenly I found this group of vivid poppies, lit by an unusually 'cold' natural light."*

Pentax Z-1 with 400mm lens; f5.6;
Fujichrome RD100

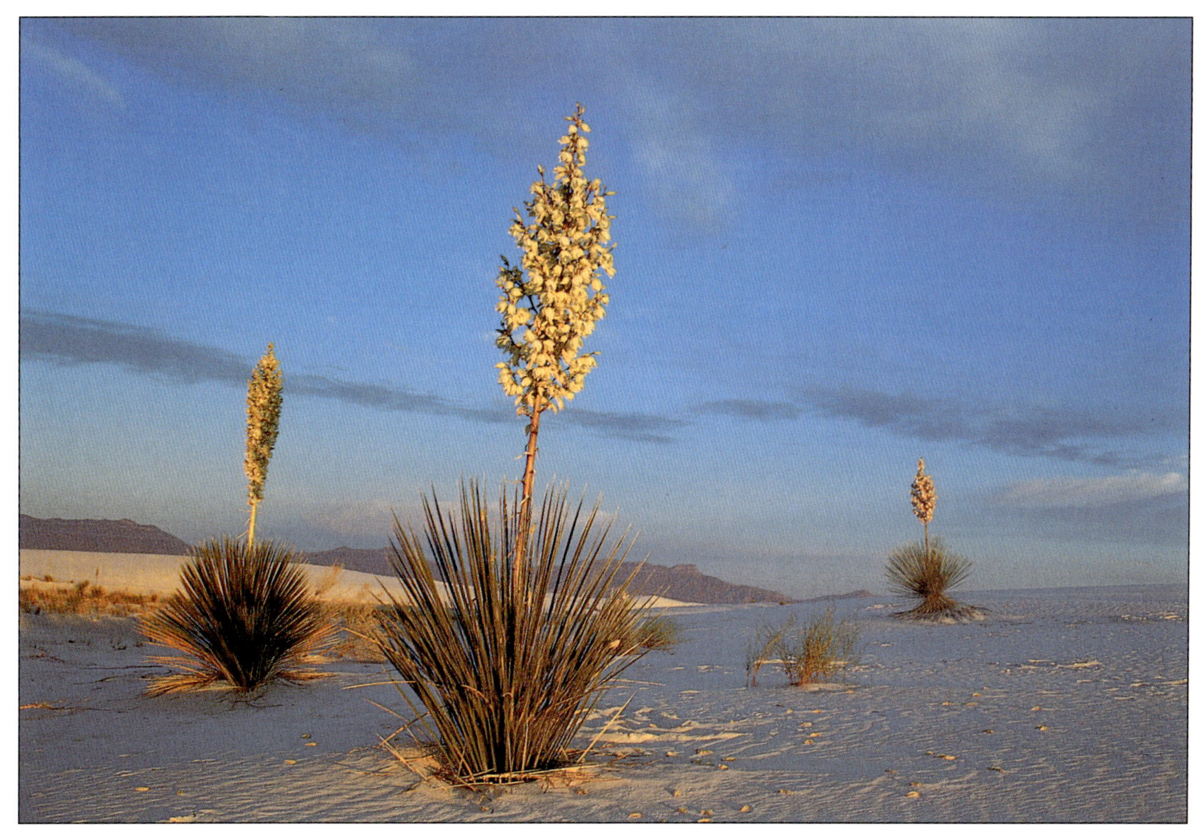

**Rosemary Calvert**
United Kingdom
HIGHLY COMMENDED

### *Banana yucca*

*"The White Sands National Monument in New Mexico is composed of continually moving dunes, and is excessively hot and dry in summer. The banana yucca survives these harsh conditions better than most plants, producing a fine erect bloom that lasts for weeks. I took this photograph one morning in late May, just as the sun rose above the horizon."*

Canon EOS 105 with 28-100mm lens; tripod; 1/8 sec at f16; Fujichrome Velvia

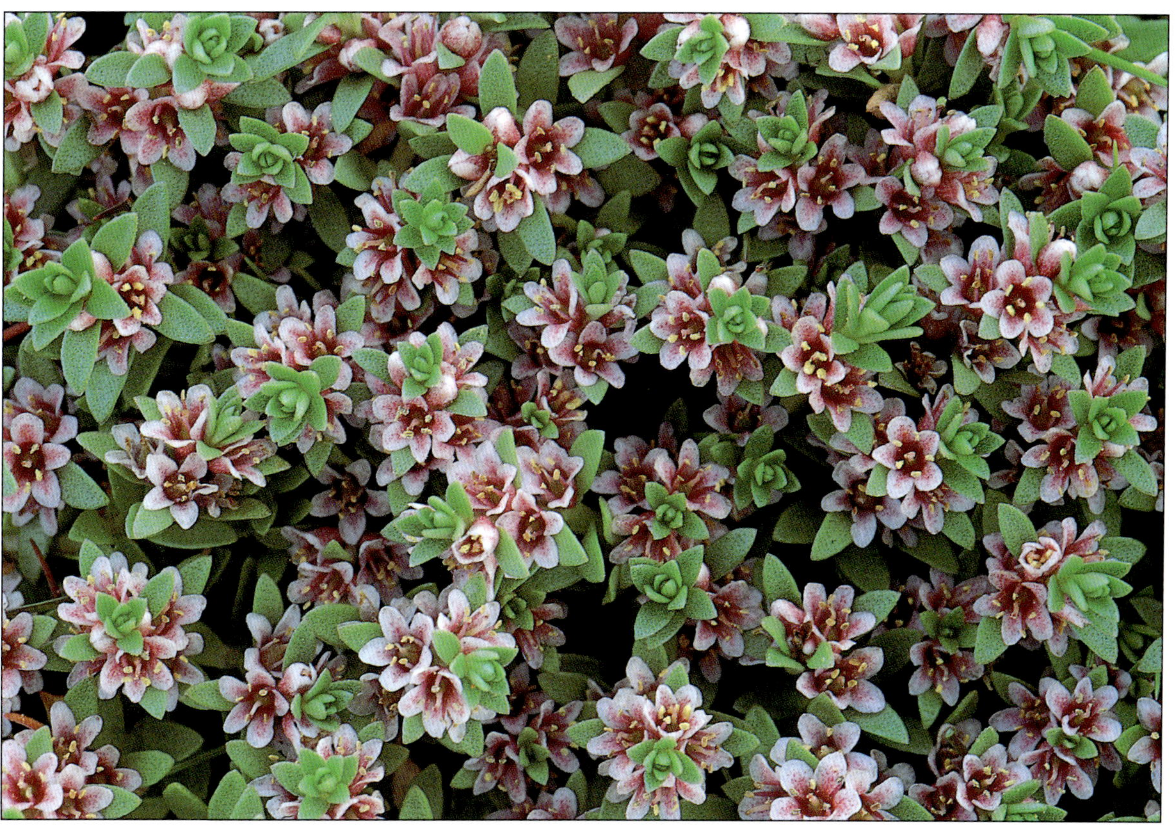

**Jörn Pilon**
The Netherlands
HIGHLY COMMENDED

### *Flowering sea milkwort*

*"Sea milkwort is a typical plant of salty or brackish coastal habitats. I particularly wanted to photograph it because I like the combination of delicate pink and fresh green. In 1993 I just couldn't find a nice regular pattern. Then, in 1994, I finally found what I was looking for."*

Nikon F-801s with 60mm lens; tripod; Fujichrome Velvia

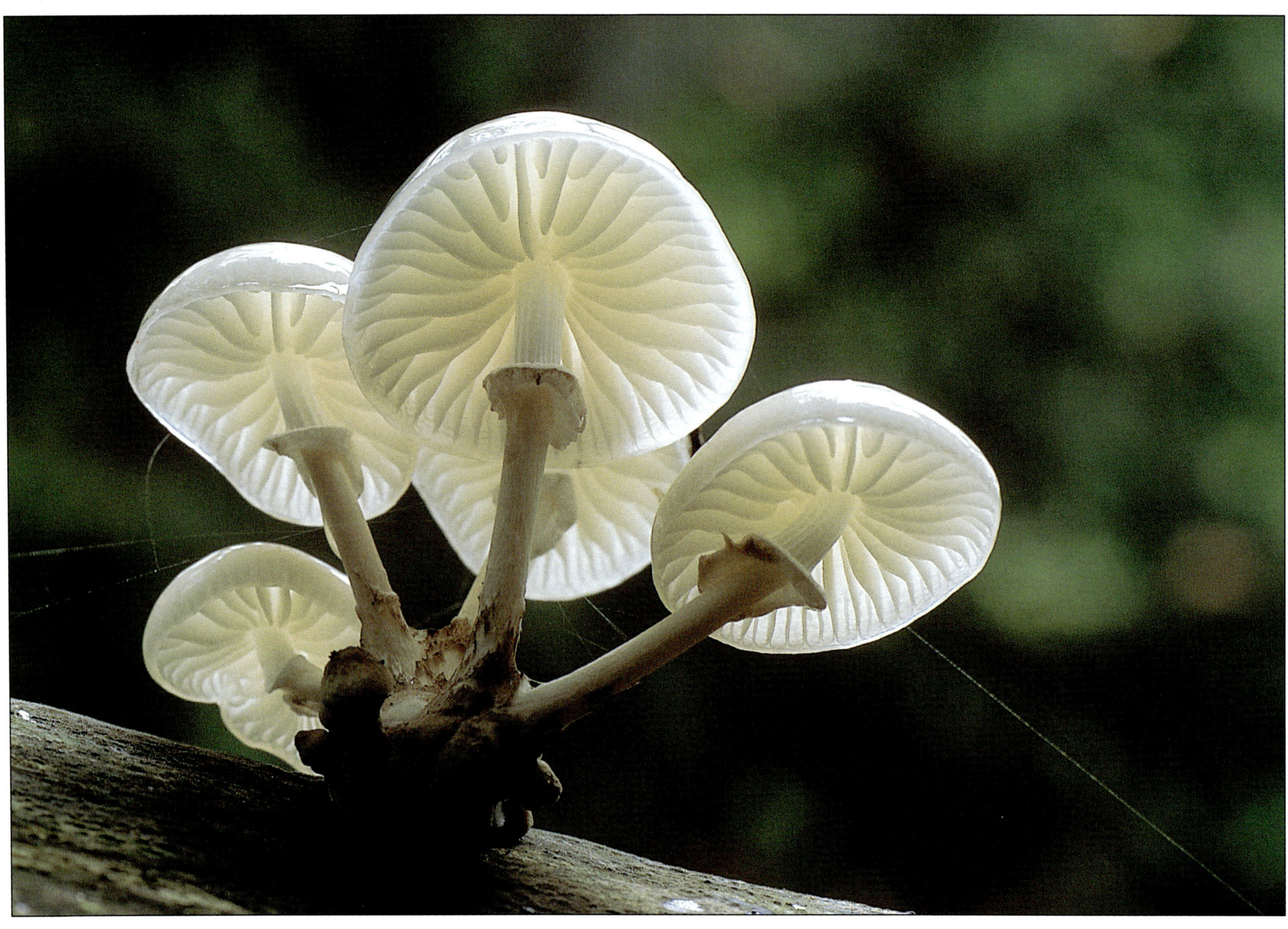

**Fritz Pölking**
Germany
HIGHLY COMMENDED

***Porcelain fungi***

*"I think this collection of Porcelain fungi Oudemansiella mucida, photographed in the Bavarian Forest, looks like a meeting of umbrellas."*

Canon EOS 1 with 100mm lens; auto-exposure at f22; Fujichrome 50

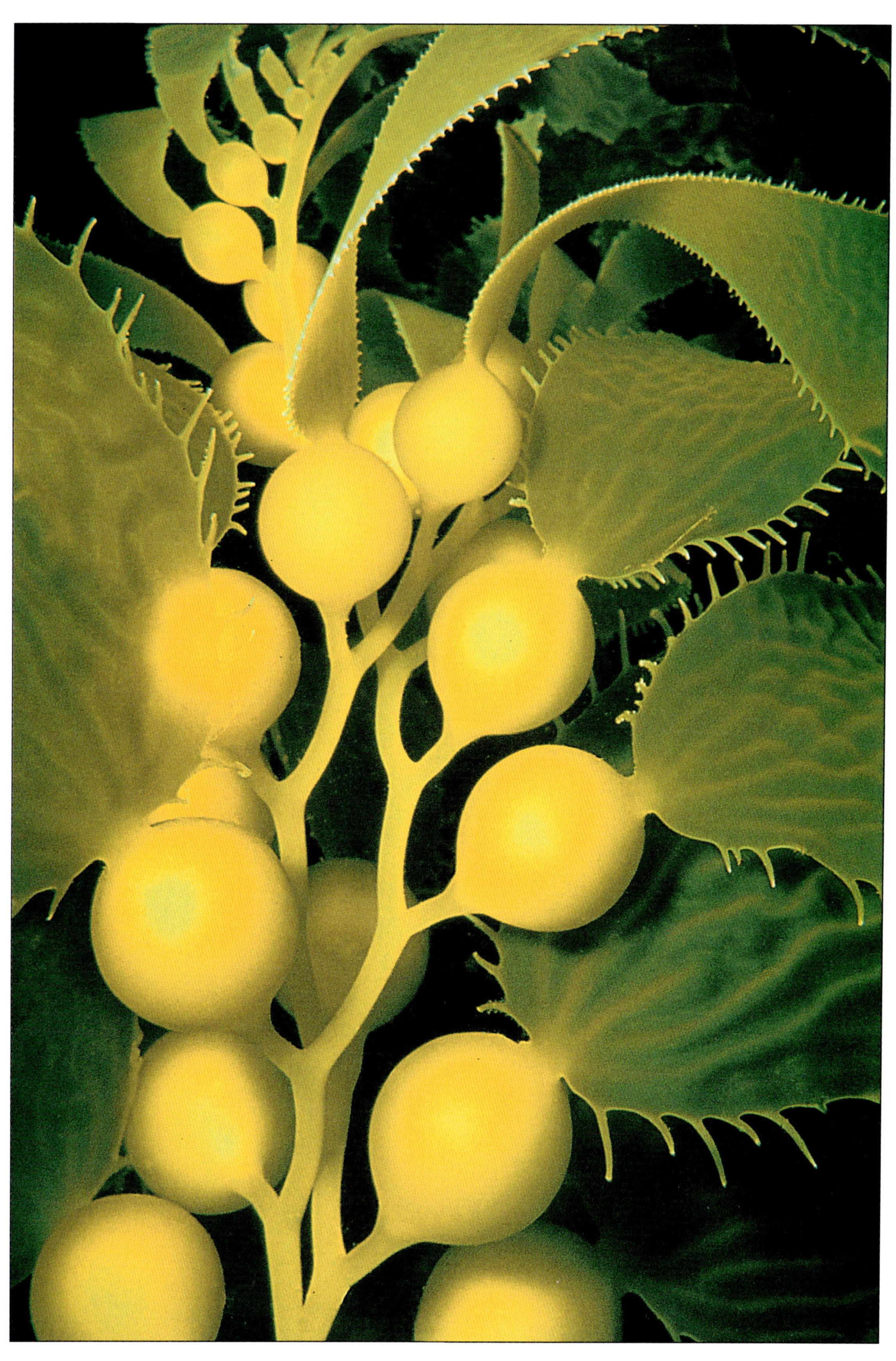

**Kenneth J Howard**
United States of America
HIGHLY COMMENDED

## *Giant kelp detail*

*"I took the picture in a kelp forest in the Pacific Ocean, off southern California. Giant kelp can grow by half a metre a day, reaching a length of 60 metres. Gas-filled bladders buoy the great fronds up, helping them to intercept sunlight."*

Nikonos V with 35mm lens and extension tube; strobe; 1/90 sec at f22; Kodak Ektachrome Lumiere 100x Professional

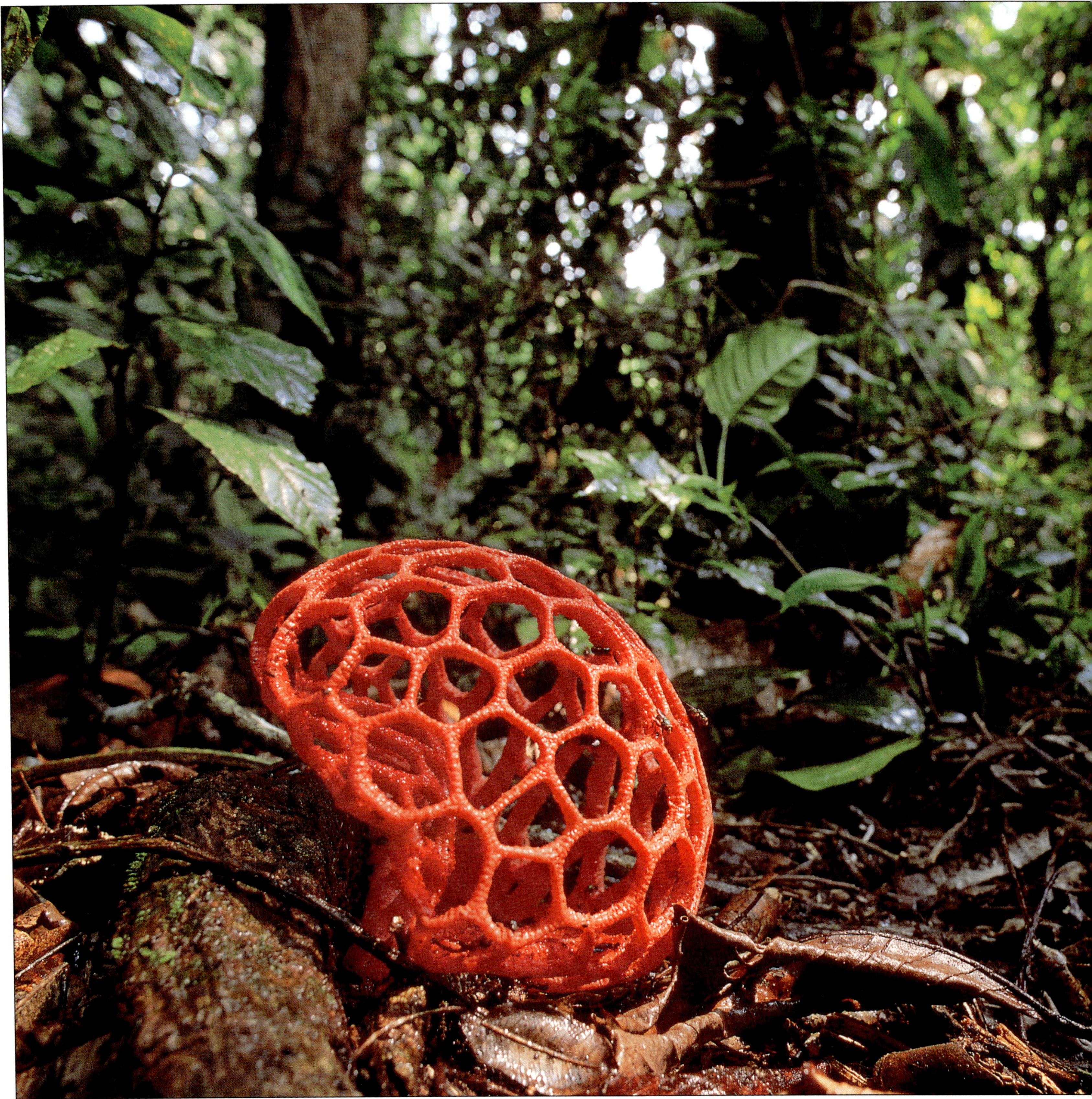

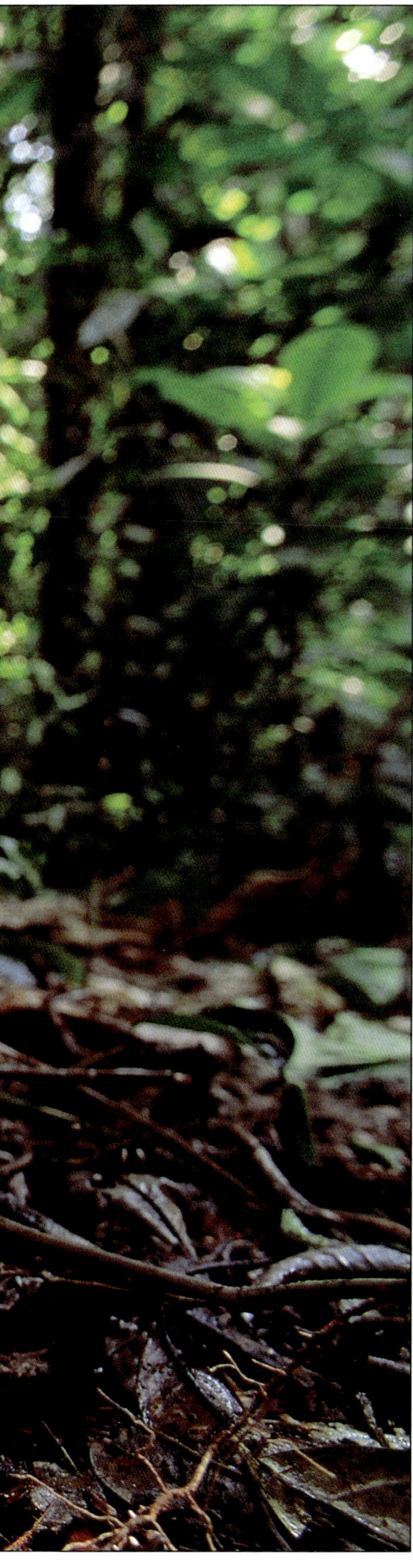

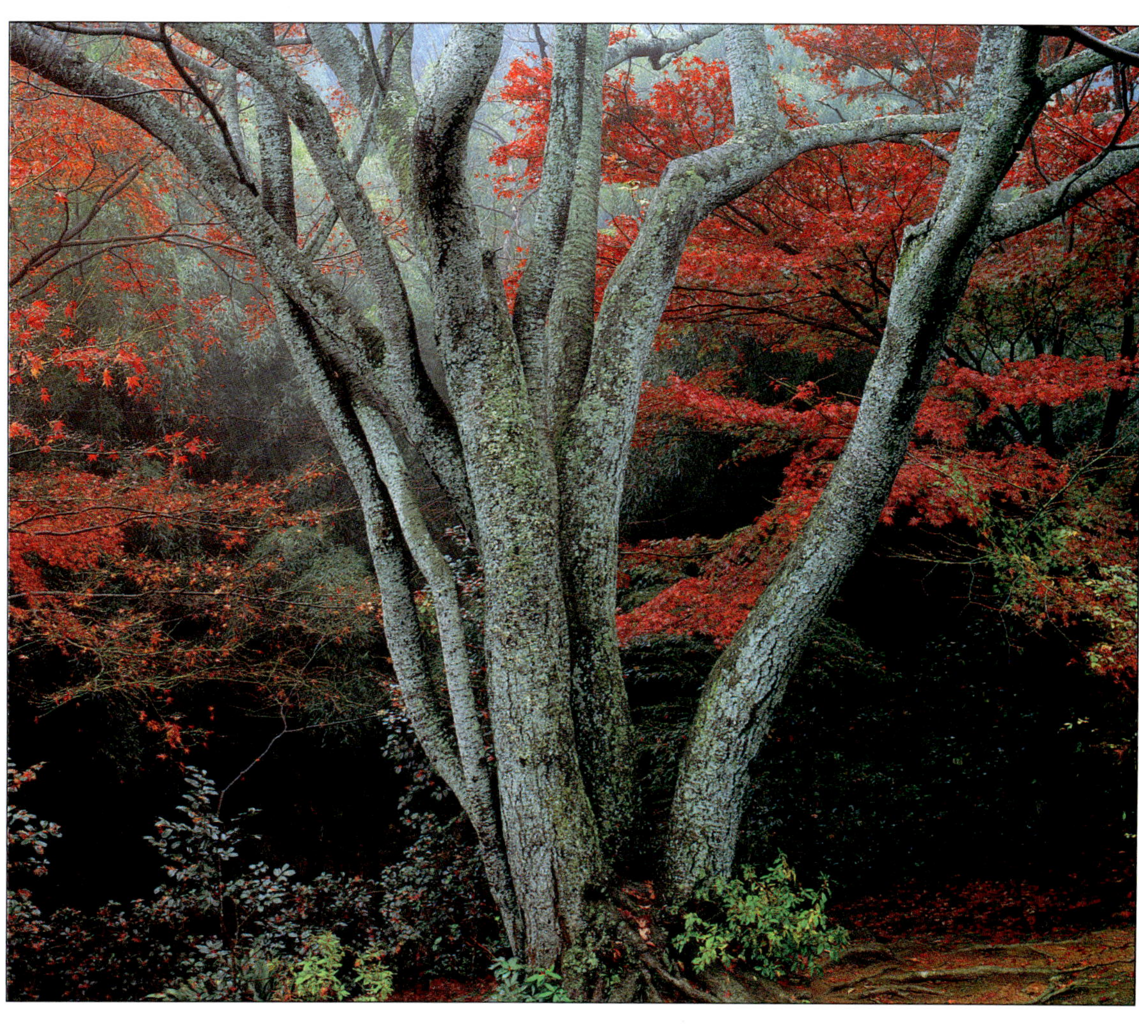

**André Bärtschi**
Liechtenstein
HIGHLY COMMENDED

**Clathraceae fungus**

*"I photographed this fungus in lowland rainforest in Tambopata-Candamo Reserve, Peru. Its bad smell attracts insects."*

**Hisaaki Mihara**
Japan
HIGHLY COMMENDED

**Yamazakura - Japanese cherry**

*"In the mysterious misty rain, I saw this old cherry tree standing quietly at a Buddhist temple in Kyoto. I felt the powerful existence of the tree, and was motivated to take a picture of it."*

Pentax 6x7 with 90mm lens; tripod; 1/4 sec at f11; Fujichrome Velvia

# Animal Portraits

The photographs entered in this category should show the subjects in close-up.

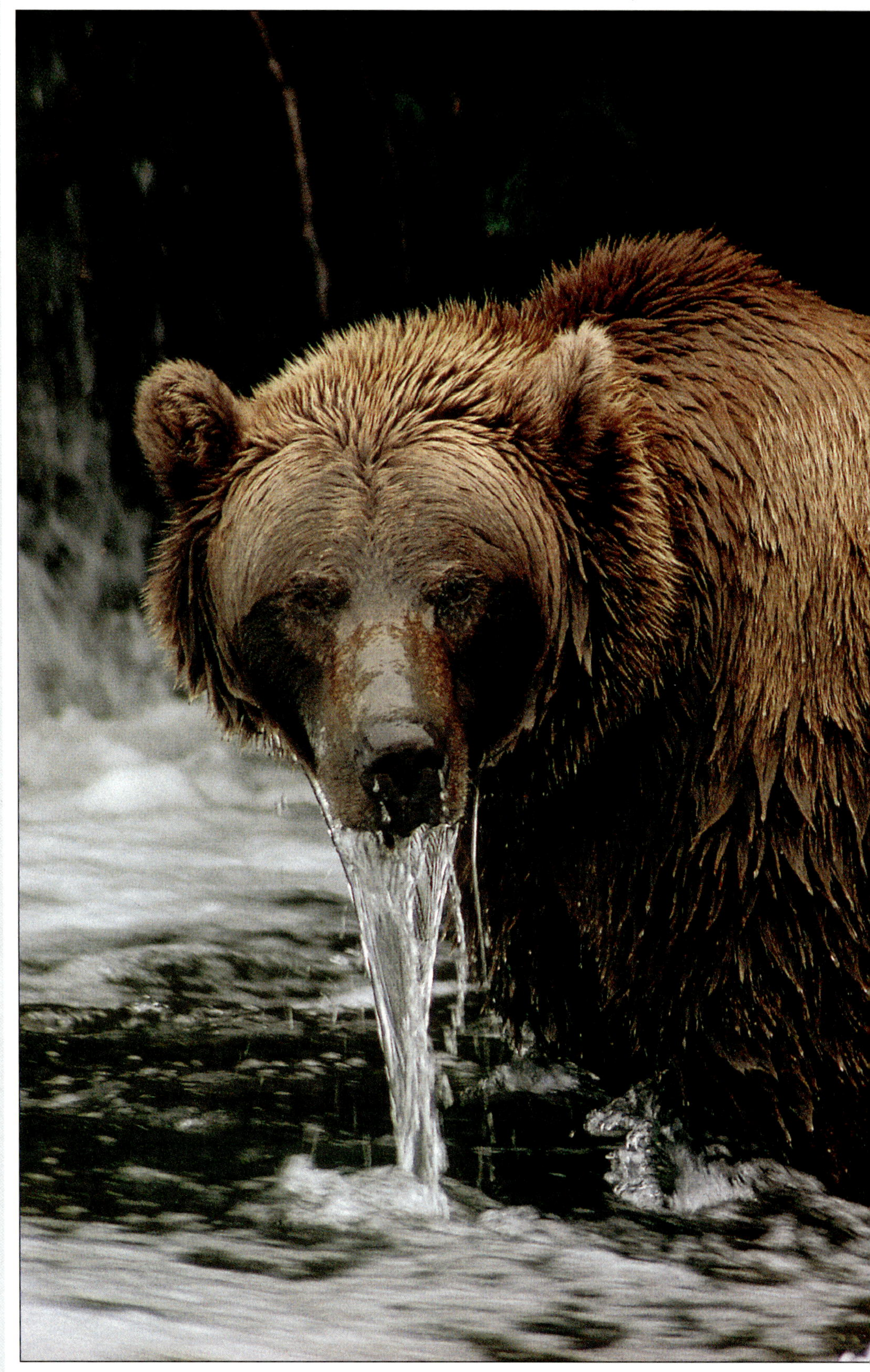

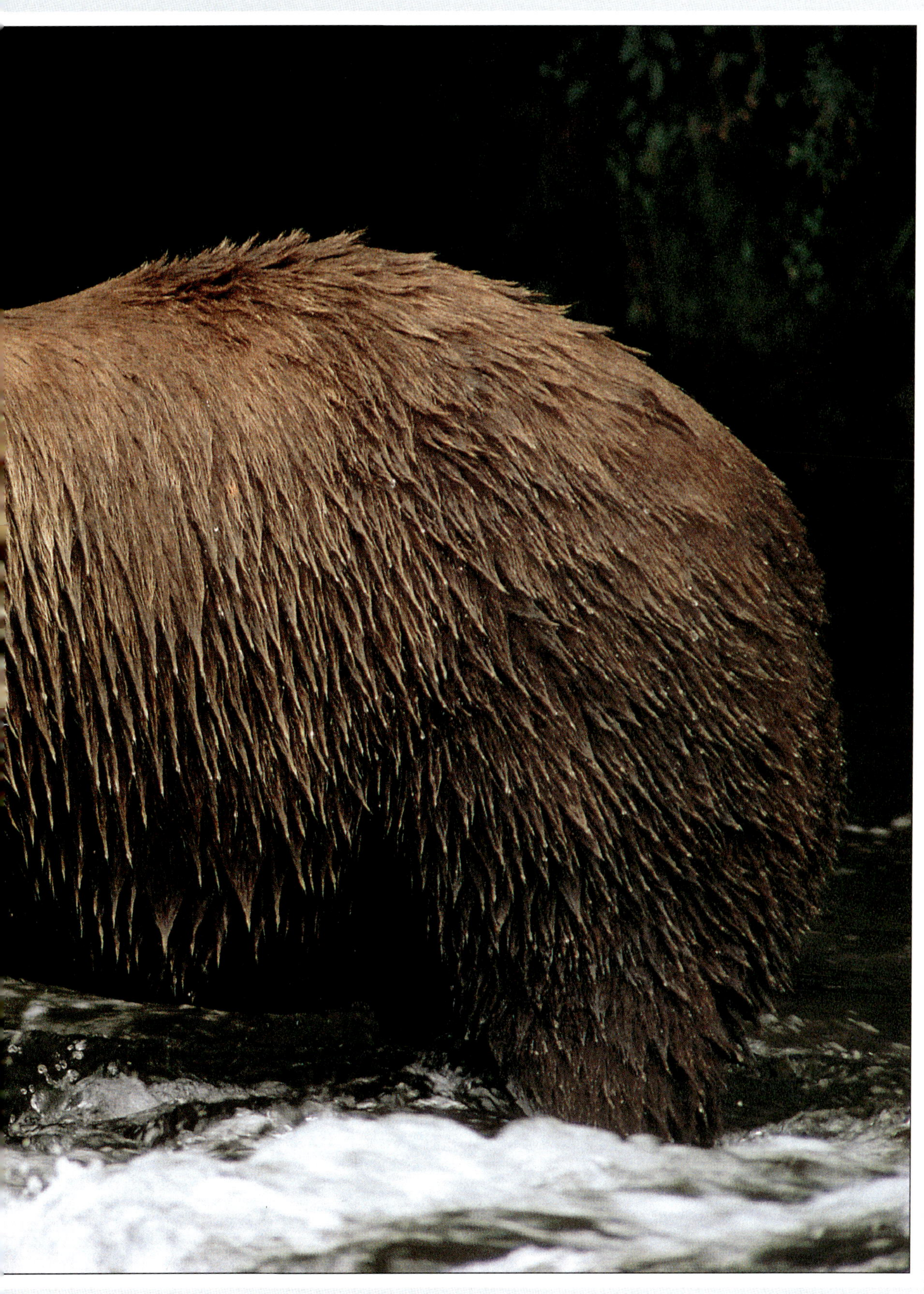

**Heidi & Hans-Jürgen Koch**
Germany
WINNER

***Brown bear waiting for salmon***

*"It wasn't a good time for salmon fishing in the Brooks River, Alaska. This bear stood for three or four hours in the same spot, sticking his head into the water and hoping for a meal. We loved the structure of his wet fur and so we pressed the button just as he lifted his head."*

Nikon F4s with 600mm lens and x1.4 converter; tripod; beanbag; Kodachrome Professional 200

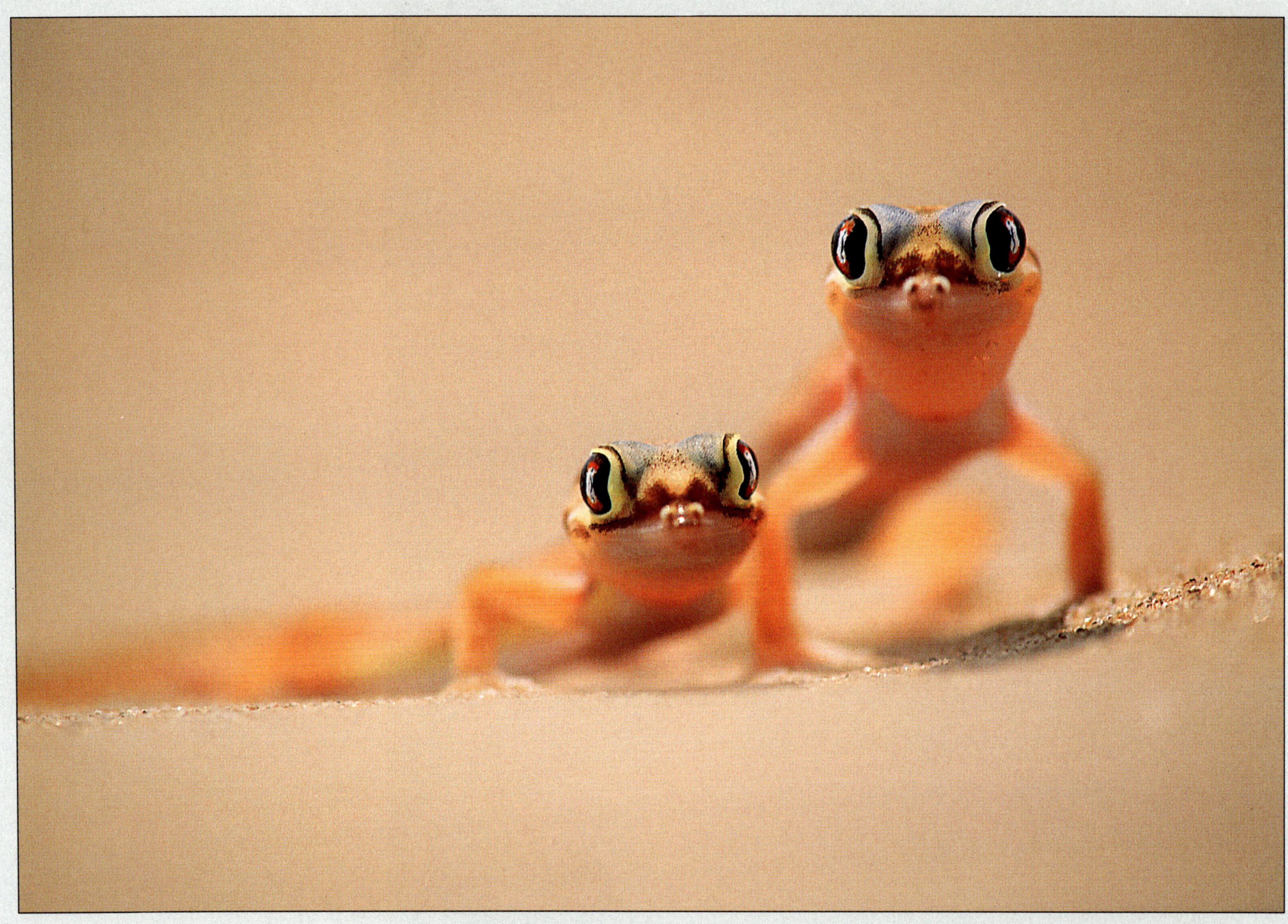

**Chris Mattison**
United Kingdom
RUNNER-UP

***Web-footed geckos***

*"These geckos are superbly adapted for life on the dunes of the Namib Desert, whisking across the shifting sand on their webbed feet. They drink droplets of water that condense on their bodies from fogs that roll in from the Atlantic Ocean."*

Canon T90

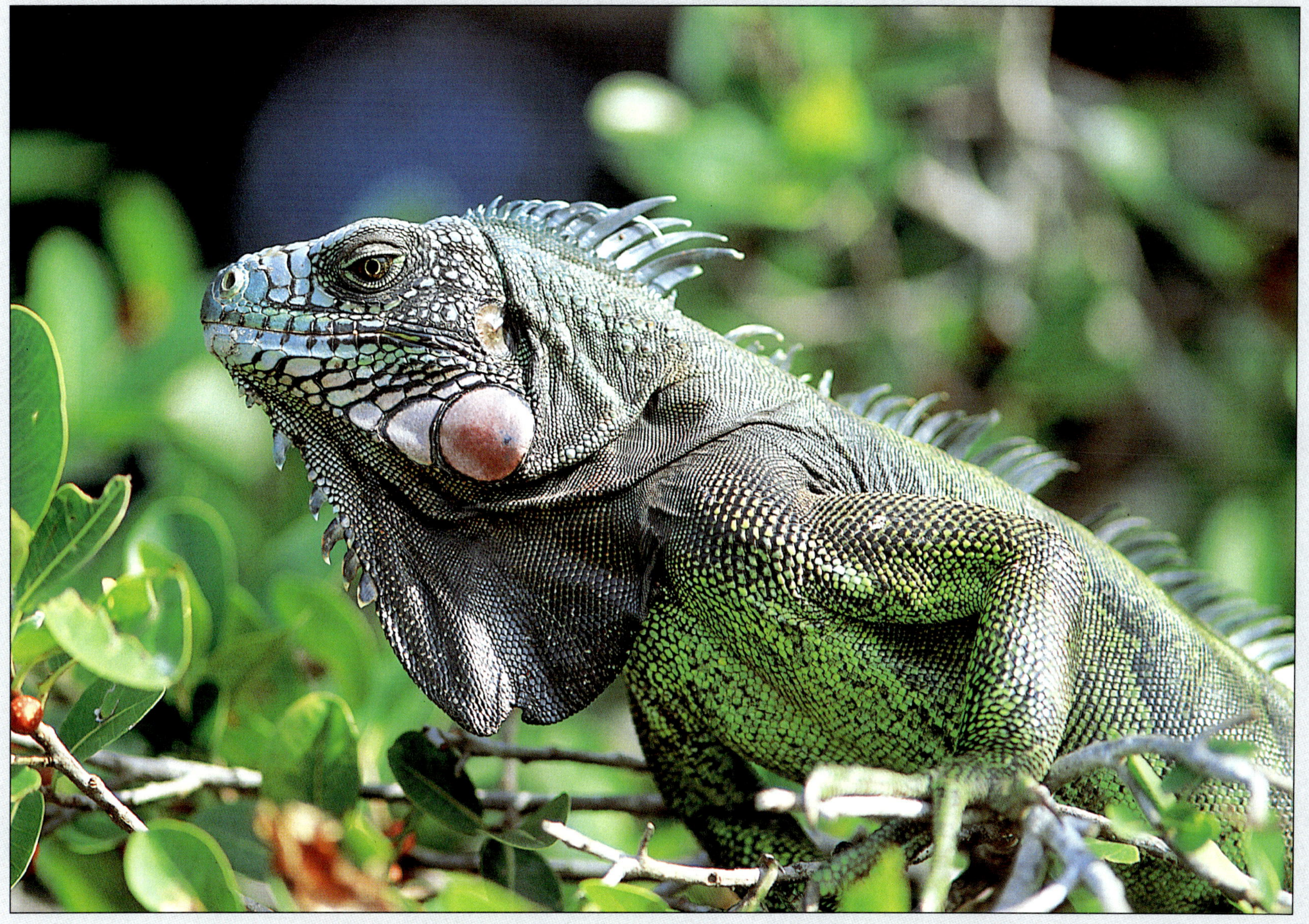

**Richard Coomber**
United Kingdom
HIGHLY COMMENDED

***Common iguana***

*"I had seen several iguanas in this part of Venezuela. I was wandering through an area of mixed trees and bushes when I suddenly came across the most colourful male I had ever seen. Thankfully, he was also the most co-operative."*

Nikon F4 with 300mm lens; Fujichrome Velvia

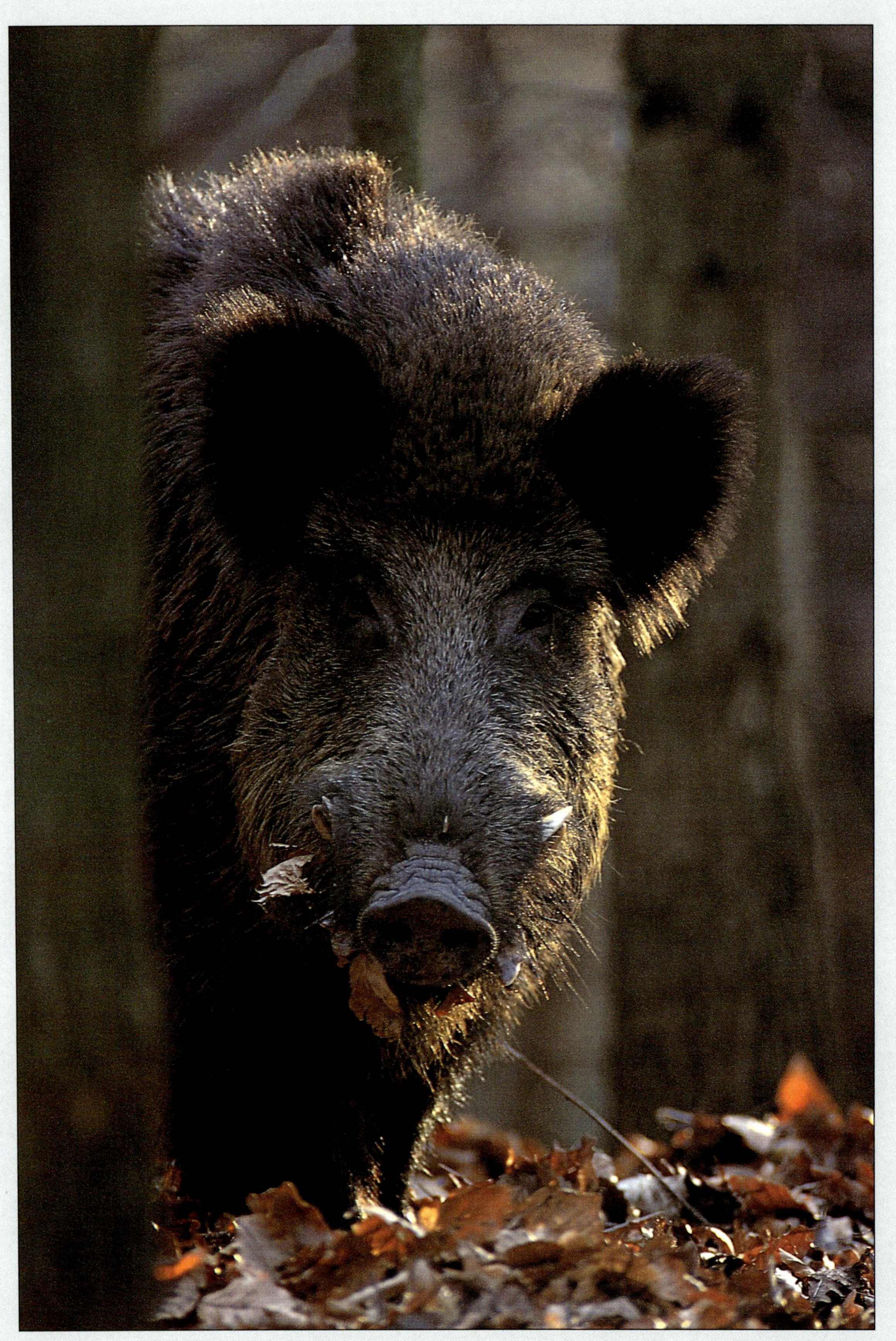

## Florian Möllers

Germany

JOINT SPECIALLY COMMENDED

### *Wild boar*

*"There is a reserve near my home, where I often take photos of wild boar. To find the animals you usually have to search for hours in the remotest parts of the park. Fortunately I knew the hiding place of this big boar."*

Canon EOS 10 with 400mm lens; tripod; 1/30 sec at f5.6; Fujichrome 100 rated at 200

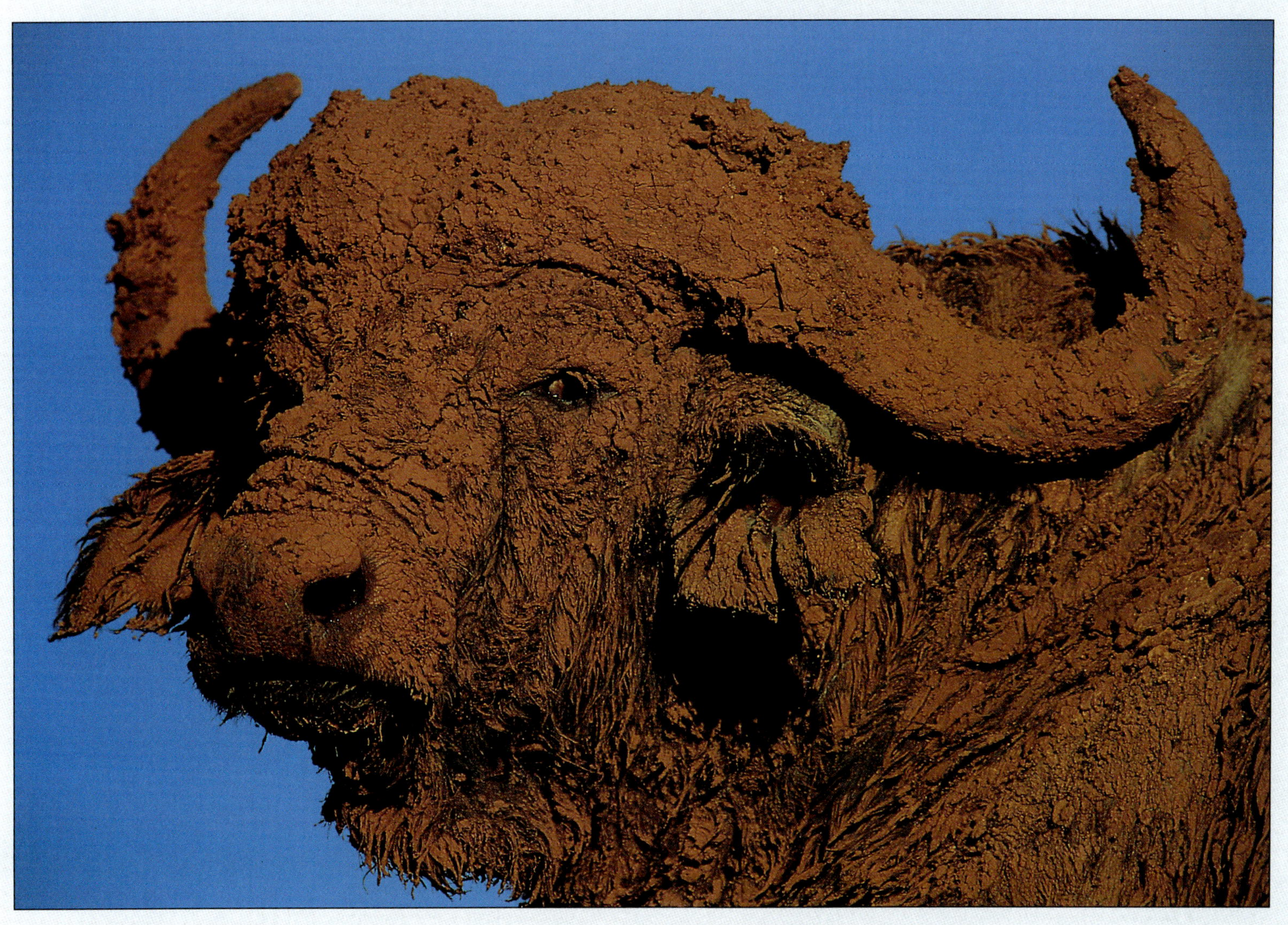

**Frank Krahmer**
Germany
JOINT SPECIALLY COMMENDED

***Mud-covered cape buffalo***

*"The sun was about to disappear behind the nearby hills, when I saw a group of buffalo cooling off in a water hole. This one was already completely dry. The red-brown Kenyan soil and the bright late-afternoon sun made an unforgettable colour combination."*

Canon EOS 1 with 500mm lens; beanbag; 1/180 sec at f4.5; Fujichrome Velvia

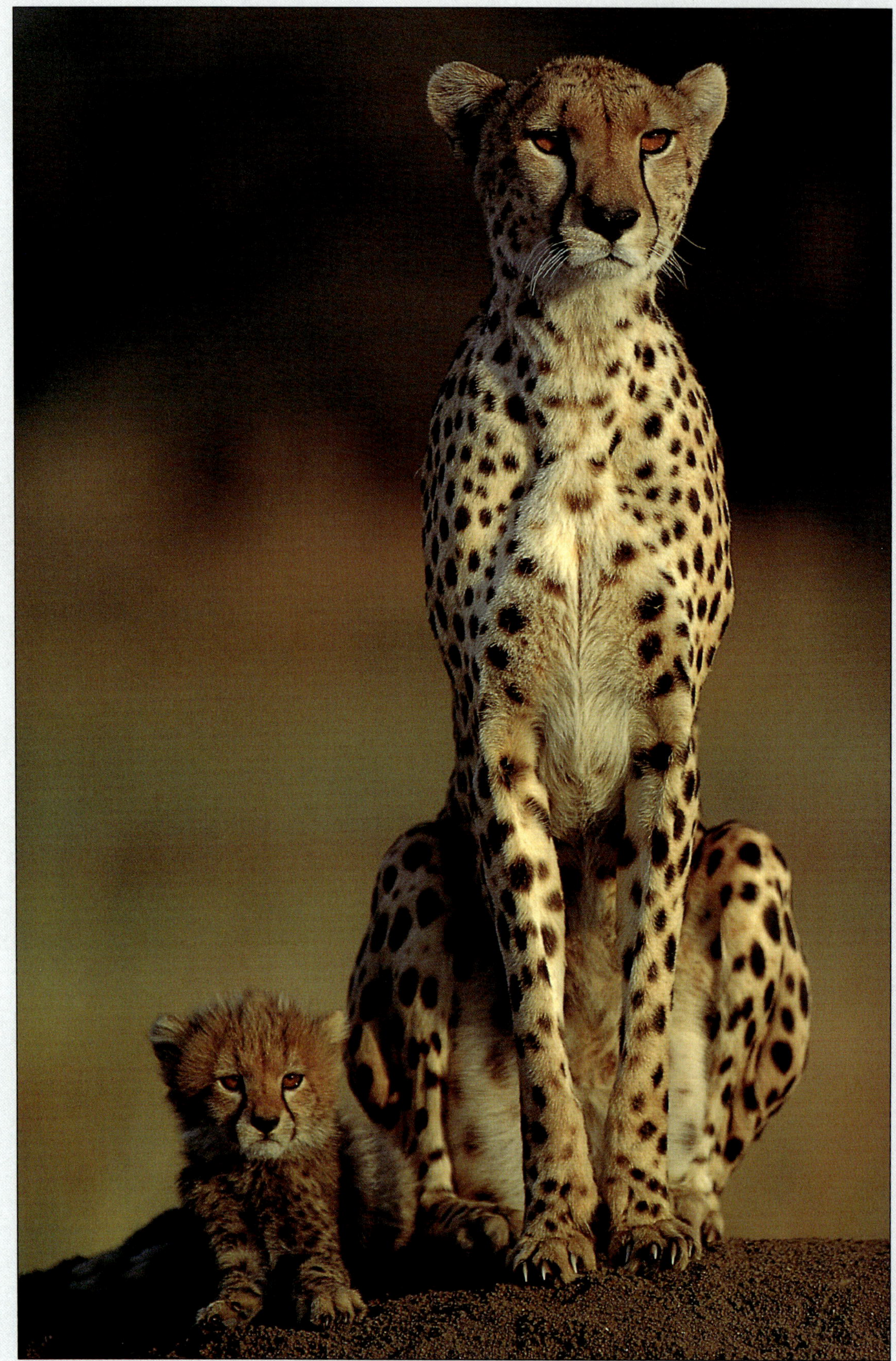

**Gabriela Staebler**

Germany

HIGHLY COMMENDED

***Cheetah mother sitting with her cub***

*"As dusk fell in the Maasai Mara, this cheetah left her three cubs under a tree and climbed a large termite mound for a better view of potential prey. For a few seconds, the sun broke through the clouds - just as one of the cubs turned up and sat down beside her. The mother went on to hunt in the fading light and got her dinner."*

Canon T90 with 500mm lens; clamp-table tripod; beanbag; 1/90 sec at f4.5; Fujichrome Sensia 100

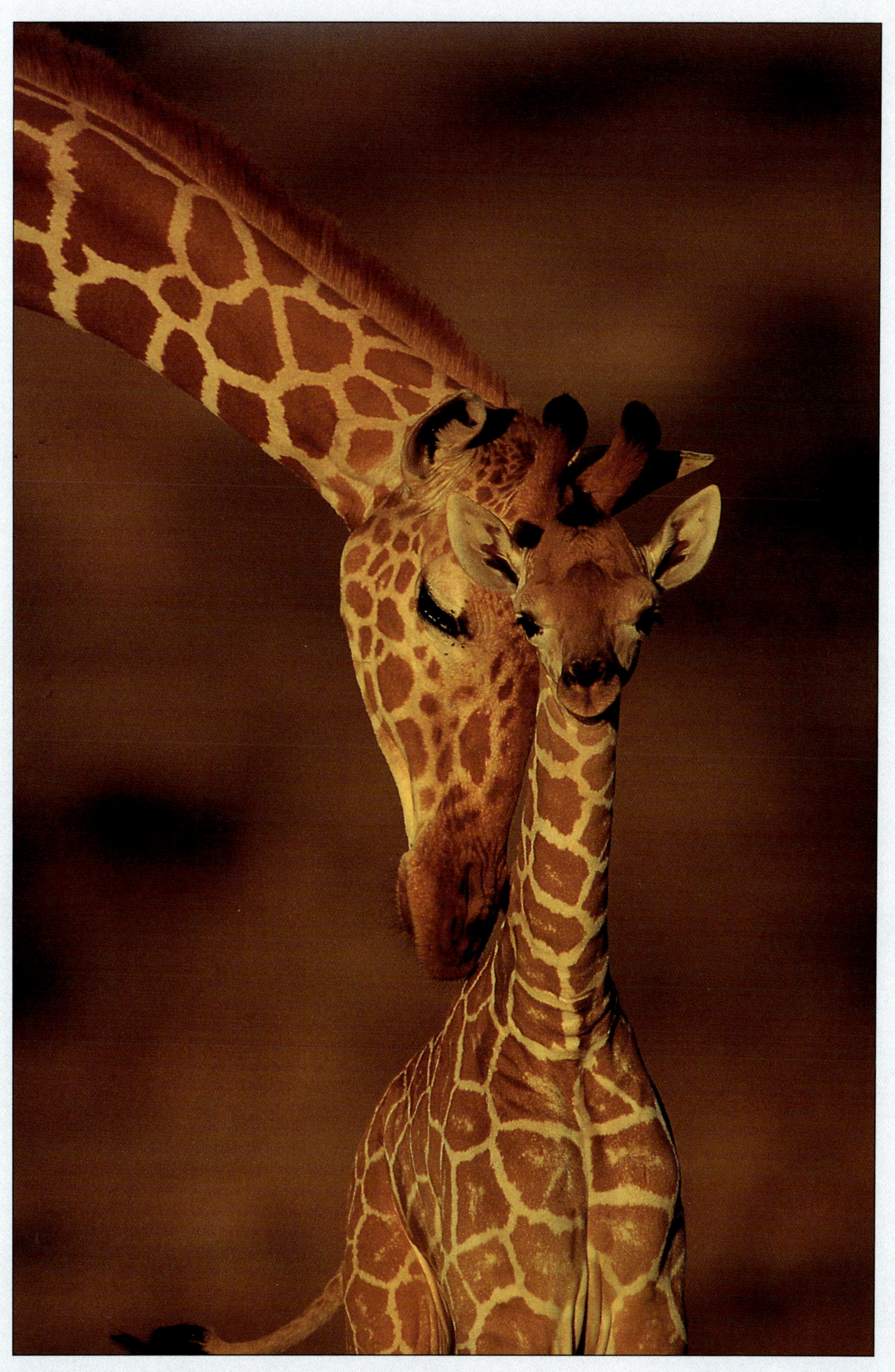

**Karl Ammann**
Switzerland
HIGHLY COMMENDED

### *Giraffe greeting*

*"A herd of reticulated giraffes was browsing in Samburu National Park when a mother and her very young calf approached from the hills. The whole herd showed interest, and this was one of several individuals that went up to investigate - perhaps smelling it, or just having a close look. To avoid affecting the behaviour, I used a very long lens and took the shot through dense acacia scrub."*

Nikon F4 with 800mm lens; Fujichrome 100

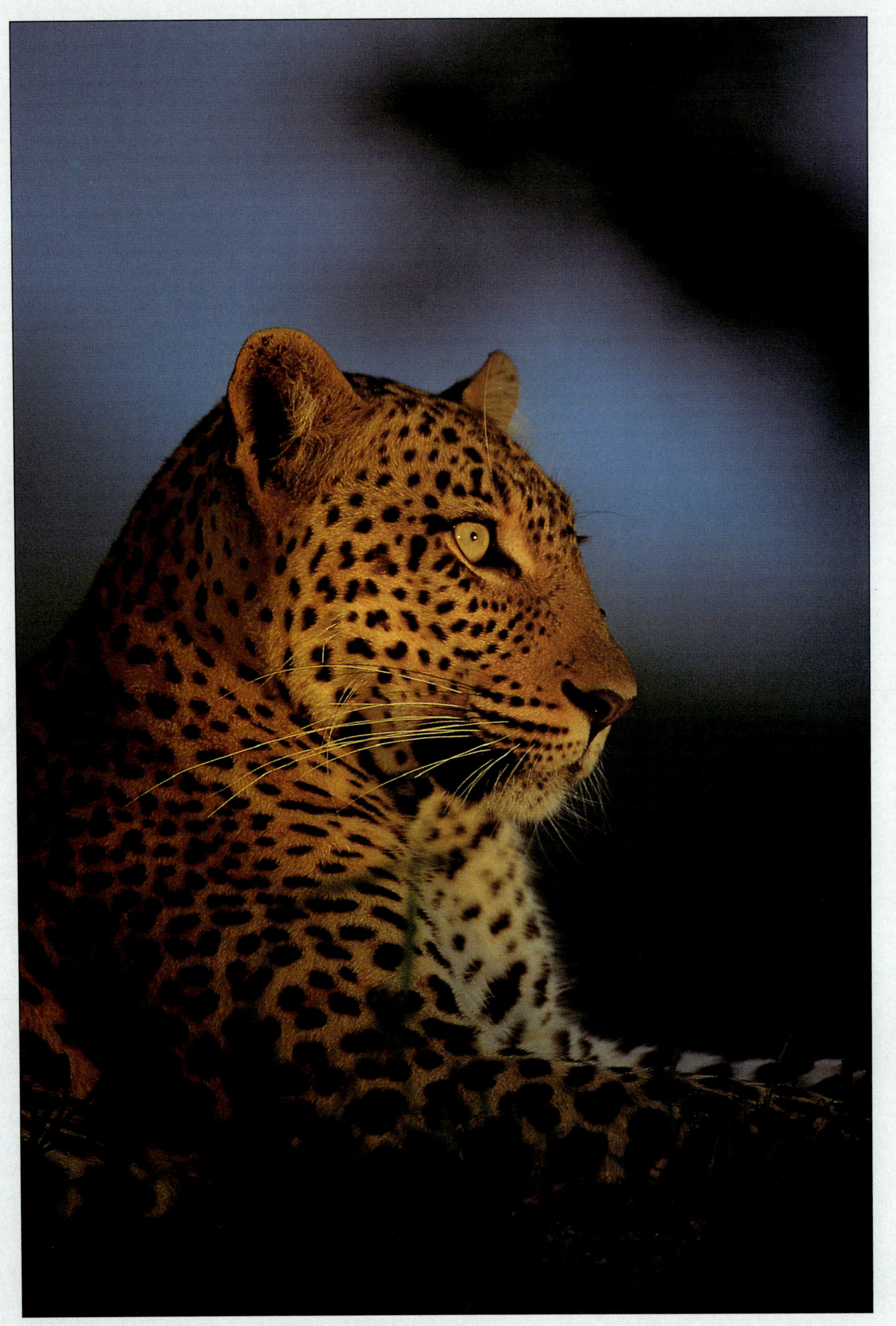

**Richard du Toit**
South Africa
HIGHLY COMMENDED

### *Leopardess*

*"It was dusk in the Mala Mala Game Reserve, South Africa, and this female leopard was sitting on a termite mound watching a pride of seven lions some 200 metres away - hence the vigilant stare. Five months later, she was seen with a cub of about four months, and so must have been pregnant at the time of the photograph."*

Nikon F-801s with 500mm lens; beanbag; spotlight; 1/30 sec at f4; Fujichrome Provia 100

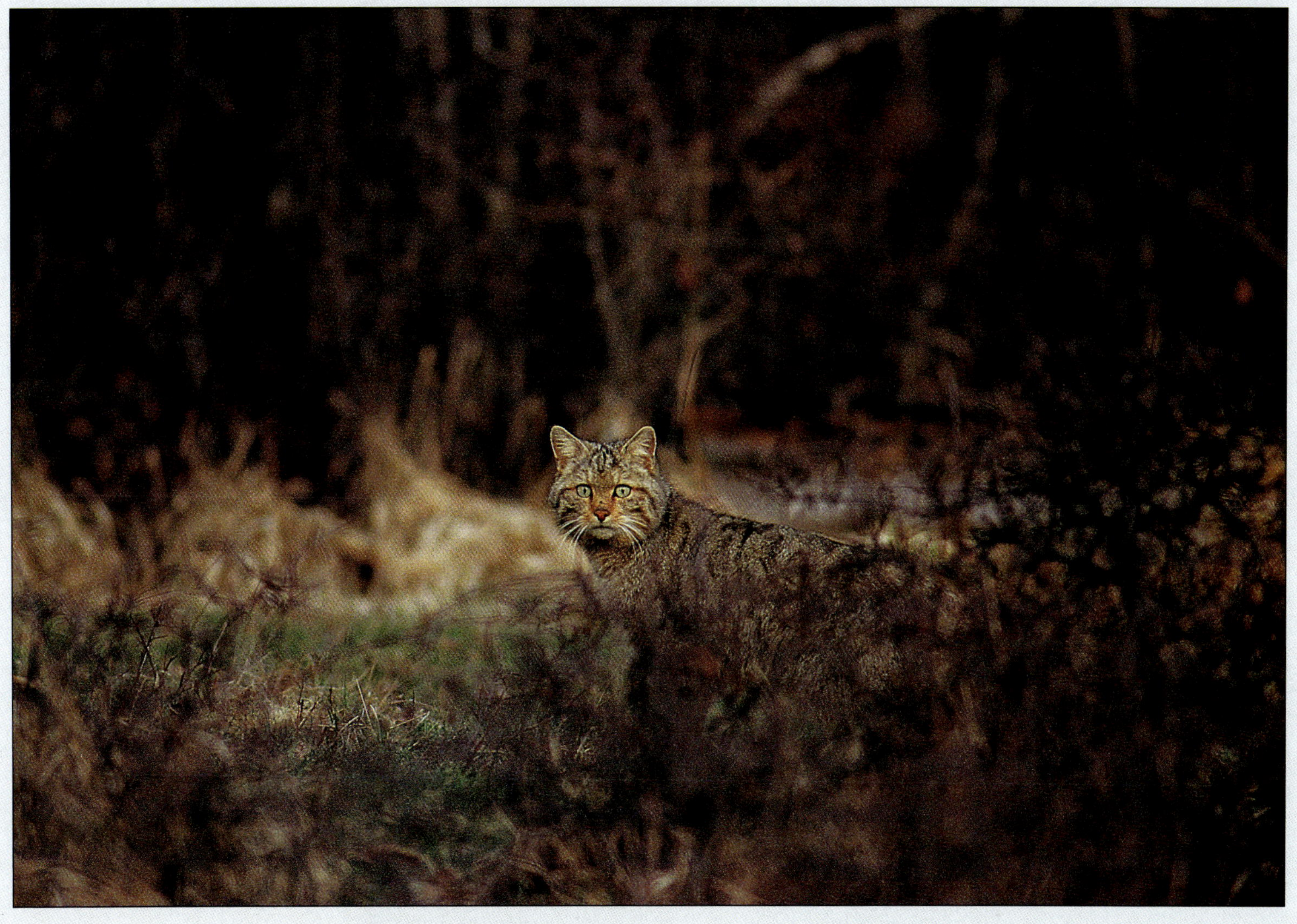

**Marko Masterl**
Slovenia
HIGHLY COMMENDED

---

***Wildcat***

*"When wandering in the forest I often come across the tracks of wildcats, but hunting here makes the animals very cautious, and so I rarely get a chance to photograph them. When I noticed this individual looking for prey on the edge of the forest one spring afternoon, I decided to wait on the spot. After a week, I got lucky."*

---

Nikon F4s with 400mm lens; tripod; hide; 1/125 sec at f4; Kodachrome 200

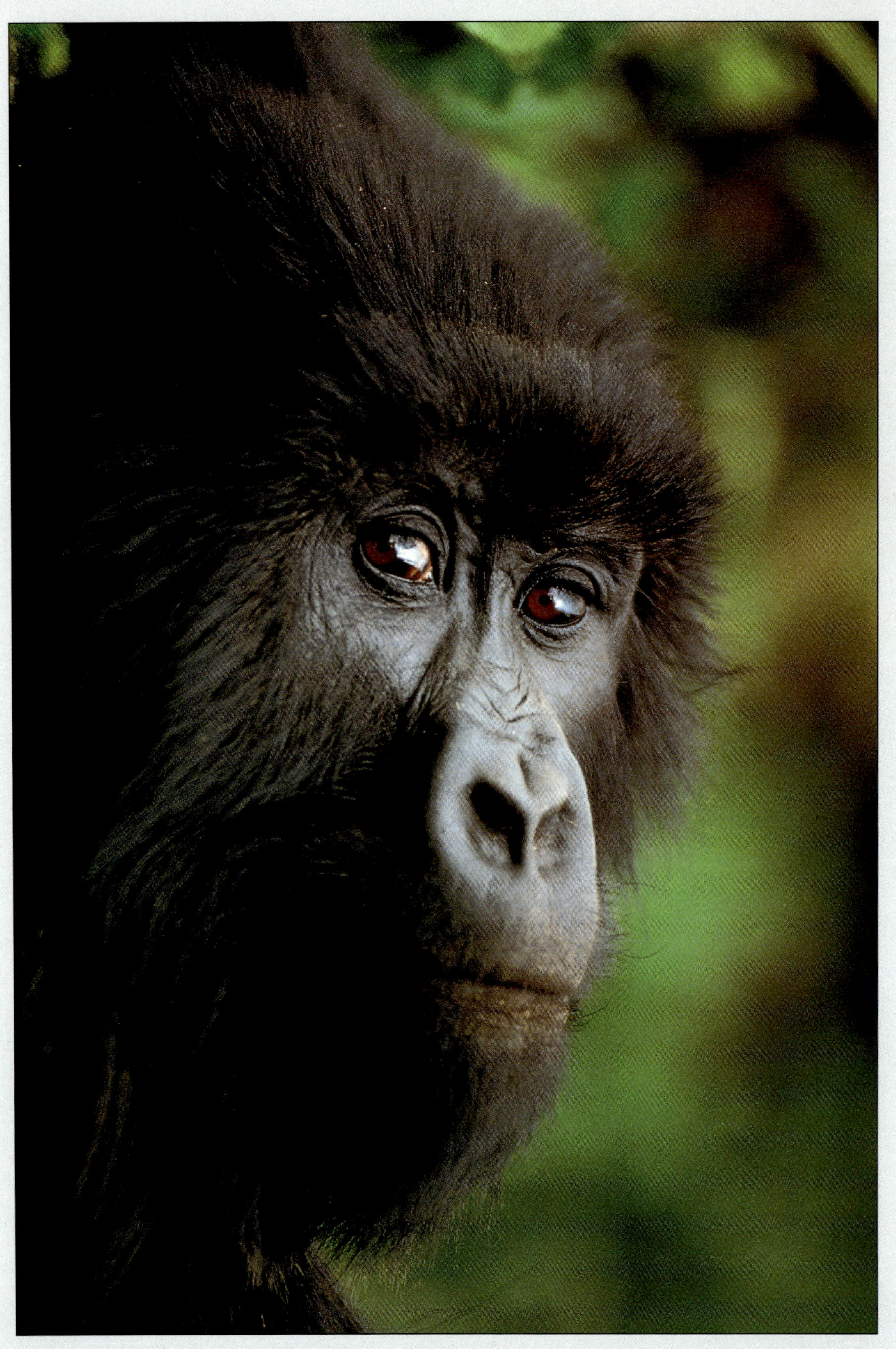

**Daniel J Cox**
United States of America
HIGHLY COMMENDED

---

***Mountain gorilla***

*"I took the picture in the forest of Volcanoes National Park in Rwanda. This female gorilla was taking a midday rest and keeping an eye on us."*

---

Nikon F4 with 300mm lens;
Fujichrome Velvia rated at 100

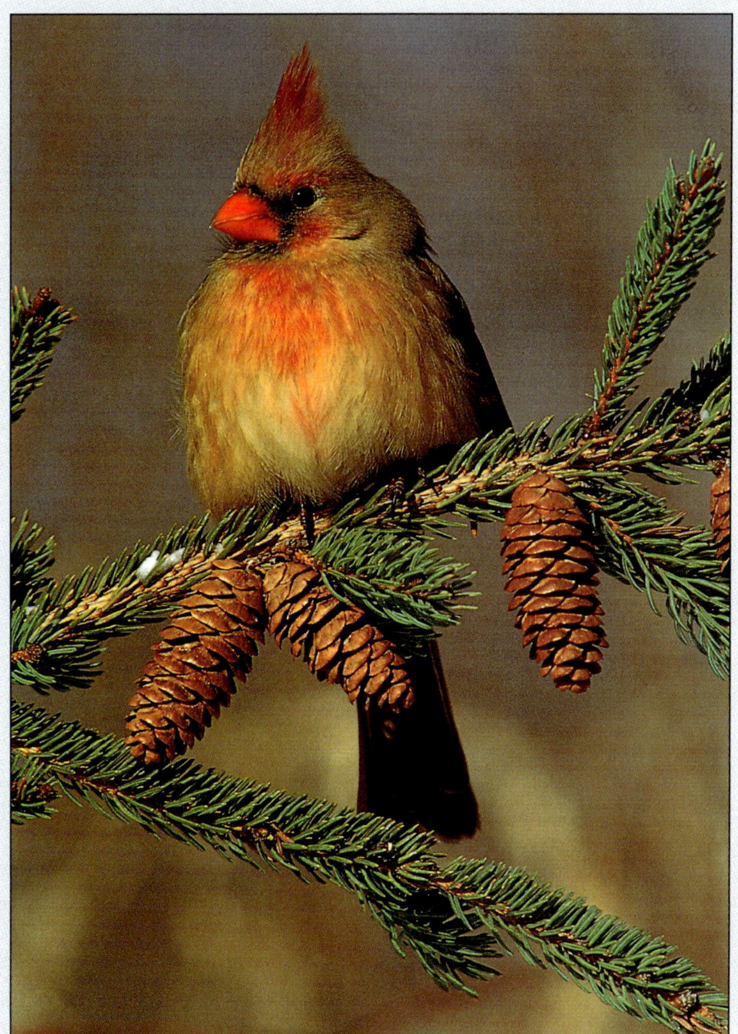

## Doug Locke

United States of America

HIGHLY COMMENDED

### *Northern cardinal*

*"Abundant in the eastern US, the northern cardinal is a favourite songbird because of its colour and songs, and regularly nests in suburban gardens. I photographed this female on a cold February morning from a blind in an area where several cardinals were visiting a feeder."*

Nikon N90s; 300mm lens with x1.4 teleconverter; tripod; Fujichrome Velvia

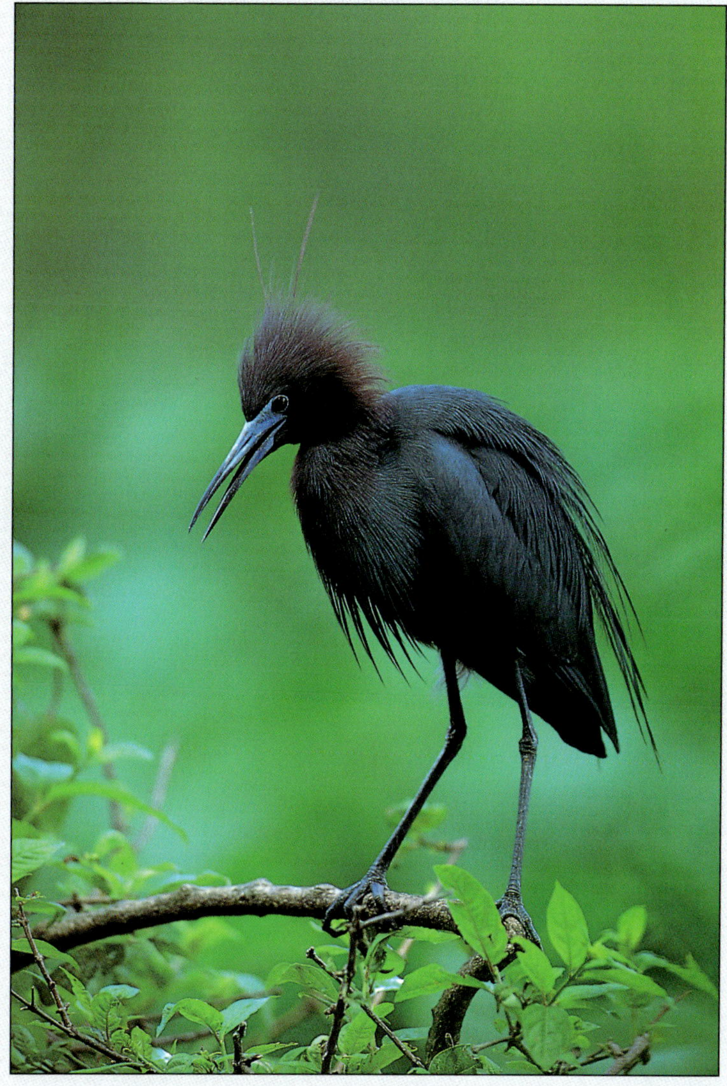

## Rosemary Calvert

United Kingdom

HIGHLY COMMENDED

### *Little blue heron in territorial display*

*"Each pair of birds in this nesting area at the edge of Bird City Lake on Avery Island, in Louisiana, has only a small area of territory. I couldn't see the little blue heron's nest, but the bird returned time and time again to the same branch where it fluffed out its feathers in territorial display and raised two feathers on its head."*

Canon EOS 105 with 500mm lens; ext. tube; tripod; 1/250 sec at f4.5; Fujichrome Velvia rated at 100

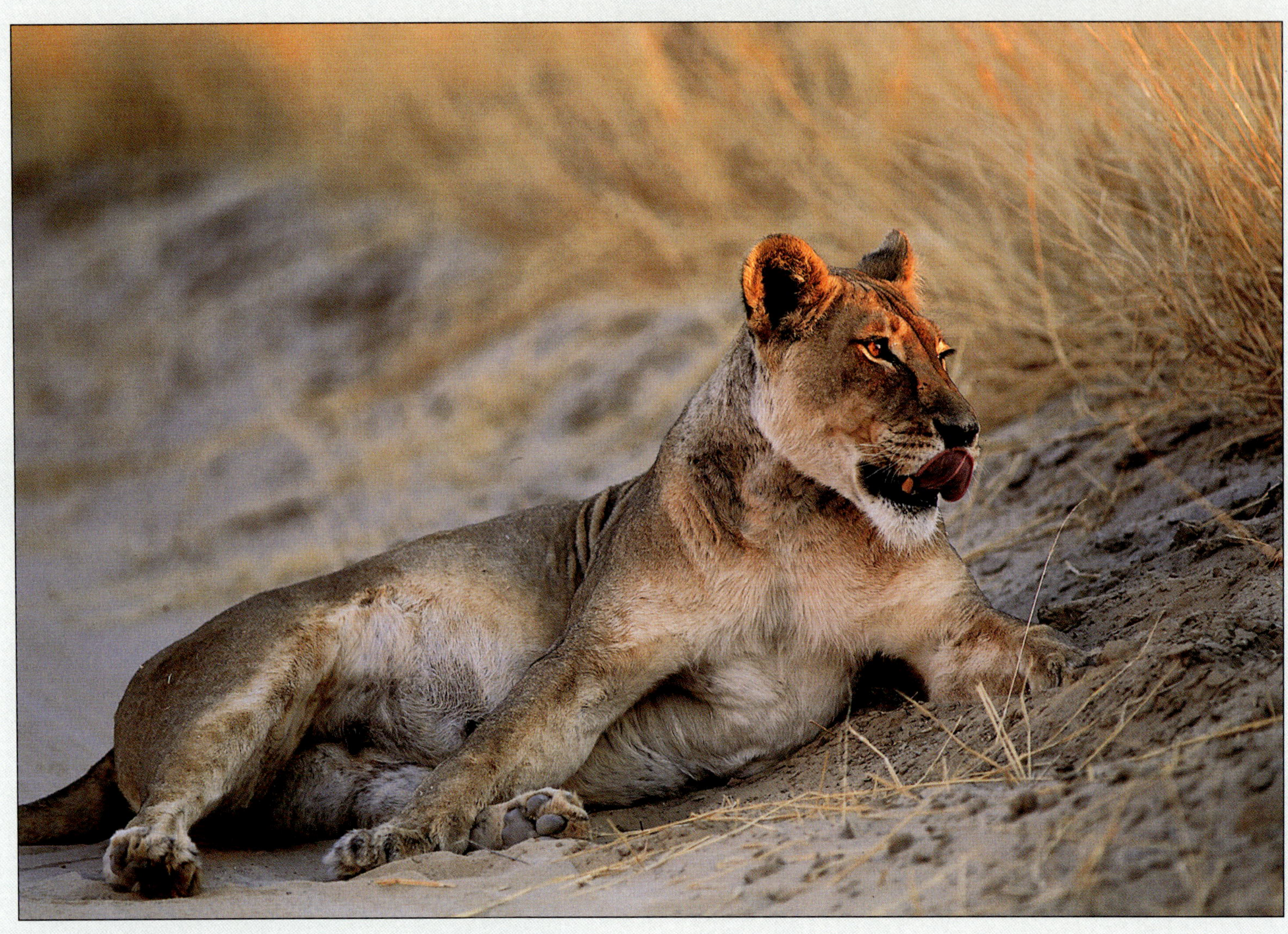

**Pete Oxford**
United Kingdom
HIGHLY COMMENDED

***Pregnant lioness***

*"This pregnant lioness in the Kalahari Gemsbok National Park simply could not get comfortable. I was particularly attracted to the light just hitting the top of her face as she looked over the rise."*

Nikon F4 with 300mm lens; 1/30 sec at f2.8-4; Fujichrome Velvia

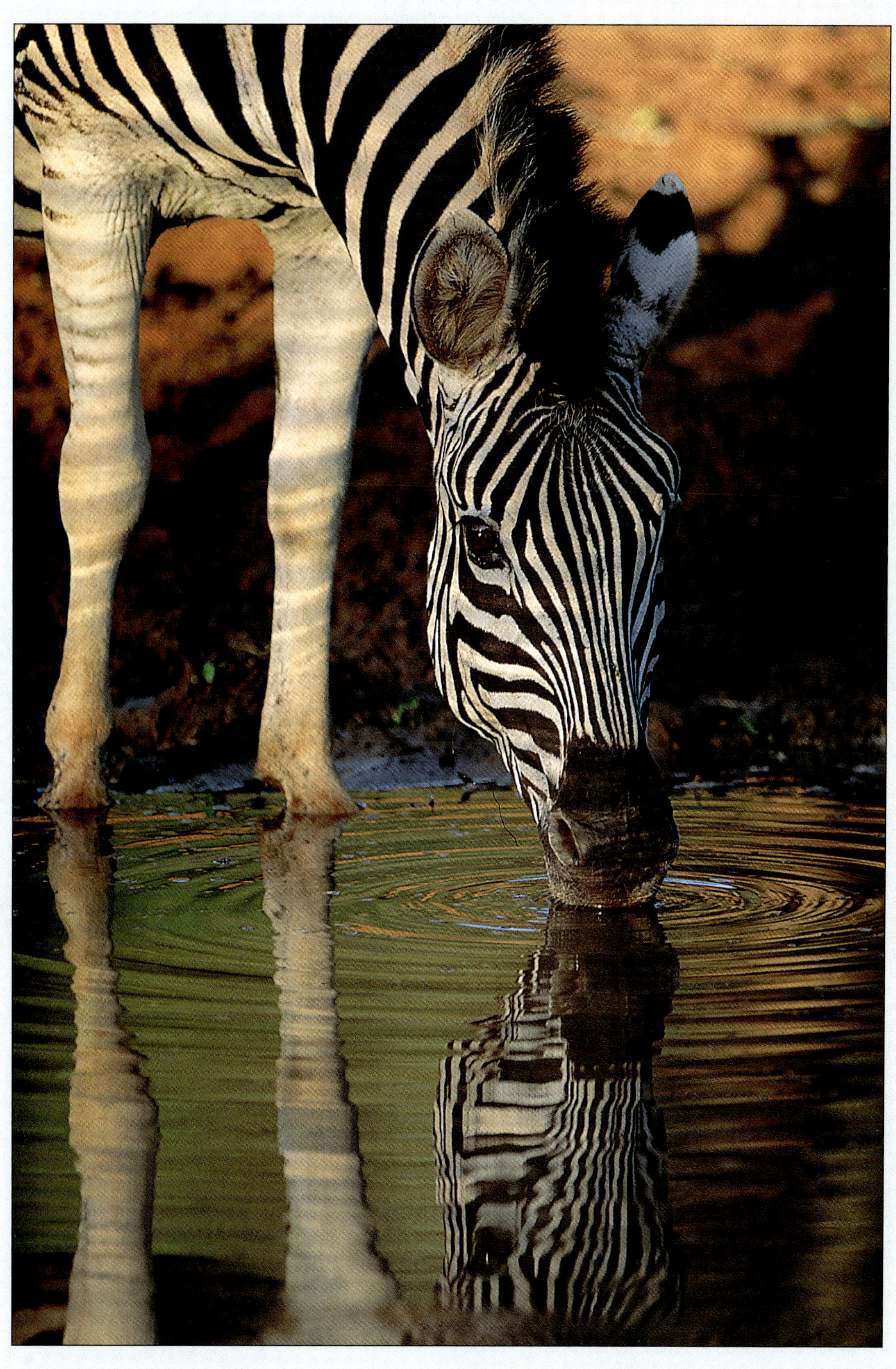

**Philip van den Berg**
South Africa
HIGHLY COMMENDED

---

**Burchell's zebra drinking**

*"I had to wait for the light to be just right. I wanted sunlight on the subject, but not on the water, so I could capture those special reflections."*

---

Canon T90 with 500mm lens; 1/250 sec at f4.5; Fujichrome Velvia

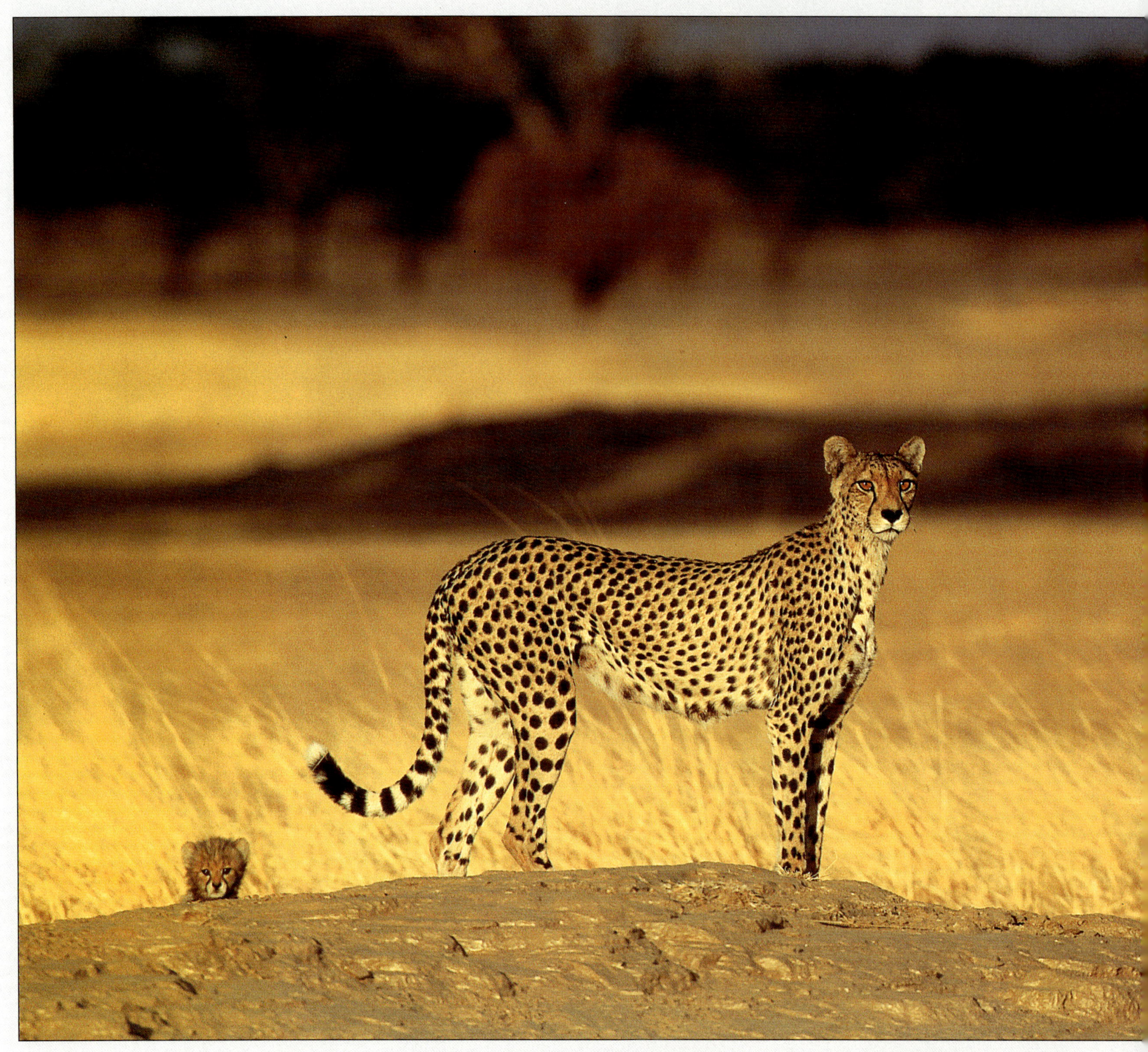

**Ronno Tramper**
The Netherlands
HIGHLY COMMENDED

***Mountain viscacha***

*"I spent three days stalking viscachas in the high Andes of northern Chile. Mountain viscachas spend most of the day dozing in an upright position, with their eyes half closed. It was terribly difficult to get the camera and tripod in position without waking this one up."*

Nikon F3 with 80-200mm lens and TC 1.4x; tripod; 1/500 sec at f5.6; Kodachrome 200

**Jill Sneesby & Barrie Wilkins**
South Africa
HIGHLY COMMENDED

***Cheetah mother and cub***

*"This is the smallest cheetah cub we have seen in the Kalahari for a long while. We were extremely pleased to find it with its mother because the previous day, we had seen it flee when its sibling was killed by a lioness."*

Canon EOS 1 with 400mm lens; car cambrac; Fujichrome Provia 100

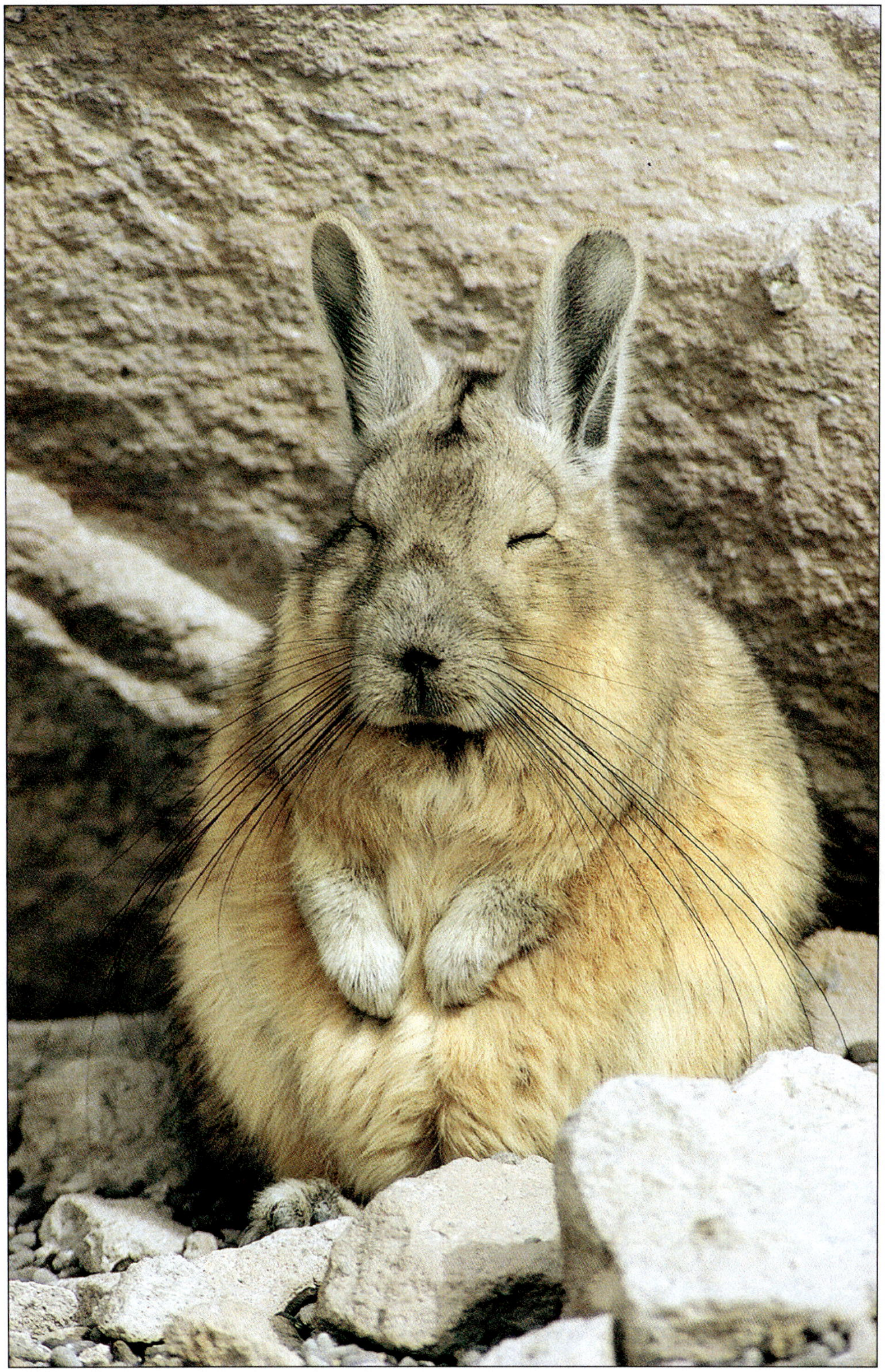

# The Underwater World

The photographs entered in this category must have been taken under water and can illustrate any marine or freshwater subject.

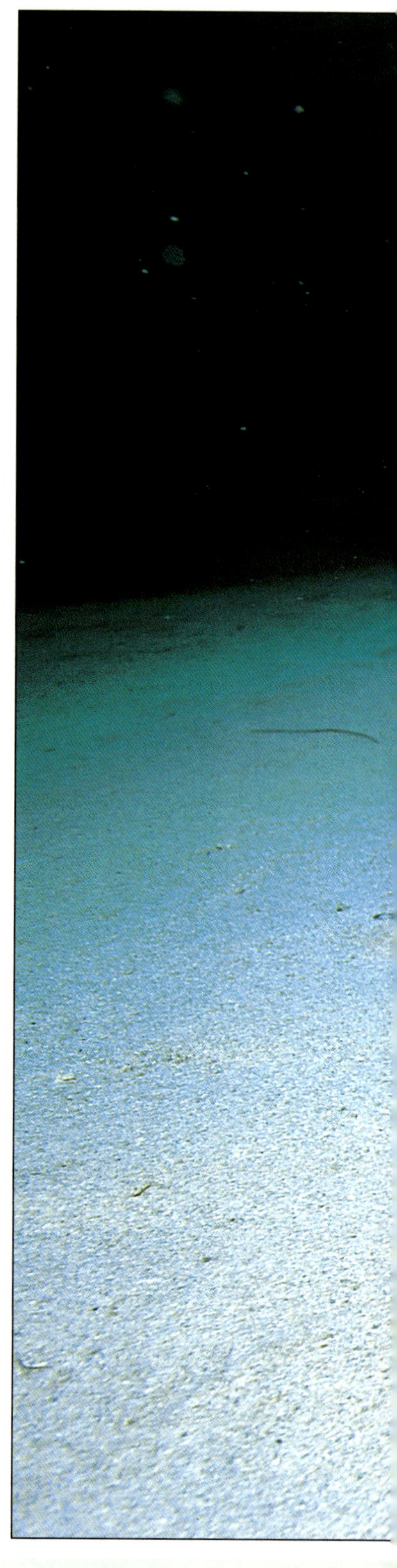

**Darryl Torckler**
New Zealand
WINNER

***Sea dragon***

*"I was on a trip to Kangaroo Island, Australia, when I came across this common sea dragon. It seemed to ghost along with no means of propulsion, sometimes hovering like a helicopter over the sea floor. A close look revealed an almost invisible clear fin on top of the body at the base of the tail."*

Canon F1 with 20mm lens in underwater housing; two strobes; 1/30 sec at f8; Fujichrome Velvia

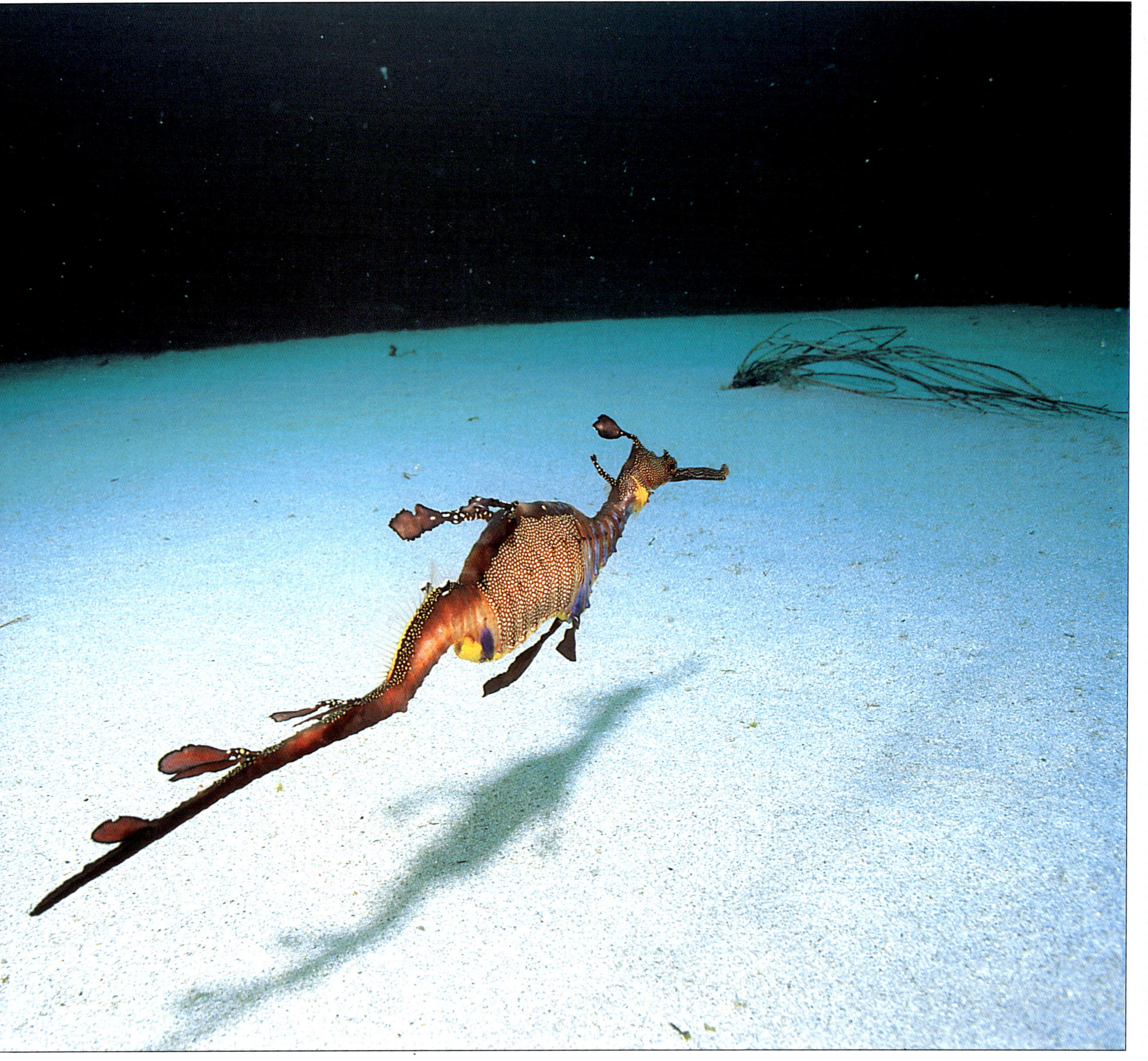

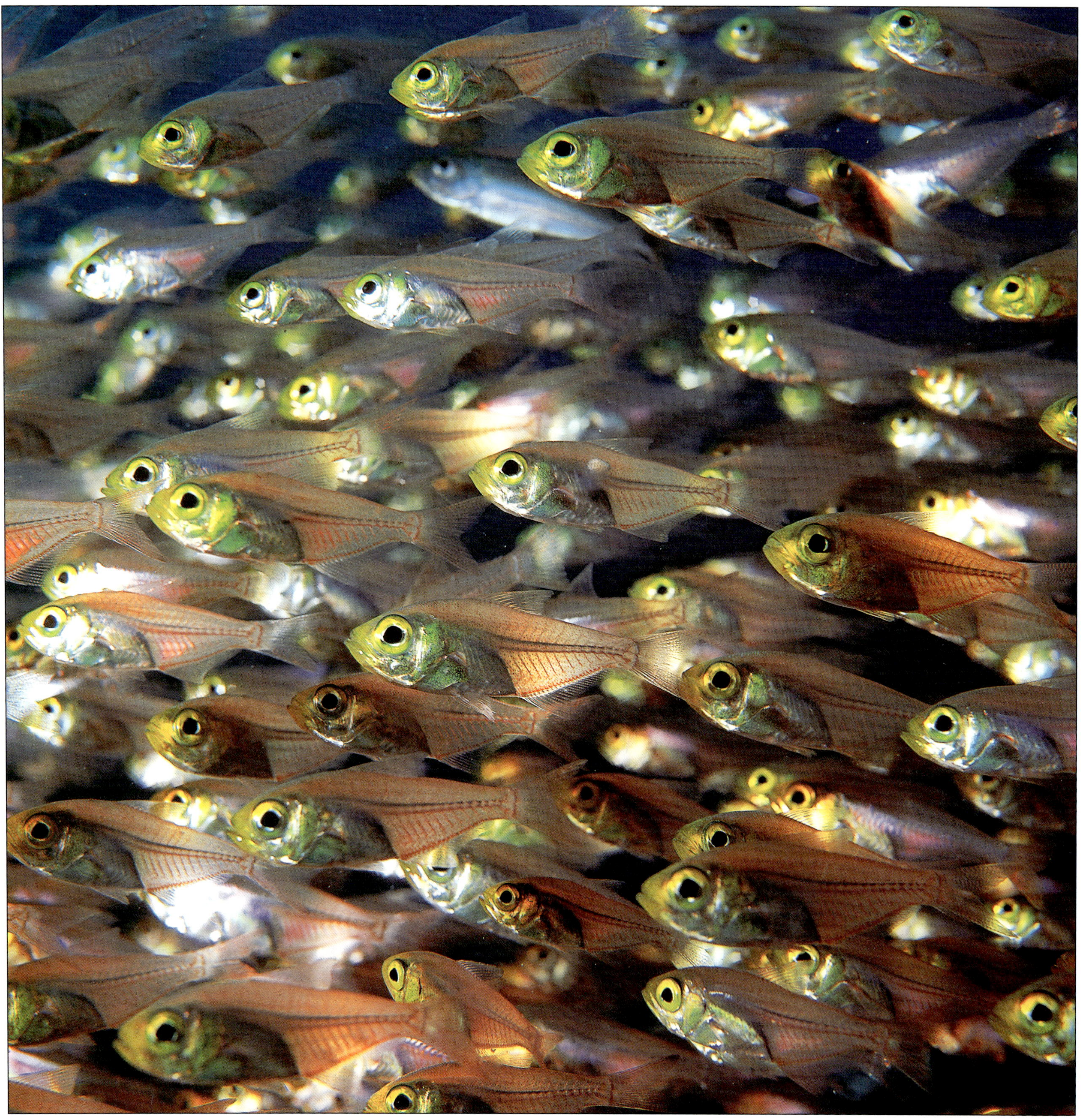

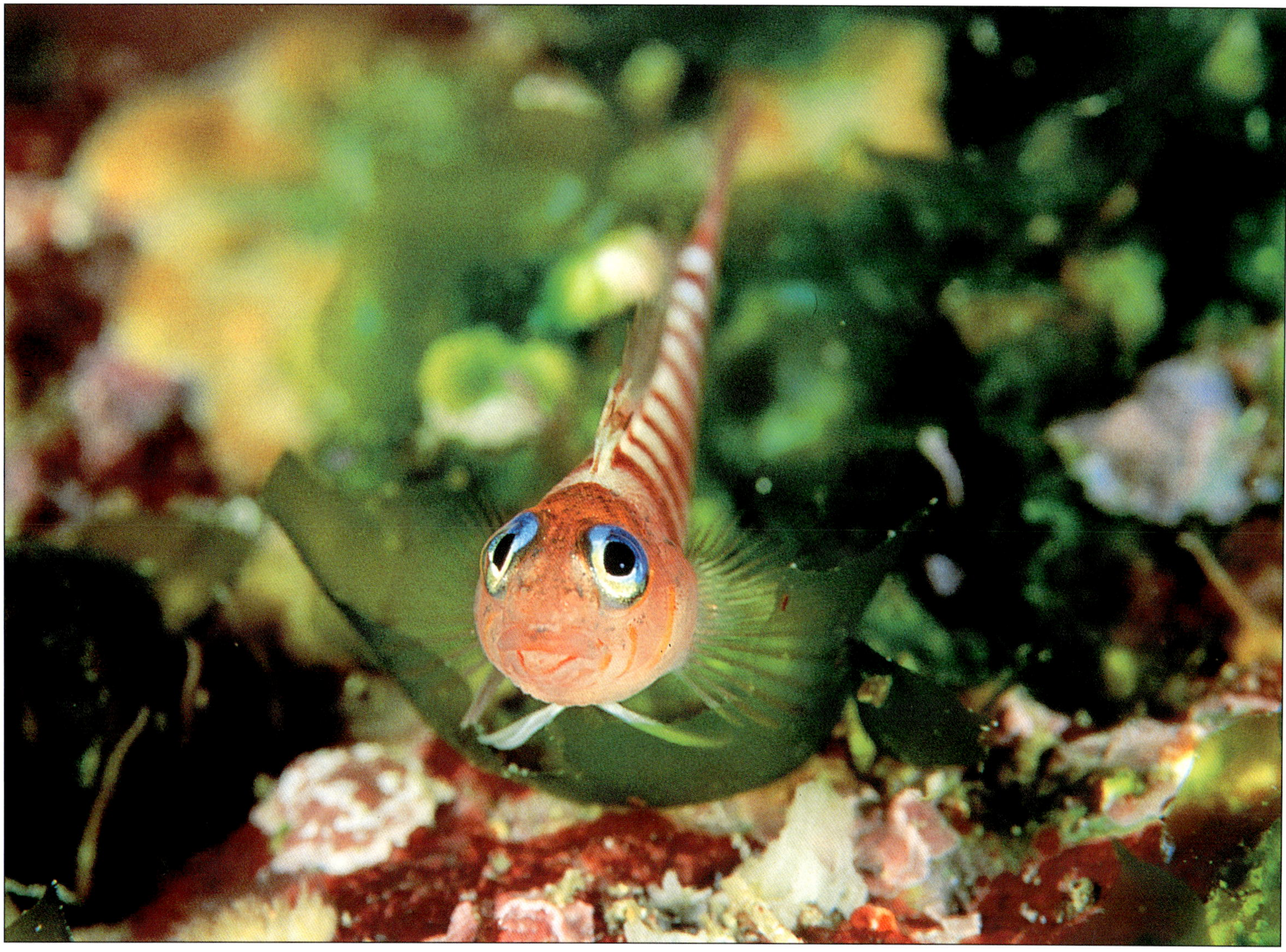

**Heinz Schimpke**
Germany
RUNNER-UP

***Slender sweepers***

*"For a long time, I have wanted to take a good shot of a school of slender sweepers that live in front of a cave in the Ari Atoll, in the Maldives. On this occasion I took a series of photos with different apertures and flash positions, finally getting the desired result when the daylight was behind the fish."*

Rollei SL66 with 50mm lens in underwater housing; flash; 1/30 sec at f22; Fujichrome Velvia

**Burt Jones & Maurine Shimlock**
United States of America
HIGHLY COMMENDED

***Blue-eyed triplefin***

*"Since they are usually no more than eight centimetres long and very secretive, the challenge is to photograph an entire fish out in the open. We especially wanted to emphasise its large protruding eyes, and so we had to wait for it to turn towards us."*

Nikon N90 with 100mm macro lens in underwater housing; two strobes; 1/60 sec at f16; Fujichrome Velvia rated at 40

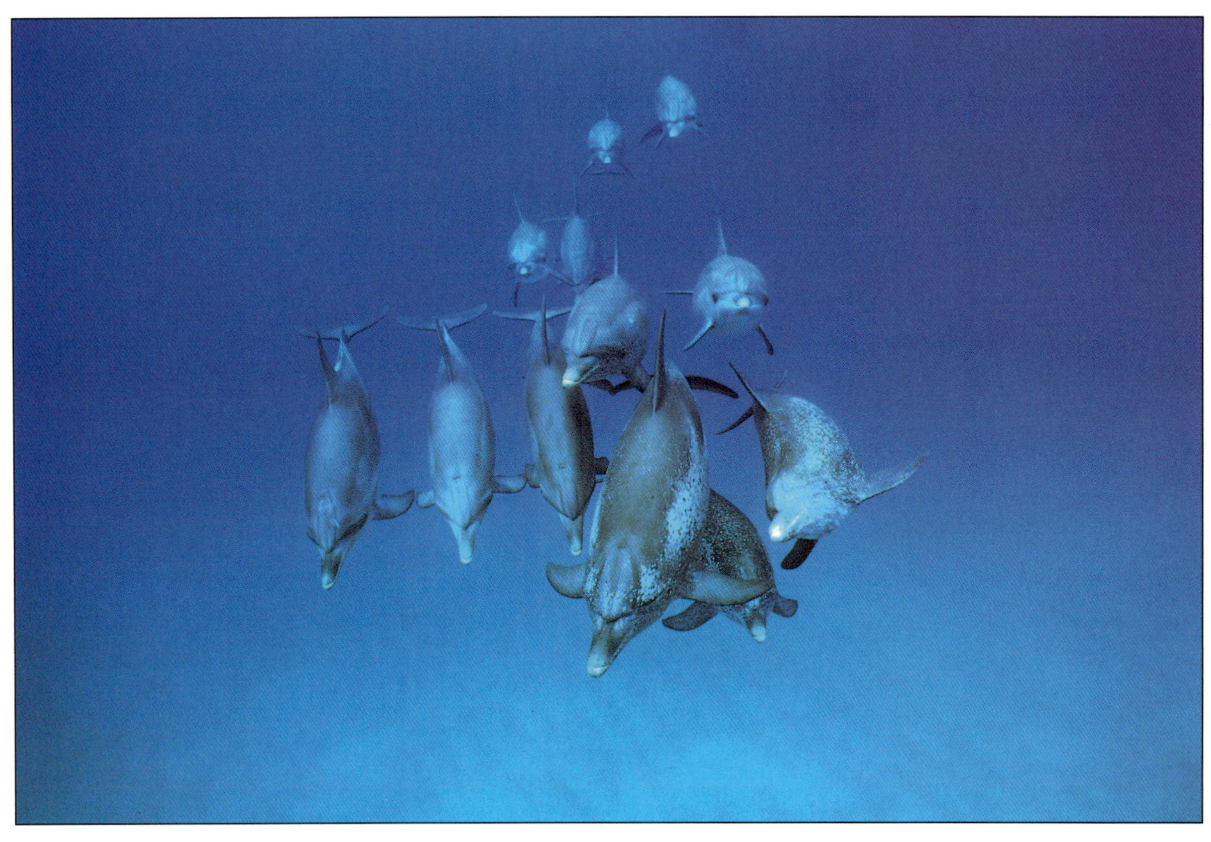

**Doug Perrine**
United States of America
HIGHLY COMMENDED

### *Atlantic spotted dolphins*

*"A pod of dolphins on Little Bahama Bank was travelling to meet another pod. Because they were so preoccupied with dolphin business, they ignored me completely, and I was able to get this unusual shot. When the two pods finally met up, the dolphins went into a frenzy of social interaction and play."*

Nikonos V with 15mm lens;
Kodak Lumiere 100 rated at 200

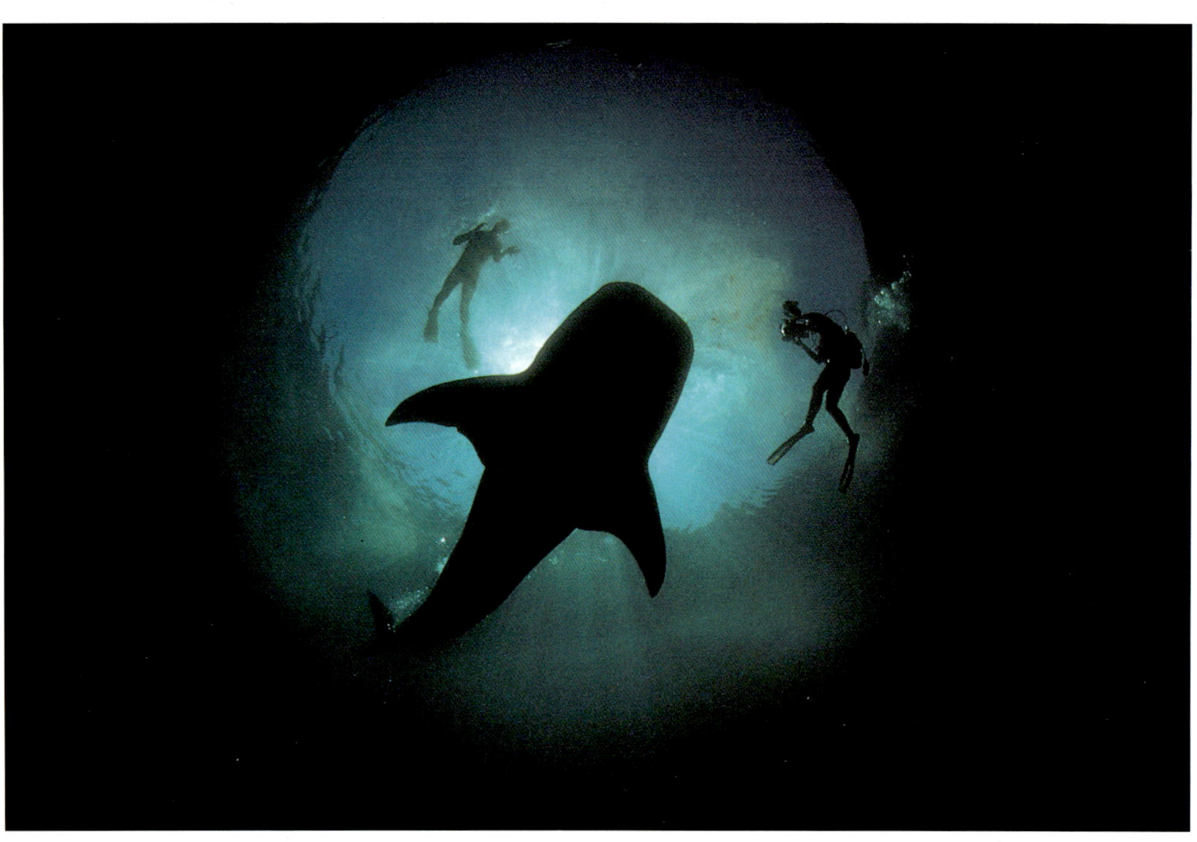

**Amos Nachoum**
United States of America
HIGHLY COMMENDED

### *Whale shark with divers*

*"Whale sharks, like this one I photographed off Western Australia, are very docile and are comfortable around swimmers, as long as nobody tries to ride on them. I used an 8mm lens so I could shoot the 10 metre shark from a metre away."*

Nikon F3 with 8mm lens;
1/250 sec at f16

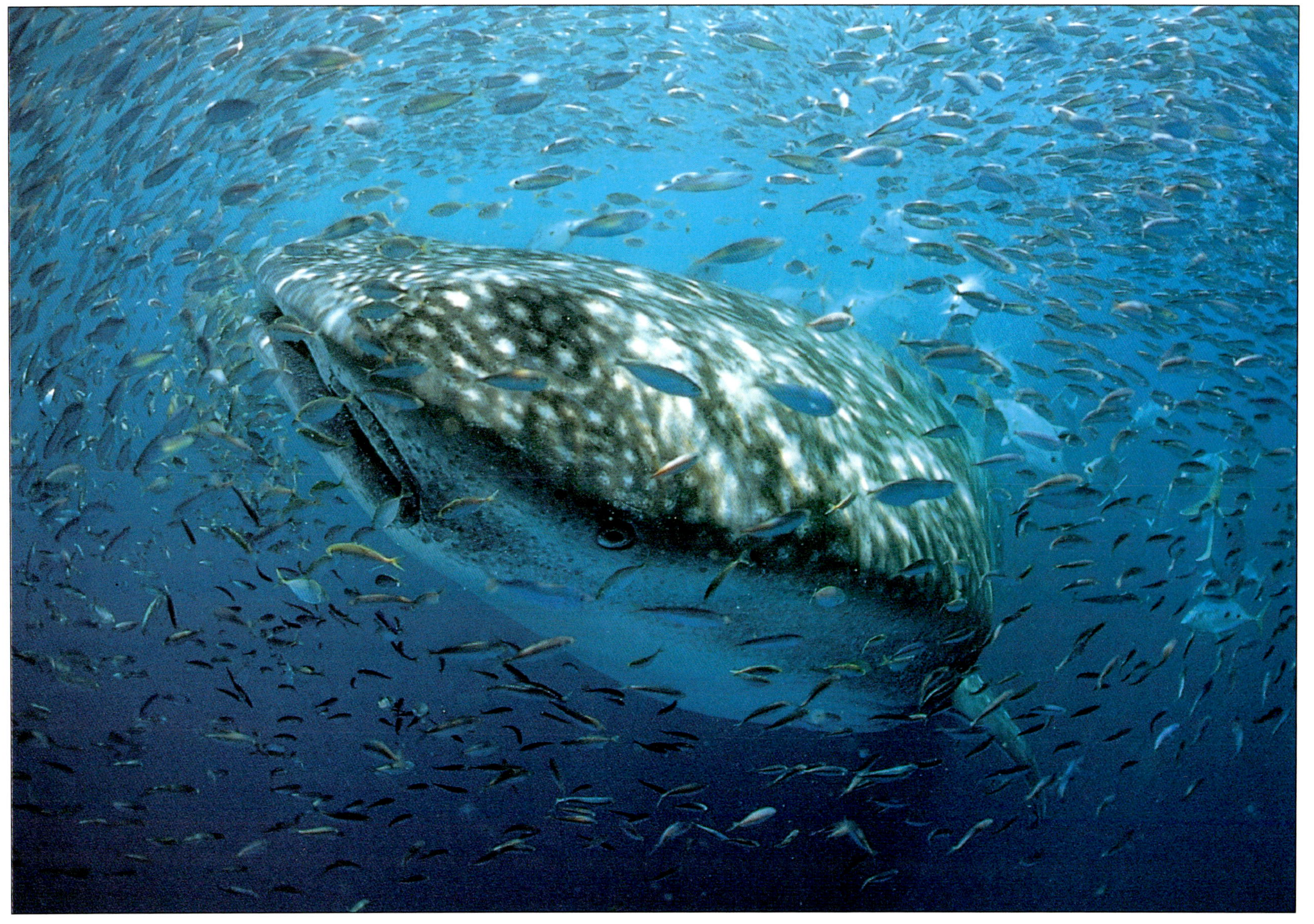

**Douglas David Seifert**
United States of America
HIGHLY COMMENDED

### *Whale shark in bait ball*

*"In April and May each year, whale sharks are attracted to the concentrations of fish known as bait balls that occur off the coast of Western Australia. I was able to watch for half an hour as this nine-metre shark swam in a six-metre diameter ball of baitfish on Ningaloo Reef - an incredible experience."*

Nikon RSAF with 13mm lens; 1/250 sec at f3.3; Kodak Lumiere 100X

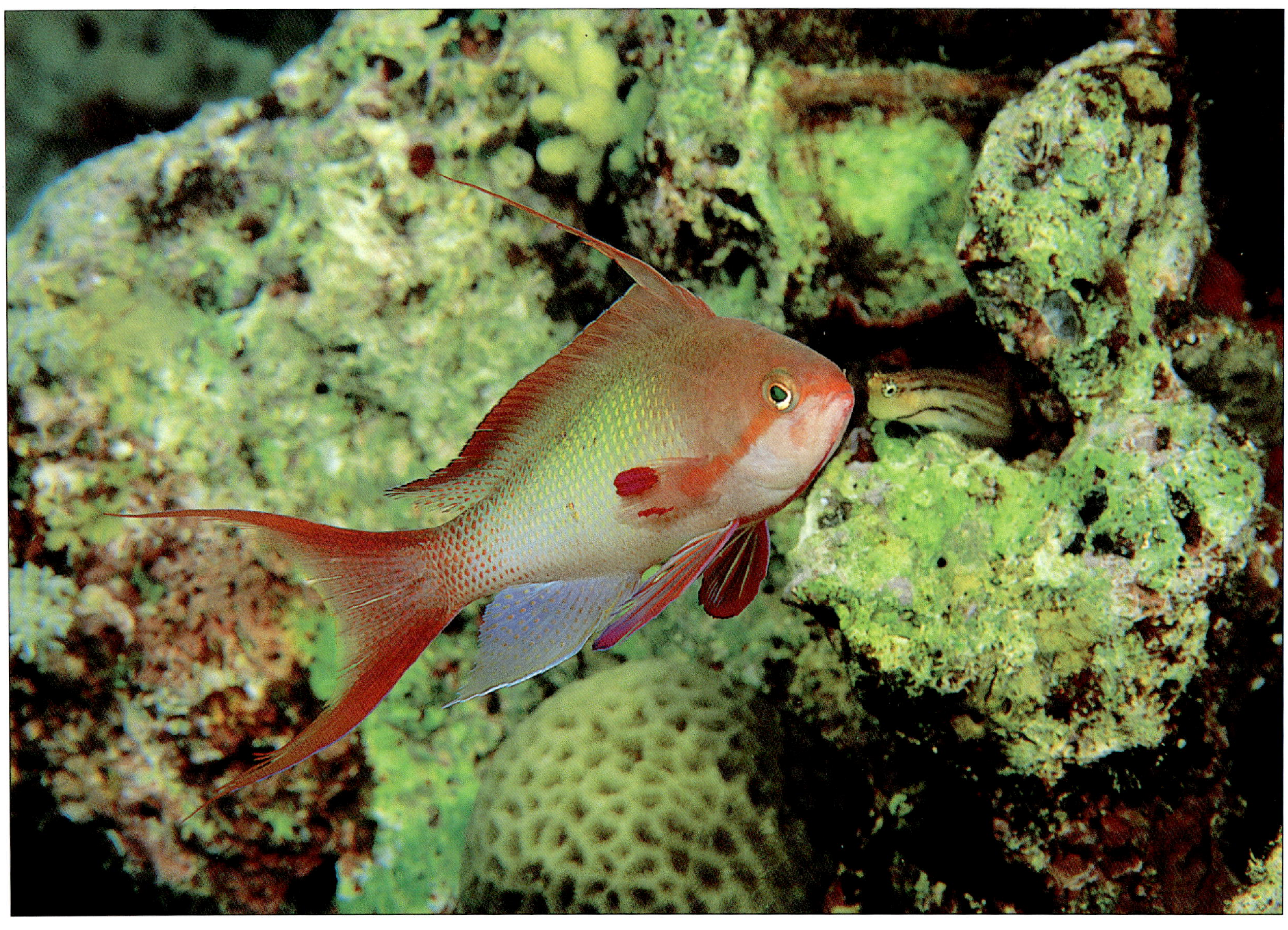

**Brent A Hedges**
Australia
HIGHLY COMMENDED

***Anthias with goby***

*"I like photographing anthias, but I am always looking for a new angle. I noticed the goby peering out from a hole in the reef and so I tried to capture the anthias in the foreground, with the goby in the background."*

Nikon F4 with 60mm lens in underwater housing; Fujichrome Velvia

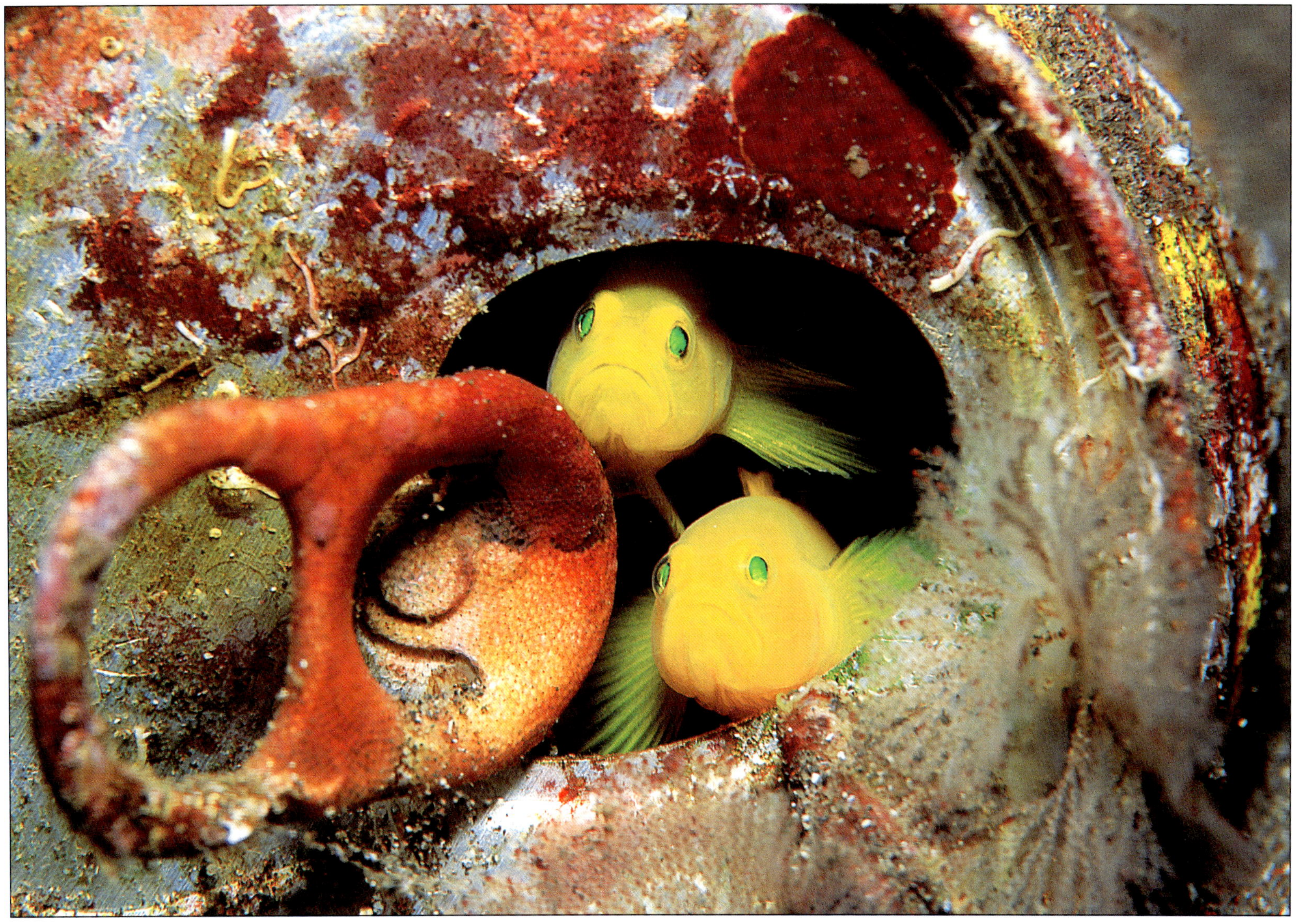

**Kimio Naito**
Japan
HIGHLY COMMENDED

***Yellow gobies in can***

*"These lovely gobies are popular fish with divers in Osezaki Bay, Japan. When I approached them, they immediately sensed my presence and hid in the can. I had to be very patient, but eventually they peeked out."*

Nikon F-801s with 105mm lens; flash; 1/60 sec at f22; Fujichrome Velvia

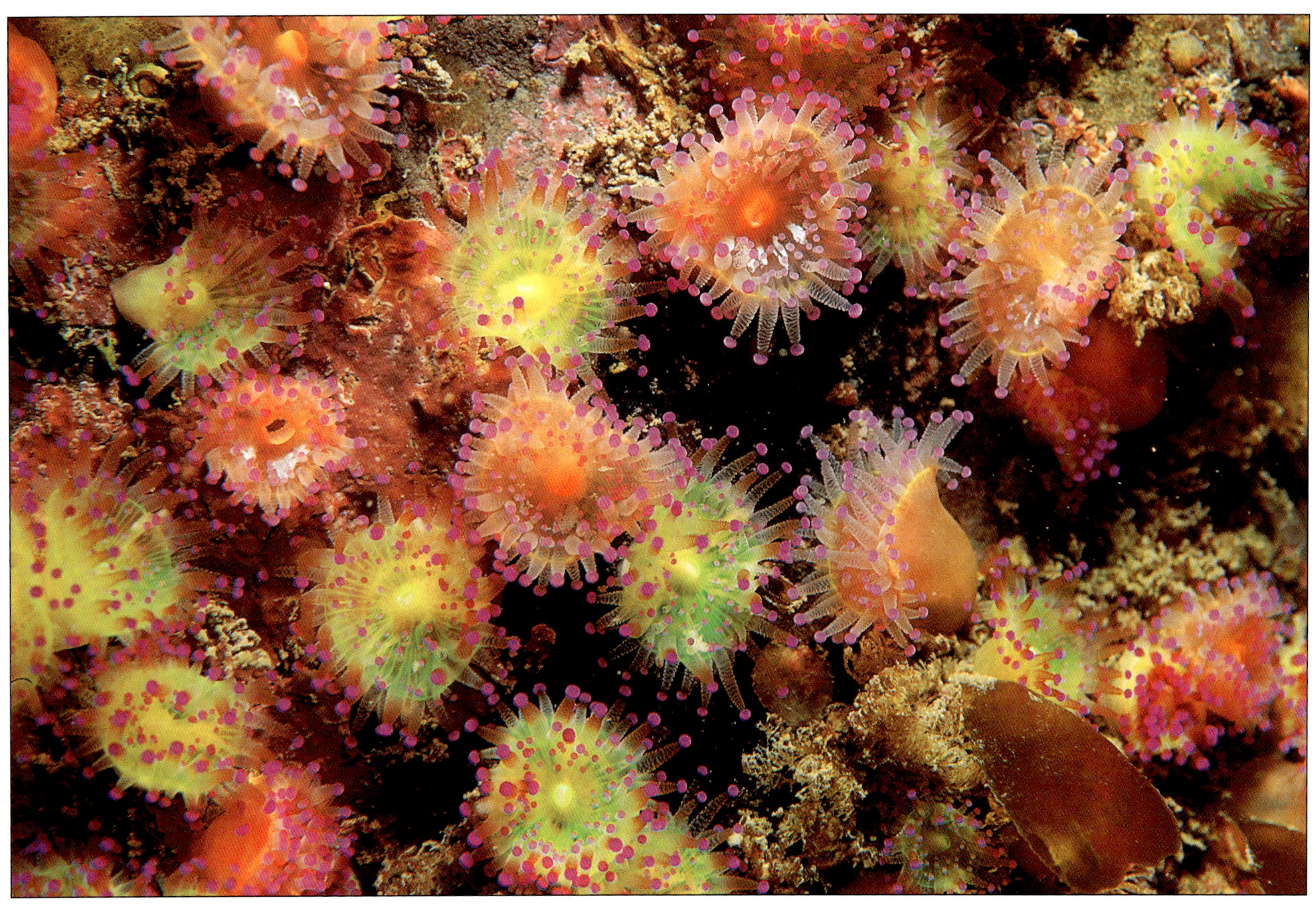

**Paul Kay**
United Kingdom
HIGHLY COMMENDED

---

***Jewel anemones***

*"Jewel anemones are a popular, but difficult, underwater subject. It is the presence of the two colour forms here that helps produce greater impact. They were photographed on the south side of Skellig Michael, in County Kerry, Ireland, on a vertical submarine cliff in a very exposed location - I was there in April for a week, and it was diveable only once."*

---

Nikon F-801 with 60mm micro lens in underwater housings; flash; 1/60 sec at f16; Fujichrome Velvia

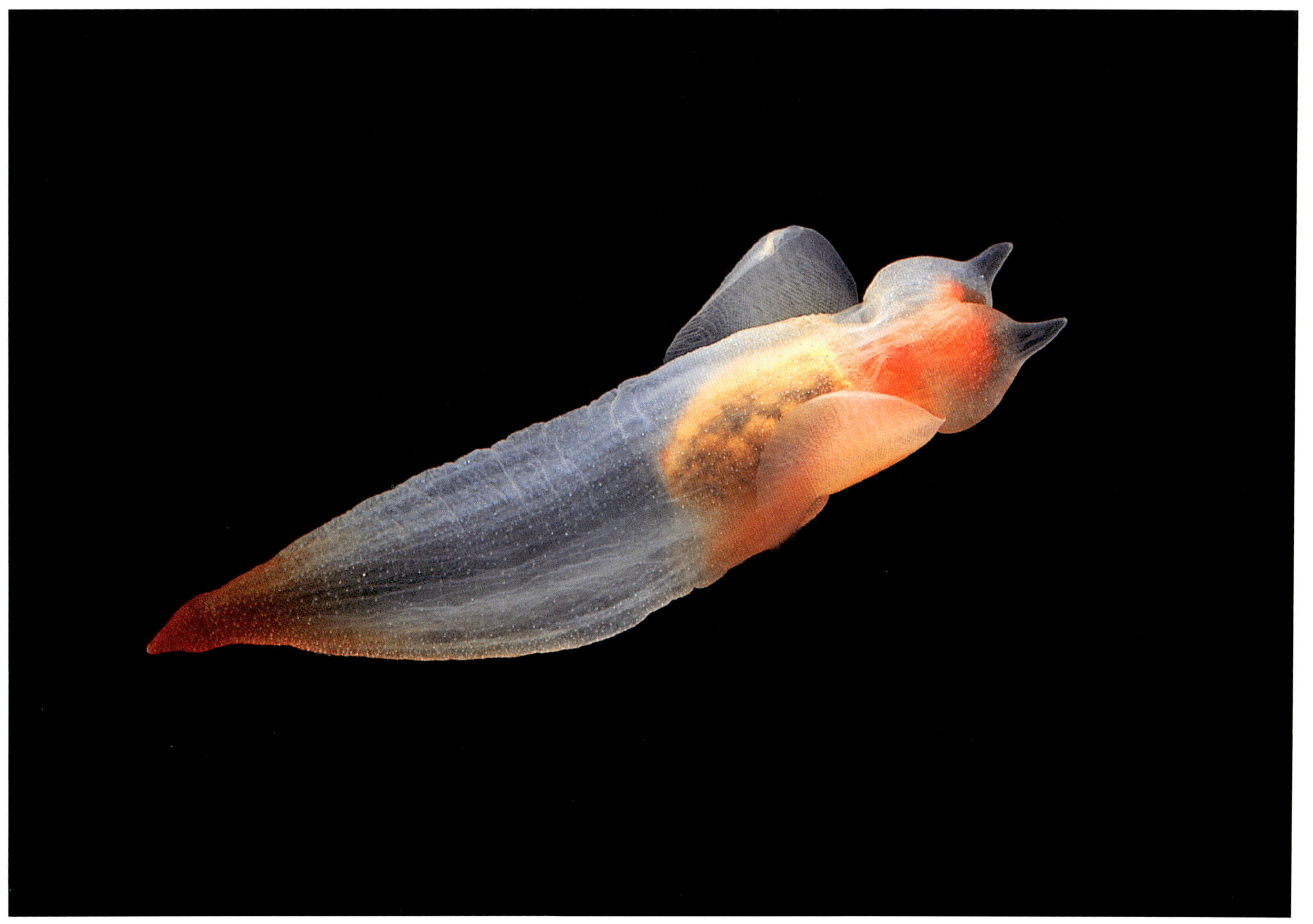

**Nikolai A Orlov**
Russia
HIGHLY COMMENDED

***Sea angel***

*"Watching this mollusc gracefully moving through the waters of the White Sea, it is hard to think of it as an active predator. But its main prey is the sea devil, another mollusc."*

Minolta 9000 with 100mm macro lens; flash; 1/250 sec at f16; Fujichrome 100

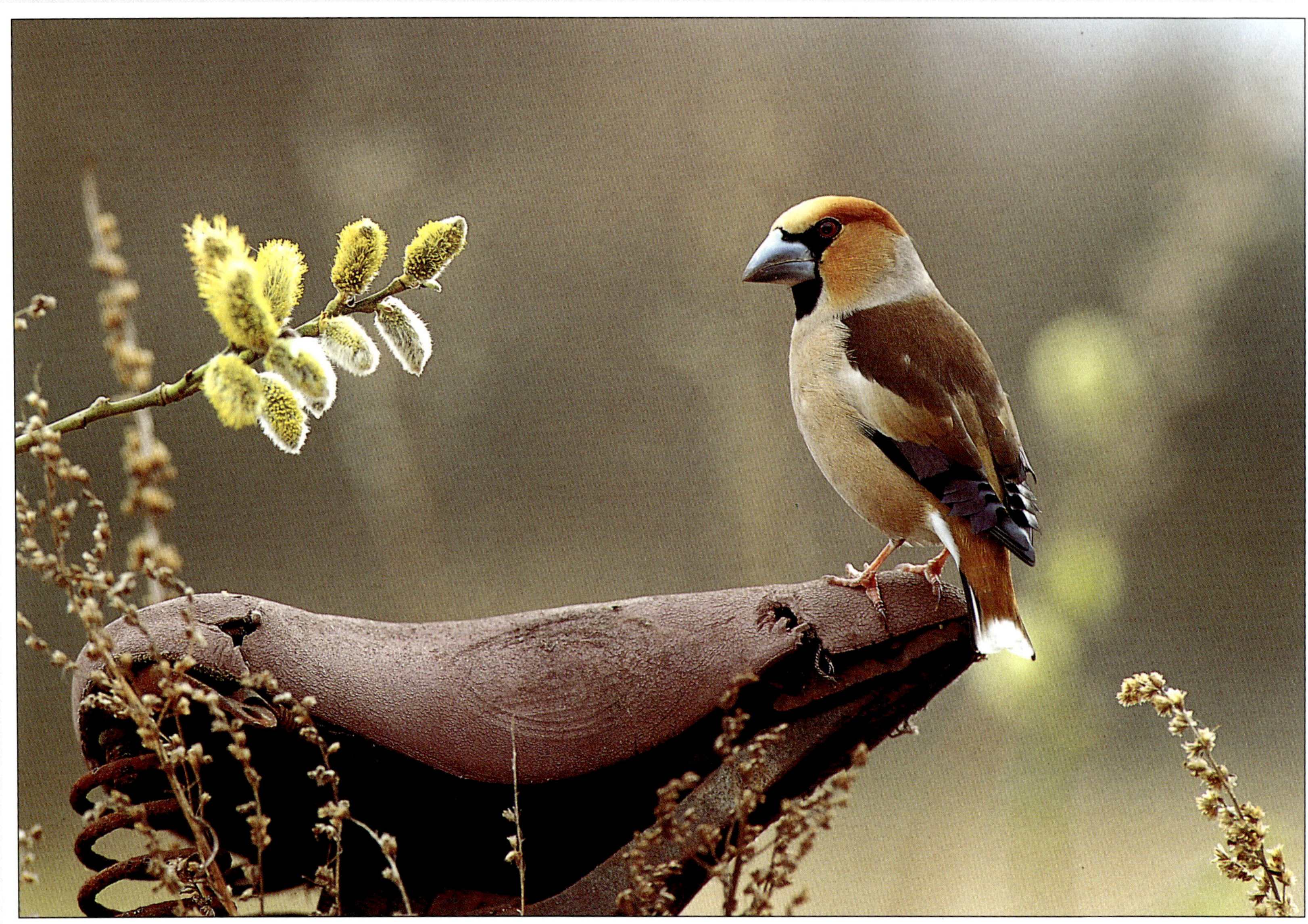

**Tapani Räsänen**
Finland
WINNER

***Hawfinch***

*"The hawfinch is quite rare in Finland, and this is only the third time I have ever seen one in my backyard. It landed on an abandoned bicycle for a few seconds - just long enough for me to get this picture."*

Canon EOS 5 with 300mm lens; tripod; 1/250 sec at f5.6; Fujichrome Provia 100

# Urban and Garden Wildlife

Pictures must show animals or plants in a garden or an obviously urban or suburban setting.

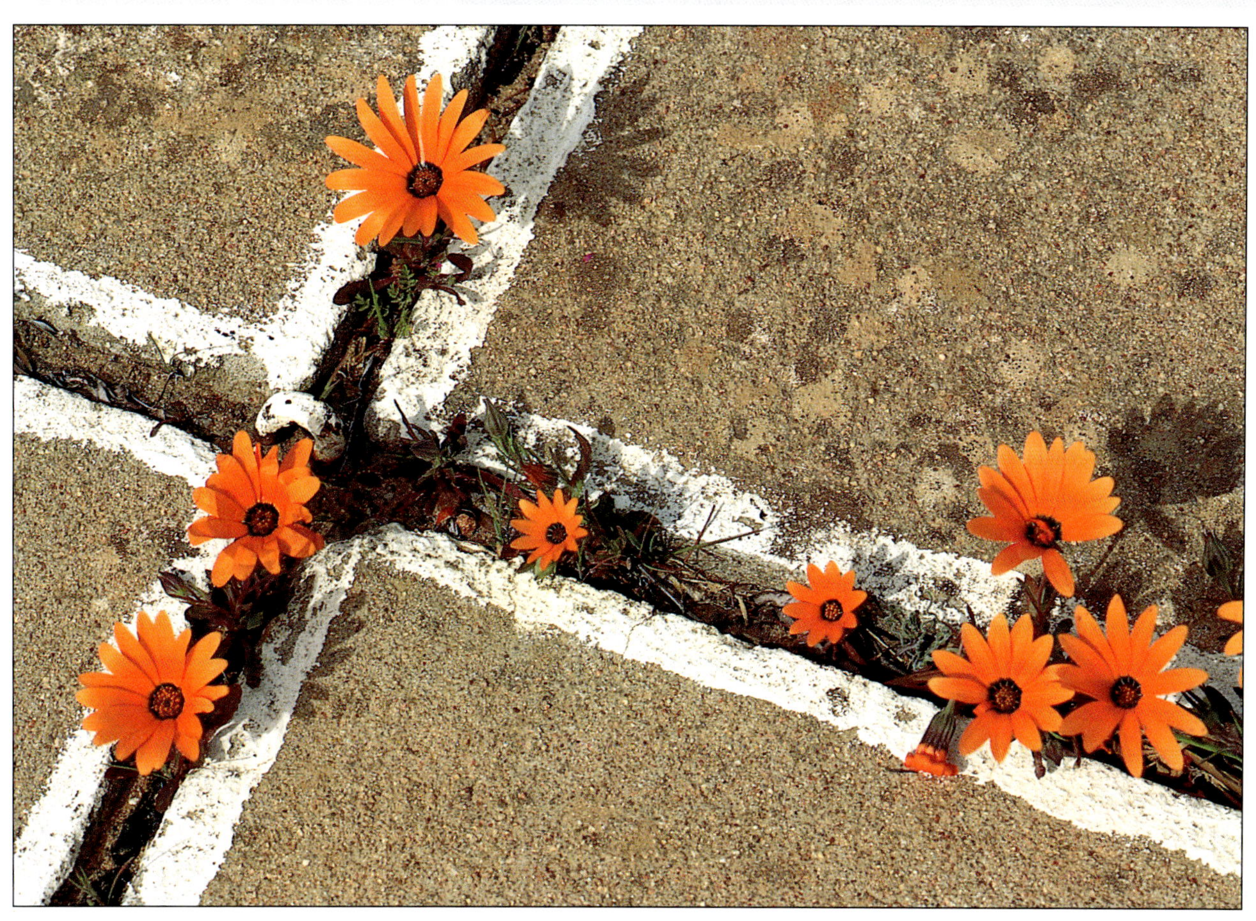

**Jill Sneesby & Barrie Wilkins**
South Africa
RUNNER-UP

***Tennis-court daisies***

*"In springtime, flowers bloom everywhere in Namaqualand. Here, seeds had lodged in crevices in the cement of a tennis court. We were intrigued by the patterns of the blooms and lines."*

Canon EOS 1 with 20-35mm lens; tripod; f16; Fujichrome Velvia

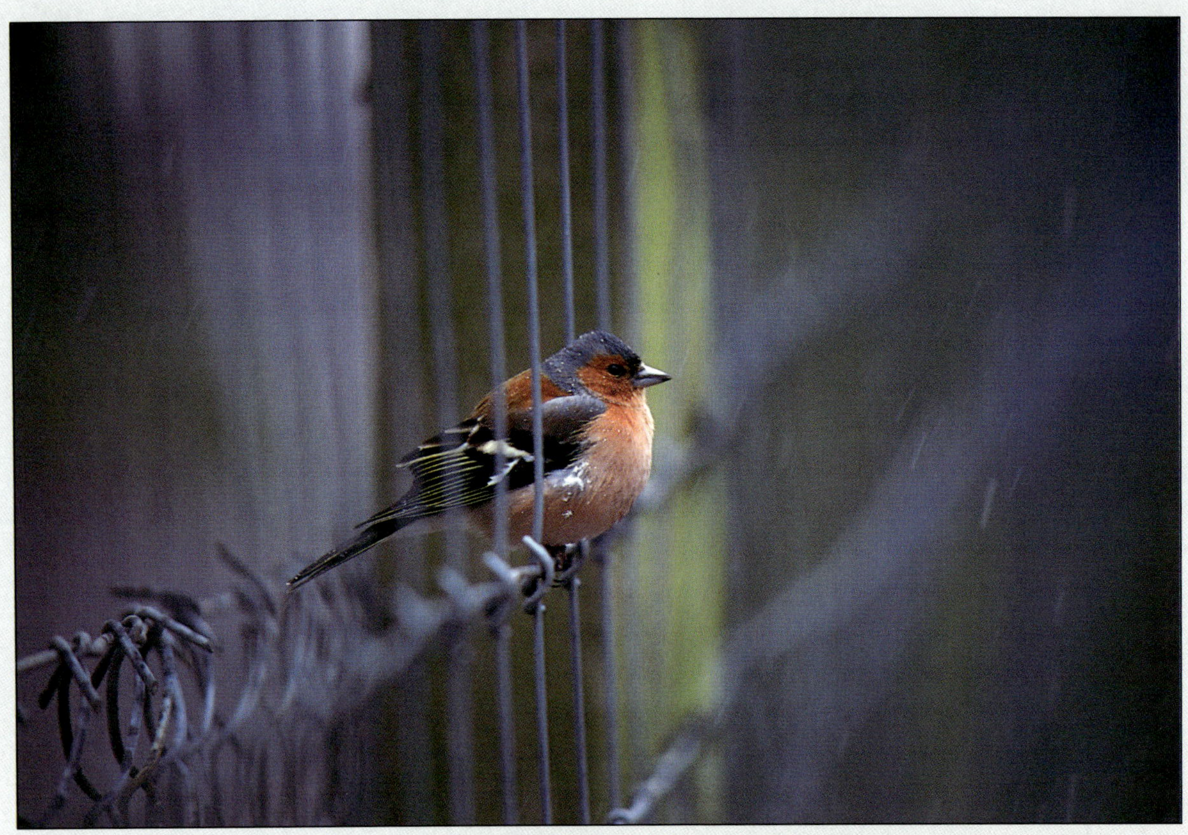

**Duncan Usher**
United Kingdom
HIGHLY COMMENDED

### *Chaffinch*

*"As I returned to my car after an unsuccessful visit to a park in Kassell to photograph mallards, a chaffinch flew up in front of me and landed on the park fence. The peculiar light and snowfall enhanced an otherwise drab urban scene, and I managed to grab two frames before he flew off."*

Nikon F4 with 300mm lens; 1/90 sec at f4.5; Fujichrome 100 rated at 200

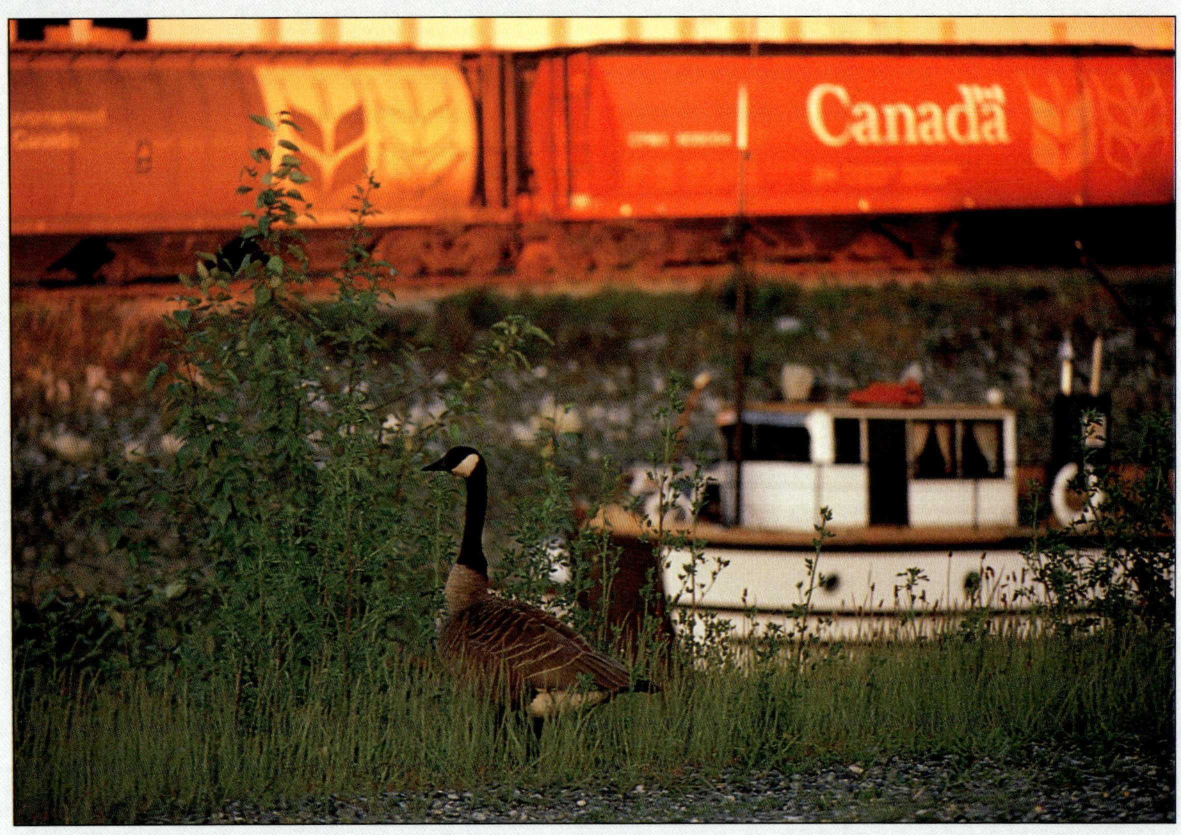


**Peter Thomas**
Canada
HIGHLY COMMENDED

### *Canada goose*

*"A grain terminal for unloading prairie wheat in Vancouver harbour was a good place to find Canada geese. Here, a parent bird keeps an eye out for danger as its family grazes at a little boat harbour which has now become a victim of development."*

Nikon FE with 105mm lens; 1/125 sec at f8/11; Kodachrome 64

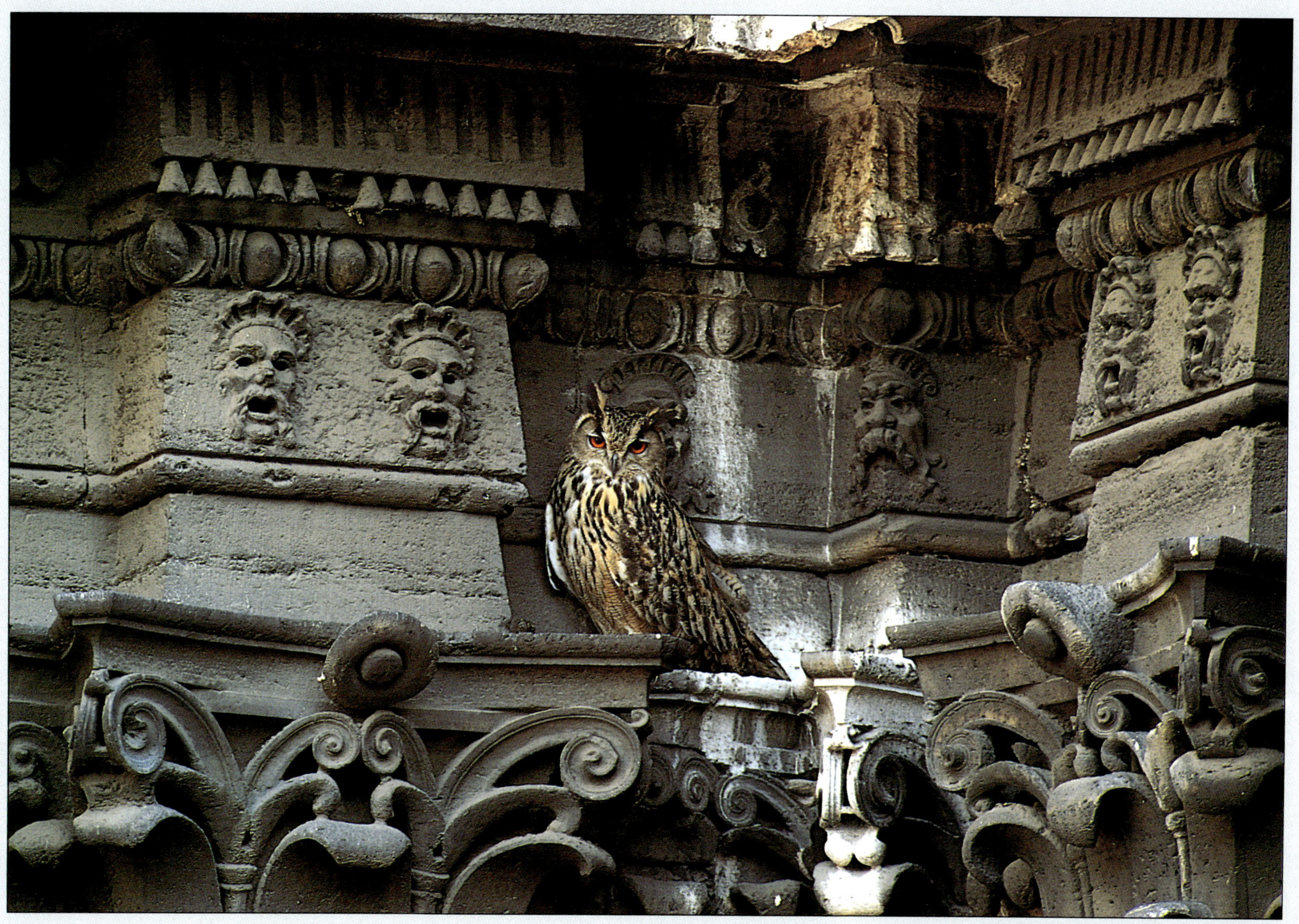

**Maurizio Lanini**
Italy
HIGHLY COMMENDED

***Eagle owl on the French Embassy***

*"In 1994, an eagle owl was spotted in Rome for the first time since the beginning of the century. It was seen on the cornice of the Palazzo Farnese, the French Embassy in Rome, where it remained until the end of the summer. The main problem with photographing it was getting authorisation to enter the building."*

Canon EOS RT with 300mm lens and x1.4 extender; tripod; 1/16 sec at f5.6; Fujichrome Velvia

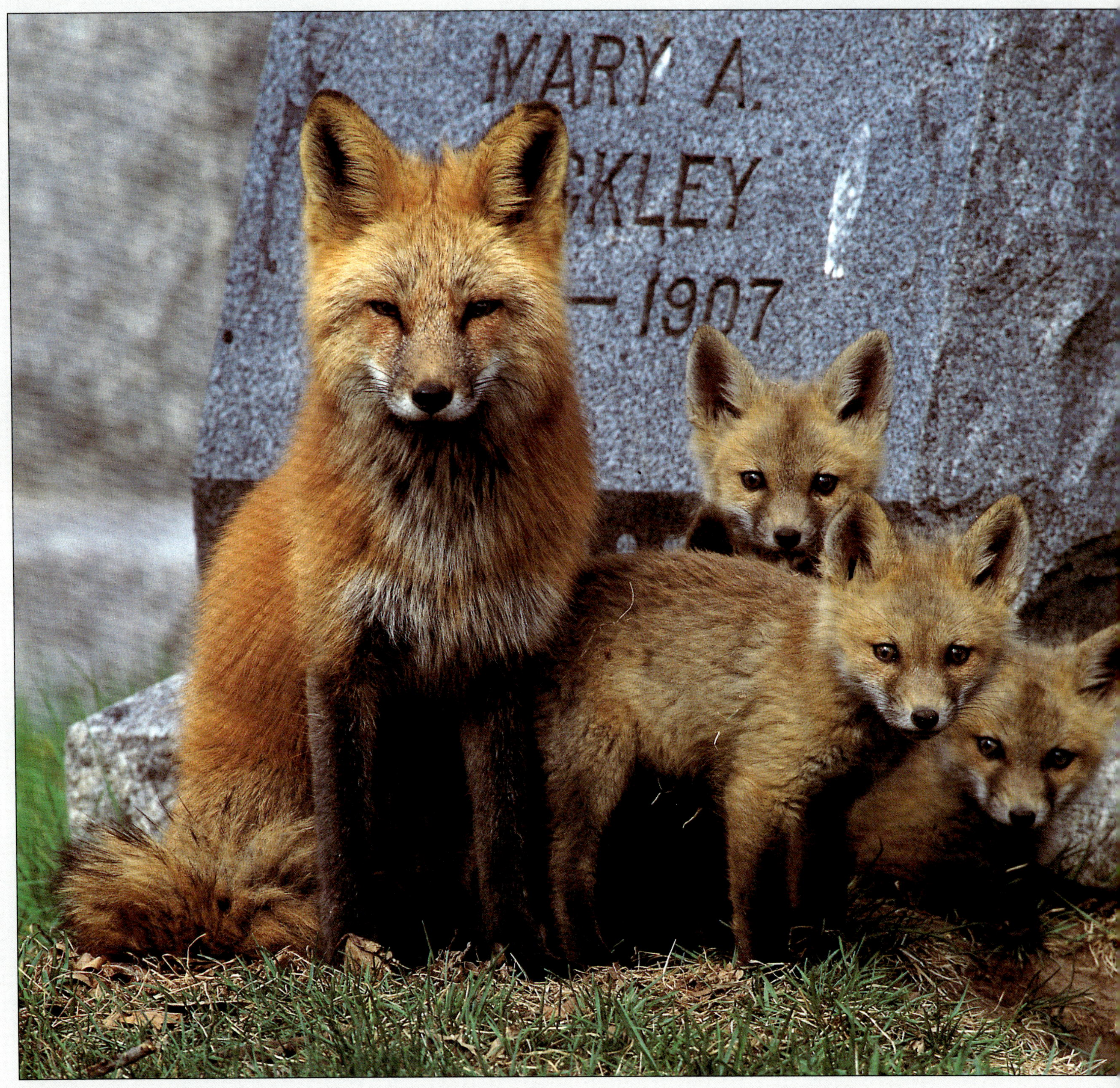
MARY A.
CKLEY
— 1907

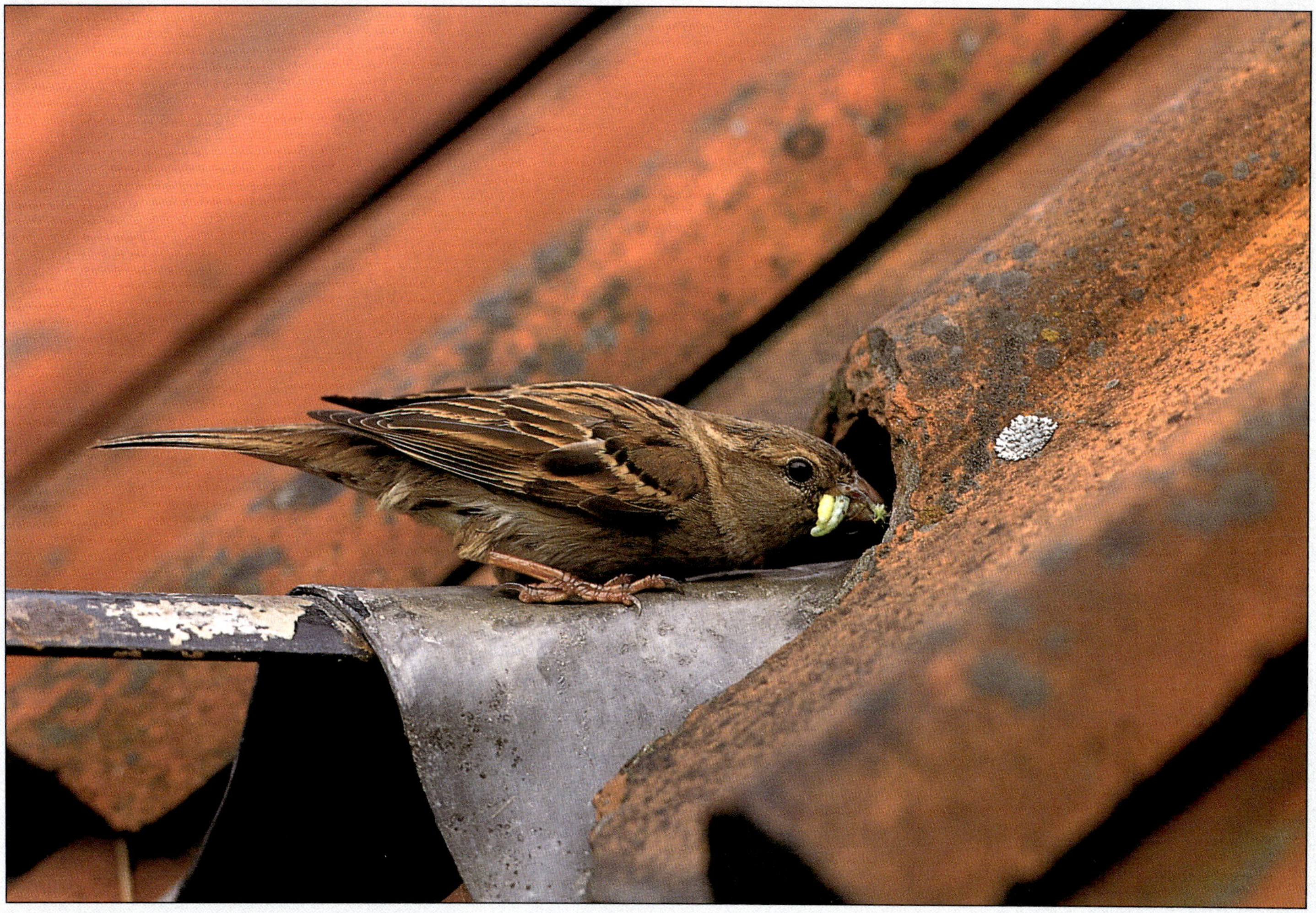

**Wendy Shattil**
**& Bob Rozinski**
United States of America
HIGHLY COMMENDED

***Red fox with cubs in cemetery***

*"Cemeteries are excellent places to find red foxes in urban areas of the United States. Trees and shrubs in the tombstoned landscape provide cover, while rodents and birds are a plentiful food source. Furthermore the foxes are not disturbed by human inhabitants."*

Canon EOS 1N with 840mm lens; 1/250 sec at f8; Fujichrome Provia

**Russell Hartwell**
United Kingdom
HIGHLY COMMENDED

***House sparrow***

*"This cavity under roof tiles has been used as a nest site by house sparrows for decades. In spring and early summer, the roof is alive with the chattering and squabbling of the sparrow community. The chicks are fed by both parents, and here, the hen sparrow is about to squeeze through the entrance with a beak full of succulent grubs."*

Nikon F4 with 180mm lens; tripod; 1/250 sec at f8; Fujichrome RDP 100

# Composition and Form

Pictures in this category must illustrate natural subjects in abstract ways, and are judged for their aesthetic values.

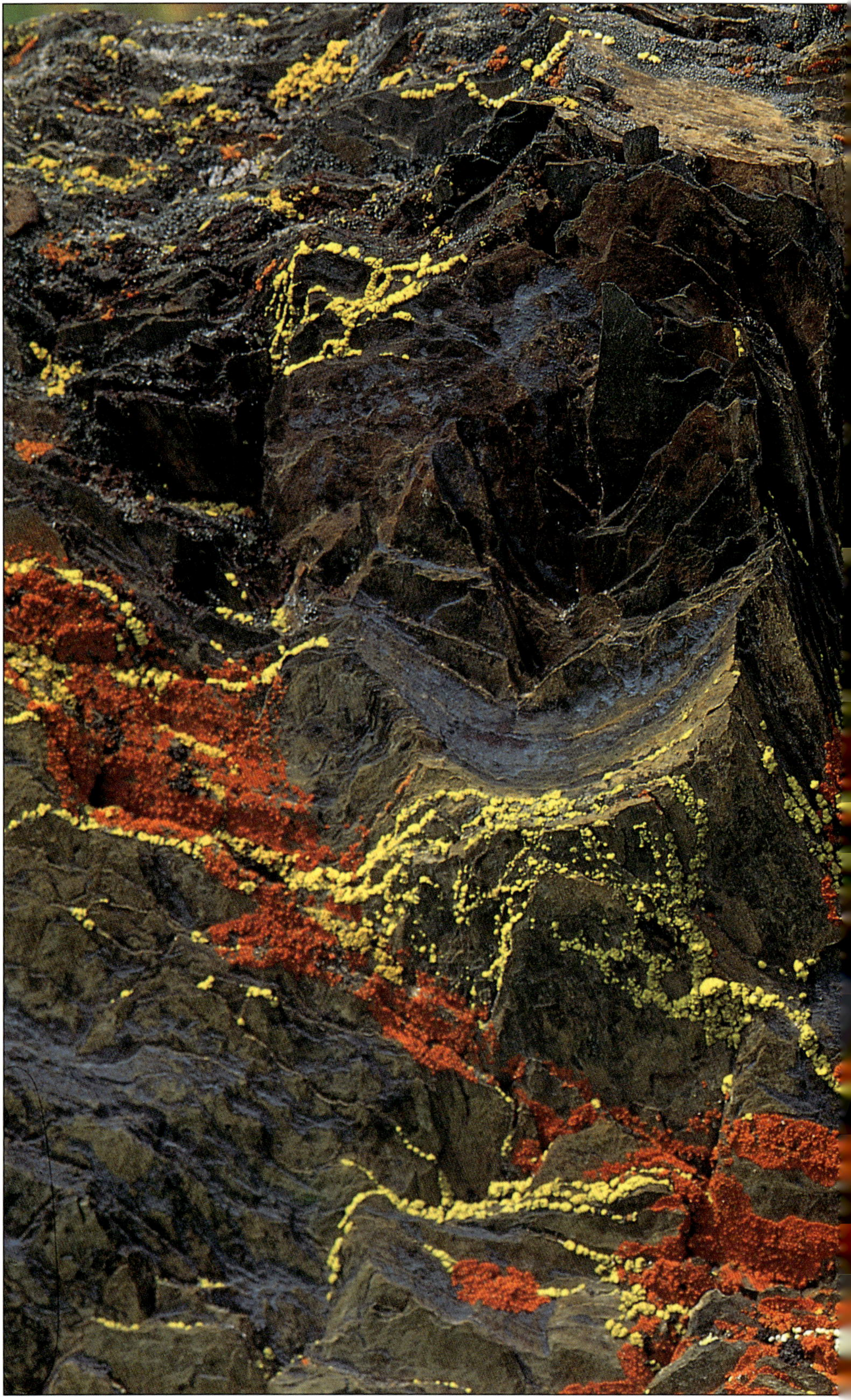

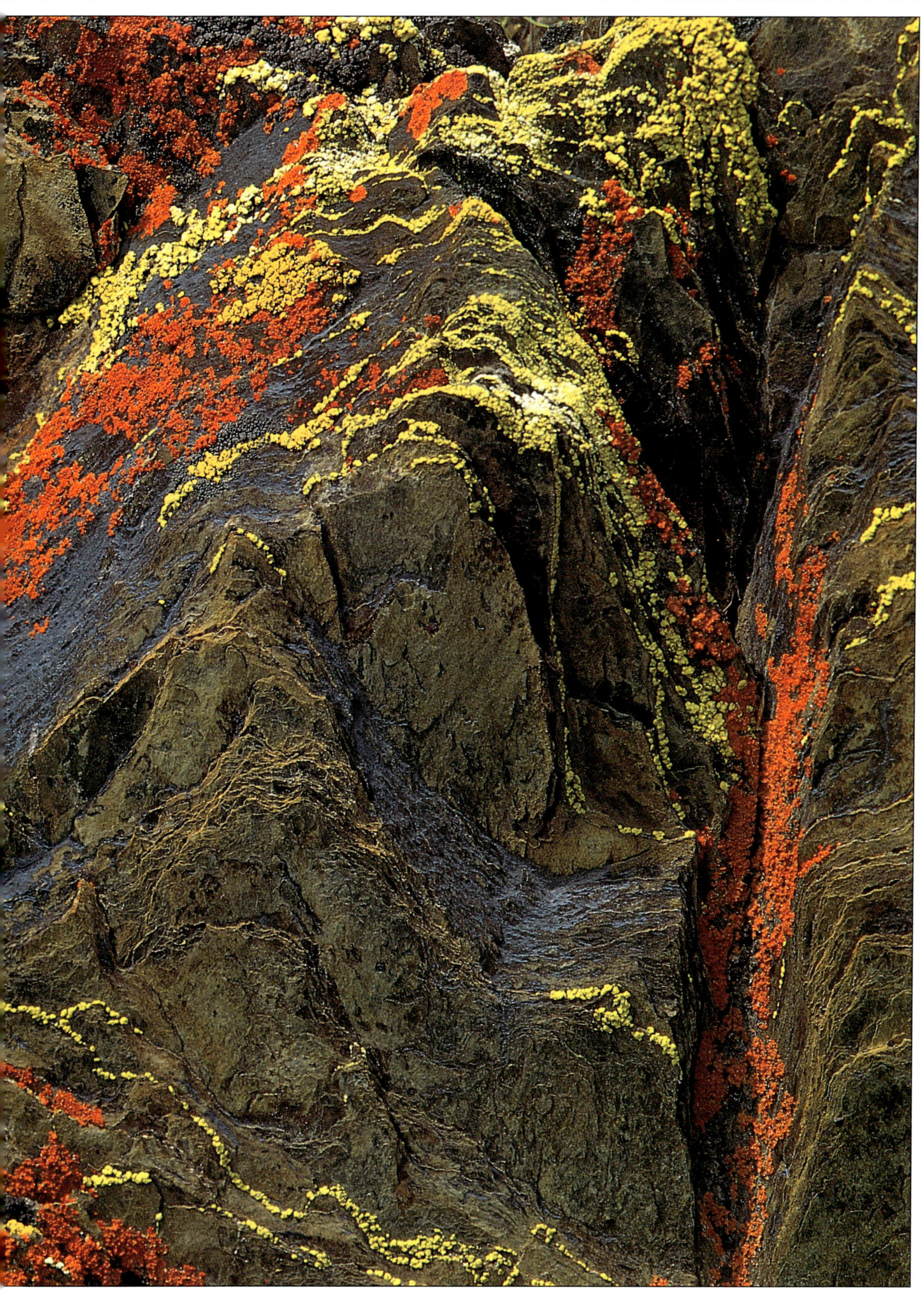

**Roger Lewis Johnson**
United States of America
WINNER

---

**Lichen on Mariposa slate**

*"This was taken in spring on the foothills of the Sierra Nevada mountains in Mariposa County, California. In this area, the colours of the lichen are so varied and bright. It was overcast and the light was even and soft - very good for colour photography. I used a soft-gold lite disk to give extra light for detail."*

---

Nikon F4s with 105mm lens; 1/60 sec at f11; Fujichrome 100

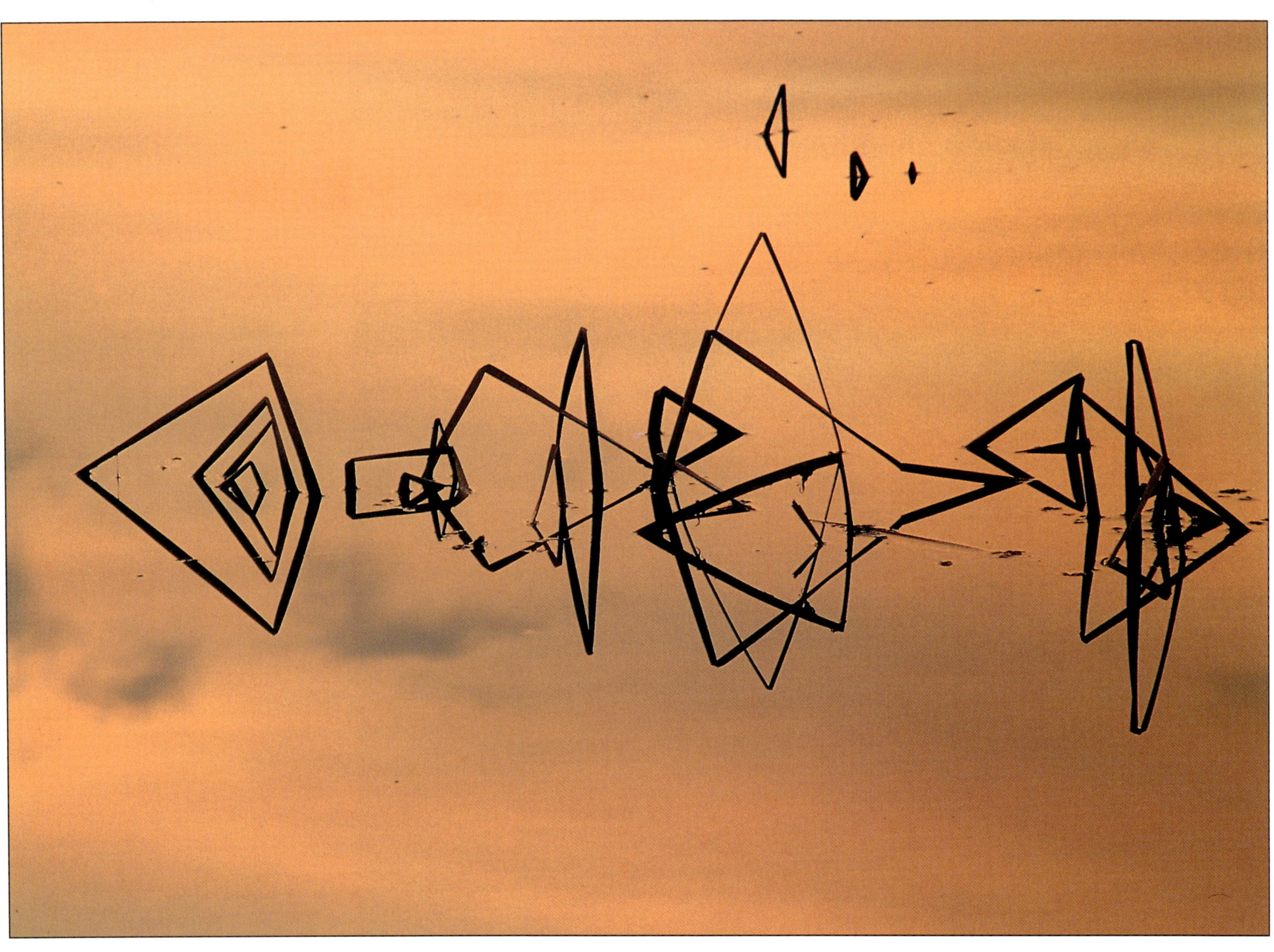

**Dr Mamoru Yoshida**
United States of America
RUNNER-UP

---

***Cattail stalks in marsh pond***

*"I live near the Arthur R Marshall Loxahatchee National Wildlife Refuge in Florida. This January morning, the dawn was special, and I was drawn to the beauty of the water, reflecting the orange cloud, and the geometric forms of the bent cattail stalks. The light that produced the rich colour only lasted a few minutes."*

---

Canon EOS A2 with 100-300mm lens; tripod; f22; Fujichrome Velvia

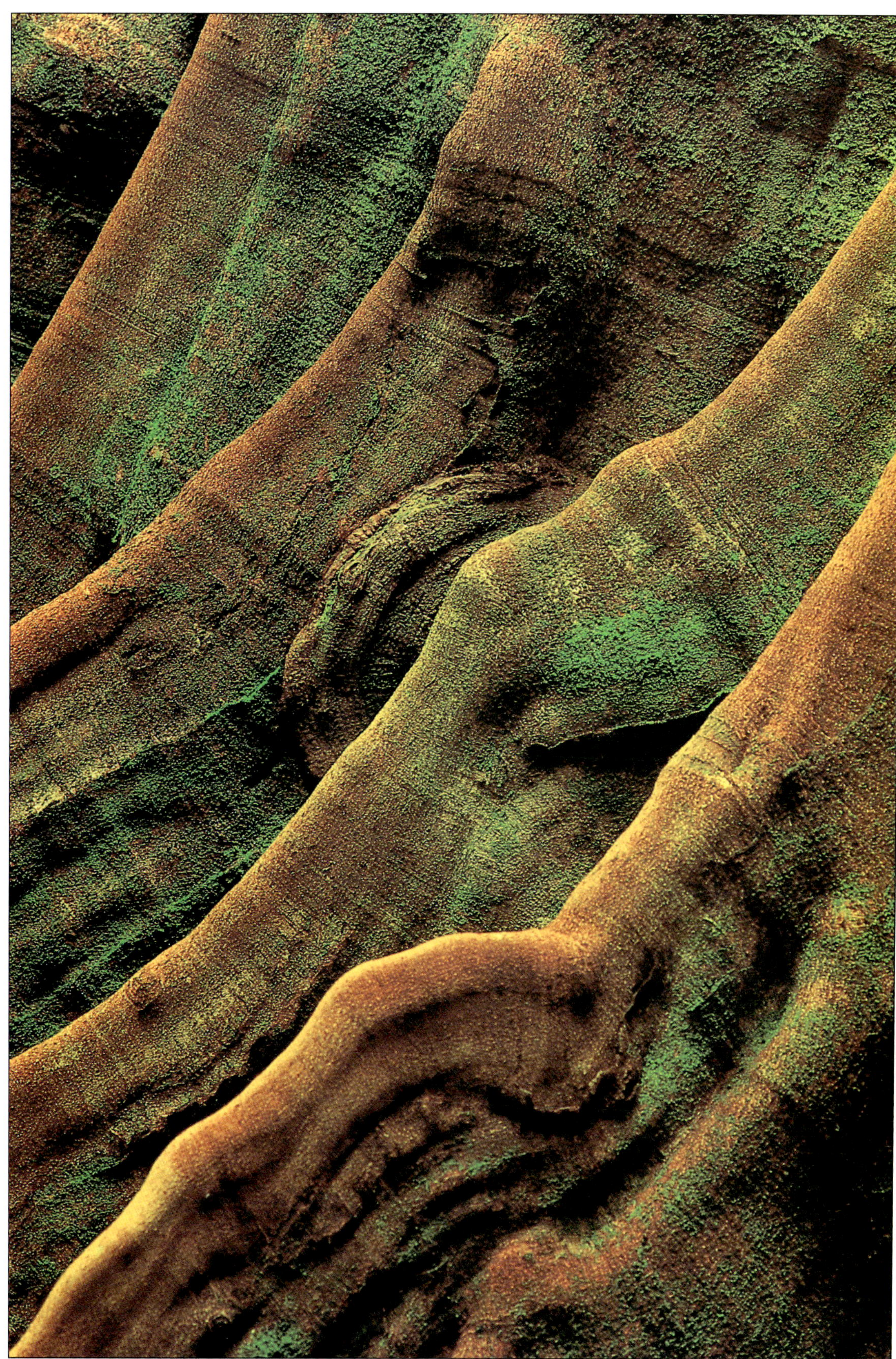

**Gary Braasch**
United States of America
SPECIALLY COMMENDED

***Reseco tree buttresses***

*"These striking buttress roots, three metres high and four metres long, were hard to resist photographically. I took this picture during a break from a tropical biodiversity assignment in Costa Rica for LIFE Magazine, framing and focusing to accentuate the 'landscape' of the root growth."*

Nikon 8008s with 105mm lens; tripod; 2 secs at f16; Fujichrome Velvia

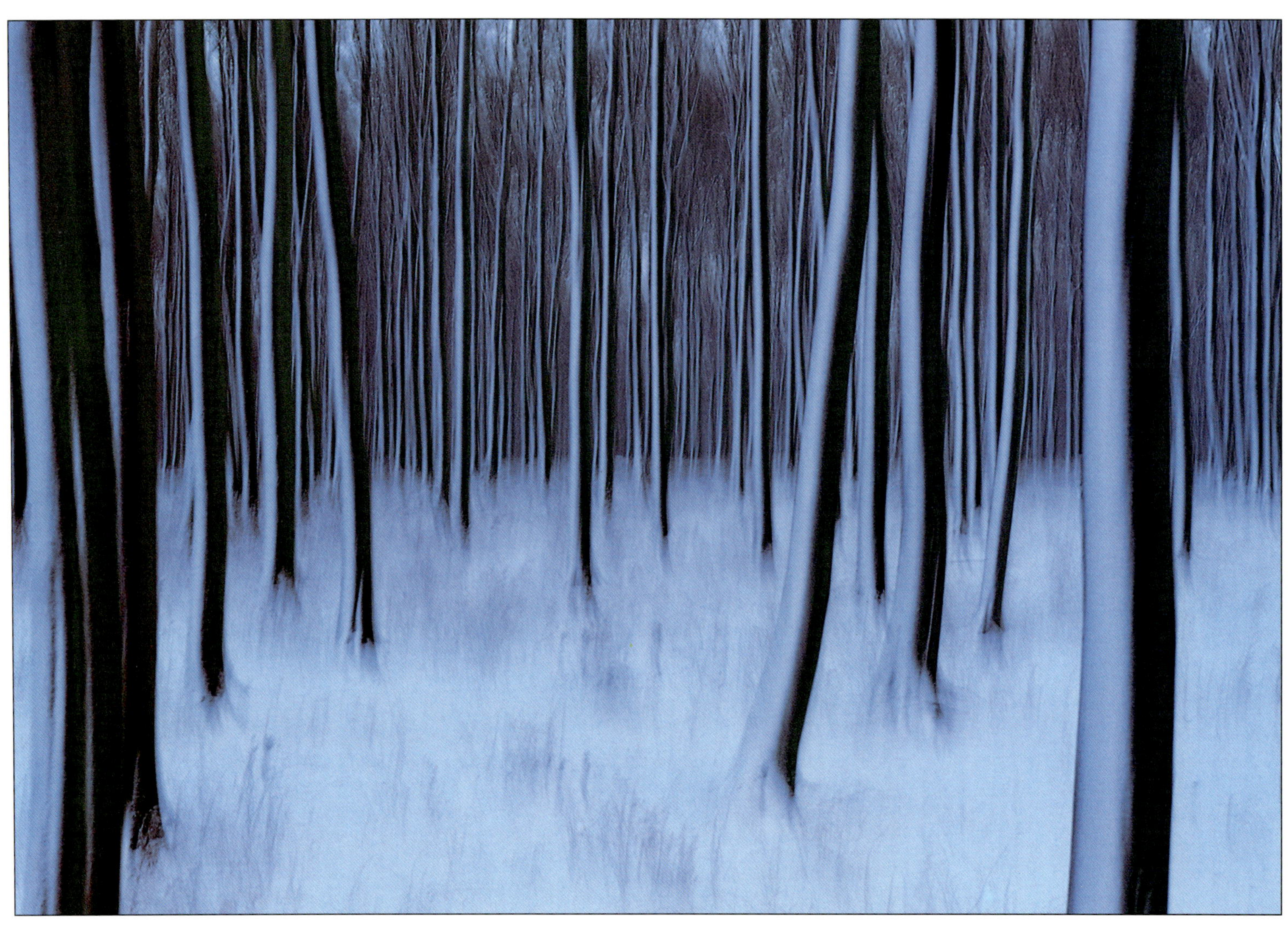

**Konrad Wothe**

Germany

HIGHLY COMMENDED

---

***Winter forest***

*"Driving home last January in northern Bavaria, I discovered this magic forest beside the highway. A snowstorm had painted the almost black trees white down one side. I tried to catch the magic atmosphere on film by moving the camera while exposing for a quarter of a second."*

---

Canon EOS 1N with 28-70mm lens;
1/4 sec auto-exposure; Fujichrome Sensia 100

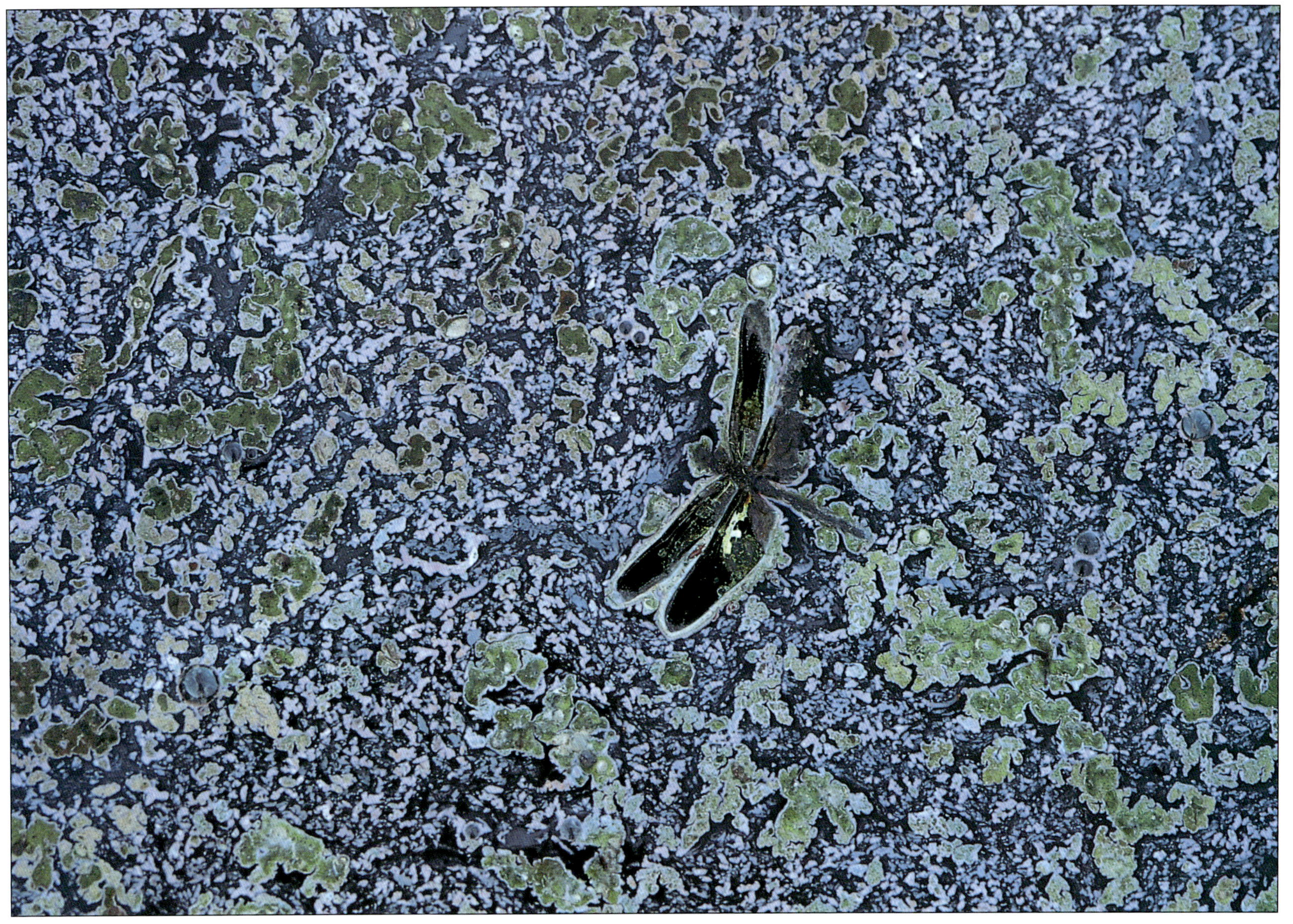

**Gertrud & Helmut Denzau**
Germany
HIGHLY COMMENDED

**_Drowned dragonfly in blue algae_**

*"During an expedition to search for Somali wild asses in the Danakil Desert, Ethiopia, we checked various waterholes for footprints. Some waterholes were covered with colourful algae in which floated dragonflies and butterflies that had died there."*

Nikon F4 with 35-70mm lens; 1/60 sec at f11; Fujichrome Sensia 100

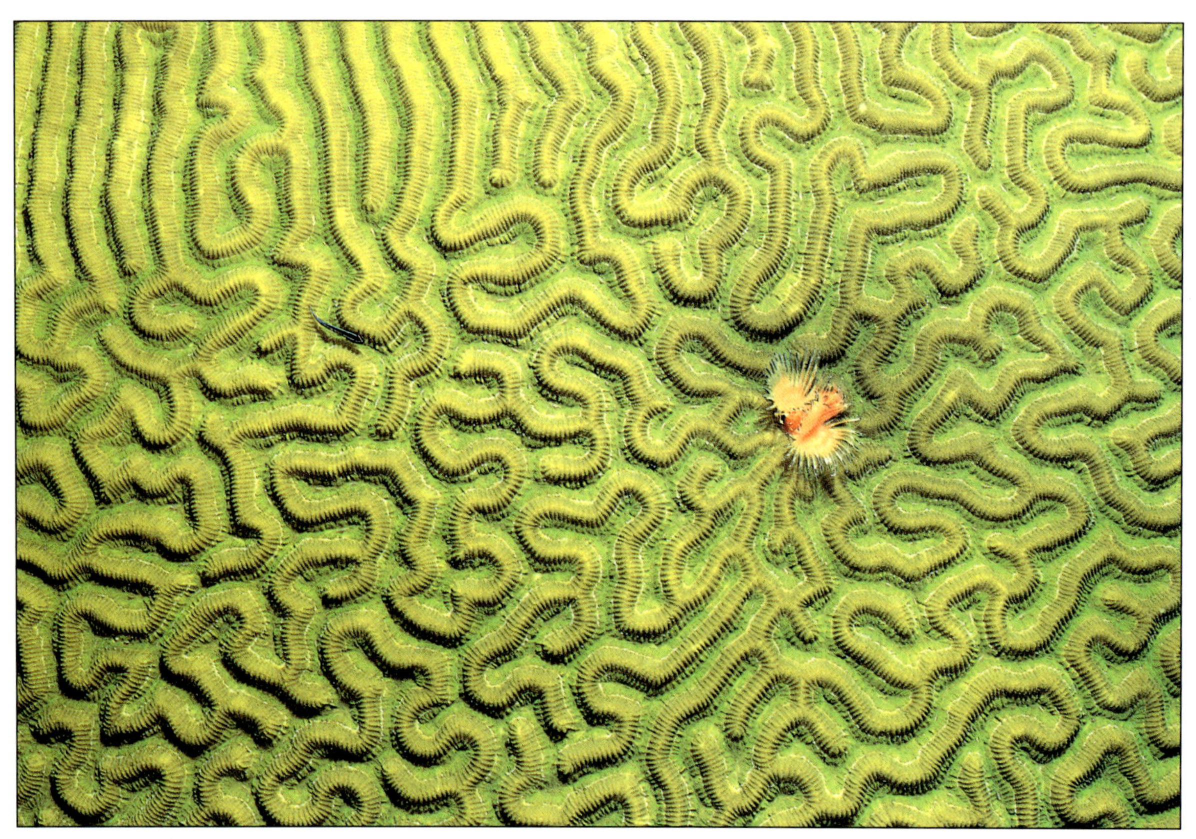

**Solvin Zankl**
Germany
HIGHLY COMMENDED

### *Horseshoe worm and goby on brain coral*

*"I photographed this brain coral on a dive off Buck Island Reef, in the US Virgin Islands, when I was looking for segmented worms. The worm in this picture lives in a tube in the centre of the brain coral and must grow at the same rate as the coral to avoid being grown over. A little goby is moving towards the tube worm."*

Nikon RSAF with 50mm lens; flash; 1/125 sec at f5.6; Fujichrome Velvia

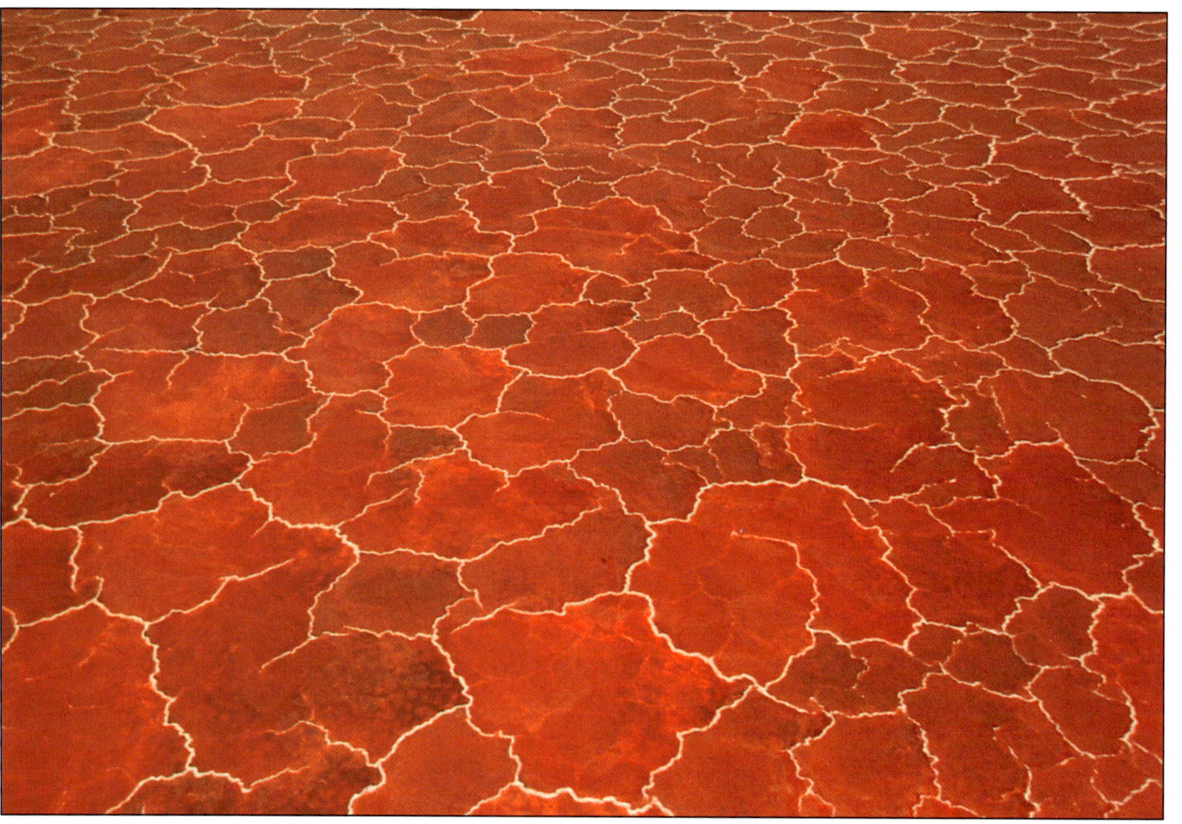

**Gerry Ellis**
United States of America
HIGHLY COMMENDED

### *Soda formation on Lake Natron*

*"This is an aerial photograph taken at Lake Natron in the Great Rift Valley, Tanzania, as part of a project to document the Rift Valley."*

Nikon F4 with 20-35mm lens; 1/250 sec at f5.6; Kodak Elite 100

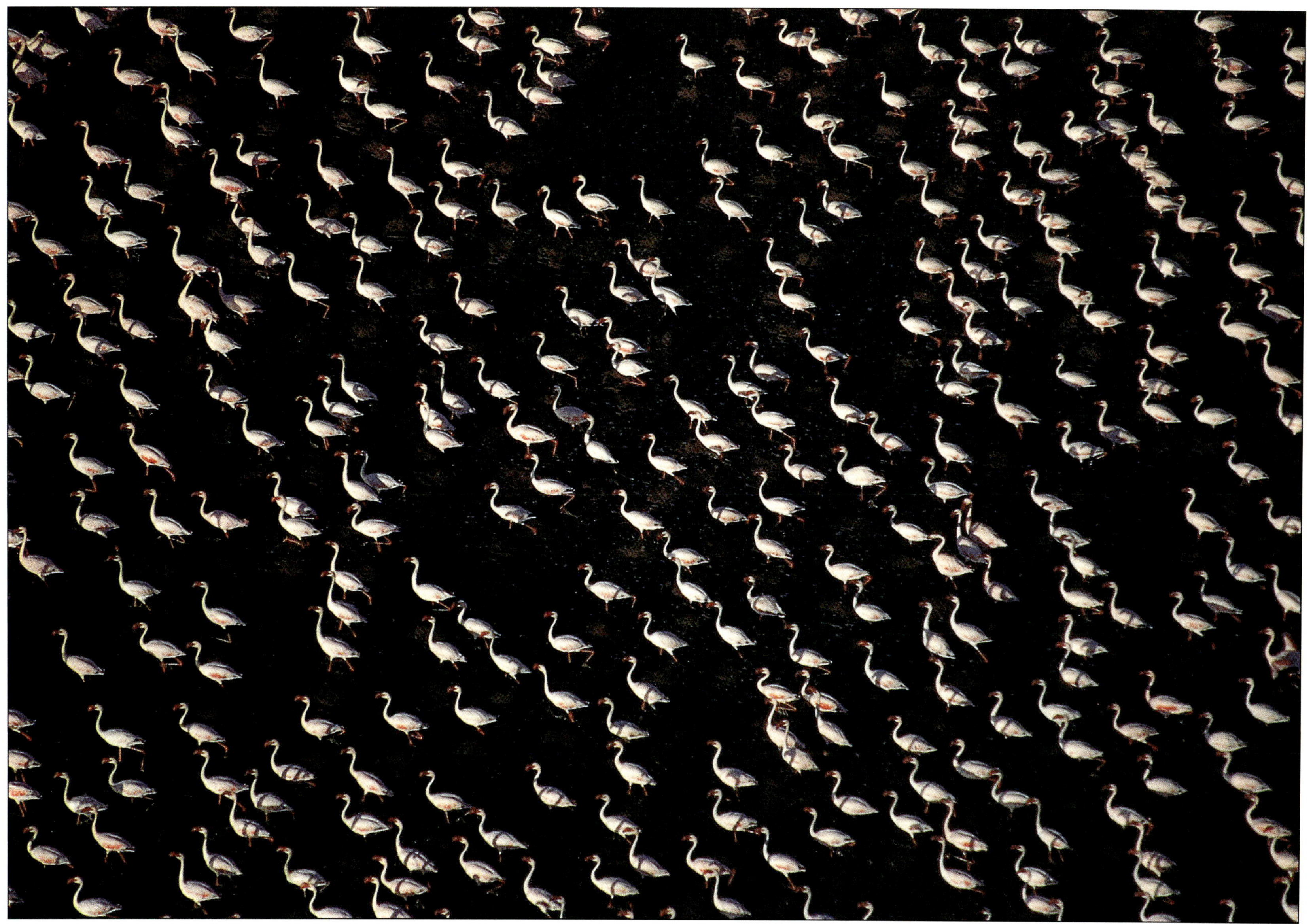

**Mike Hill**
United Kingdom
HIGHLY COMMENDED

***Lesser flamingos***

*"We hired an ultralight aircraft and flew over Lake Magadi, in Kenya. Most aerial shots of flamingos show them fleeing in panic from the aircraft and so, anxious not to disturb this flock, we approached carefully, allowing time for them to get used to us."*

Nikon F4 with 80-200mm lens; autofocus; Fujichrome Sensia

# The World In Our Hands

Pictures must illustrate in a symbolic or graphic way our dependence on the natural world or our capability of inflicting harm on it.

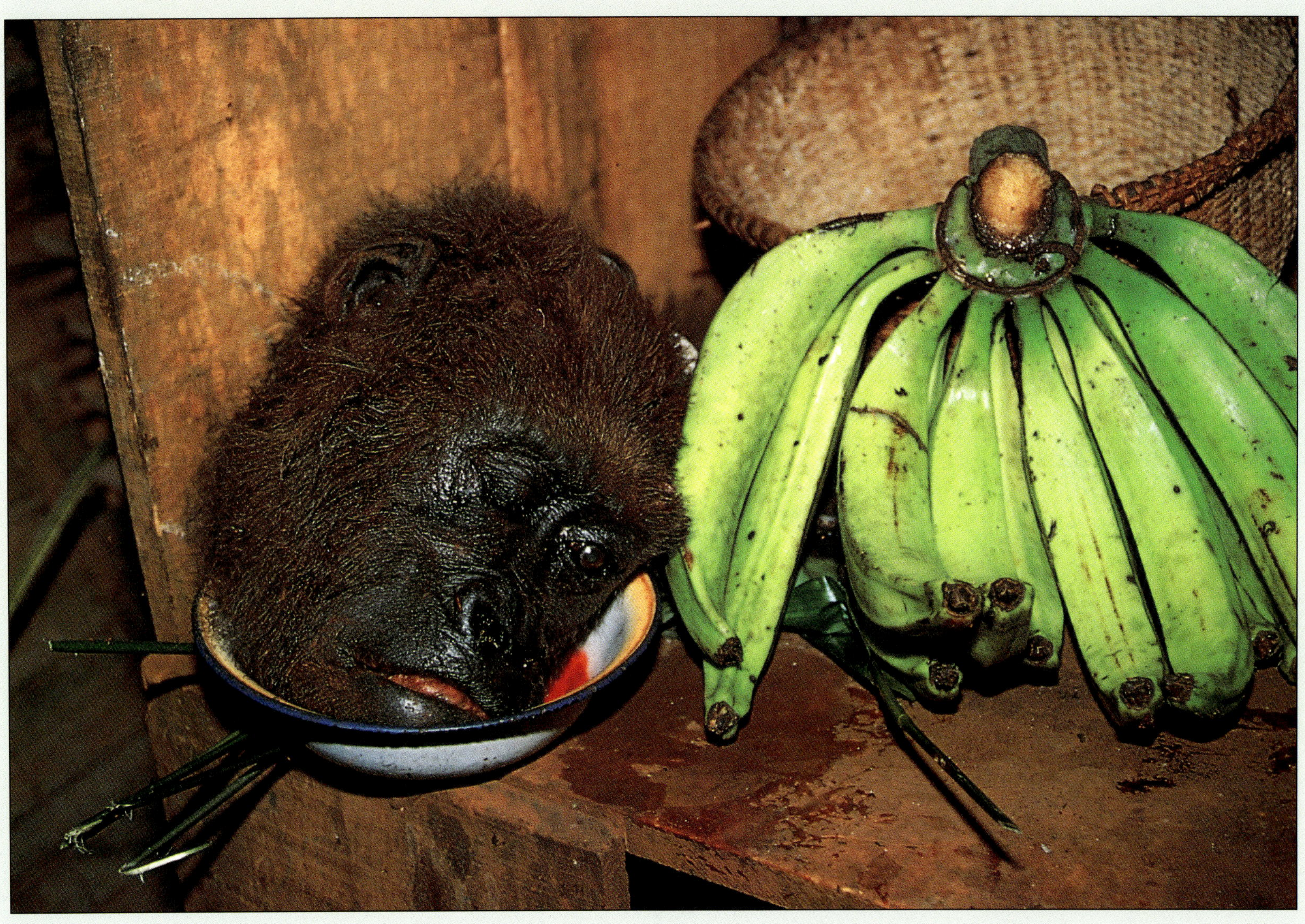

## David Woodfall
United Kingdom
RUNNER-UP

### *Rainforest clearcutting*

*"Clayquot Sound, on Vancouver Island, has seen a number of confrontations between conservationists and industrial logging companies over clearcutting of its temperate rainforests, among the most important examples of their kind in the world. The day I arrived, it was exceptionally clear, and I spent two hours flying around recently clearcut areas in a chartered Cessna - one of the most depressing and exhilarating experiences of my life."*

Mamiya 645 with 80mm lens; 1/1,000 sec at f2.8; Fujichrome Provia 100

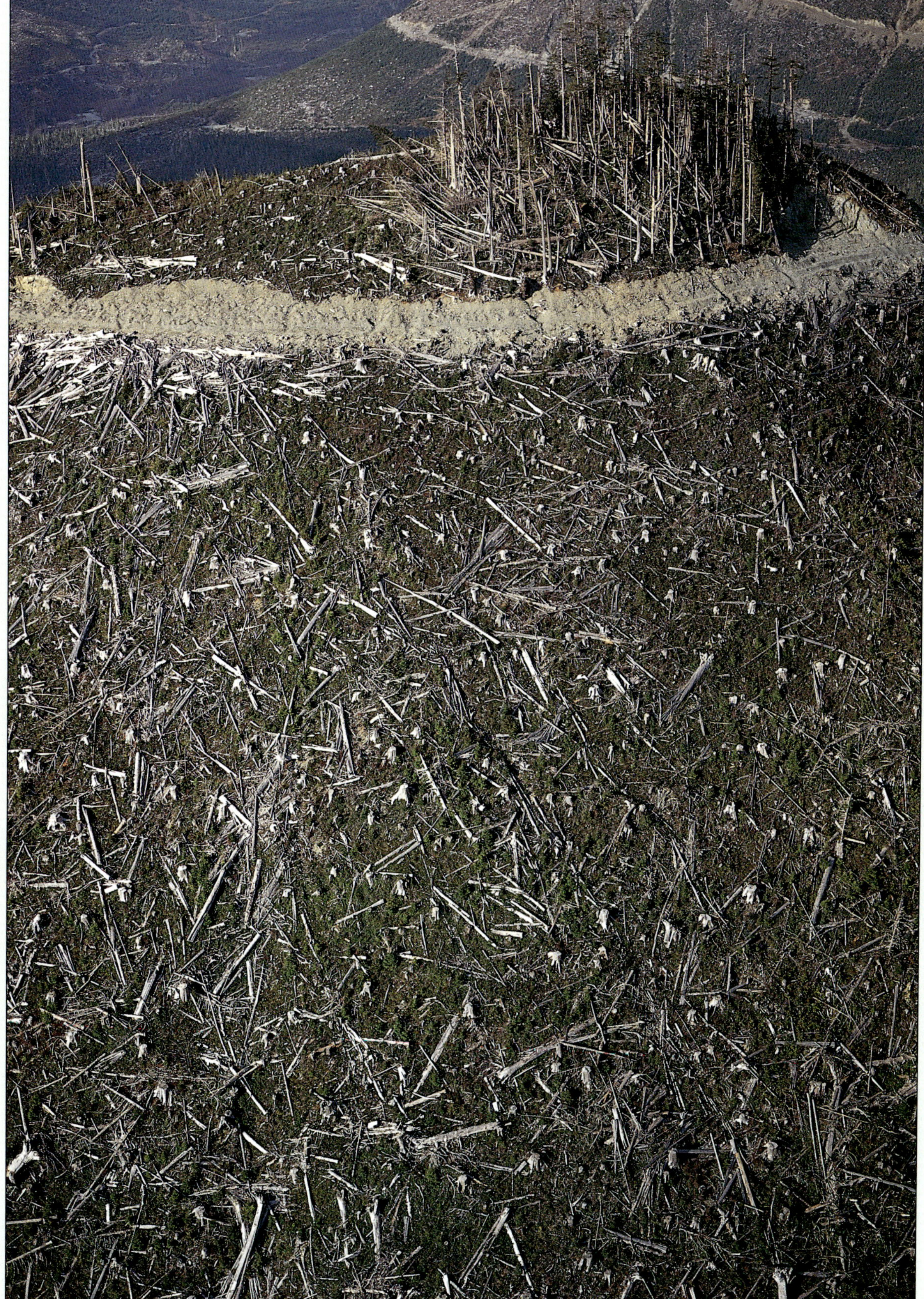

## Karl Ammann
Switzerland
WINNER

### *Gorilla head*

*"I took this photograph to draw attention to the question, 'Do conservation initiatives in West Africa work?'*
*I was staying in a village in southern Cameroon to get footage for the campaign run by the World Society for the Protection of Animals (WSPA) to discourage the killing and eating of great apes. Early one morning, I heard that a local man had just shot a female gorilla on behalf of the police chief in the next village. As payment, he got to keep the head and one arm.*
*By the afternoon, when I arrived at his hut, the arm had already been eaten. The head was in the kitchen hut on a shelf exactly as I photographed it."*

Nikon F4 with 24-50mm lens; fill-in flash; Fujichrome Velvia

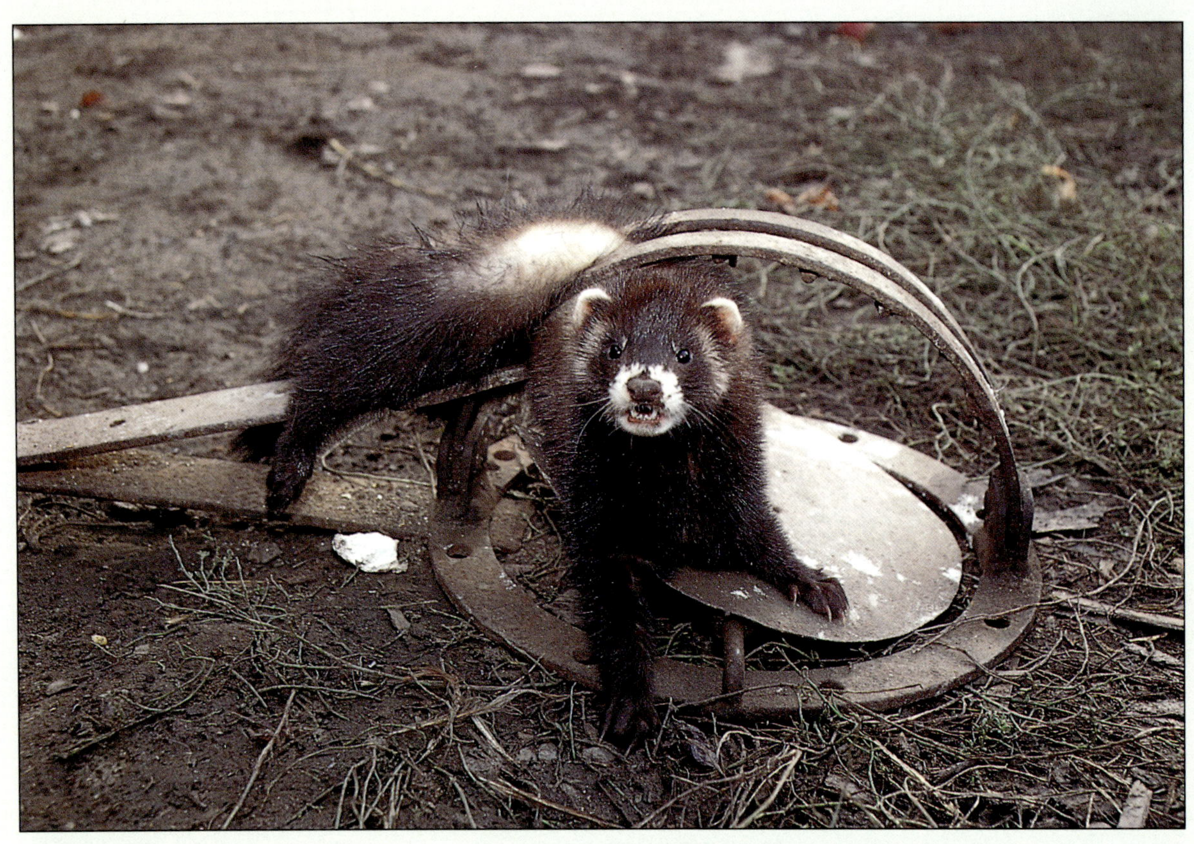

**Manfred Delpho**
Germany
HIGHLY COMMENDED

**_Polecat in trap_**

*"I was staying on a farm in the Carpathian Hills, Romania, where I had gone to photograph brown bears. One morning I discovered this polecat in a trap in the farmyard. Immediately afterwards, the farmer struck the polecat dead with a piece of wood. He said he set the trap because polecats frequently stole eggs from his hens."*

Nikon F4 with 35-135mm lens; 1/125 sec at f8; Fujichrome Sensia 100

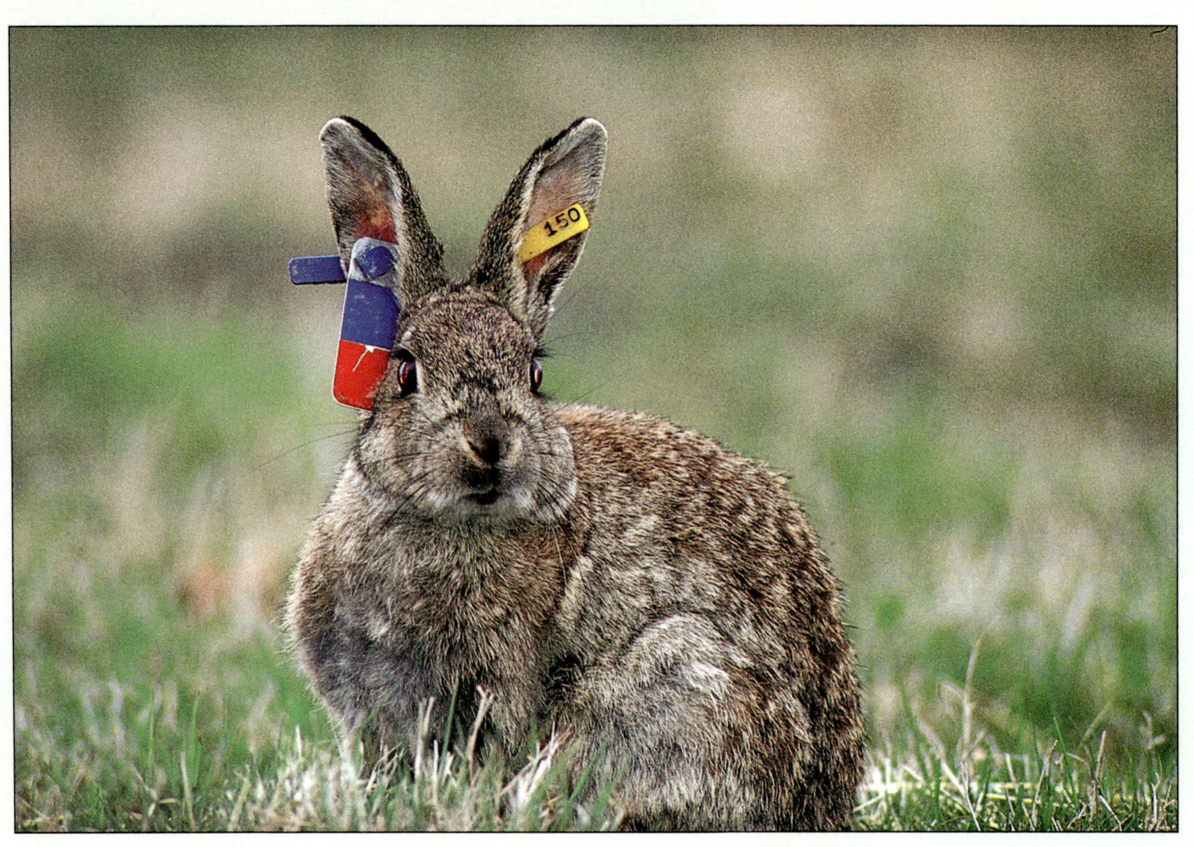


**Heidi & Hans-Jürgen Koch**
Germany
HIGHLY COMMENDED

**_Tagged wild rabbit_**

*"We were trying to photograph different aspects of a rabbit's daily life for a German magazine, and spent some time at the study site of biologists from the University of Bayreuth, in southern Germany, who have been observing the behaviour of wild rabbits nearby. The scientists' tagging efforts certainly give the normally well-camouflaged creatures a strange appearance."*

Nikon F4s with 500mm lens and x1.4 converter; tripod; hide; Kodachrome Professional 200

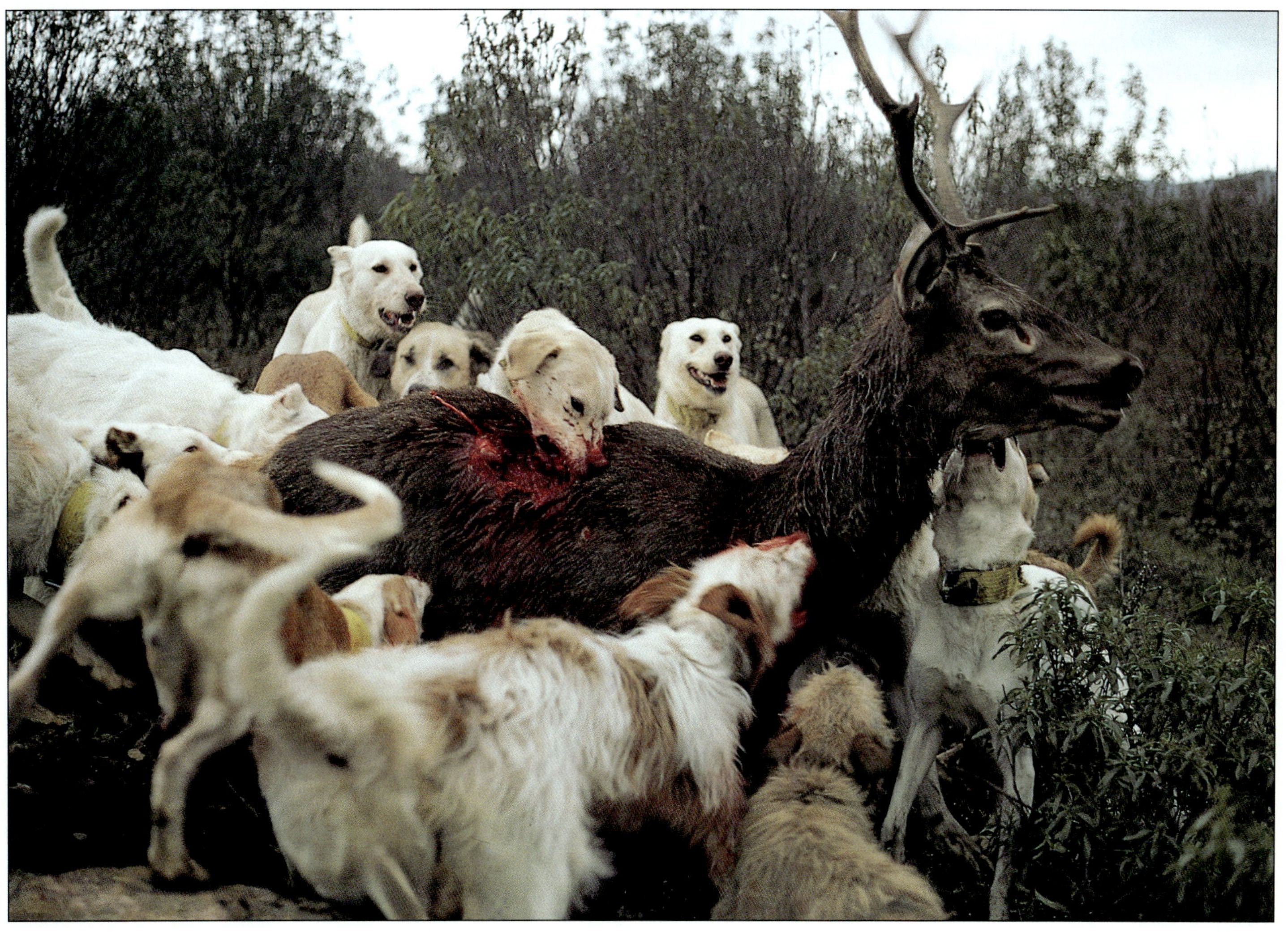

**Roberto Travesi Ydañez**
Spain
HIGHLY COMMENDED

***Deer hunt***

*"The picture was taken in Sierra Morena, in southern Spain, during a 'Monteria', a typical Spanish hunting trip. Hunting with dogs is a tradition in our mountains, where thousands of dogs can be seen each year as the hunting season approaches."*

Canon T90 with 50mm lens; 1/60 sec at f1.4; Kodachrome 64

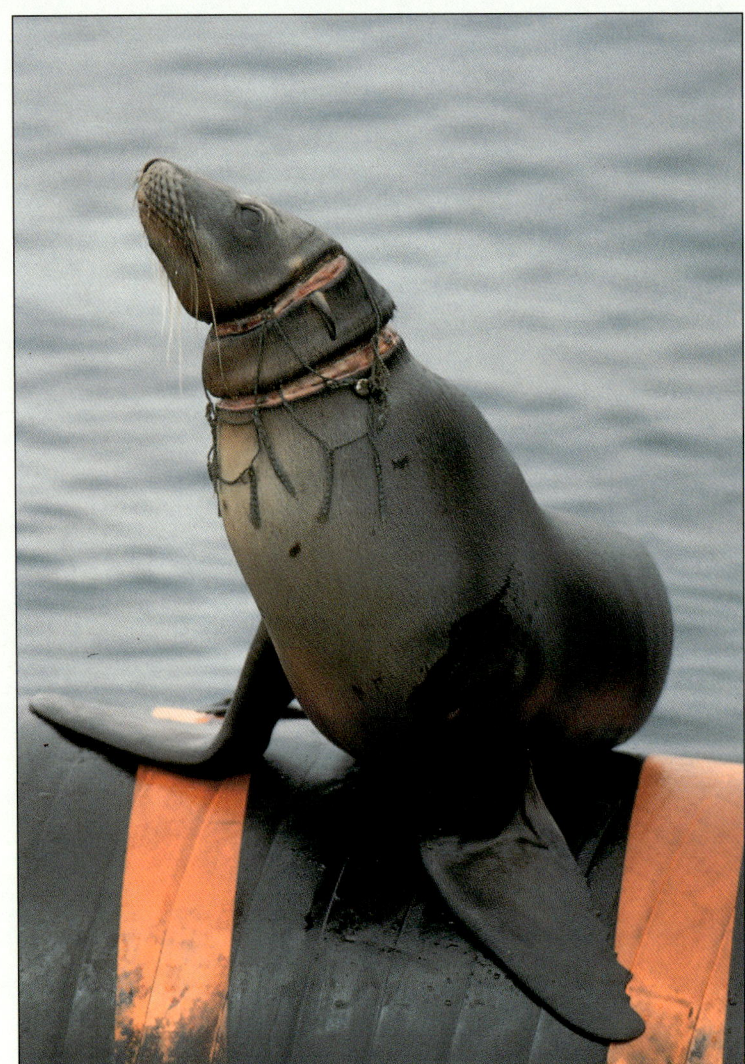

## Tom Campbell

United States of America

HIGHLY COMMENDED

### *Californian sealion entangled in gillnet*

*"This image, taken off the coast of Santa Barbara, California, graphically shows the sort of environmental damage that is often out of sight and out of mind. The animal was never captured, but its photograph, used in a poster campaign, helped push through legislation to reduce the indiscriminate use of gillnets in California."*

Nikon F3 with 80-200mm lens; 1/250 sec at f4; Kodachrome 64

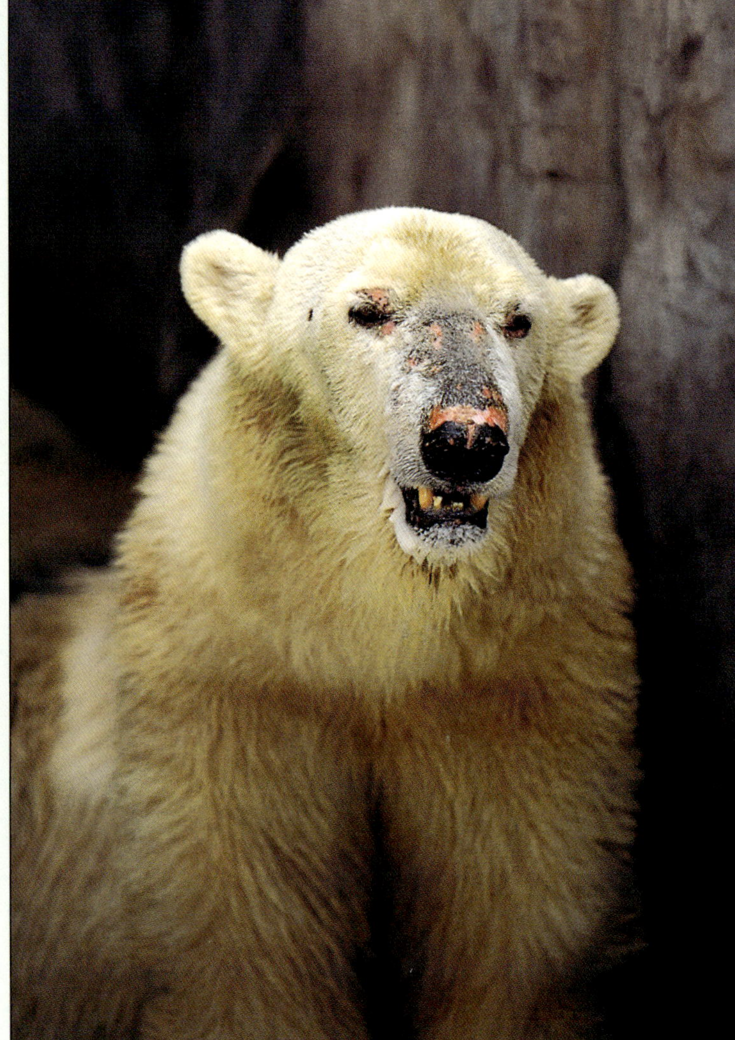

## Andy Rouse

United Kingdom

HIGHLY COMMENDED

### *Polar bear in Pata Zoo, Bangkok*

*"Pata Zoo is a disgusting zoo on the top two floors of a department store in central Bangkok. This polar bear was on its own in a bare concrete pit, open to the sun and with no water. The camera had to be hidden from the authorities."*

Canon EOS 1N with 300mm lens; 1/125 sec at f4; Fujichrome Velvia rated at 40

**Eric Robert**
**& Sylvia Bergerot**
France
HIGHLY COMMENDED

### *Monkey theatre, Thailand*

*"We took this picture during a rehearsal of a 'Lakhon Link' (monkey theatre). Although popular with Thai people because of the special place monkeys hold in Buddhism, the troupe is the last in Thailand and has been banished from tourist areas due to pressure from Westerners."*

Nikon F4 with 105mm lens; 1/125 sec at f11; flash; Fujichrome Provia 100

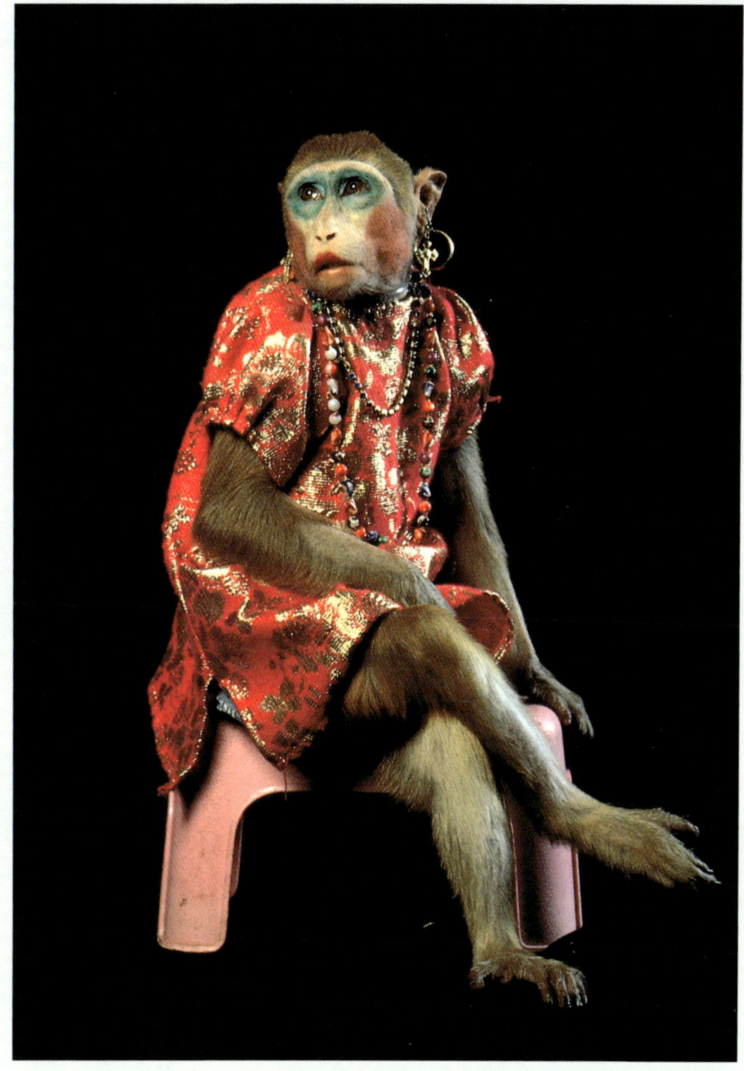

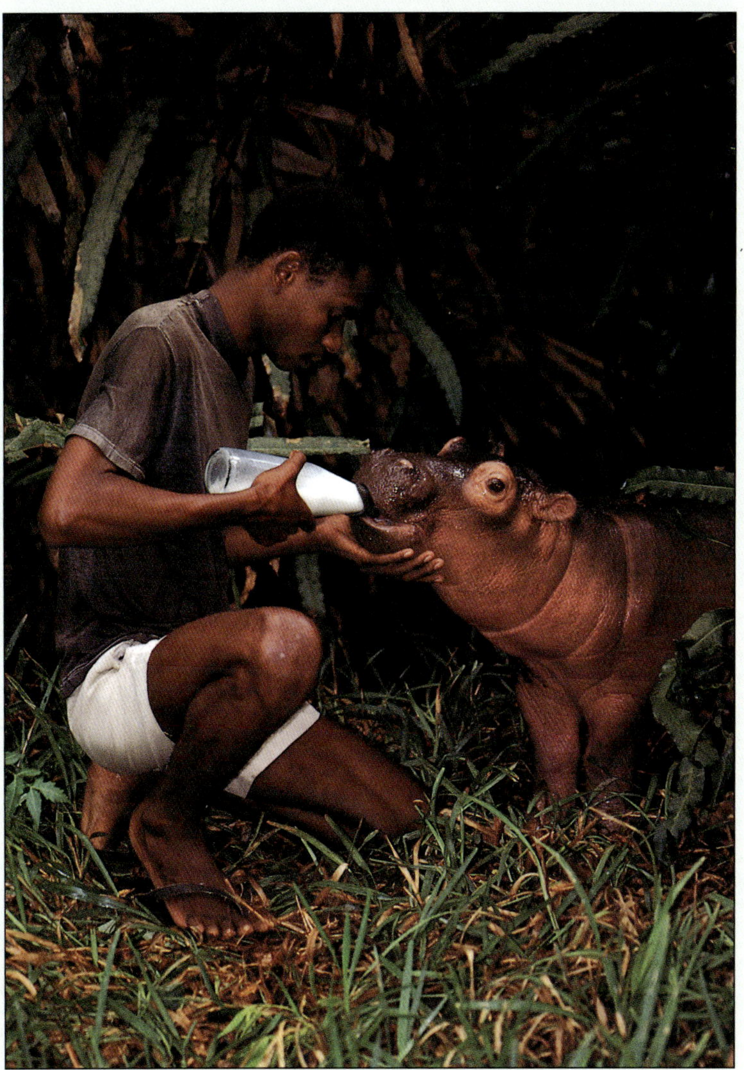

**Hilary G Mackay**
United Kingdom
HIGHLY COMMENDED

### *Young hippo being bottle fed*

*"John, the young hippo, had been attacked by an adult hippo and needed extensive treatment when he arrived at the Bamburi Nature Trail in Kenya. The picture shows him at three months with Begarri, his keeper. He is now fully recovered."*

Canon EOS 1000 with 28-80mm lens; flash; Ektachrome 100

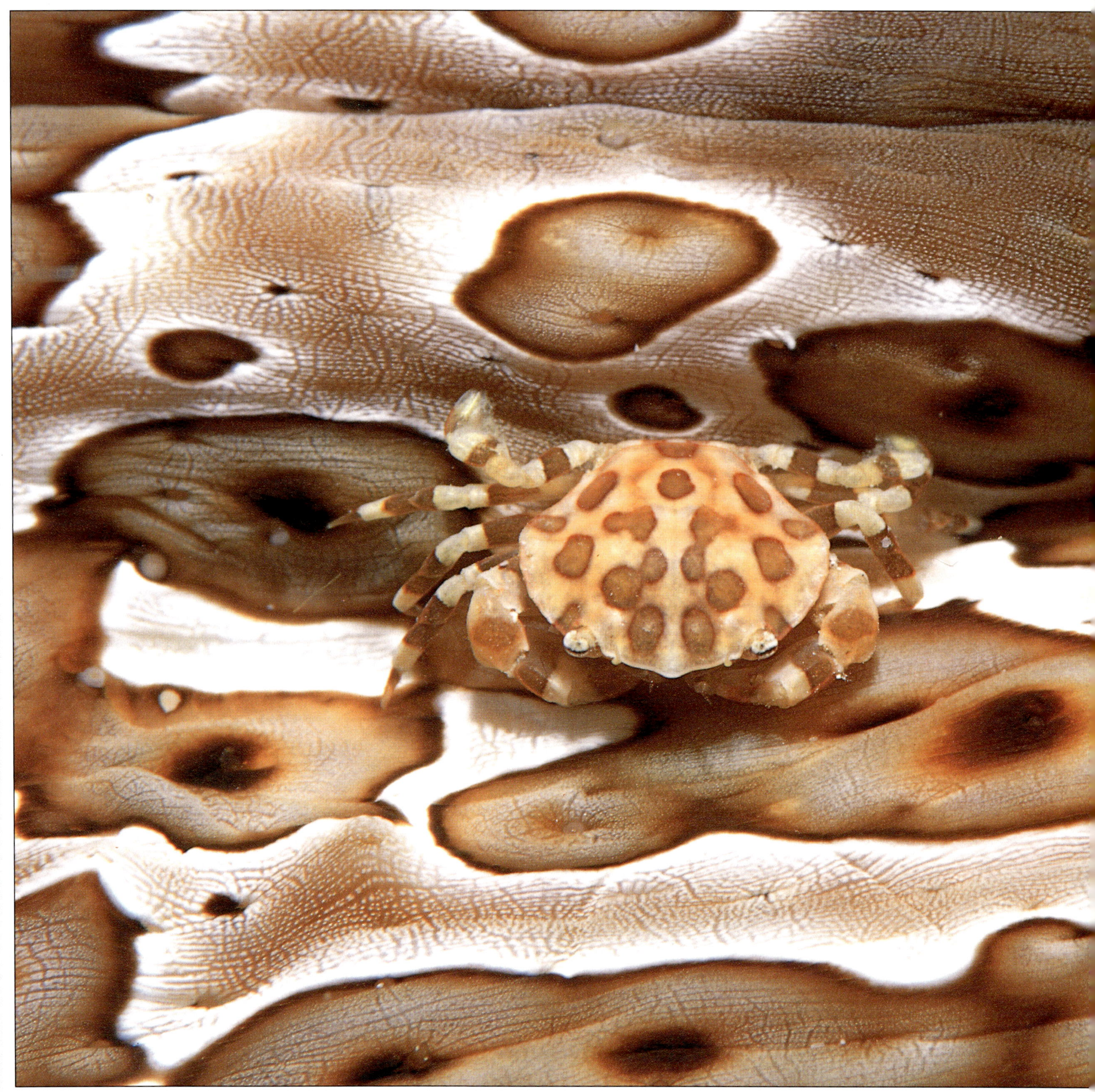

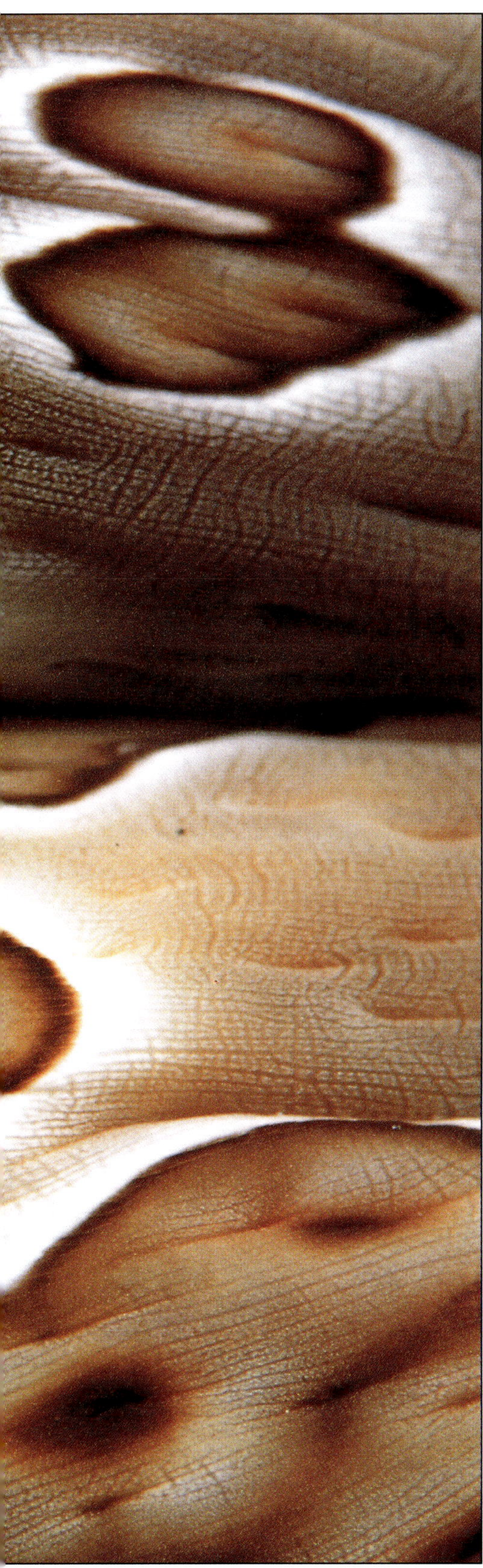

# The Eric Hosking Award

This award goes to the best portfolio of six images taken by a photographer aged 26 or under. The award was introduced in 1991 in memory of Eric Hosking - probably Britain's most famous wildlife photographer. Eric was a supporter of the competition from its earliest days. He presented the prizes for the Dusk to Dawn category, and before 1983 the judging sessions were often held in his house in north London. The prize is a specially commissioned wood carving presented by David Bellamy, £1,000 and a holiday for two to the Seychelles.

The 1995 winner, Brandon D Cole from the United States, is a freelance photojournalist who specialises in the marine environment. He has a degree in marine biology from the University of California and has carried out underwater scientific research for that institution as well as the National Park Service and the Australian Institute of Marine Science. He has travelled much of the world for his work and counts among his favourite places the kelp beds of California, the coral reefs of Indonesia, the dizzying blue of the South Pacific and the current-swept, icy waters of British Columbia and Alaska.

**Brandon D Cole**
United States of America
WINNER

***Crab and sea cucumber***

*"I was diving in Bunaken Marine Park, in the Sulawesi Sea, Indonesia, when my dive guide pointed out this crab Lissocarcinus orbicularis tucked among the folds on a sea cucumber's underside."*

Canon F1 with 105mm macro lens in underwater housing; two strobes; 1/60 sec at f22; Fujichrome Velvia

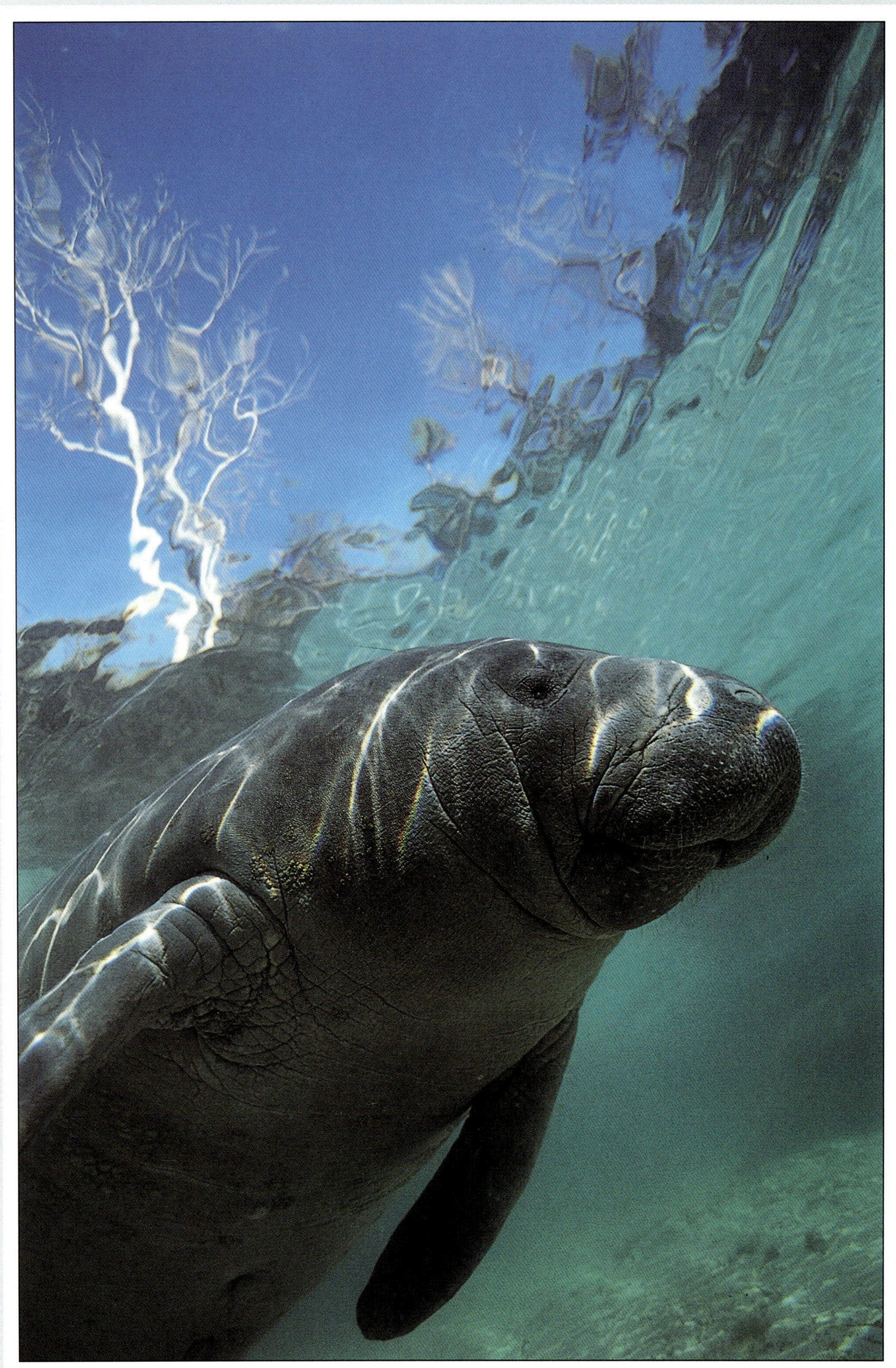

**Florida manatee**

*"In winter, Florida manatees leave their ocean haunts for warmer spring-fed waters such as Crystal River, on Florida's west coast. They are very co-operative photographic subjects - slow, trusting, curious. I was concentrating on facial shots of this manatee when I suddenly noticed the view above."*

---

Nikon 8008s with 20mm lens in underwater housing; 1/125 sec at f8; Fujichrome 100

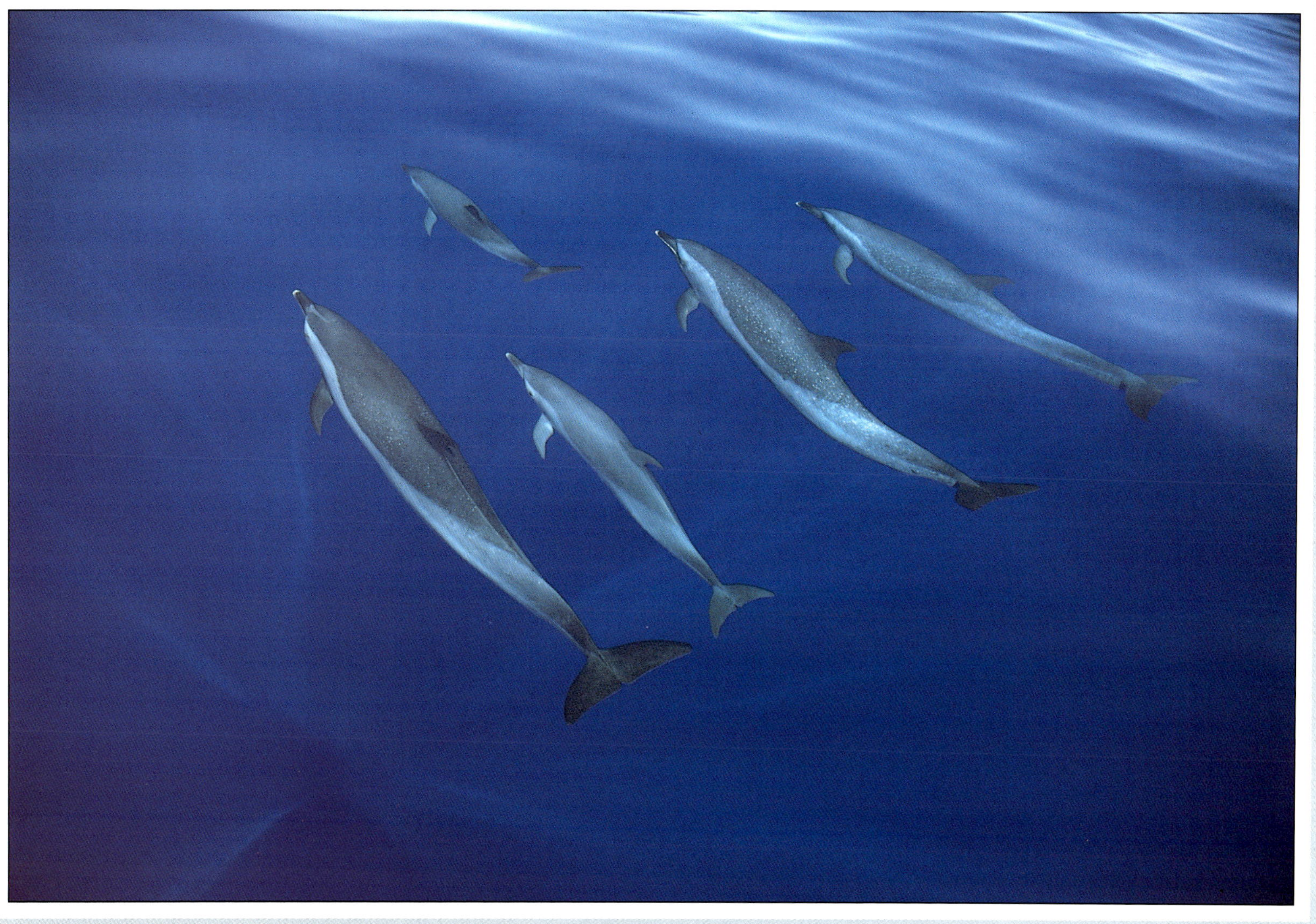

**Dolphin pyramid**

*"I was out cruising off the Kona Coast of the Big Island, in Hawaii, when I found a group of about 20 Pacific spotted dolphins. They paralleled the boat for nearly an hour, but only once came together in such perfect formation."*

Canon EOS A2 with 28-105mm lens; 1/250 sec at f4.5; Fujichrome 100

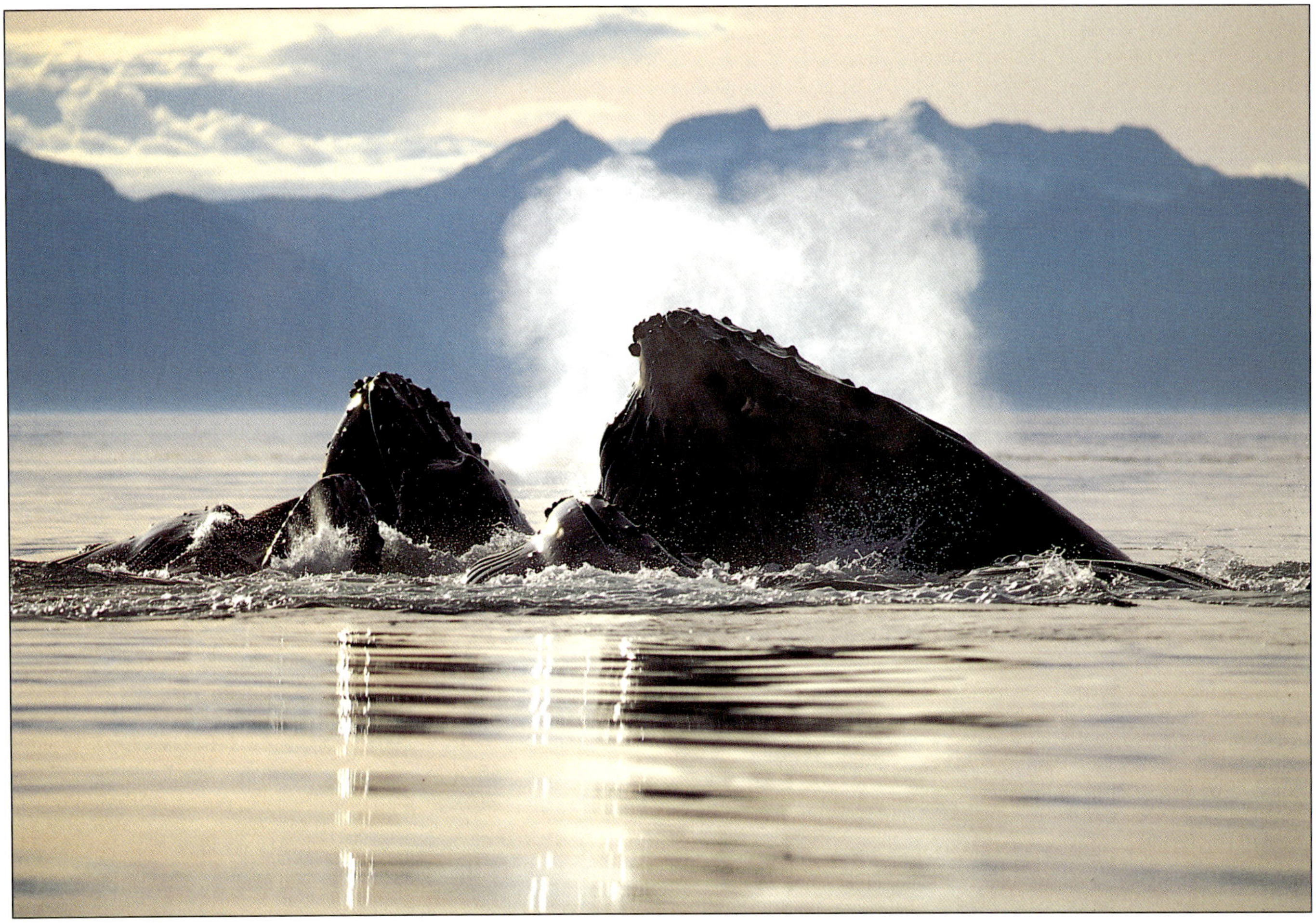

**Humpbacks bubble-net feeding**

*"It was sunset on a midsummer's evening in Frederick Sound, south-east Alaska, and I was watching the ultimate candlelit dinner. A group of humpback whales dived down together, blew a ring of bubbles which rose to stun and trap herring, then swam upward, mouths open, to swallow their meal."*

Canon EOS A2 with 300mm lens; 1/750 sec at f4; Fujichrome 100

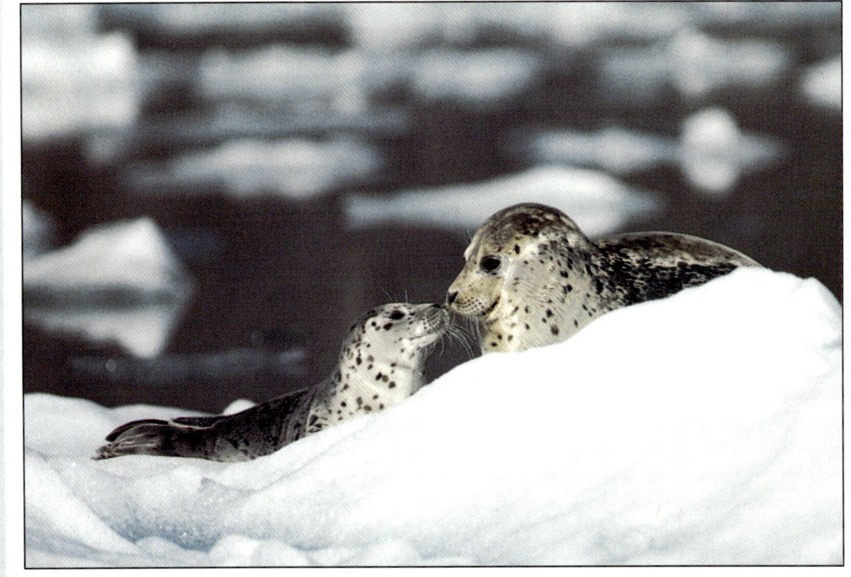

**Harbor seal mother and pup**

*"I spotted this mother and her 3-4-week-old pup afloat on their own little icy palace at Le Conte glacier, in Alaska. The pup would nurse for a few minutes, then squirm around, yawn, stick out its pink tongue, and return to sucking."*

Canon EOS A2 with 300mm lens; 1/750 sec at f4; Fujichrome 100

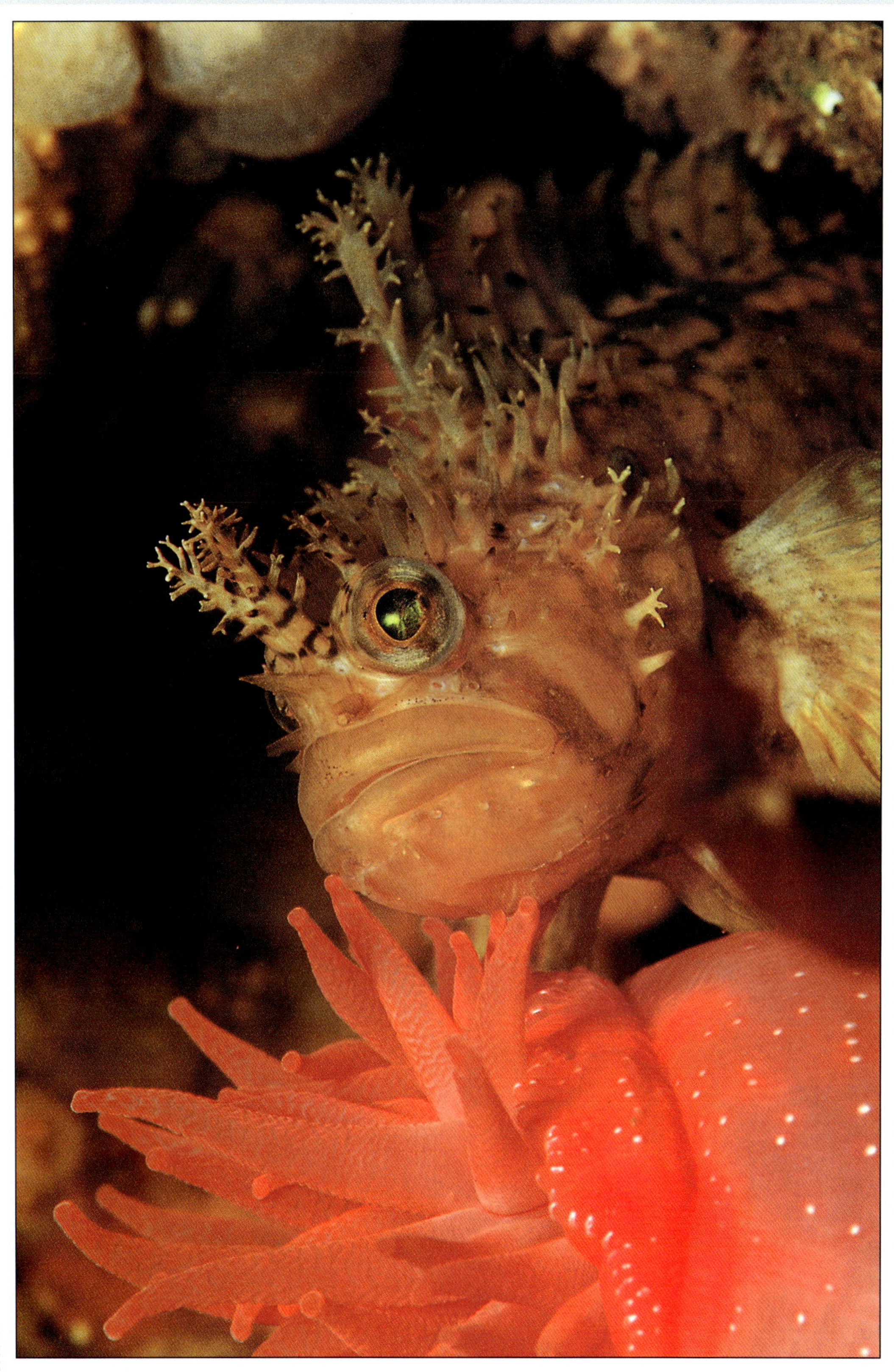

**Decorated warbonnet**

*"I am ever drawn to weird little fishes all over the world, but the decorated warbonnet* Chirolophis decorulus *- here photographed with a sea anemone, off* Vancouver Island *- is one of my favourite photo subjects. One must look past the bulging eyes, puffy lips, carelessly groomed hair and warty skin flaps to the true beauty within."*

Canon F1 with 50mm macro lens in underwater housing; two strobes; 1/60 sec at f16; Fujichrome Velvia

# Humorous Views

Pictures should show a light-hearted view of the subject but should not ridicule it. No prizes were awarded this year

**Wayne R Bilenduke**
Canada
HIGHLY COMMENDED

***Polar bear playing with tyre***

*"While out on the frozen tundra near Churchill, Manitoba, I came upon three polar bears playing tug-of-war with an old tyre. After about five minutes (and much film), this one rolled the tyre away from the others, then lay on his back and raised it in the air as if to say 'I am the champion!' "*

Nikon F-801s with 500mm lens; beanbag; 1/250 sec at f4; Fujichrome Velvia rated at 100

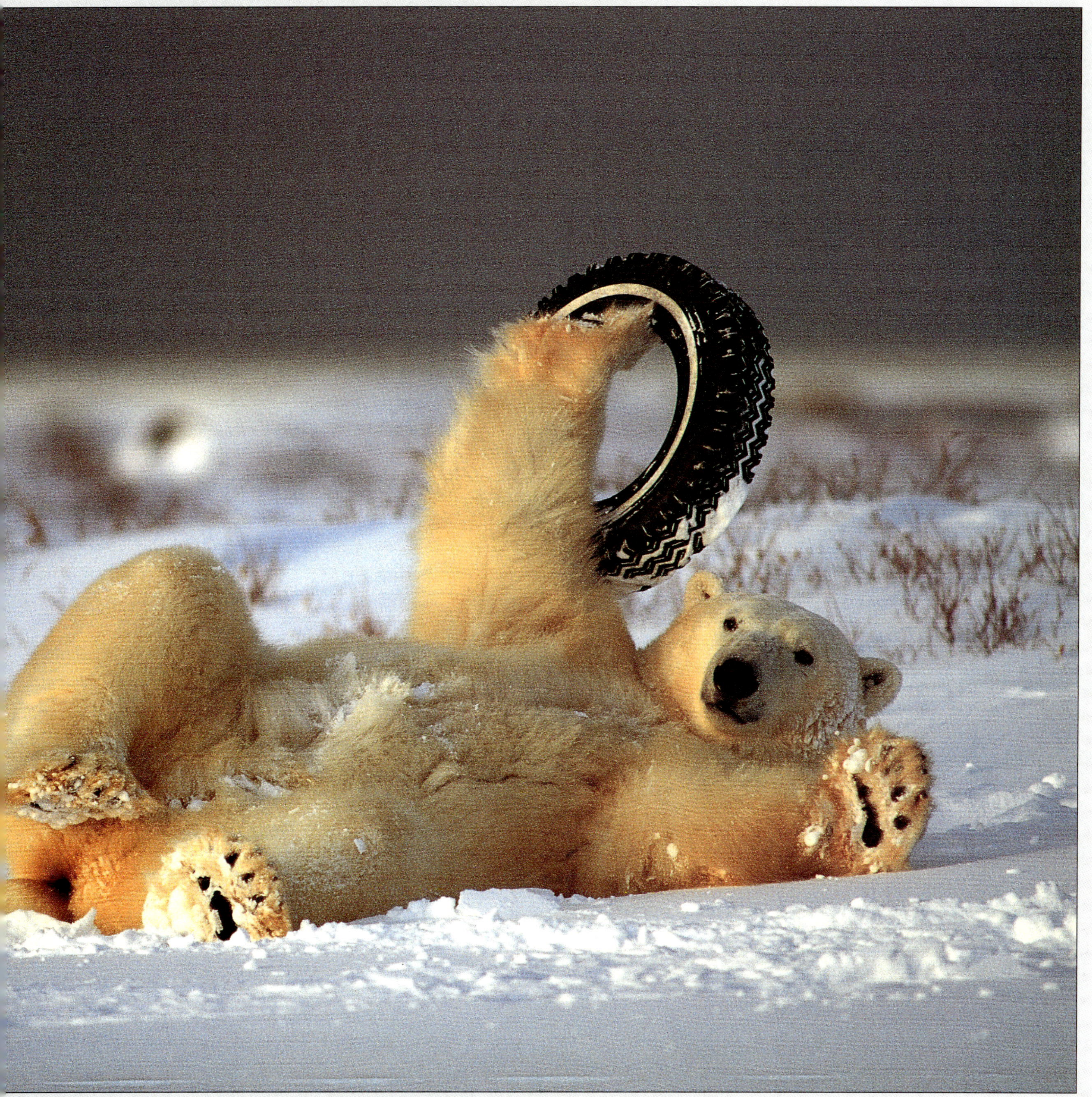

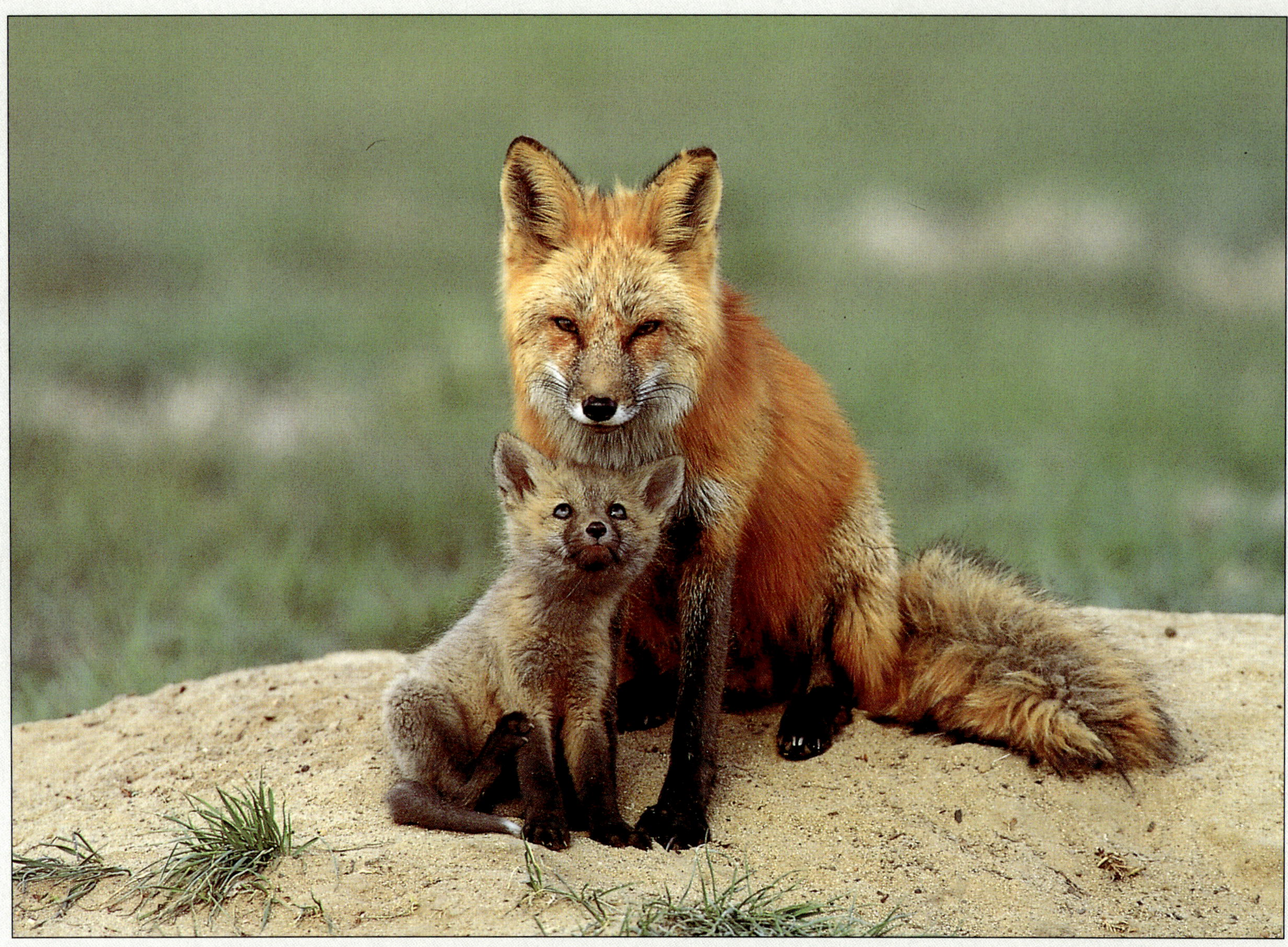

**Wendy Shattil & Bob Rozinski**
United States of America
HIGHLY COMMENDED

***Mother fox and adoring cub***

*"Foxes are a speciality of ours. This spring we discovered a perfect den and were able to follow the growth and behaviour of a fox family. The four cubs had just finished nursing and all but one had returned to the den. While the mother tried to nap, the cub persistently sought ways to get her attention."*

Canon EOS with 840mm lens; 1/250 at f8; Fujichrome Provia

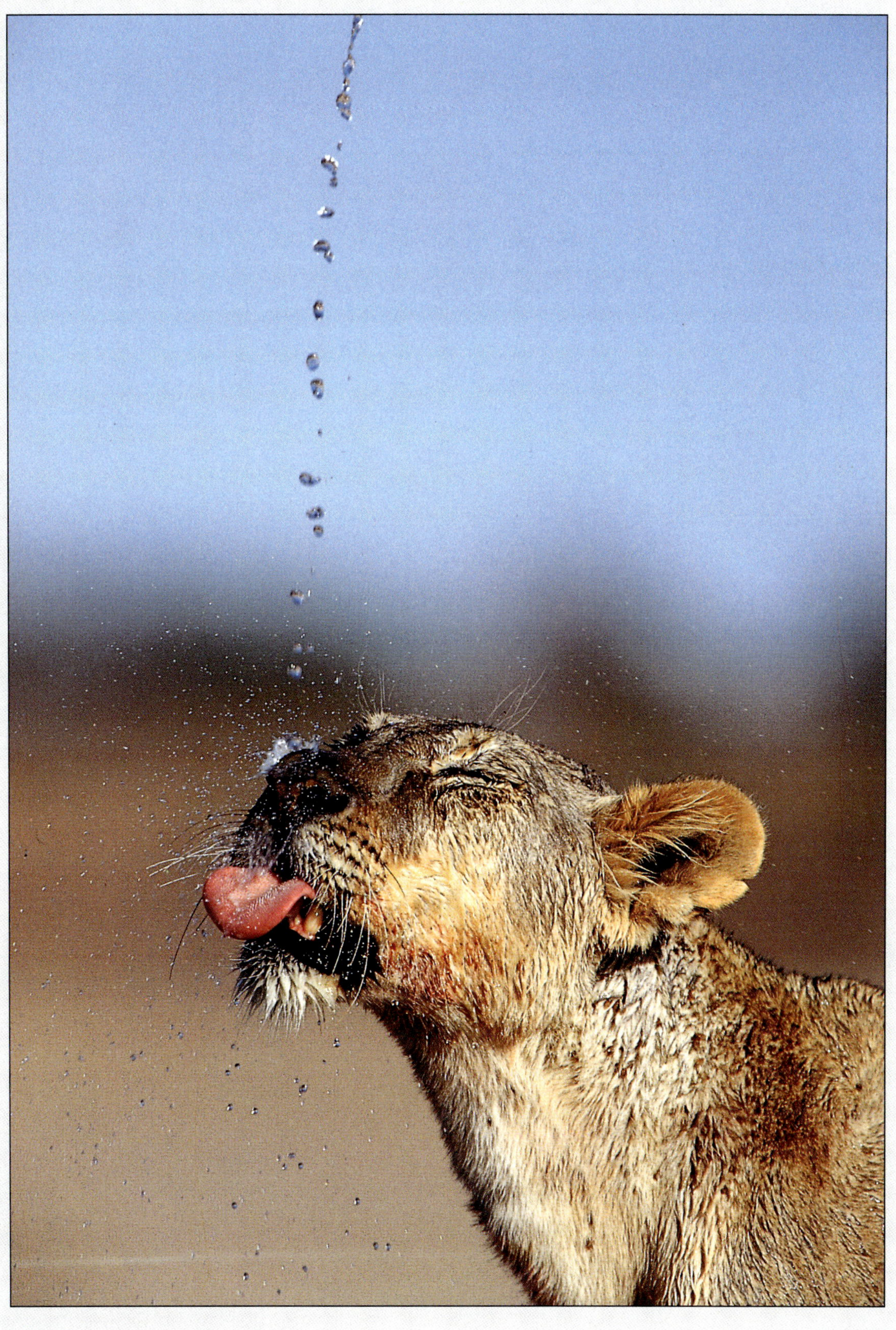

**Eliot Lyons**
South Africa
HIGHLY COMMENDED

***Lioness drinking***

*"The Bedinkt waterhole in the Kalahari Gemsbok Park has no permanent surface water, and so wind-driven pumps are used to fill fibreglass tanks. Various animals come in regularly from the sand dunes to drink the overflow. In the park, lighting suitable for photography lasts only a short time in the early morning and evening, and at the waterhole, there's a greater chance of catching the action."*

Canon EOS 1 with 600mm lens; 1/1,200 sec at f5.6; Ektachrome 100 EPP

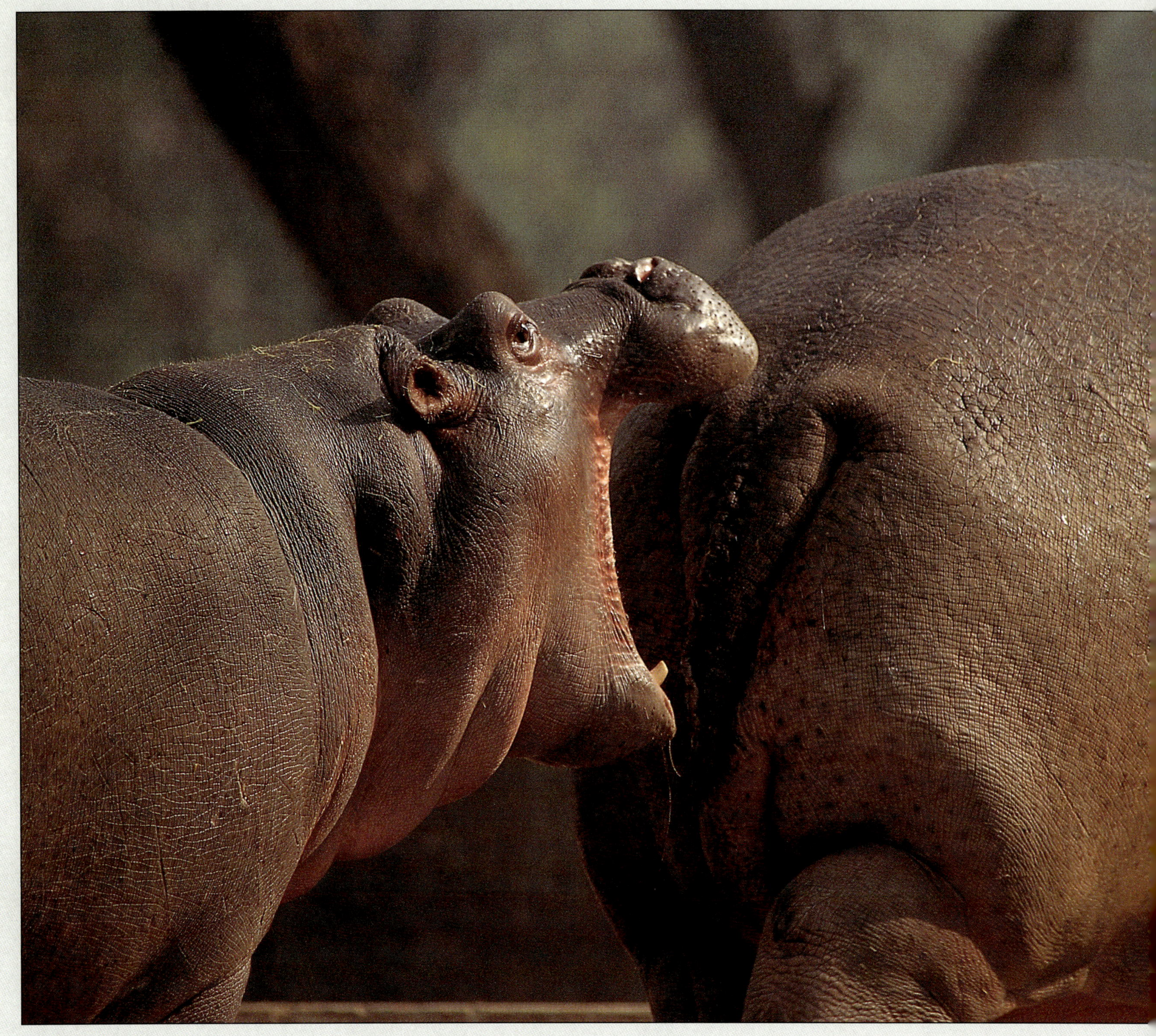

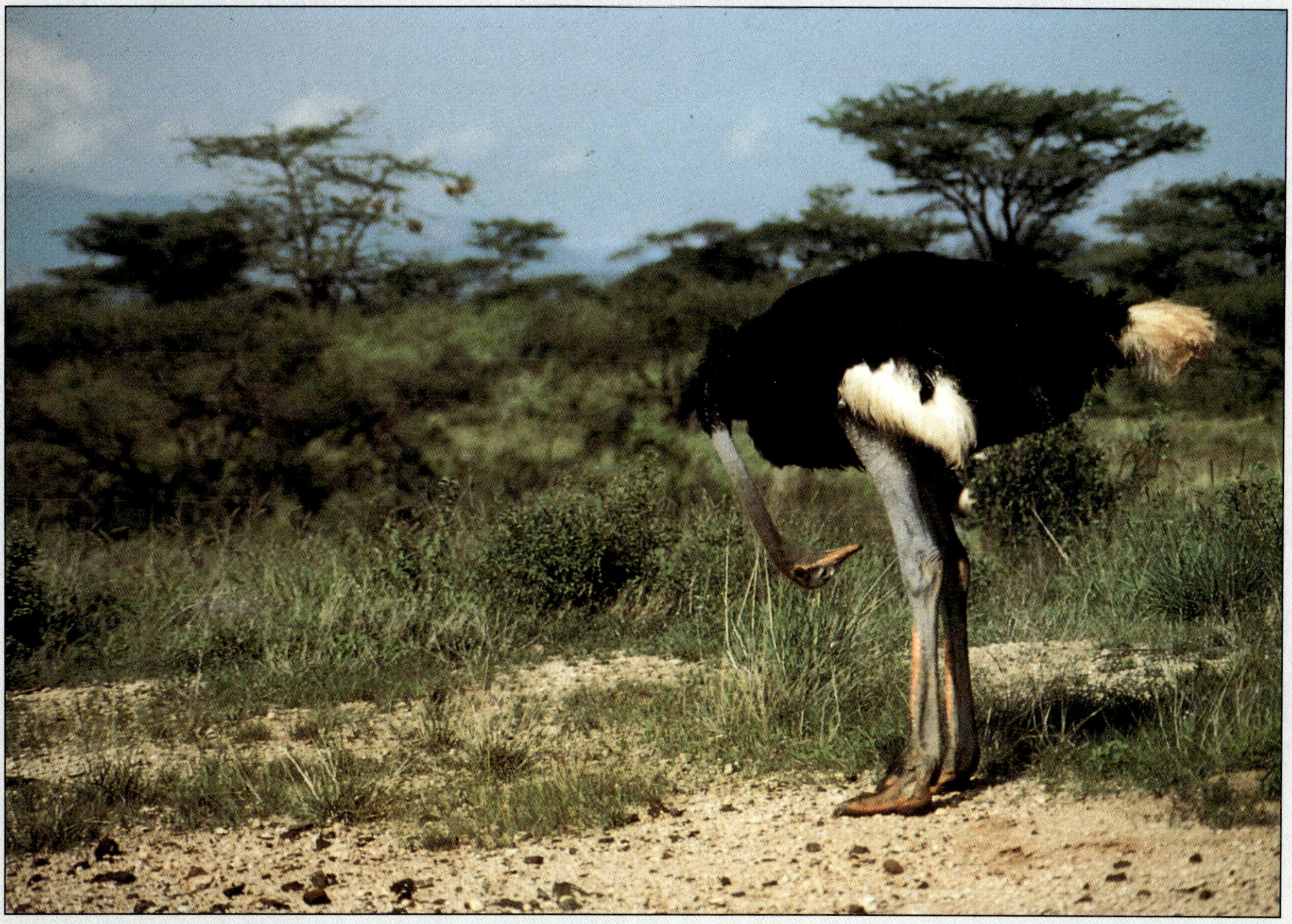

**Dr P Kumar**
India
HIGHLY COMMENDED

***Measured yawn***

*"I took this shot at the National Zoological Park, New Delhi, just for the yawn. It was only later I realised the humour of the young hippo standing behind its mother slowly stretching its jaws apart - almost a measured act, as if to bite off its mother's stumpy tail."*

Nikon F-801 with 180mm lens; shoulderpod; 1/250 sec at f11; Fujichrome Provia

**Karl Ammann**
Switzerland
HIGHLY COMMENDED

***Male ostrich finding himself***

*"In the process of grooming, a male ostrich in Kenya's Samburu National Park assumed this pose. For me, it was a lucky shot - I have tried to duplicate it several times when I've come across ostrich grooming sessions, but have never seen this particular pose again."*

Nikon F4 with 300mm lens; Kodachrome 64

# Wild Places

Pictures in this category should be landscapes which convey a feeling of wildness and create a sense of wonder or awe.

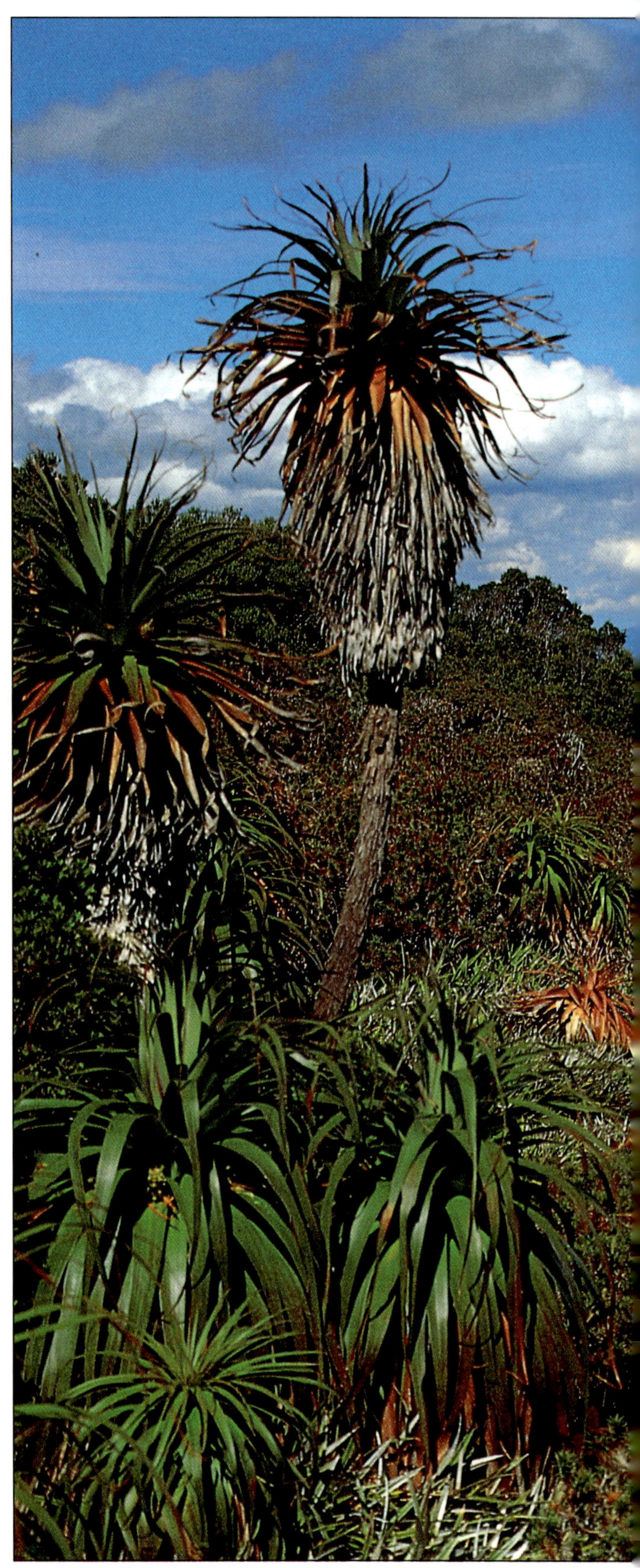

**Gilbert Hays**
Australia
WINNER

**Pandani Shelf, South West Tasmania**

*"I took this photo of pandani plants and cushion plants at the base of Mount Anne, looking across Pandani Shelf. I had been to the area before in bad weather, but this time conditions were ideal, with good afternoon light and high white fluffy clouds."*

Nikon FM with 35-105mm lens; tripod; polarising filter; 1 sec at f16; Fujichrome Velvia

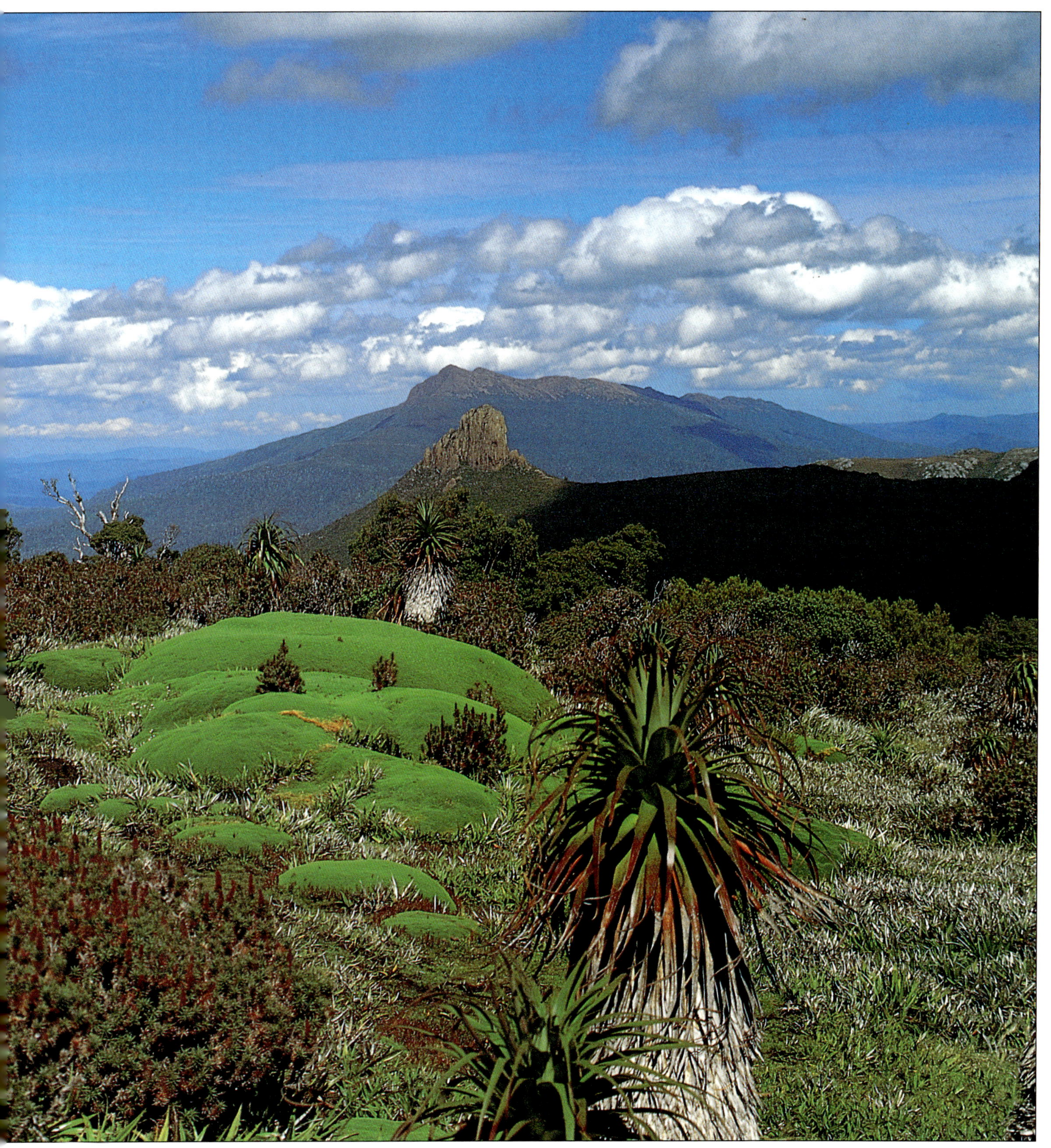

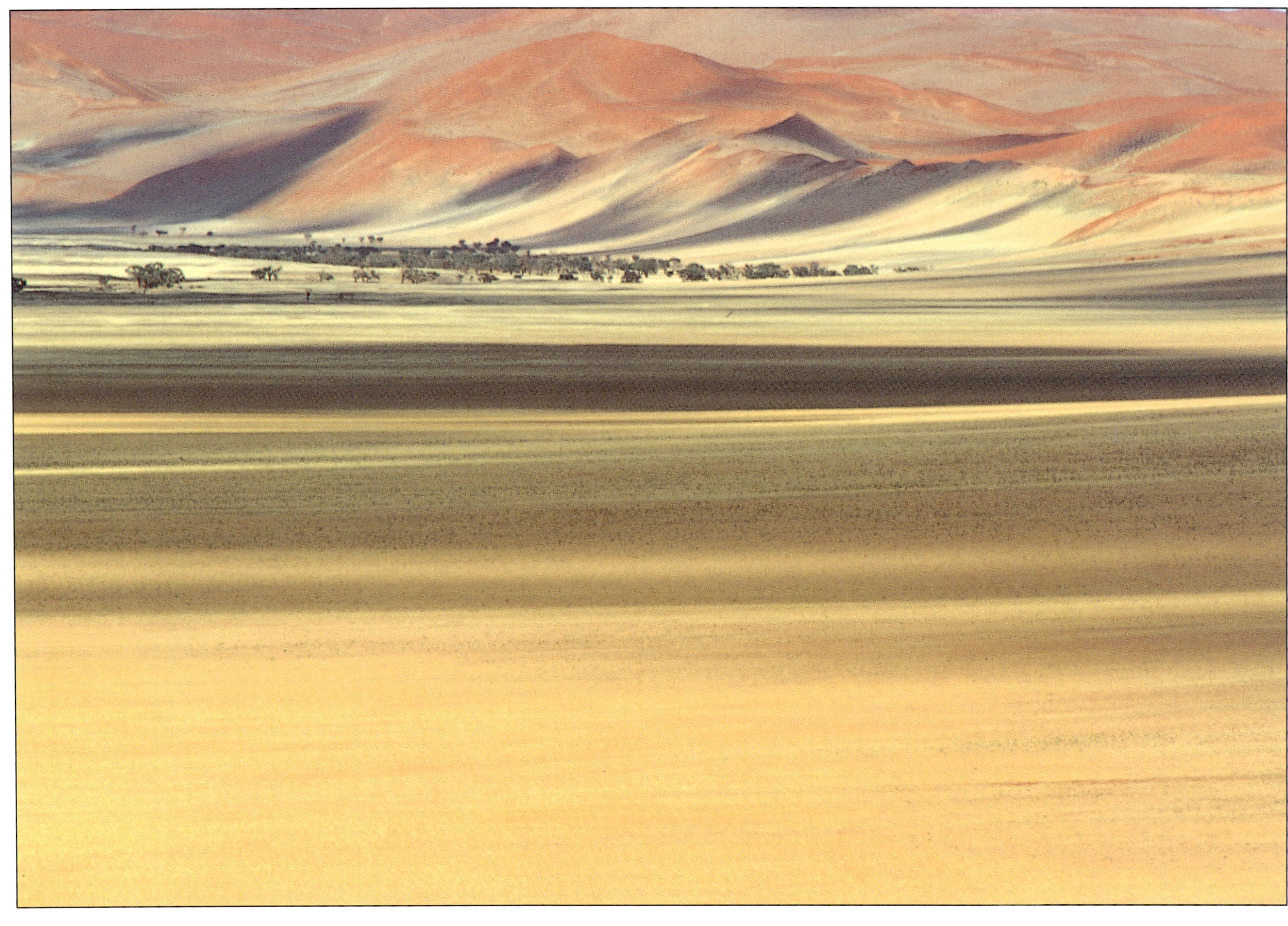

**Claudia Auer**
Germany
RUNNER-UP

---

***Shades of the Namib***

*"The dunes of the Namib Desert are my favourite subject. For most of the year the sky is clear and the sun burns down mercilessly. Occasionally scattered clouds appear, providing a little shade, but they usually disappear again without bringing the long awaited rains."*

---

Nikon FG20 with 400mm lens; beanbag; 1/125 sec at f8; Fujichrome Velvia

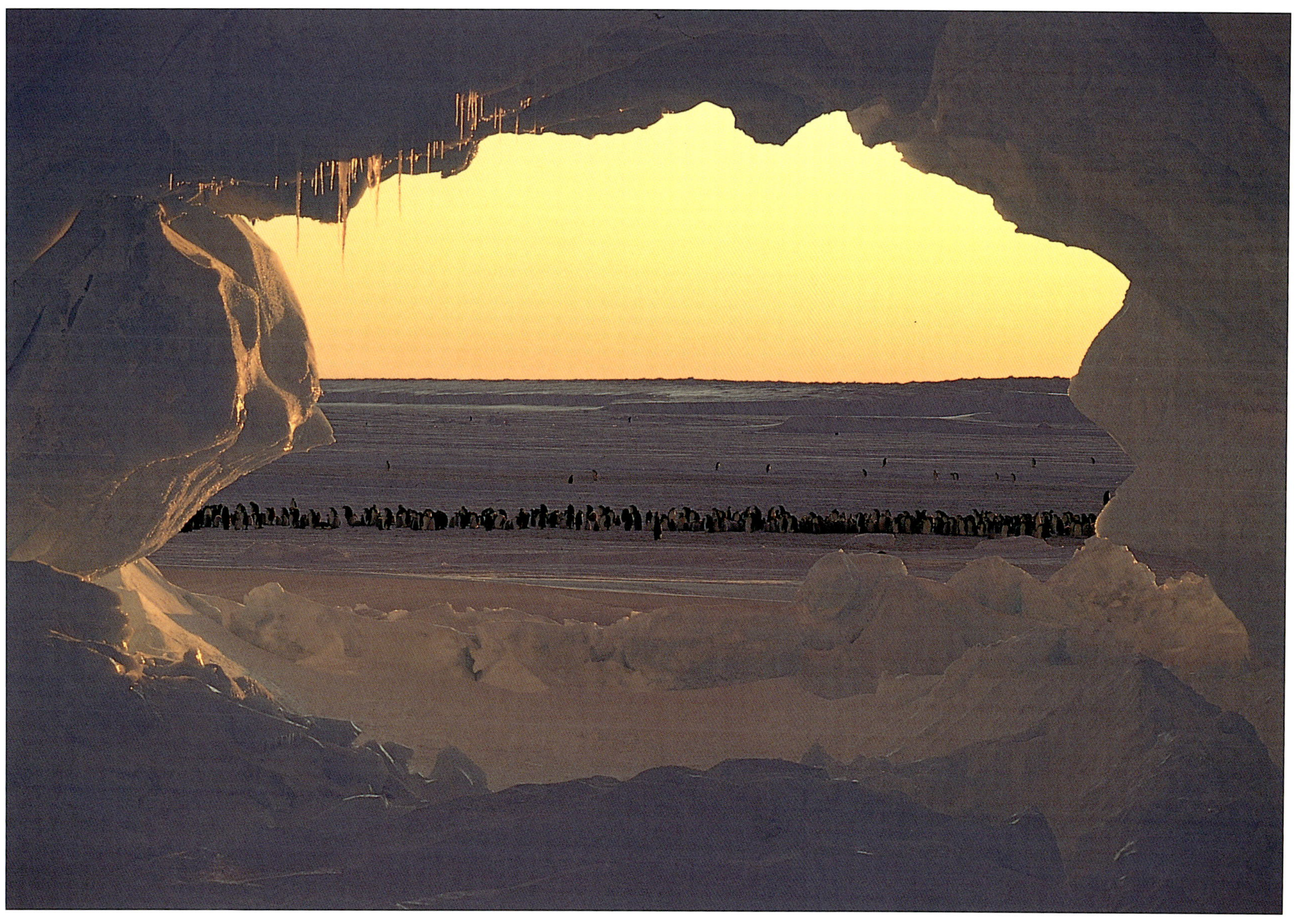

**Daniel J Cox**
United States of America
HIGHLY COMMENDED

***Emperor penguins***

*"I took this photo at Atka Bay, Antarctica, at midnight, when the temperature was 5-10 degrees below freezing. The wind had eroded a hole in a tabular iceberg, making a perfect frame for the penguin colony."*

Nikon N90s with 300mm lens; Fujichrome Provia

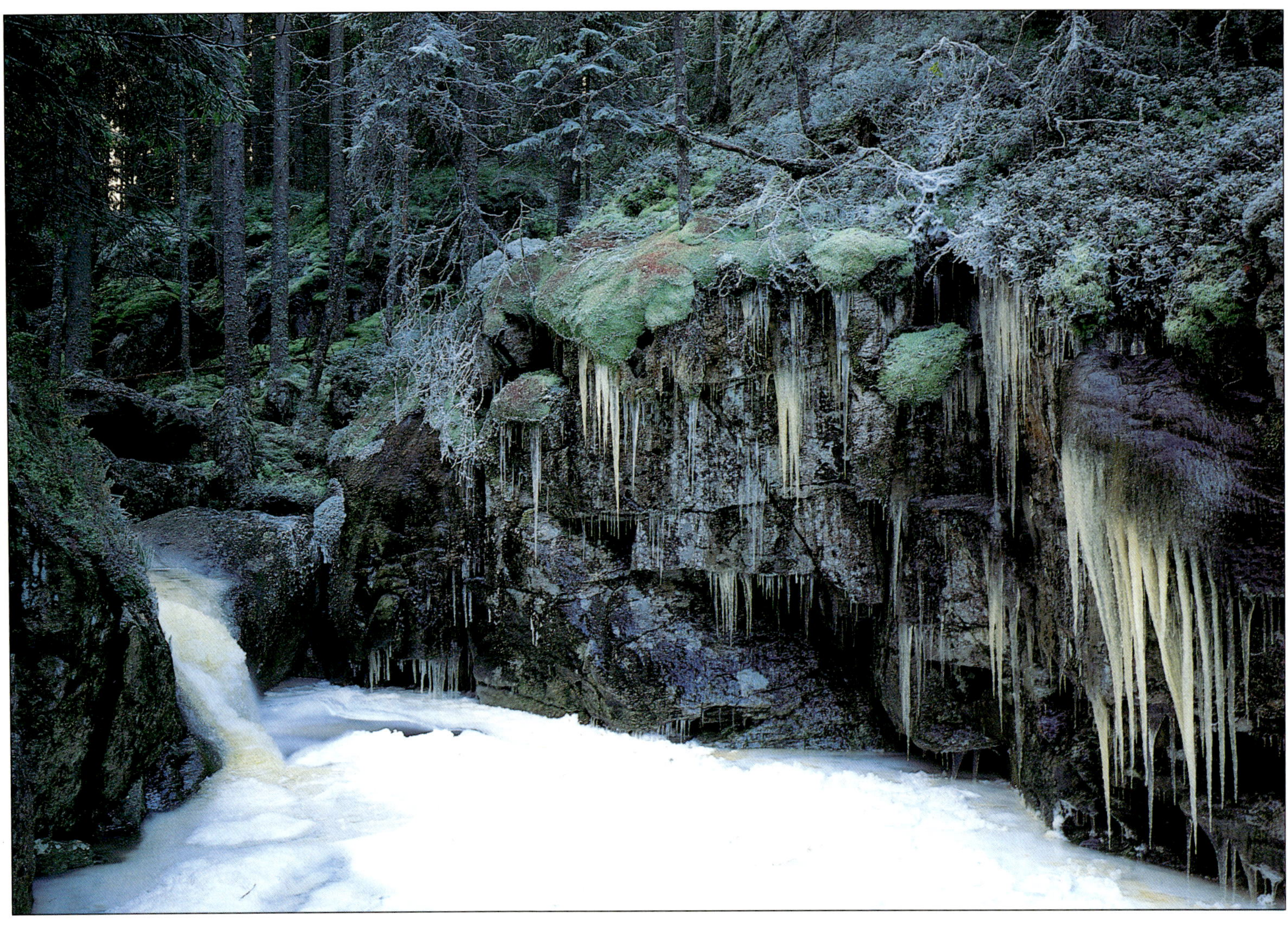

**Jørn Areklett Omre**
Norway
HIGHLY COMMENDED

***Frost in the deep forest***

*"I had seen this image in my mind for a long time, and after returning 20 times to the same place, in forest outside Oslo, I was lucky. It was a bitterly cold December day (-20°C), and it was all perfect, with frost and ice on the ground. I had had to cross the frozen stream, and was wet up to my waist. I returned home cold, wet and exhausted, but that is what it takes to get the picture."*

Arca Swiss 6/9 with 65mm lens; 10 secs at f22; Fujichrome Velvia

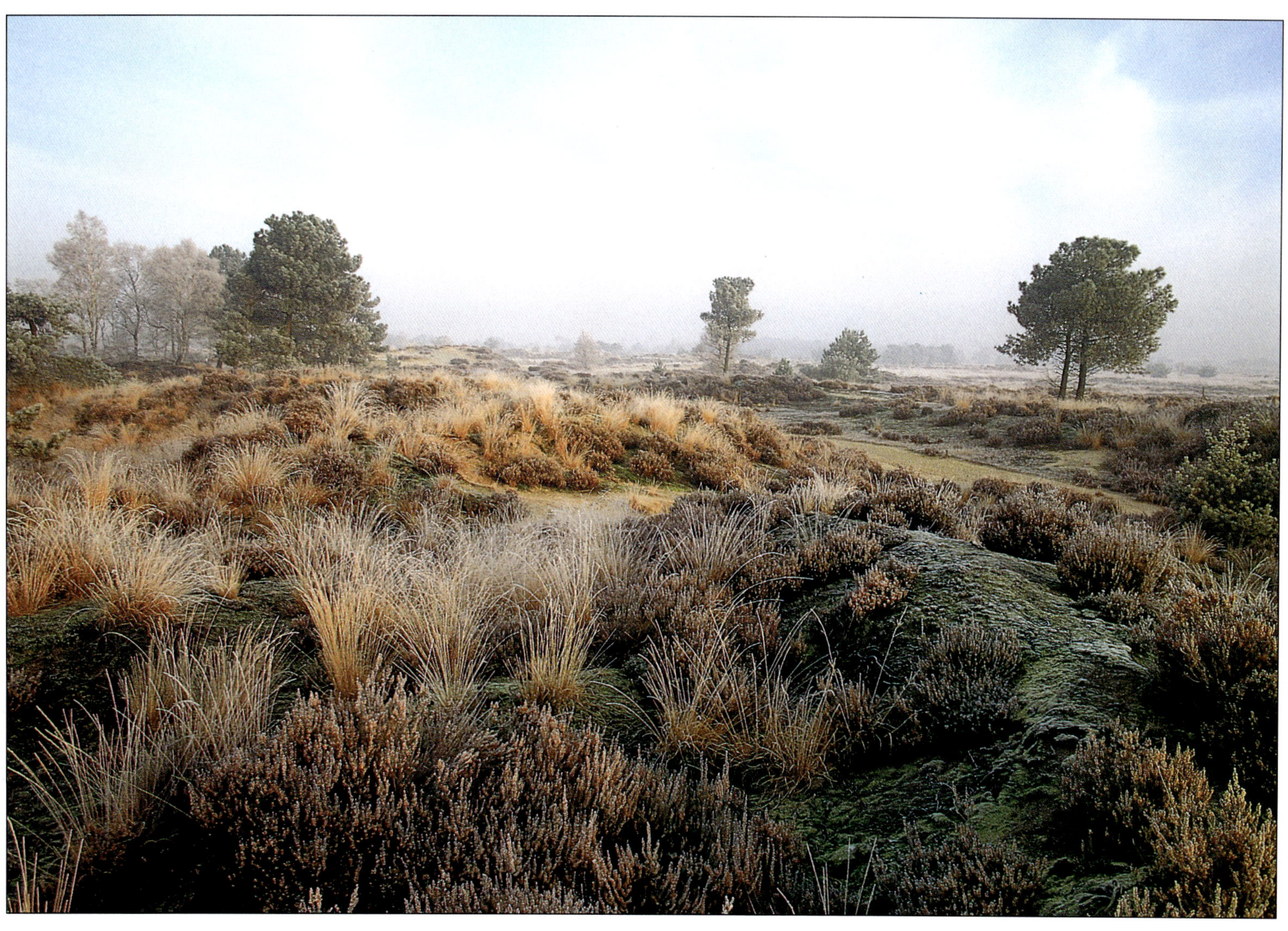

**Bob Jorens**
Belgium
HIGHLY COMMENDED

***Mystic morning, Kalmthoutse Heide***

*"I had passed this part of the nature reserve many times before, but this time it seemed irresistibly mystical. I had to be quick, because the sun was coming through and the mist was clearing up. A few moments later, everything had changed. The rime frost was gone, the mist was gone and the sun began to shine."*

Pentax LX with 24mm lens; 1/8 sec at f16; Fujichrome Velvia

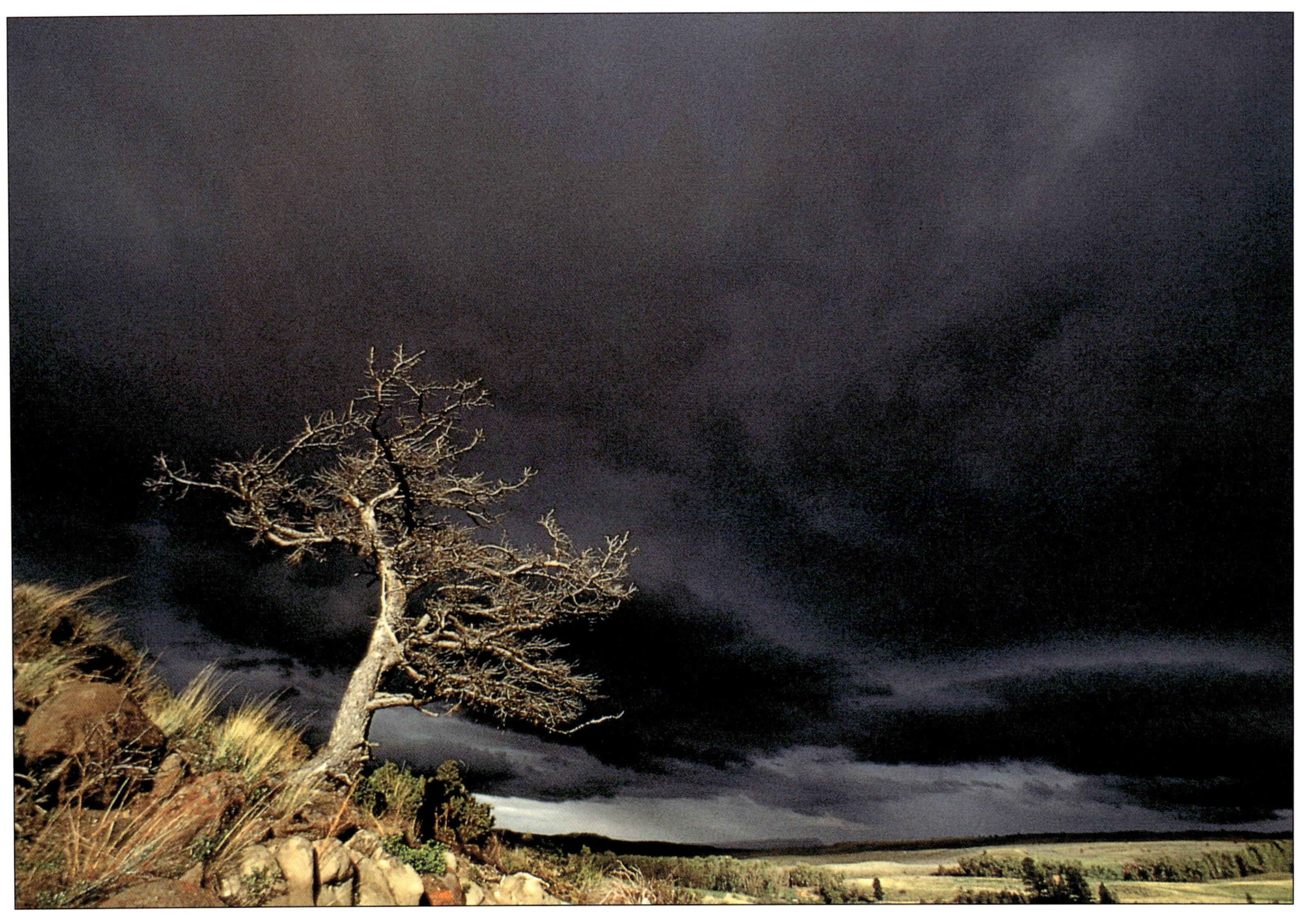

**Gerry Ellis**
United States of America
HIGHLY COMMENDED

***Juniper and stormfront***

*"Late in the afternoon, spectacular lighting began to build as I was photographing near the edge of Bridger National Forest, in Montana. I remembered this tree from earlier in the day, and raced back to catch it before the sun retreated into the approaching storm."*

Nikon F-90s with 20-35mm lens; tripod; 1/15 sec at f11; Kodak Elite 100

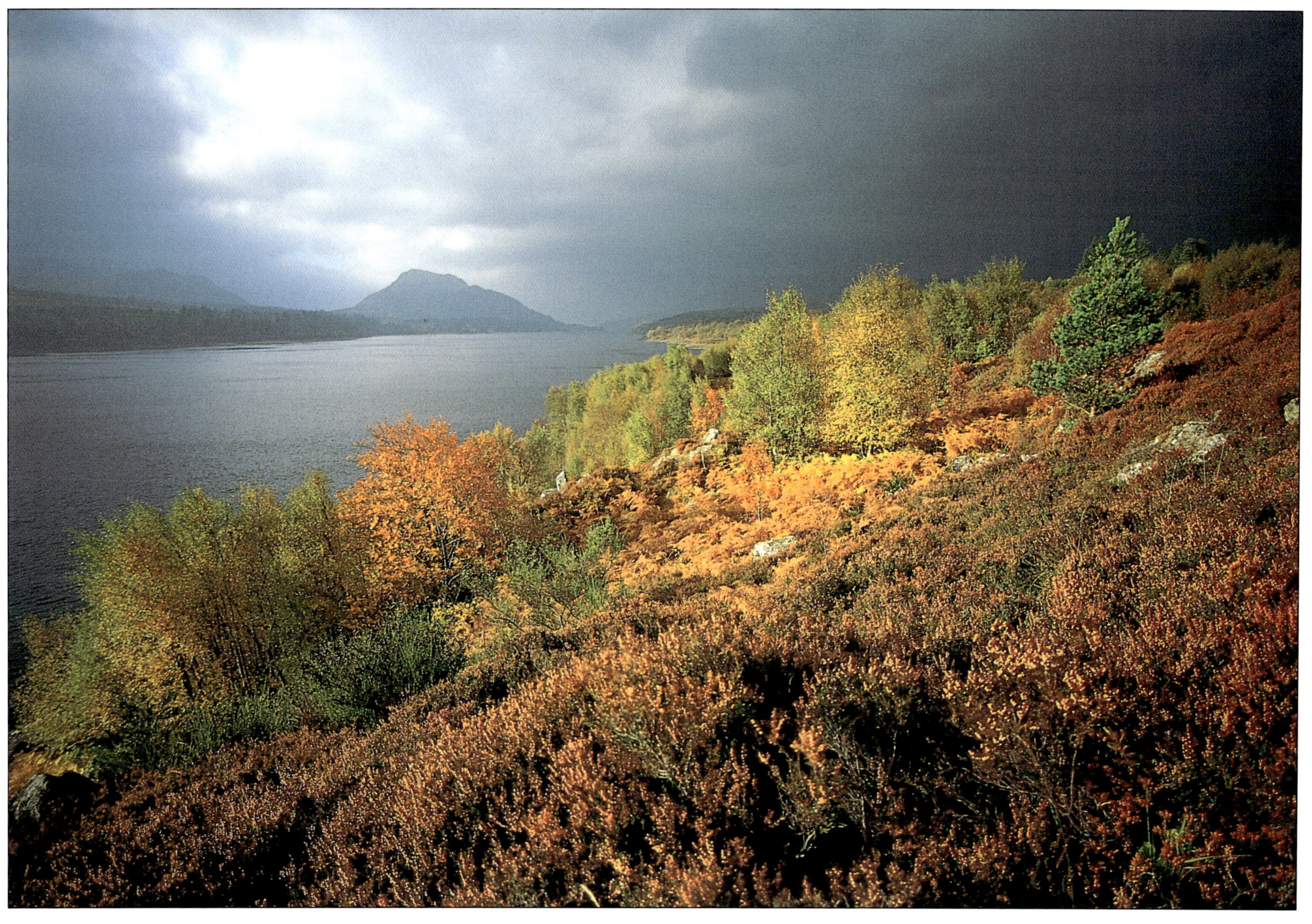

**Steve Austin**
United Kingdom
HIGHLY COMMENDED

**Autumn, Loch Laggan**

*"I was driving along the edge of Loch Laggan, in the Scottish Highlands, when suddenly the sun came through a gap in the clouds. I remember running around trying to find a suitable viewpoint when I came upon this scene of silver birch scrub in heather. Minutes later, it was raining again."*

Ricoh XR-X with 28-70mm lens; tripod; 1/30 sec at f9.6; Fujichrome Velvia

# Wildlife in Trade

This category was introduced for 1995 only, to highlight the work of the Environmental Investigation Agency by illustrating the problems faced by wild animals through trade.

**Martin Harvey**
South Africa
WINNER

***Poached white rhino***

*"Growing demand for rhino horn for traditional Chinese medicine is the driving force behind this catastrophe; all five species may soon be extinct in the wild. This was taken in the Umfolozi Game Reserve, South Africa."*

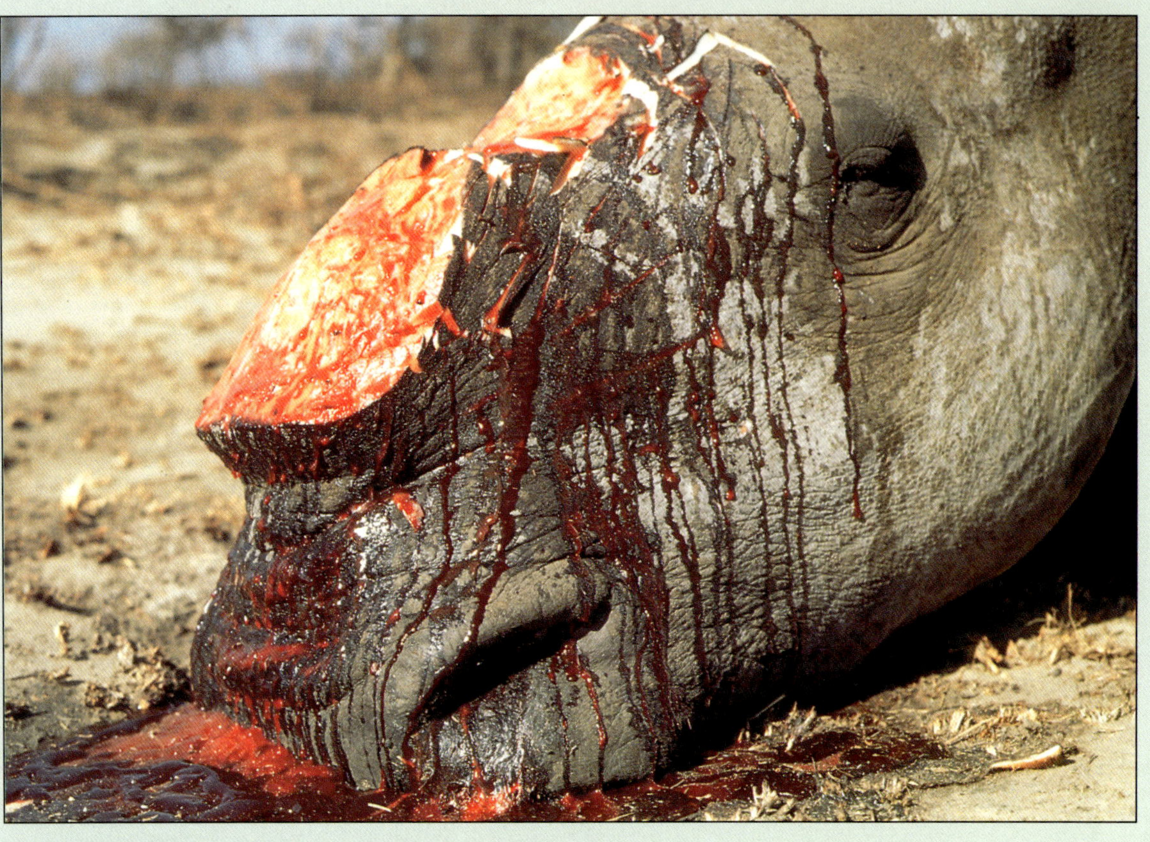

**Pete Oxford**
United Kingdom
RUNNER-UP

***Dead walrus***

*"This adult male walrus was killed at Inchoun on the Chukchi Peninsula, Russia, to feed foxes on government-sponsored fur farms. The ivory is also carved for Far Eastern markets."*

Nikon F4 with 24mm lens; flash; 1/125 sec at f5.6; Fujichrome Velvia

**Andy Rouse**
United Kingdom
HIGHLY COMMENDED

***Asiatic black bear cub***

*"Last year the Thai authorities seized a shipment of 23 cubs caught in Burma and destined for restaurants in Korea."*

Canon EOS 1N with 28-80mm lens; flash; 1/60 sec at f4; Fujichrome Velvia rated at 40

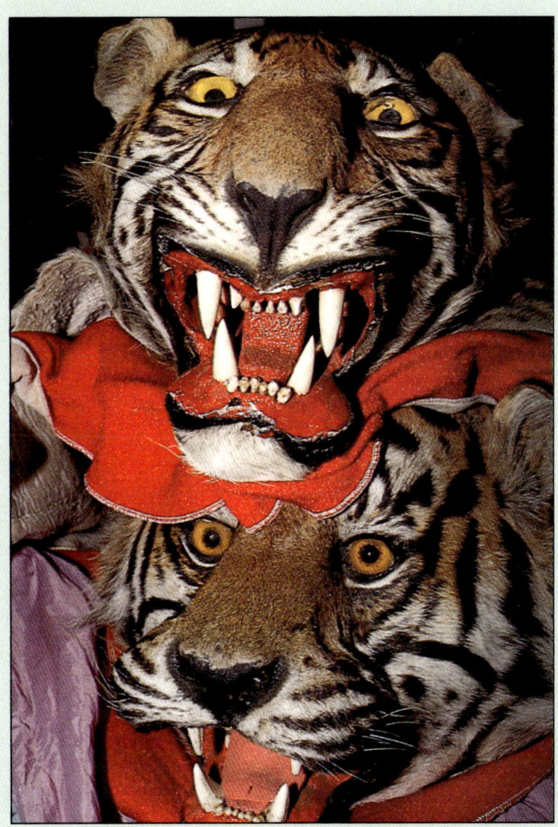

**Martin Wright**
United Kingdom
HIGHLY COMMENDED

***Bengal tiger skins, South Korea***

*"Posing as a representative of a British fur importer, I was offered the two Bengal tiger skins in Seoul for US$2,500 each."*

Canon EOS 600 with 28-80mm lens; flash; Fujichrome Professional 100

**Steve Morgan**
United Kingdom
HIGHLY COMMENDED

***Siberian tiger and its skin***

*"This Siberian tiger had been illegally hunted. Its skin was recovered from poachers in the forests of Primorskii Krai, Russia, and photographed in Lazo village."*

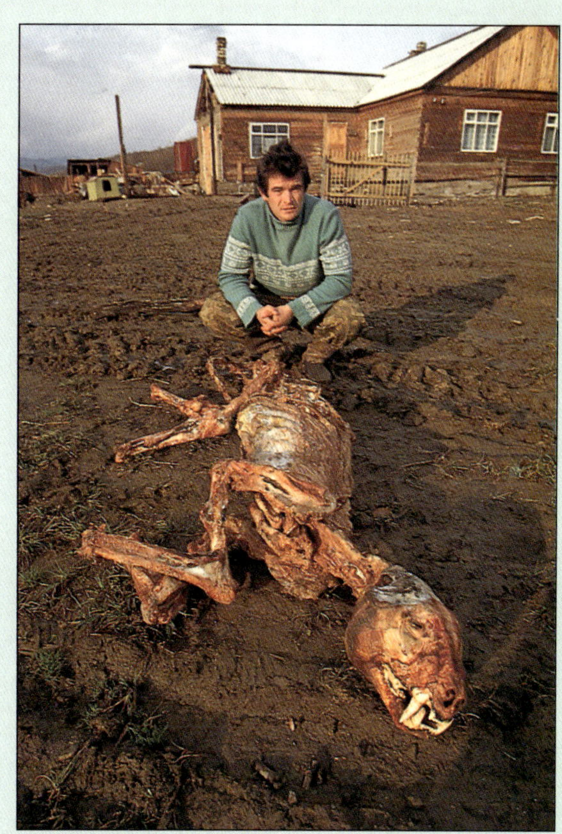

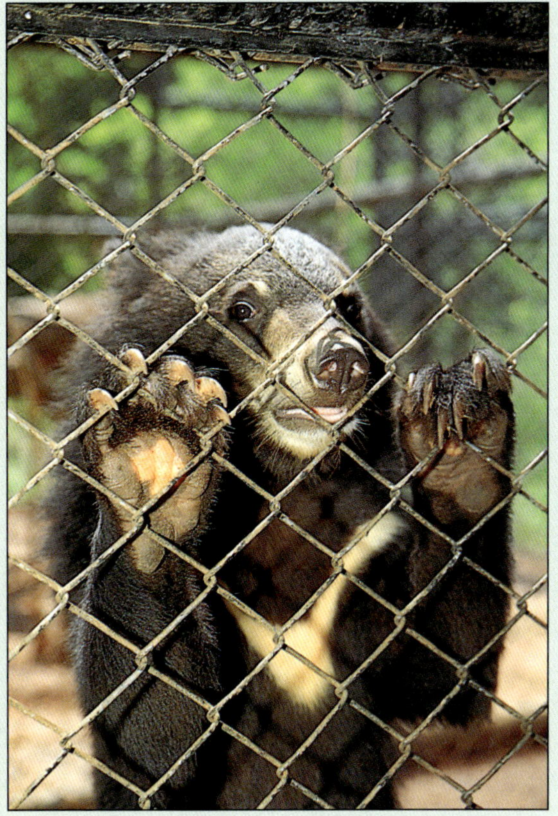

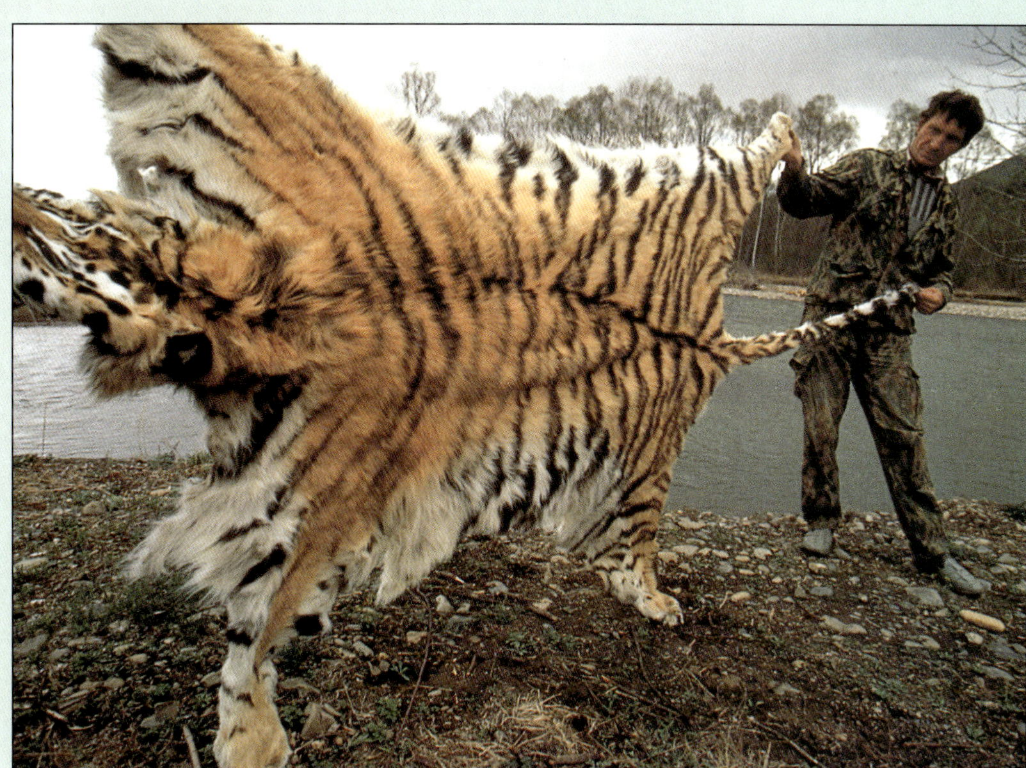

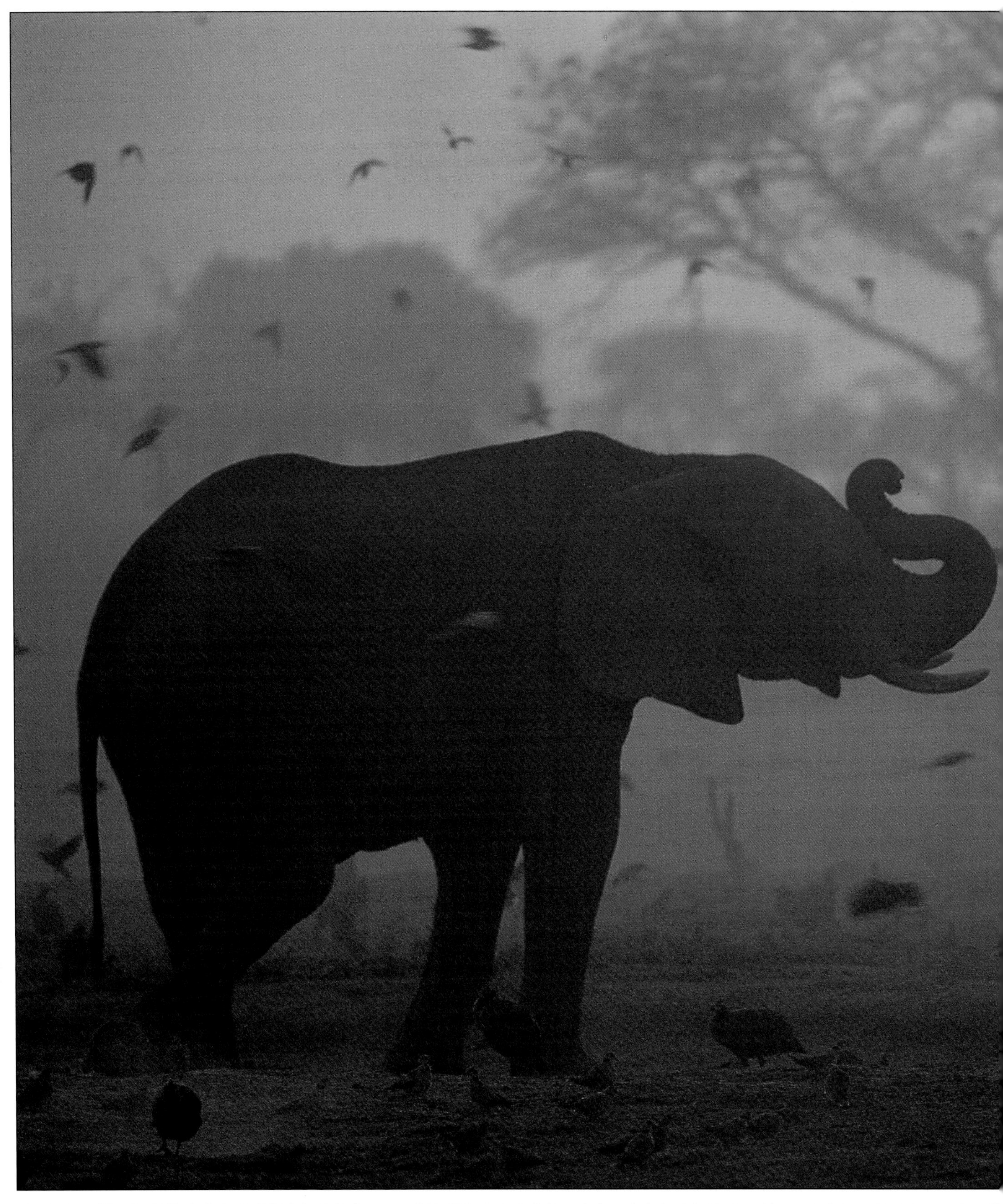

# From Dusk to Dawn

Pictures must have been taken between sunset and sunrise (the sun may be on but not above the horizon) and must feature animals.

**Richard Coomber**
United Kingdom
WINNER

**_Dawn in Savuti_**

*"This is dawn by a waterhole in Savuti, Botswana, at the end of the dry season - it is always a magic time. Elephants, wary of lions, drink as hundreds of turtle doves fly in from the surrounding bush, and helmeted guinea fowl scurry about raising dust that hangs in the still air."*

Nikon F4 with 300mm lens; Fujichrome Velvia

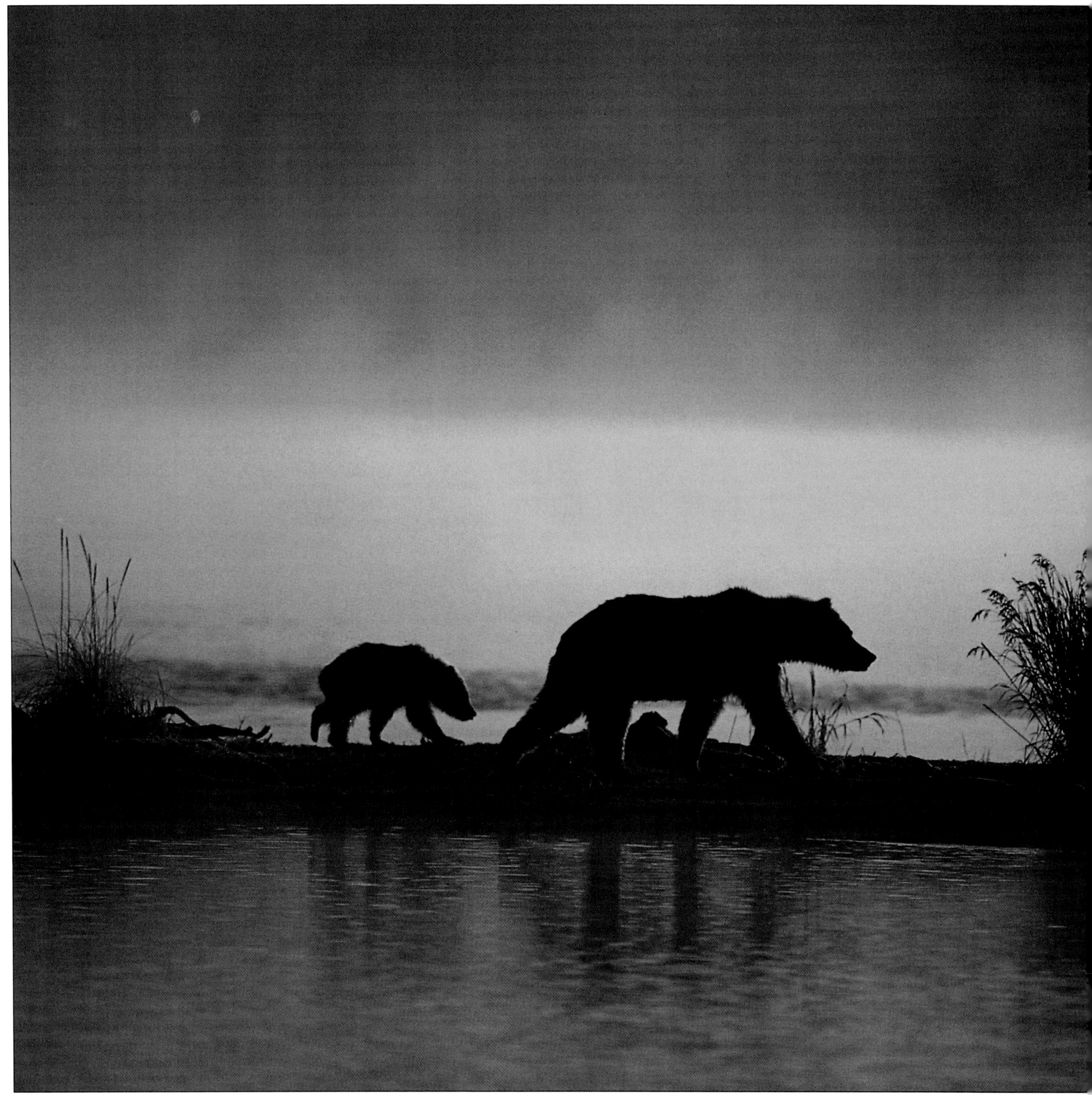

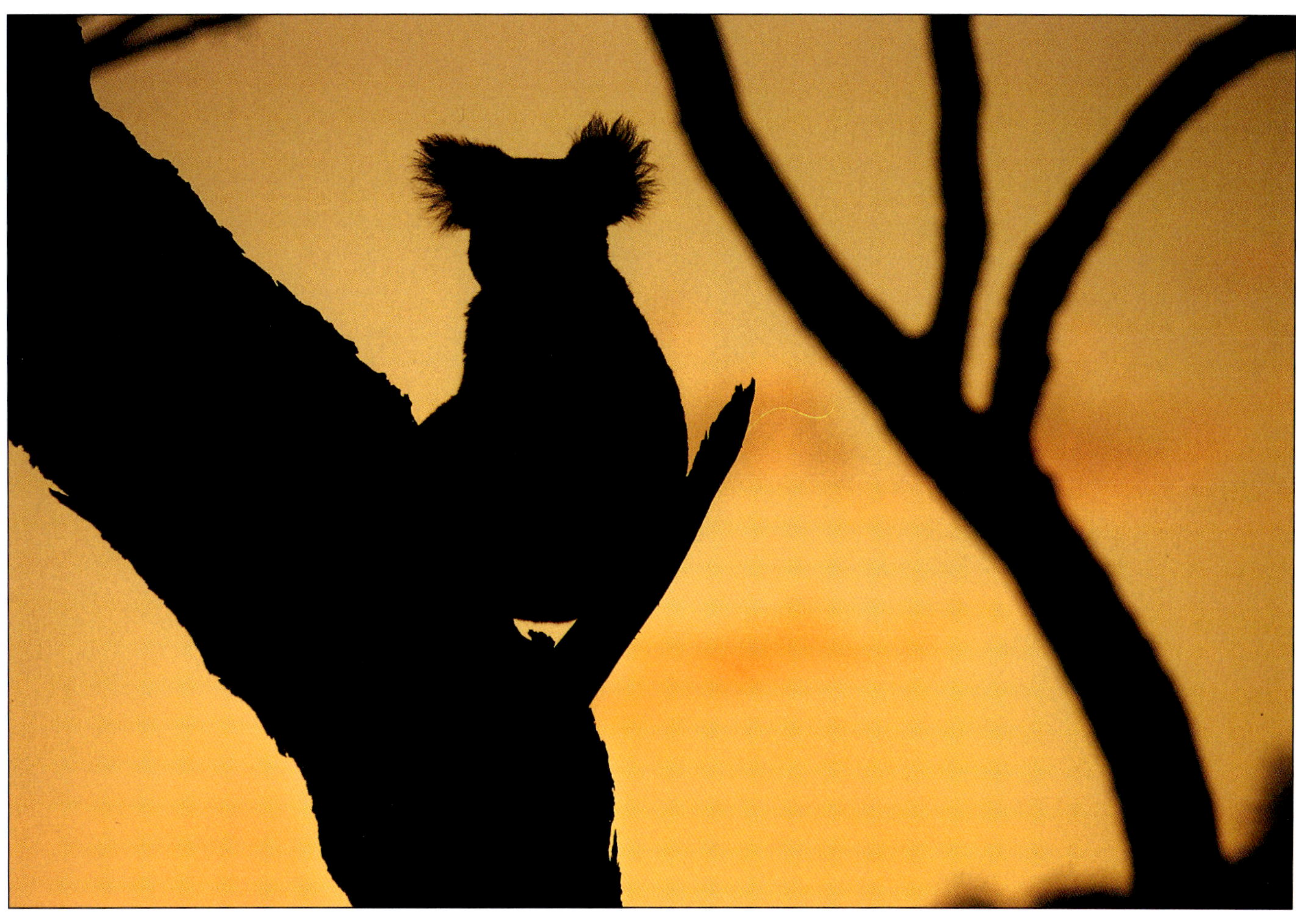

**Dominic Chaplin**
United Kingdom
HIGHLY COMMENDED

***Koala at sunset***

*"I spent a day walking in baking heat on Magnetic Island in Queensland, Australia, looking for koalas. These animals are hard to photograph, not because they are difficult to approach, but because they sleep for 20 hours a day and it is hard to find one doing anything of interest. I had just given up and was walking home when I spotted this individual on the move."*

Canon EOS 100 with 100-200mm lens; tripod; 1/60 sec at f5.6; Kodachrome 64

**Gary Schultz**
United States of America
RUNNER-UP

***Brown bear and cub at dawn***

*"I had been watching this bear and her cub for several days in the Katmai National Park, Alaska. Their morning route often led along this spit of land to Naknek Lake, where they looked for salmon. On this particular morning, the bears showed up just as light started breaking through the fog, putting a golden glow on the surroundings."*

Nikon F4s with 500mm lens; tripod; 1/500 sec at f5.6; Fujichrome Velvia

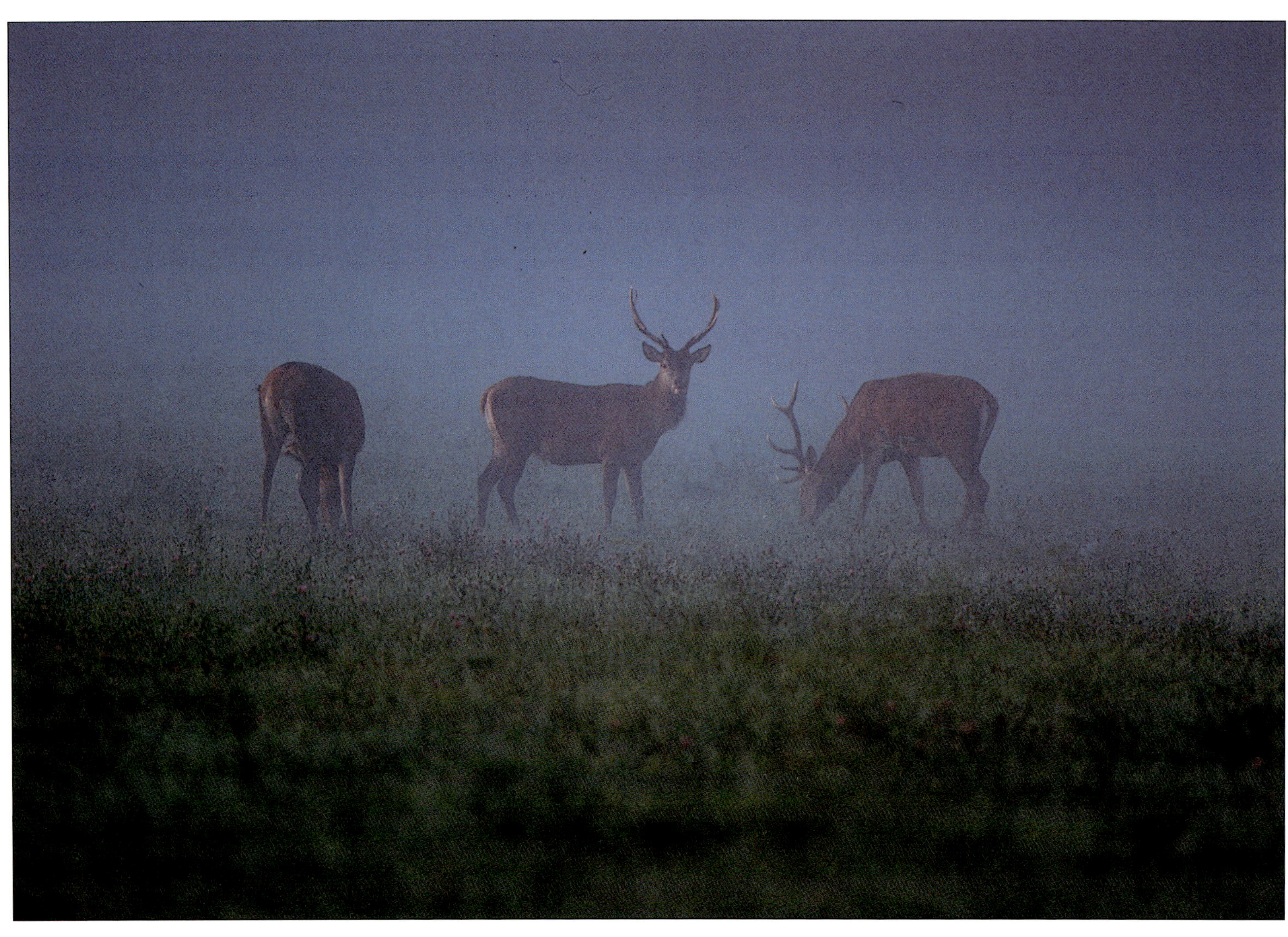

**Frédéric Fève**

France

HIGHLY COMMENDED

***Deer at dawn***

*"This picture was taken at the edge of a forest in eastern France at the beginning of the rutting season. I arrived there while it was still night and quietly approached a group of deer. An hour after daybreak, the sunrise and morning mist gave this special atmosphere, and I took about 15 photos."*

Nikon F-301 with 300mm lens; tripod; 1/2 sec at f4; Fujichrome 100

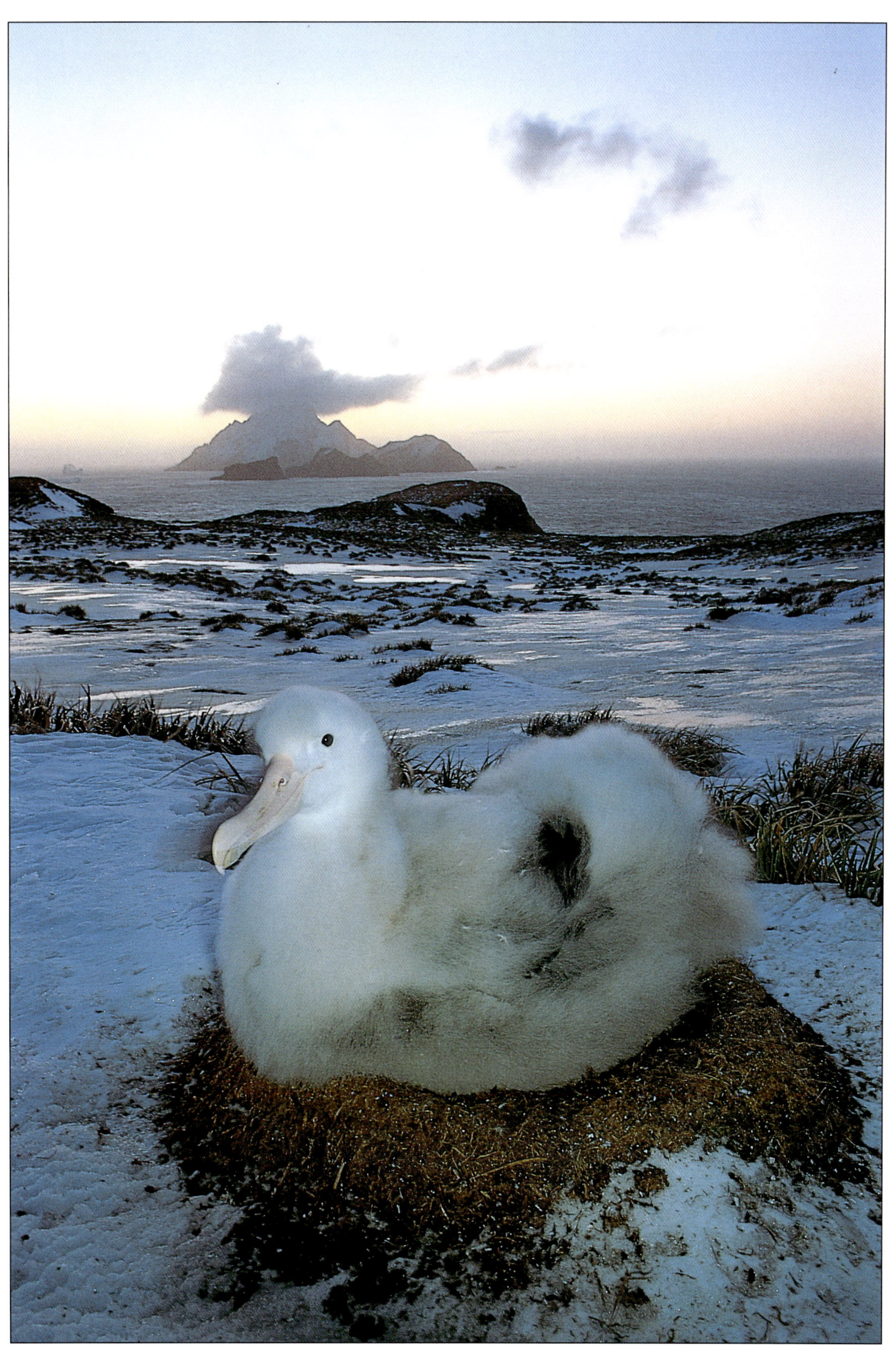

**Ben Osborne**

United Kingdom

HIGHLY COMMENDED

***Wandering albatross chick***

*"Wandering albatross chicks take nine months to grow, and so, unlike other southern ocean seabirds, are reared through the long cold winter. The parent birds have to travel to warmer waters to find food, flying round trips of up to 5,000 kilometres, lasting on average 10 days, during which the chick - as in this picture - sits alone on the nest."*

Nikon F4s with 28mm lens; flash; 1/2 sec at f16; Fujichrome Velvia

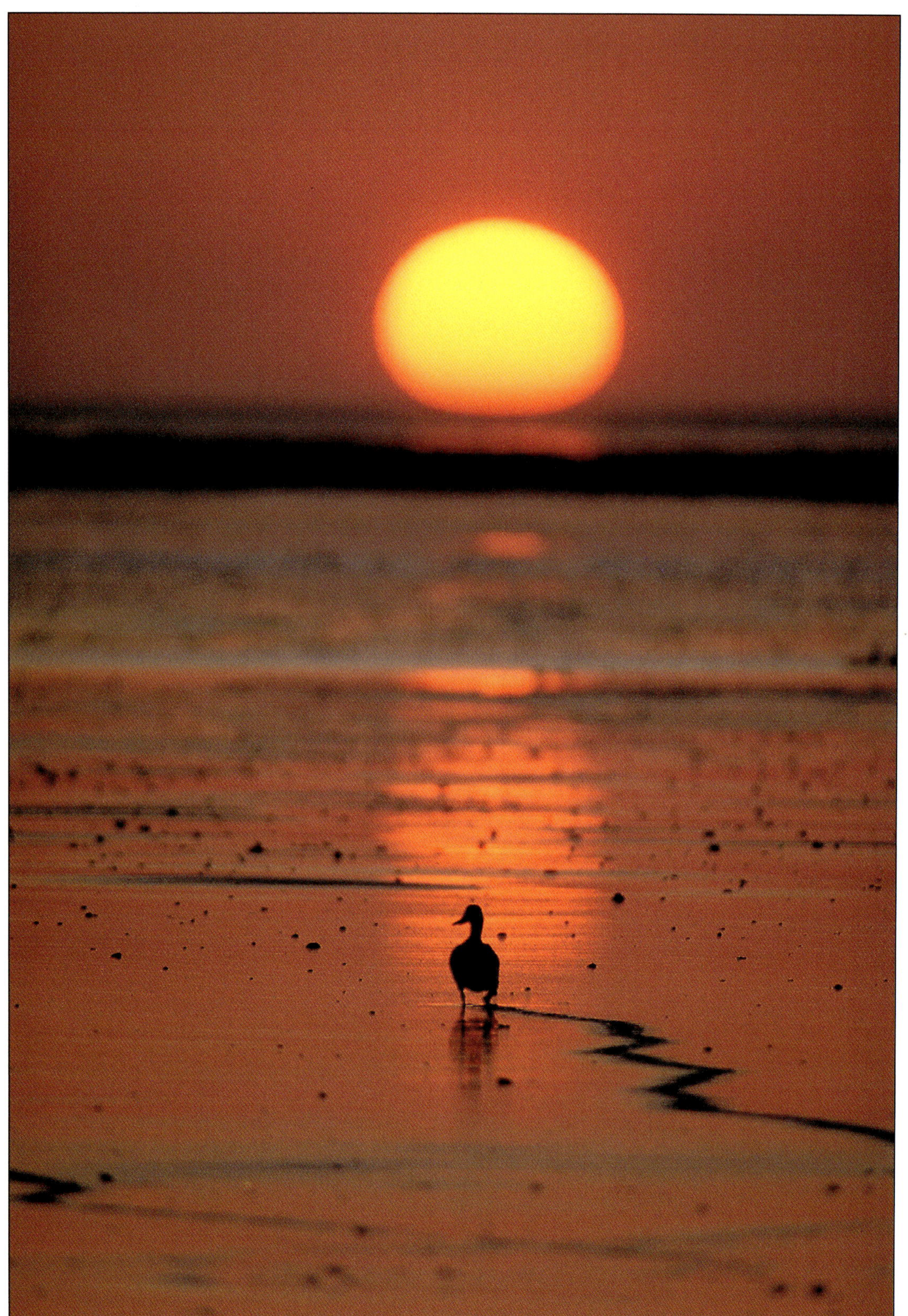

**Solvin Zankl**
Germany
HIGHLY COMMENDED

### Duck on mudflats

*"At low tide, large areas of mud flats are exposed along the shore of Pellworm Island in the North Sea. I was an ornithological warden there for a year and used to take people onto the mud to show them the rich wildlife there. I took photographs, such as this one of a duck searching for food, to illustrate talks I gave in the evenings."*

Nikon F4 with 300mm lens and x2 extender; tripod; 1/350 sec at f2.8; Ektachrome Panther 100X

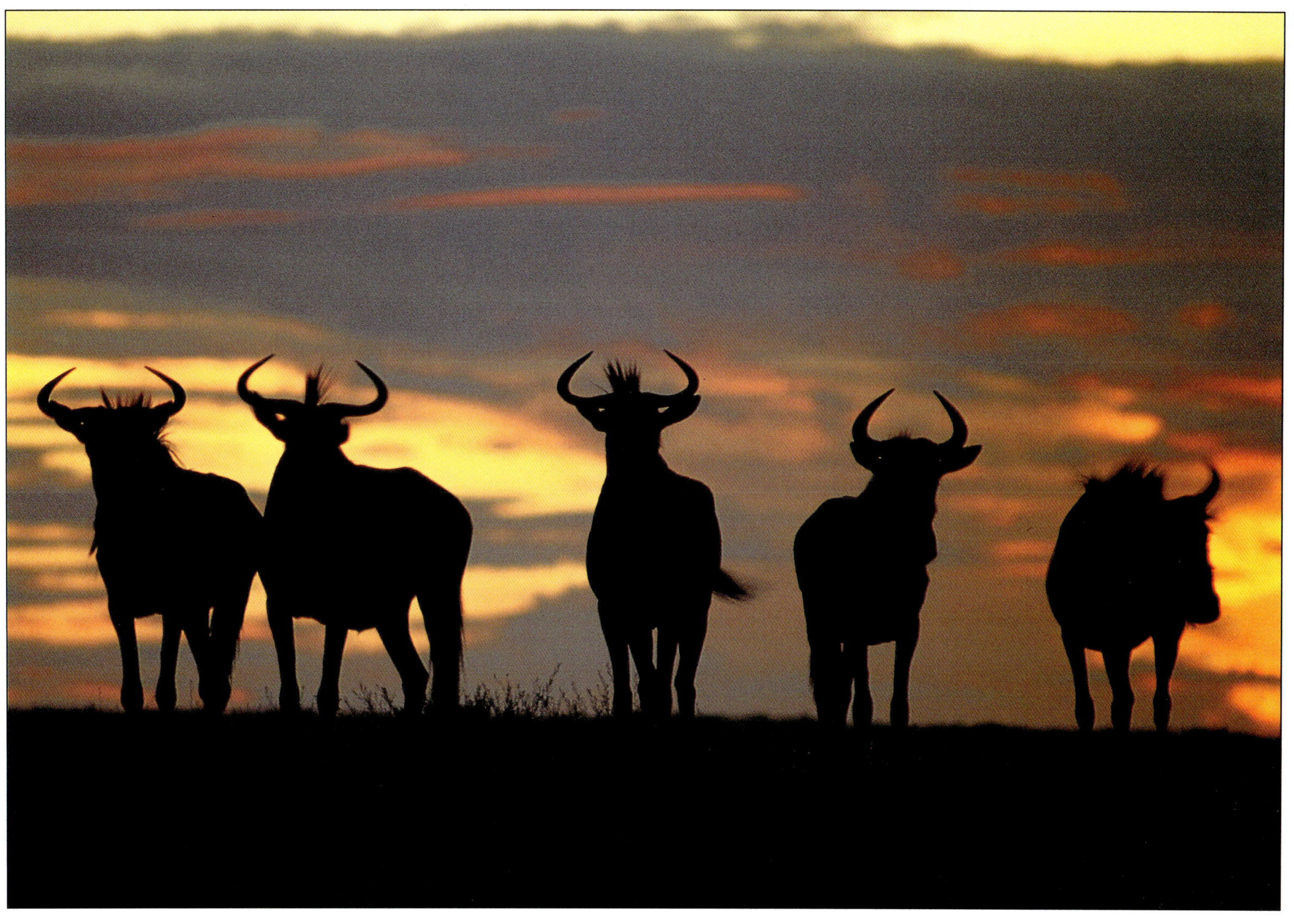

**Claudia Auer**

Germany

HIGHLY COMMENDED

***Wildebeest at dusk***

*"As part of my research in Etosha National Park, Namibia, I followed a group of wildebeest to observe their feeding and drinking behaviour. At dusk I stepped out of my car to photograph them against the sunset. They turned towards me, snorted and watched - behaviour typical of wildebeest when they first sight a predator."*

Nikon FG20 with 80-200mm lens; beanbag; 1/60 sec at f2.8; Fujichrome Velvia

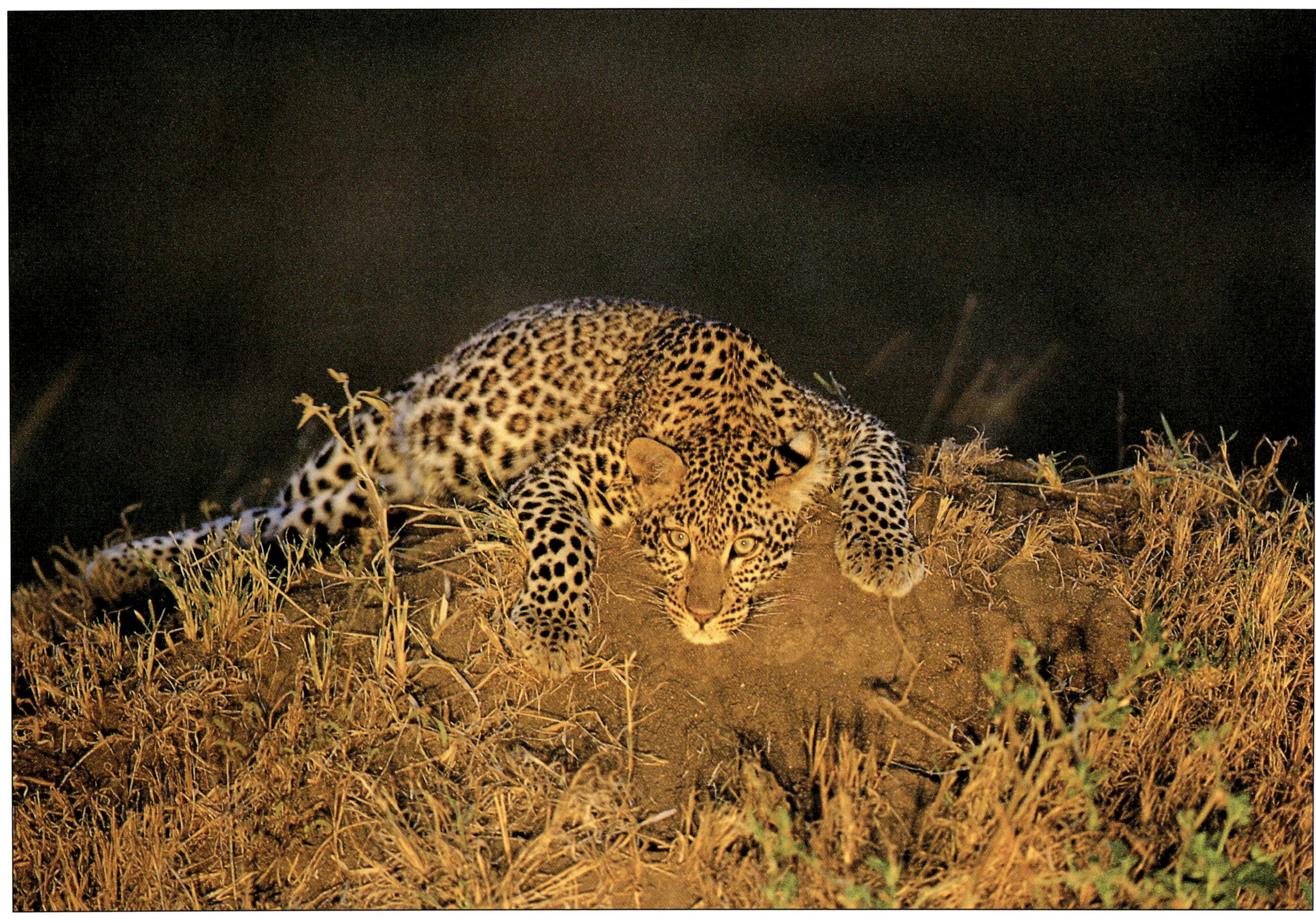

**Bijal Patel**

Kenya

HIGHLY COMMENDED

***Leopard cub at night***

*"I came across this leopard cub late one afternoon in the Maasai Mara, Kenya. Just as the sun set, the cub got up and perched on top of an anthill. I cautiously approached in my car and managed three exposures in the last few minutes of twilight."*

Nikon F4s with 300mm lens; 1/60 sec at f2.8; Fujichrome RDP100 rated at 200

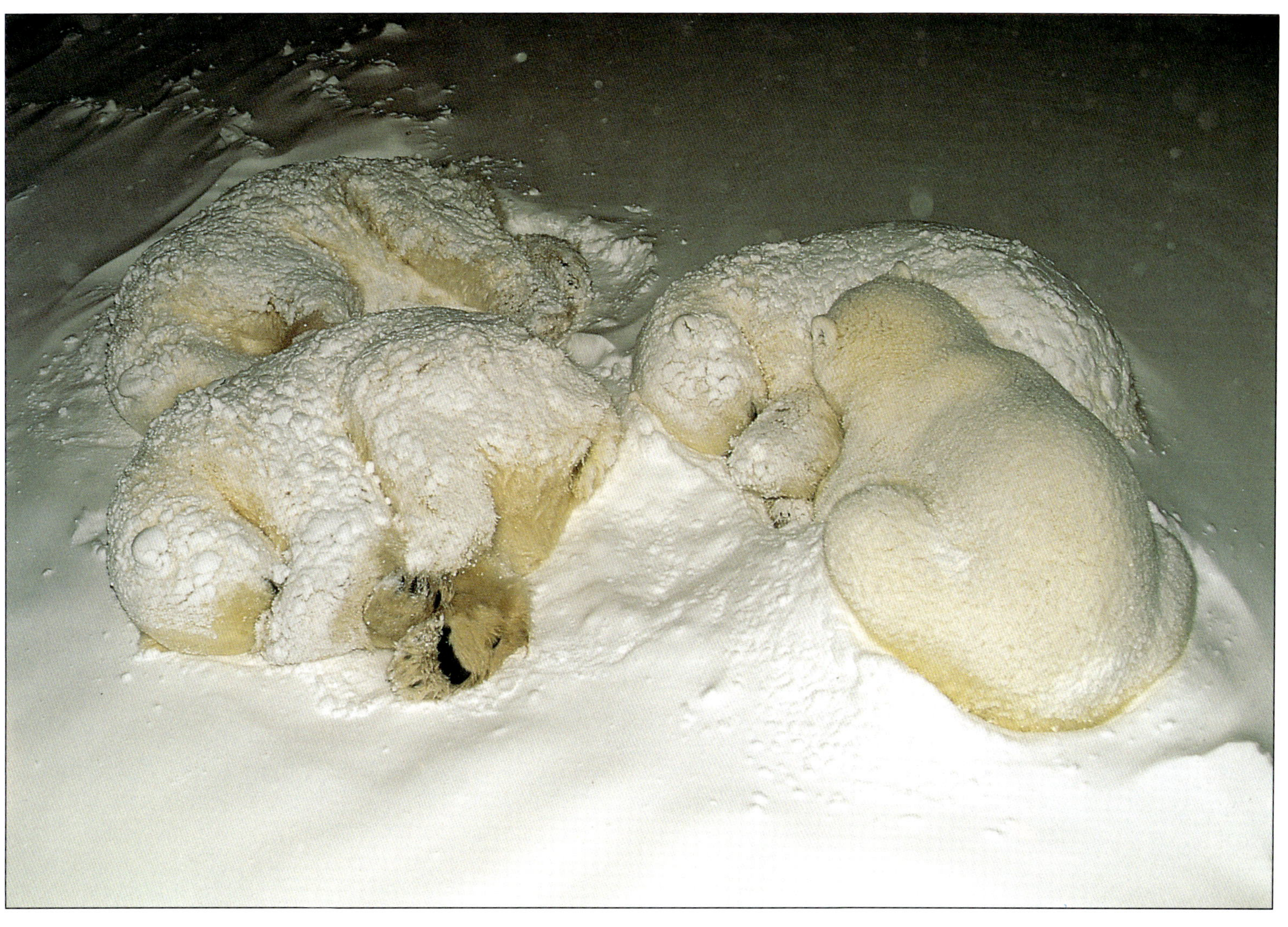

**Thomas D Mangelsen**
United States of America
HIGHLY COMMENDED

***Sleeping polar bears***

*"A major windstorm forced these bears to seek shelter in a snow drift for the night. I thought it interesting that these adult bears, who would normally be solitary, came together to shelter from the storm. I took the picture in Hudson Bay, Canada."*

Nikon F4 with 24-50mm lens; flash; Fujichrome Velvia

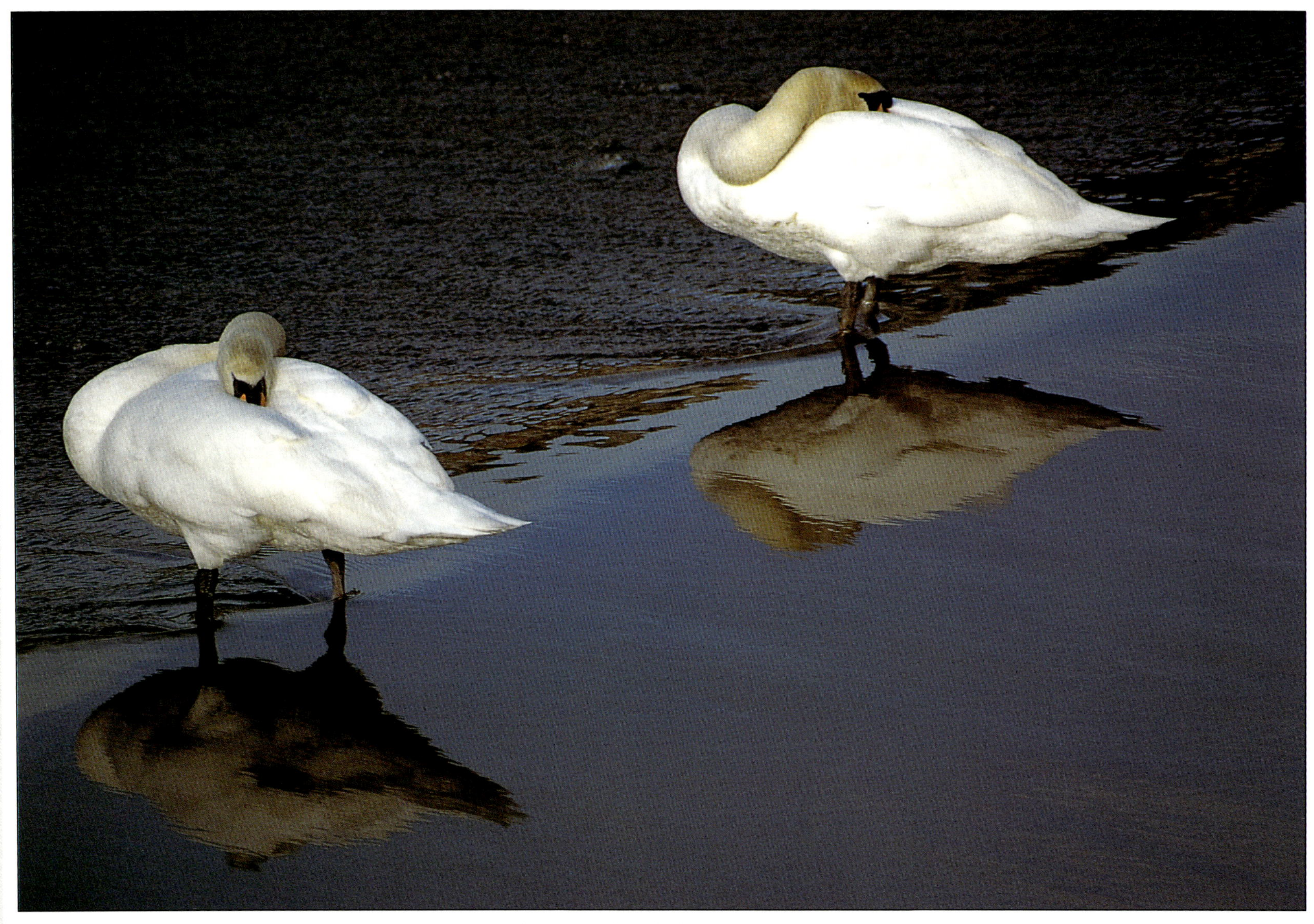

**Ross Hoddinott**
United Kingdom
YOUNG WILDLIFE PHOTOGRAPHER OF THE YEAR 1995

***Reflected swans***

*"I frequently enjoy the walk around Tamar Lakes, our local reservoir, to photograph wildlife. It was the soft spring light, and the symmetry of the mute swans and their reflection, that drew me to this resident pair resting on the weir."*

Minolta Dynax 7000i with 70-210mm lens; tripod; 1/250 sec at f5.6; Fujichrome Sensia 100

# Young Wildlife Photographer of the Year

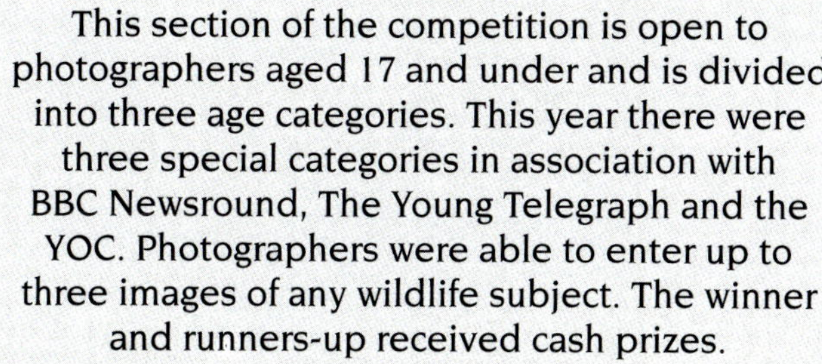

This section of the competition is open to photographers aged 17 and under and is divided into three age categories. This year there were three special categories in association with BBC Newsround, The Young Telegraph and the YOC. Photographers were able to enter up to three images of any wildlife subject. The winner and runners-up received cash prizes.

Neil Davy, the winner of the BBC Newsround Young Wildlife Photojournalist Award, won a cheque and a camera. Louise Dean, winner of the Young Telegraph Award, won a cheque, a trophy and a day with a Young Telegraph photographer. Michael Hill, the winner of the YOC Award, won a cheque and a trophy.

The overall winner of the competition, 17-year-old Ross Hoddinott, received the British Gas award - a bronze sculpture of a scarlet ibis - a cheque and the opportunity to spend a day on location with wildlife photographer Heather Angel.

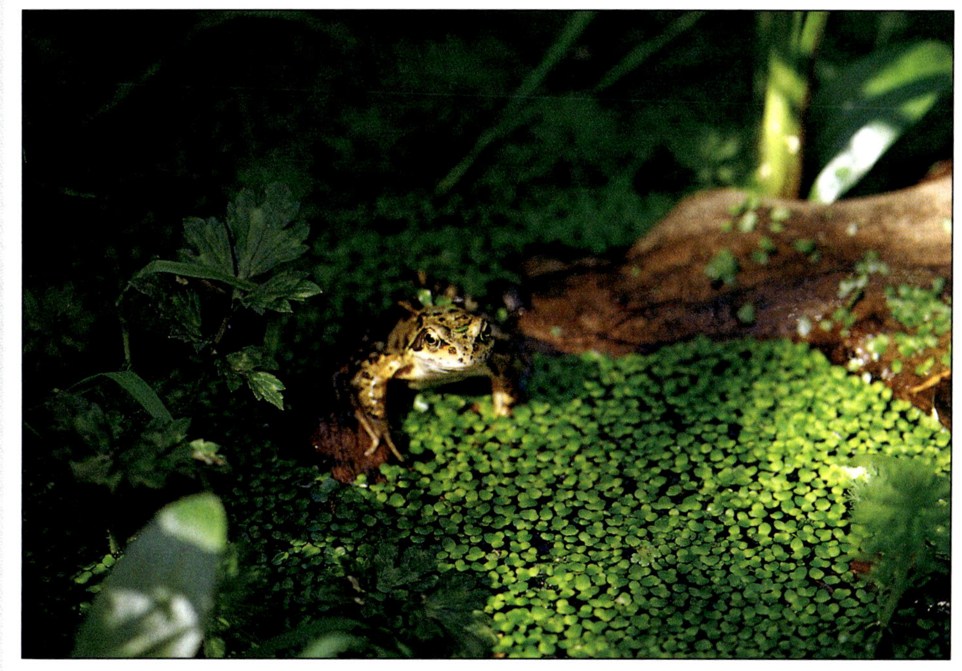

**Iwan T Fletcher**
United Kingdom
WINNER: 10 YEARS & UNDER

***Common frog***

*"Four years ago, we built a wildlife pond in our rear garden to provide a habitat for the frogs whose original marsh had been drained. I took the photograph of a common frog there in spring to enter the competition. The soft evening light made the subject particularly attractive."*

Nikkormat FT2 with 105mm lens; tripod; 1/125 sec at f8; Kodachrome 64

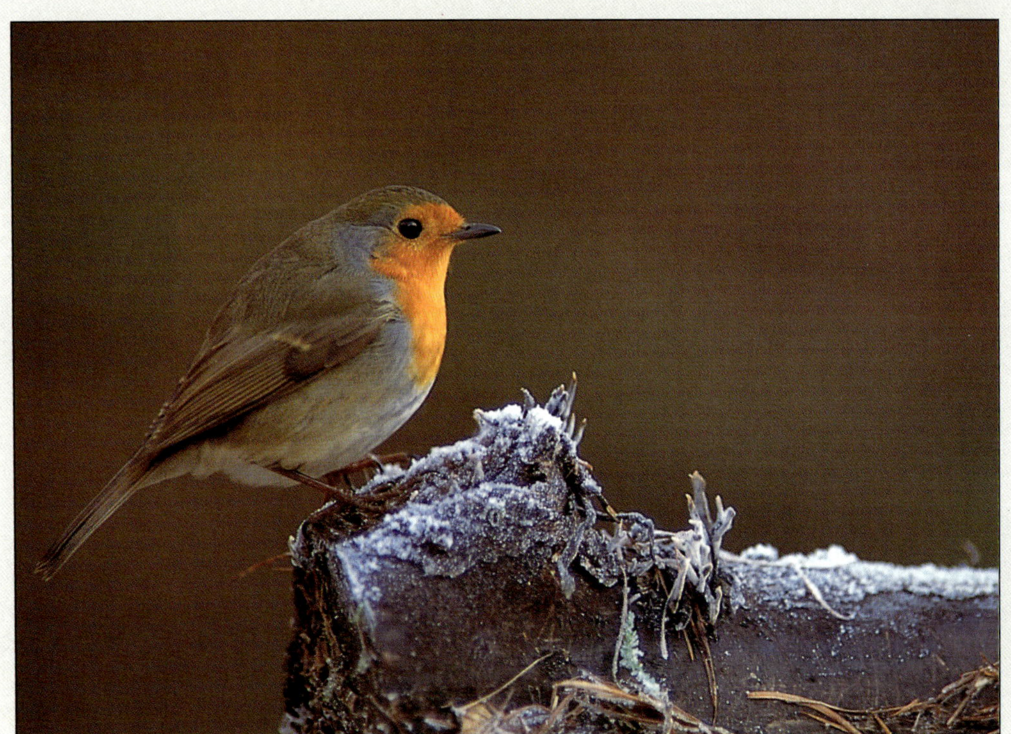

## Rachel Hingley
United Kingdom

WINNER: 11-14 YEARS

### *Robin on log*

*"I had been going regularly to the Castle Eden Walkway Country Park, in Cleveland County, to photograph birds near a tree stump used as a bird-feeding station. One January morning I decided to set up a hide there. I found a log covered in hoar frost and put it on the stump with some food. The robin was landing before I had even got into the hide."*

Contax 167MT with 300mm lens and x1.4 converter; tripod; hide; Fujichrome Provia 100

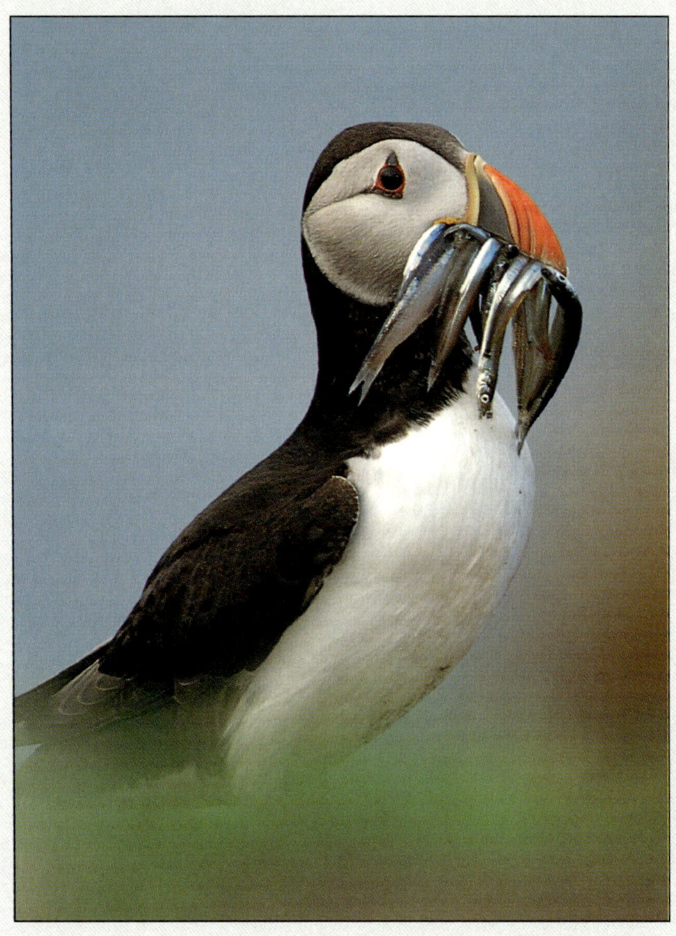

## Richard Hill
United Kingdom

RUNNER-UP: 11-14 YEARS

### *Puffin with sandeels*

*"I spent a week in July on Skokholm Island, in Pembrokeshire, Wales, on a family holiday to photograph seabirds. This puffin was returning from the sea to its nest burrow with a beak full of sandeels to feed its chicks."*

Nikon F50 with 600mm lens; tripod; flash; auto-exposure; Fujichrome Sensia

## Michael Hill

United Kingdom

WINNER: 15-17 YEARS

### *Wildebeest and rainbow*

*"I was in Amboseli National Park, Kenya, on a family photographic holiday when we came across this lone wildebeest just after a rainstorm. I liked the shadows on the flanks of the wildebeest and the dramatic lighting."*

Nikon F-601 with 300mm lens; beanbag; auto-exposure; Fujichrome Sensia

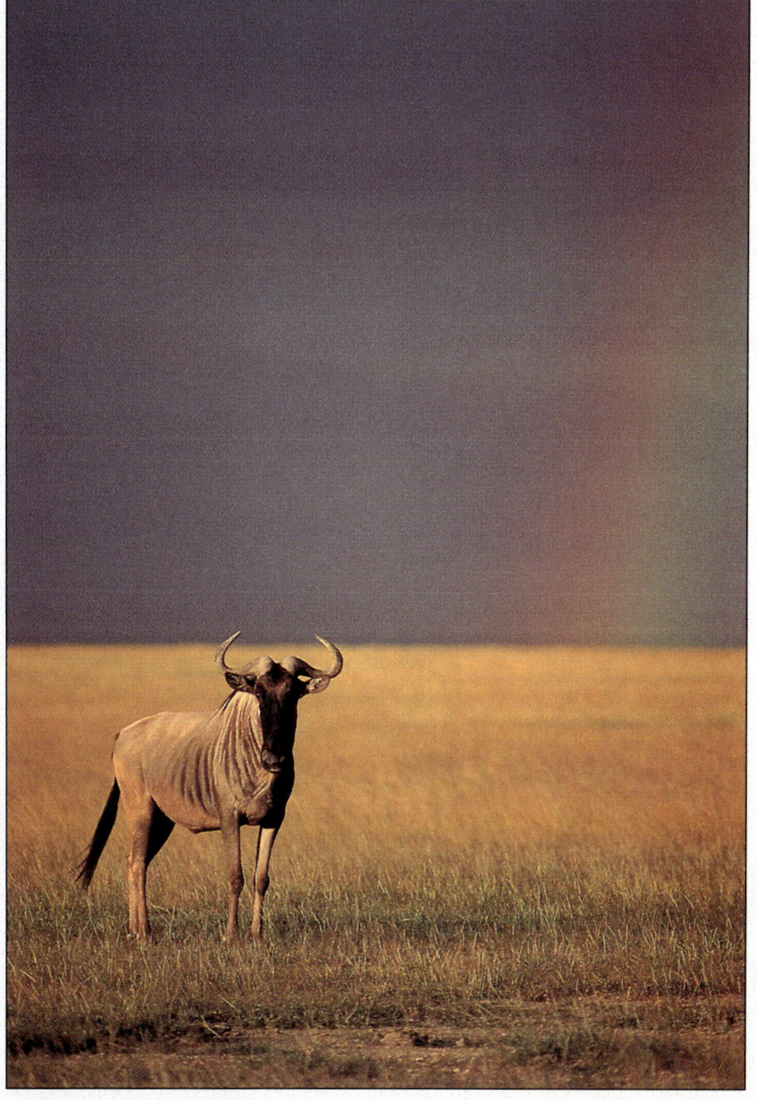

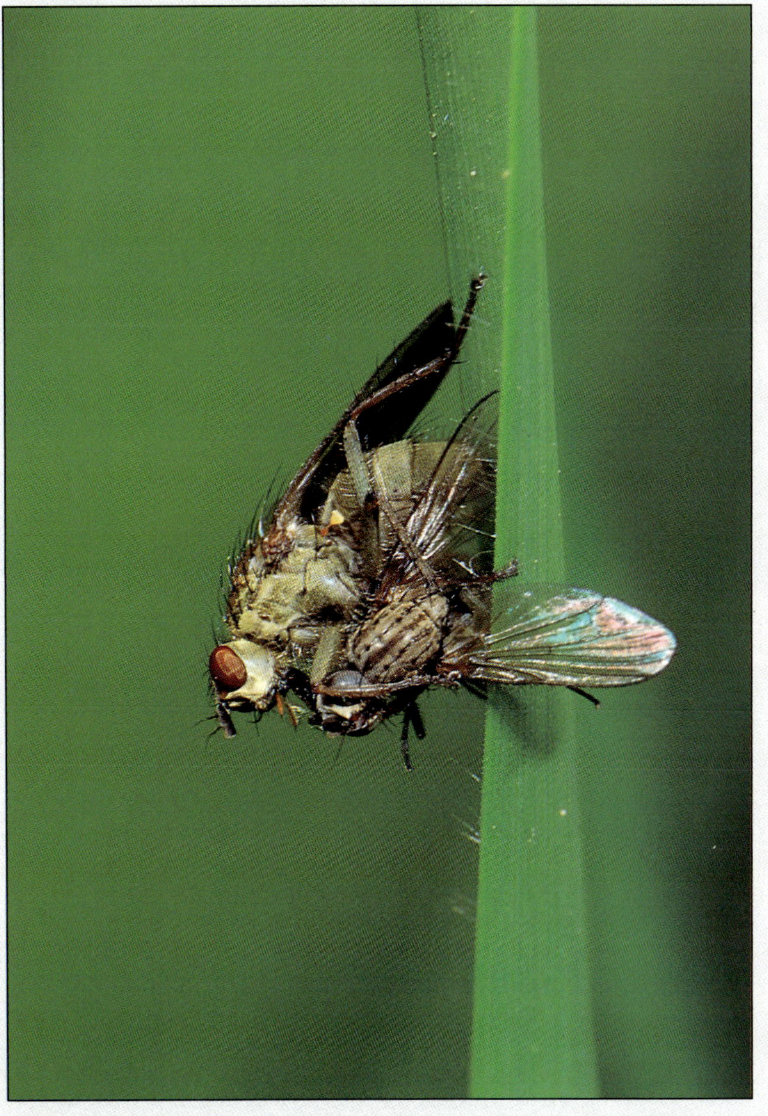

## Sven Zellner

Germany

RUNNER-UP: 15-17 YEARS

### *Dung fly with prey*

*"In spring, dung flies can often be found on meadows near my home in Trier. I try to document biological relations, and so decided to take this photograph of a dung fly eating a smaller fly."*

Nikon F-801s with 180mm macro lens and bellows; tripod; flash; 1/60 sec at f16; Kodak Elite 100

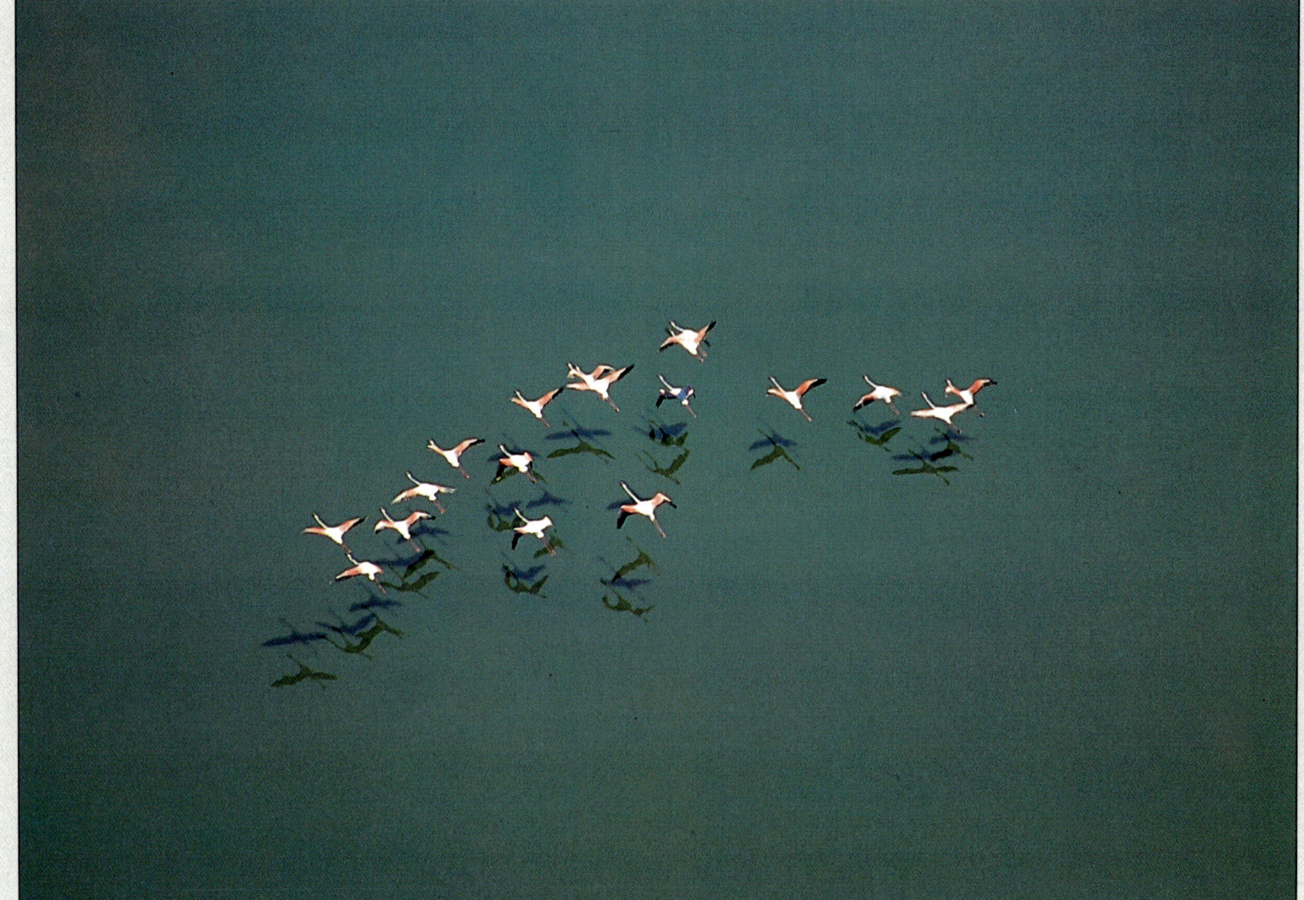

**Michael Hill**
United Kingdom
WINNER: YOC AWARD

### *Lesser flamingos*

*"Lesser flamingos migrate up and down the African Rift Valley lakes, and we went to Lake Magadi, Kenya, in an ultralight aircraft, specifically to photograph them in flight. These birds were already in the air - they were not put up by the ultralight."*

Nikon F-601 with 70-210mm lens; auto-exposure; Fujichrome Sensia

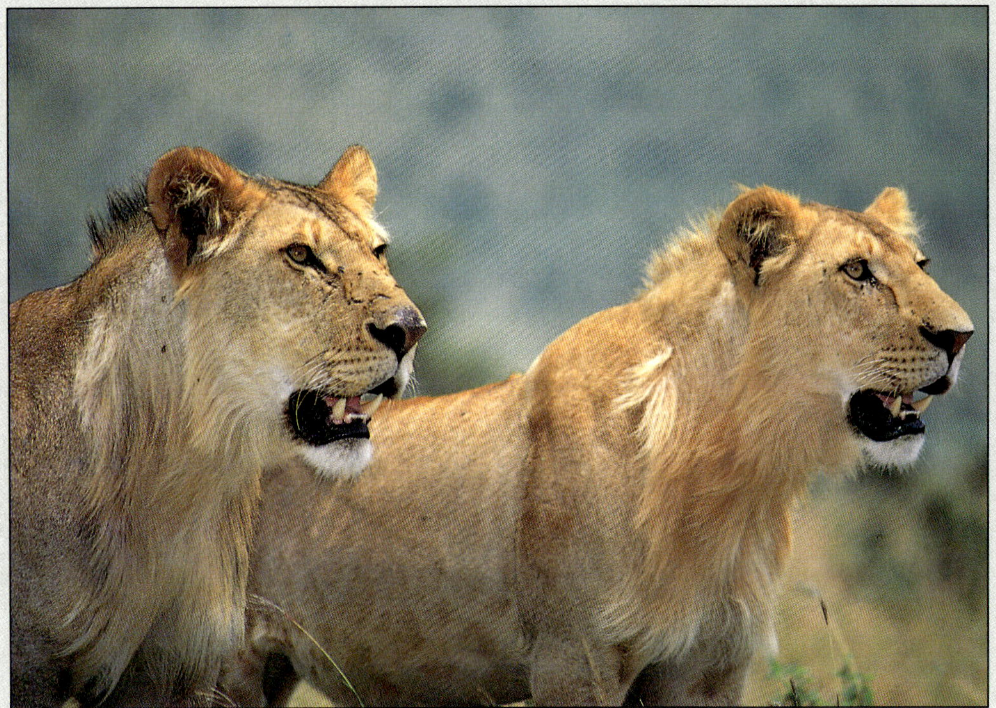

**Michael Hill**
United Kingdom
HIGHLY COMMENDED: 15-17 YEARS

### *Lions watching prey*

*"I saw many lions on a recent trip to the Maasai Mara, in Kenya, but they seemed to be asleep most of the time. These two were sleeping at the base of a bush when an impala came into view in the long grass ahead. They suddenly sat up and became alert before attempting an unsuccessful stalk."*

Nikon F-601 with 300mm lens; beanbag; flash; auto-exposure; Fujichrome Sensia

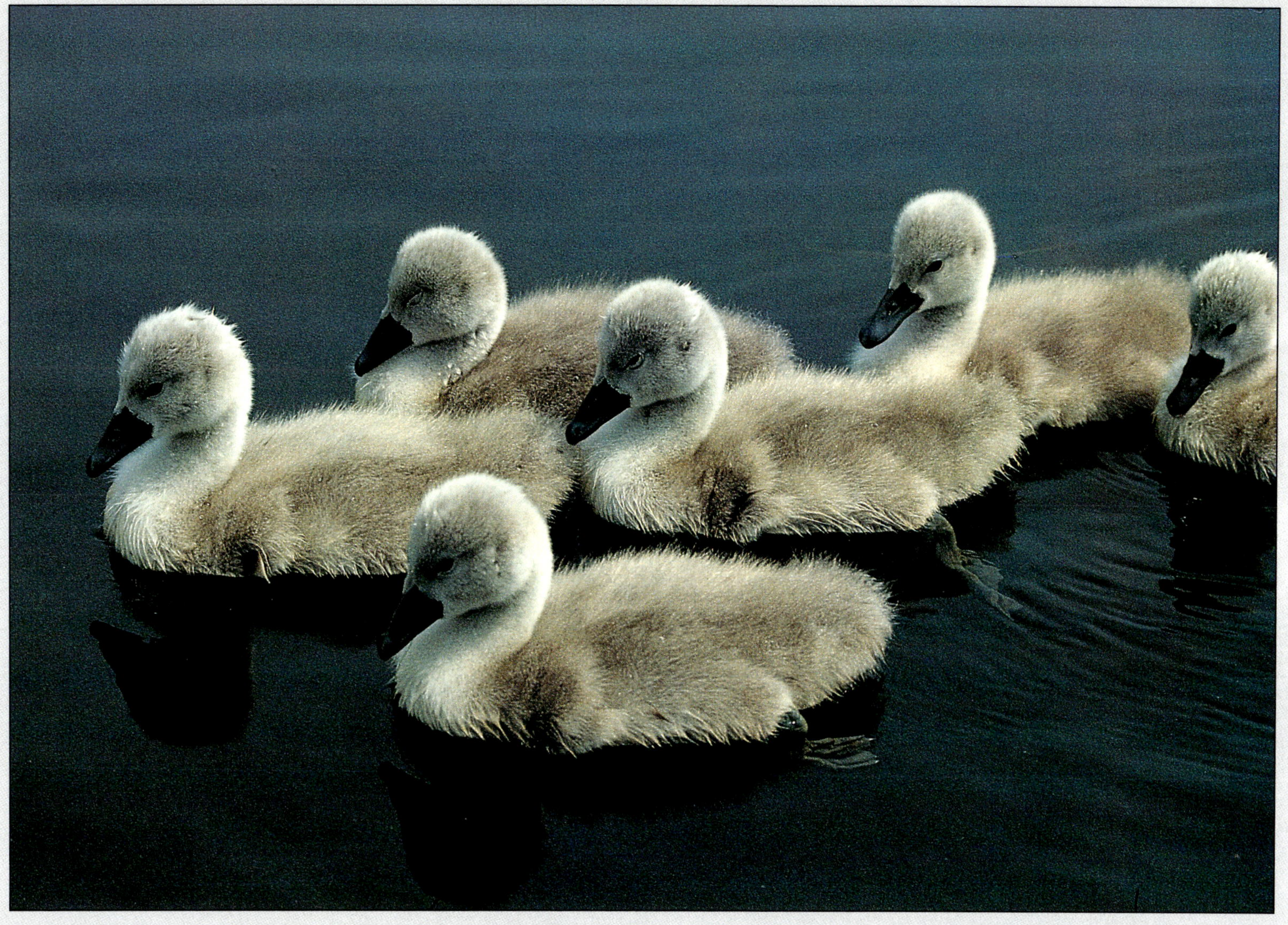

**Louise Dean**
United Kingdom
WINNER: YOUNG TELEGRAPH AWARD

### *Cygnets*

*"I often go for walks at Slapton Ley when I am on holiday in Devon. I had been watching a family of swans, and walked out on to a jetty to get closer. It was a clear day with a blue sky, which made the water appear blue, and highlighted the water droplets on the cygnets' fluffy down."*

Nikon F-601 with 75-300mm lens; 1/125 sec at f8; Kodachrome 200

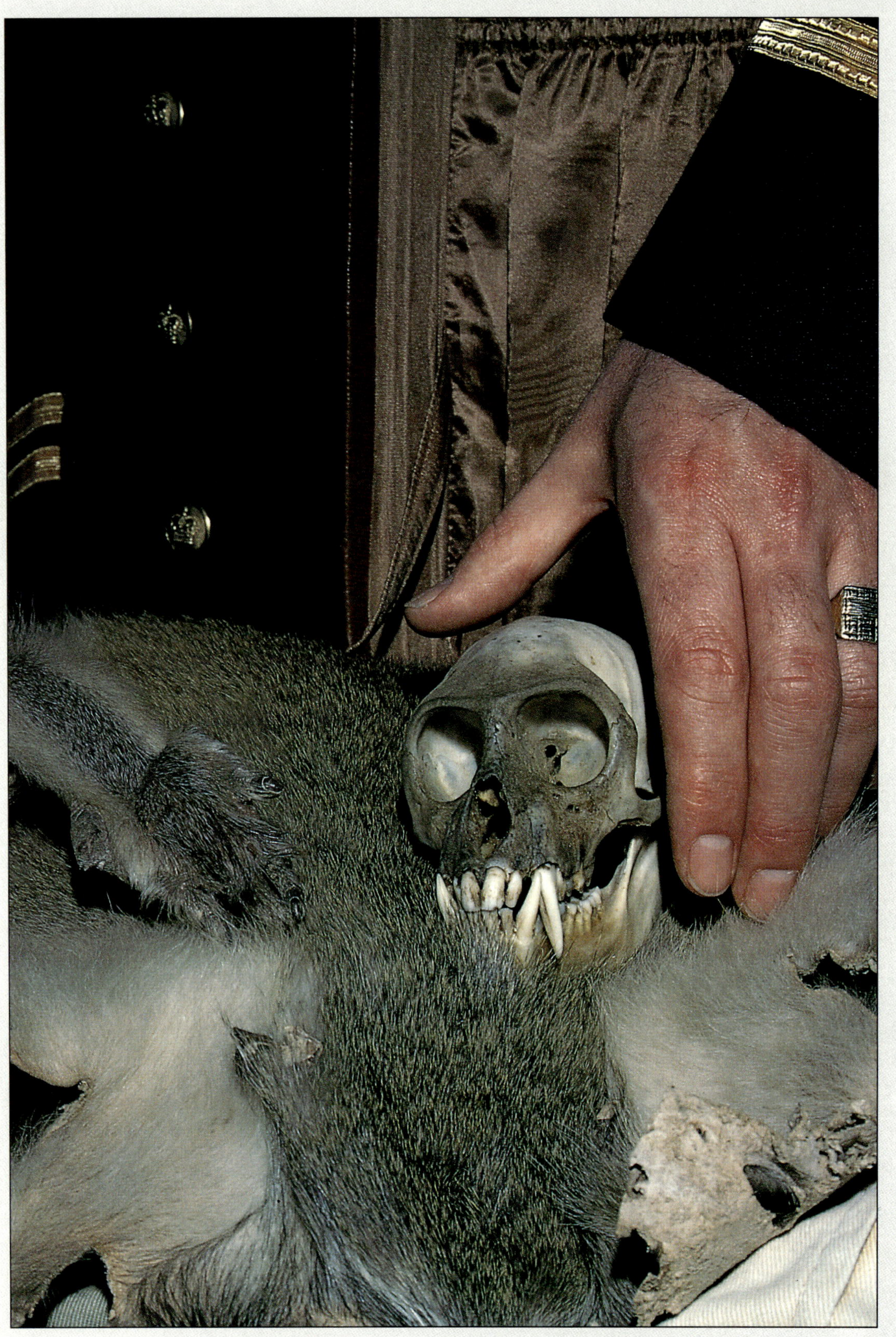

**Neil Davy**
United Kingdom
WINNER: BBC NEWSROUND YOUNG WILDLIFE PHOTOJOURNALIST AWARD

***Monkey skull and fur at Customs***

*"This monkey skull and fur were confiscated at Customs in Manchester Airport. In spite of the publicity, many people still bring back illegal souvenirs such as bones and coral, not realising they are further endangering rare species. They don't seem to realise that their money pays poachers to go out and kill another rare animal. I hope that this photograph will make people think twice about buying souvenirs such as skin handbags and ivory ornaments when on holiday."*

Pentax Z1 with 28-105mm lens; tripod; flash; 1/250 sec at f8; Kodachrome 64

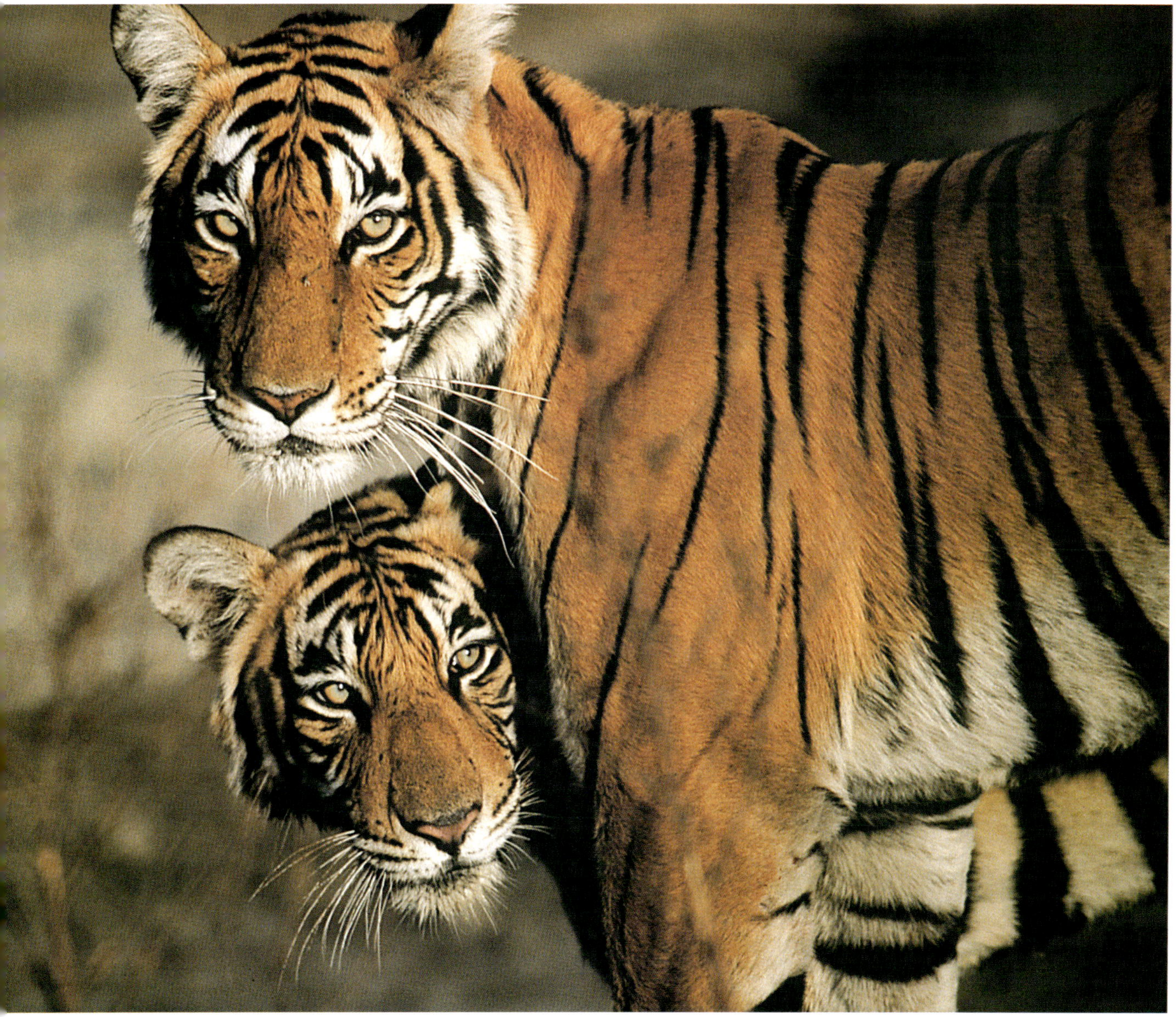

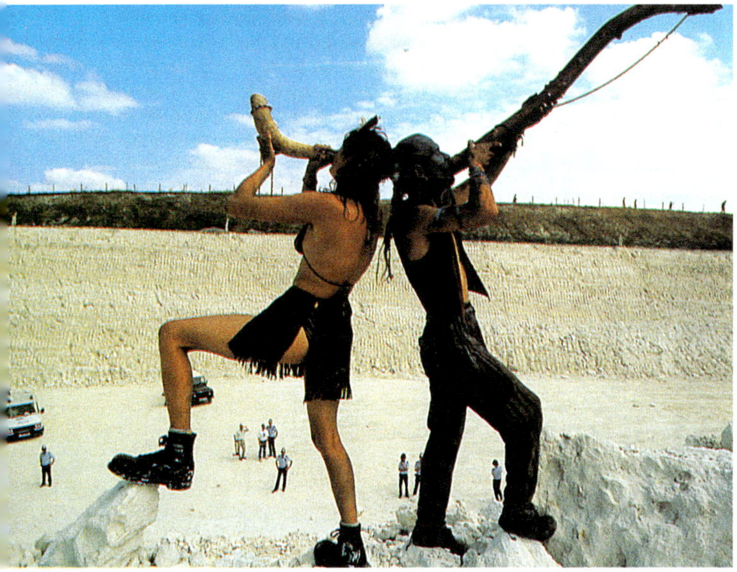

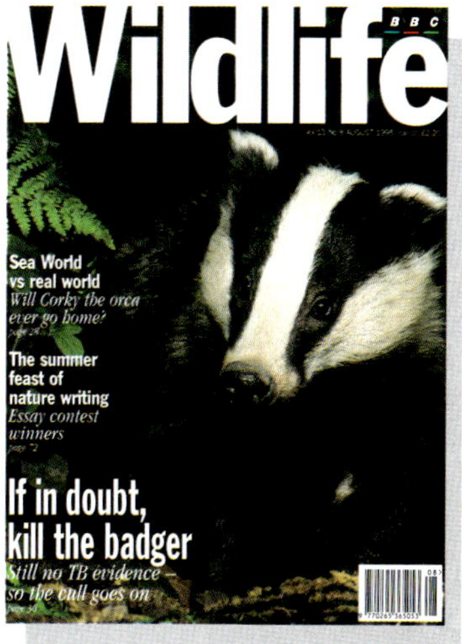

# THE NATURAL HISTORY MUSEUM

## South Kensington London

The Natural History Museum, one of the most striking Victorian buildings in the country, was designed by the architect Alfred Waterhouse to house the ever growing natural history collections from the British Museum, bequeathed to the nation by Sir Hans Sloane, and opened to the public in 1881.

Central to the Museum's mission is furthering the understanding of the natural world. It is at the forefront of modern exhibition development, making effective use of the latest techniques such as interactive computers and robotics, which can be seen in many of its exhibitions from Creepy Crawlies to Ecology. An annual highlight of its exhibition programme is the Wildlife Photographer of the Year Exhibition.

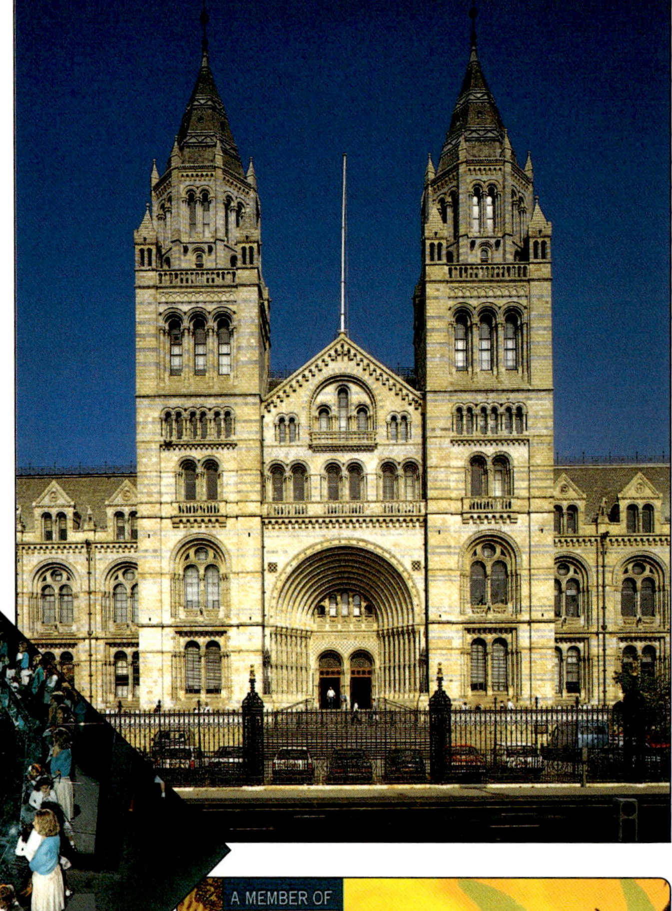

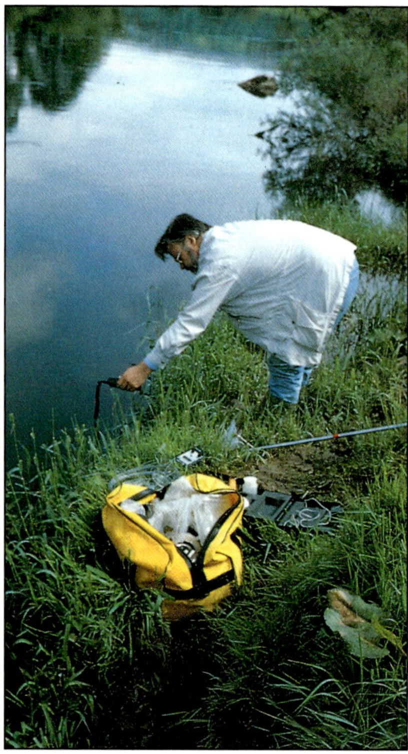

The Natural History Museum houses 68 million specimens in its collections providing an unrivalled taxonomic database for the work of over 350 scientists. Scientists at the Museum are involved on a global scale helping to tackle many of the environmental, sustainable resource use and health problems which threaten our planet. There are ten research and curation programmes ranging from conserving biodiversity and improving human health to maintaining environmental quality and efficient use of mineral resources.

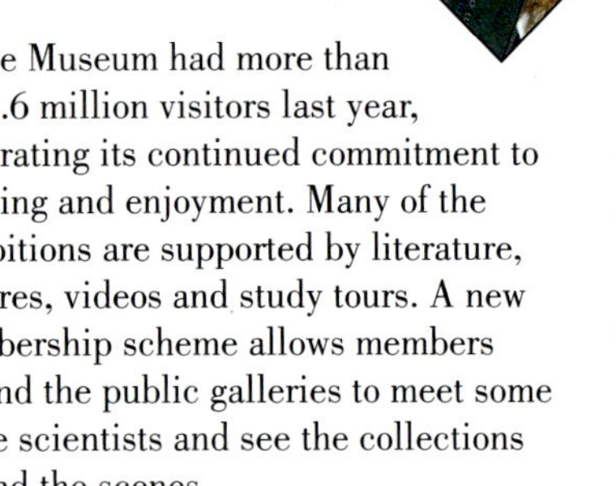

The Museum had more than 1.6 million visitors last year, illustrating its continued commitment to learning and enjoyment. Many of the exhibitions are supported by literature, lectures, videos and study tours. A new membership scheme allows members beyond the public galleries to meet some of the scientists and see the collections behind the scenes.

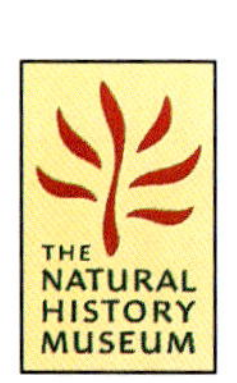

# Index of Photographers

*The numbers after the photographers' names indicate the pages on which their work can be found.*

*Telephone numbers are listed with international dialling codes from the UK in brackets - these should be replaced when dialling from other countries.*

**Cherry Alexander**
Front Jacket, 8/9
(Overall Winner 1995)

Higher Cottage
Manston
Sturminster Newton
Dorset
DT10 1EZ
UK

Tel: 01258 473006
Fax: 01258 473333

**Karl Ammann**
73, 106, 123

Box 437
Nanyuki
KENYA

Tel: (00254) 176 22448
Fax: (00254) 176 32407

**Claudia Auer**
126, 141

Etosha Ecological Institute
PO Okaukuejo via Outjo
NAMIBIA

Fax: (00264) 671 29853

**Steve Austin**
131

10 Burn Brae Avenue
Westhill
Inverness
IV1 2RG
UK

Tel: 01463 790533

**Andrew Bailey**
54

4 Buckingham House
Bois Lane
Chesham Bois
Amersham
Bucks
HP6 6BN
UK

Tel: 01494 432170

**André Bärtschi**
7, 64
(Overall Winner 1992)

Bannholzstrasse 10
FL-9490 Vaduz
LIECHTENSTEIN

Tel: (004175) 232 0338
Fax: (004175) 232 0339

Agent:
Planet Earth Pictures
4 Harcourt Street
London
W1H 1DS
UK

Tel: 0171 262 4427
Fax: 0171 706 4042

**Rajesh Bedi**
7 (Overall Winner 1986)

Bedi Films
E-19 Rajouri Gardens
New Delhi 110 027
INDIA

**Wayne R Bilenduke**
118/119

91 James Street
Churchill
Manitoba
R0B 0E0
CANADA

Tel: (001) 204 675 2834
Fax: (001) 204 675 2738

**Gary Braasch**
101

35700 Ninth Street, PO Box 400
Nehalem
Oregon 97131
USA

Tel: (001) 503 368 5091
Fax: (001) 503 368 5075

**Jim Brandenburg**
7 (Overall Winner 1988)

c/o Minden Pictures
24 Seascape Village
Aptos
CA 95003
USA

Tel: (001) 408 685 1911
Fax: (001) 408 685 1913

**Wolfgang Braunstein**
32

Schulstr. 18a
67435 Neustadt
GERMANY

Tel: (0049) 6321 69319

**Rosemary Calvert**
61, 77

2710G Holly Hall
Houston
Texas 77054
USA

Tel: (001) 713 741 4206
Fax: (001) 713 245 7850

**Laurie Campbell**
54

Rosewell Cottage
Paxton
Berwick-upon-Tweed
Scotland TD15 1TE
UK

Tel: 01289 386736
Fax: 01289 386736

**Tom Campbell**
110

238 Las Alturas Road
Santa Barbara
CA 93103
USA

Tel: (001) 805 965 4951/4901
Fax: (001) 805 563 4953

**Dominic Chaplin**
137

c/o Fermo
PO Box 108
Gordonvale
Queensland 4865
AUSTRALIA
Tel: (0061) 70 562658

**Martyn Colbeck**
7 (Overall winner 1993)

Julian Villa
West Hill
Wincanton
Somerset BA9 9BY
UK

Tel: 01963 32443

Agent:
Oxford Scientific Films
Lower Road
Long Hanborough
Witney
Oxfordshire 0X8 8LL
UK

Tel: 01993 881881

**Brandon D Cole**
112-117

S. 4822 Farr Road
Spokane
WA 99206
USA

Tel: (001) 509 922 4855
Fax: (001) 509 926 3746

**Richard Coomber**
69, 134/135

1 Haglane Copse
Pennington
Lymington
Hants
SO41 8DT
UK

Tel: 01590 674471

**Warren K Corning**
13

26 Tory Hole Road
Dorien
CT 06820
USA

Tel daytime: (001) 212 837 1765
Tel evening: (001) 203 656 1952
Fax: (001) 212 819 1169

**Daniel Cox**
76, 127

16595 Brackett Cree Road
Bozeman
Montana 59715
USA

Tel: (001) 406 686 4448
Fax: (001) 406 686 4448

**Neil Davy**
150

*35 Elm Avenue*
*Crosby*
*Liverpool*
L23 2SX
UK

*Tel:* 0151 924 9868

**Louise Dean**
149

*Tall Trees*
*Ellesmere Road*
*Weybridge*
*Surrey*
KT13 0HY
UK

*Tel:* 01932 847418

**Manfred Delpho**
108

*Am Rain 10*
*34281 Gudensberg*
GERMANY

*Tel:* (0049) 5603 3132

**Gertrud & Helmut Denzau**
103

*Memelstrasse 61*
*45259 Essen*
GERMANY

*Tel:* (0049) 201 465188
*Fax:* (0049) 201 465188

**Richard du Toit**
10/11, 74

*Box 100090*
*Scottsville 3209*
SOUTH AFRICA

*Tel:* (0027) 331 903 043

**Gerry Ellis**
104, 130

*4045A N. Massachusetts Avenue*
*Portland*
*Oregon 97227*
USA

*Tel daytime:* (001) 503 287 4179
*Tel evening:* (001) 503 287 3619
*Fax:* (001) 503 287 5087

**Frédéric Fève**
138

*06 Rue des Pres*
*54110 Dombasle*
FRANCE

*Tel daytime:* (0033) 87 33 26 24
*Tel evening:* (0033) 83 40 48 85

**Iwan T Fletcher**
145

*Pen Lon*
*Maes-y-Llan*
*Llandwrog*
*Gwynedd*
LL54 5TT
UK

*Tel:* 01286 830378
*Fax:* 01286 830378

**Csaba Forràsy**
60

*Nagytetenyi ut 234/F*
*Budapest*
H-1225
HUNGARY

*Tel daytime:* (0036) 1 463 1404
*Tel evening:* (0036) 1 226 8470
*Fax:* (0036) 1 463 3800

**Malcolm Freeman**
55

*5 West Ridge*
*Bourne End*
*Bucks*
SL8 5BU
UK

*Tel:* 016285 20104

**Jürgen Freund**
51

*Riezlerweg 23*
*80997 München*
GERMANY

*Tel:* (0049) 89 145479
*Fax:* (0049) 89 1411325

**Andrew Hadley**
56

*35 Belvedere Crescent*
*Bewdley*
*Worcs*
DY12 1JX
UK

*Tel:* 01229 400344

**Richard R Hansen**
34

*485 Shasta #25*
*Morro Bay*
CA 93442
USA

*Tel:* (001) 805 772 1705

**Frants Hartmann**
39

*PO Box 30181*
*Nairobi*
KENYA

*Tel:* (00254) 151 47252
*Fax:* (00254) 2 762178

**Russell Hartwell**
97

*11 Orchard Drive*
*Wooburn Green*
*Bucks*
HP10 0QN
UK

*Tel daytime:* 01753 889911
*Tel evening:* 01628 527996
*Fax:* 01753 887496

**Martin Harvey**
132

*Box 8945*
*Hennopsmeer*
*0046 Pretoria*
SOUTH AFRICA

*Tel:* (0027) 12 664 2241

**Hannu Hautala**
32

*Kiestingintie 12*
*93600 Kuusamo*
FINLAND

*Tel:* (00358) 89 8511 056
*Fax:* (00358) 89 8523 031

**Gilbert Hays**
124/125

*114 Berrigan Road*
*Devonport*
*Tasmania 7310*
AUSTRALIA

*Tel daytime:* (0061) 04 246510
*Tel evening:* (0061) 04 246750

**Brent Hedges**
88

*71 Arabella Street*
*Longueville*
NSW 2066
AUSTRALIA

*Tel daytime:* (0061) 2 231 4166
*Tel evening:* (0061) 2 428 4156
*Fax:* (0061) 2 221 3720

**Paul Hicks**
52/53

*26 Bridgestone Drive*
*Bourne End*
*Buckinghamshire*
SL8 5XH
UK

*Tel daytime:* 01753 889911
*Tel evening:* 01628 524996

**Michael Hill**
147, 148

*Benson House*
*Wellington College*
*Crowthorne*
*Berkshire*
RG11 7PU
UK

*Tel:* 01344 780650

**Dr Mike Hill**
19, 105

*PO Box 25005*
*Awali*
BAHRAIN

*Tel:* (00973) 756292
*Fax:* (00973) 753624

**Richard Hill**
146

*PO Box 25005*
*Awali*
BAHRAIN

*Tel:* (00973) 756292
*Fax:* (00973) 753624

**Rachel Hingley**
146

*19 Mount Pleasant Road*
*Norton*
*Stockton-on-Tees*
TS20 2HX
UK

*Tel:* 01642 531724

**Ross Hoddinott**
144

*Higher Broxwater*
*Kilkhampton*
*Bude*
*Cornwall*
EX23 9RL
UK

*Tel:* 01288 321328

**Klaus Honal**
33

*Lehenfeldstr. 20*
*91717 Wassertrüdingen*
GERMANY

*Tel daytime:* (0049) 9853 339173
*Tel evening:* (0049) 9832 1246
*Fax:* (0049) 9832 1246

**Kenneth Howard**
63

*10 Woodside Court*
*San Anselmo*
CA 94960
USA

*Tel daytime:* (001) 510 271 7504
*Tel evening:* (001) 415 453 0377
*Fax:* (001) 510 208 2683

**Ernie Janes**
22

*Park House Studio*
*Northchurch Common*
*Berkhamsted*
*Hertfordshire*
HP4 1LR
UK

*Tel:* 01442 871342

**Roger L Johnson**
98/99

*813 Orange Blossom Way*
*Danville*
CA 94526
USA

*Tel:* (001) 510 820 6135
*Fax:* (001) 510 820 6535

**Adam Jones**
58

*3415 Rems Road*
*Louisville*
KY 40241
USA

*Tel:* (001) 502 327 0416
*Fax:* (001) 502 327 8032

**Burt Jones**
**& Maurine Shimlock**
85

PO Box 162931
*Austin*
TX 78716
USA

*Tel:* (001) 512 328 1201
*Fax:* (001) 512 328 1201

**Rob Jordan**
57

*Stonechats*
*Espley Hall*
*Morpeth*
*Northumberland*
NE61 3DJ
UK

*Tel:* 01670 512761
*Fax:* 01670 510277

**Bob Jorens**
129

*Berkensweg 3*
*B-2950 Kapellen*
BELGIUM

*Tel daytime:* (0032) 3 664 2712
*Tel evening:* (0032) 3 664 9991

**Hans C Kappel**
40

*Hugo-Preuss-Strasse 32*
*D-34131 Kassel*
GERMANY

*Tel daytime:* (0049) 5594 1864
*Tel evening:* (0049) 561 313943
*Fax:* (0049) 561 313943

**Paul Kay**
90

*Bodwyn*
*Radcliffe Road*
*Criccieth*
*Gwynedd*
LL52 0BE
UK

*Tel:* 01766 522404
*Fax:* 01766 522404

**Richard & Julia Kemp**
7 (*Overall winners* 1984)

*Valley Farmhouse*
*Whitwell*
*Norwich* NR10 4SQ
UK

*Tel:* 01603 872498

**Brian Kenney**
30

*9067 Hilolo Lane*
*Venice*
*Florida 34293*
USA

*Tel:* (001) 941 426 4284
*Fax:* (001) 941 492 9724

**Stephen Kirkpatrick**
14

PO Box 31414
*Jackson*
MS 39286-1414
USA

*Tel:* (001) 601 362 7100
*Fax:* (001) 601 981 0055

**Heidi & Hans-Jürgen Koch**
18, 66/67, 108

*Schillerstr. 6*
*D-27472 Cuxhaven*
GERMANY

*Tel:* (0049) 4721 34352
*Fax:* (0049) 4721 33426

*Agent:*
*Bilderberg*
*Hoheluftchaussee 139*
*20253 Hamburg*
GERMANY

*Tel:* (0049) 40 420 6655
*Fax:* (0049) 40 420 7876

**Frank Krahmer**
71

*Bahnhofstr. 13F*
*D-82024 Taufkirchen*
GERMANY

*Tel:* (0049) 89 4133 2996

**Dr P Kumar**
122

*2/81 Roop Nagar*
*Delhi*
INDIA 110 007

*Tel:* (0091) 11 251 5852
*Fax:* (0091) 11 713 7060

*Agent:*
*Planet Earth Pictures*
*4 Harcourt Street*
*London* W1H 1DS
UK

*Tel:* 0171 262 4427
*Fax:* 0171 706 4042

**Maurizio Lanini**
95

*Via Trevignano Snc*
*00066 Manziana (Rm)*
ITALY

*Tel:* (0039) 6 9967 4260

**Frans Lanting**
7 (Overall winner 1991)

Frans Lanting Photography
1985 Smith Grade
Santa Cruz
California 95060
USA

Tel: (001) 408 427 9707
Fax: (001) 408 423 8324

**Antti Leinonen**
15

Koirisärkäntie 4 C 10
88900 Kuhmo
FINLAND

Tel: (00358) 866 551775

**Brian Lightfoot**
59

Parkhead Croft
Balandro
Johnshaven
Montrose
DD10 0PU
UK

Tel daytime: 01674 830736
Tel evening: 01561 362017
Fax: 01674 830736

**Doug Locke**
41, 77

1415 Oakbrook East
Rochester Hills
Michigan 48307-1127
USA

Tel daytime: (001) 810 656 1625
Tel evening: (001) 810 826 6286

**Eliot Lyons**
121

Box 92153
Norwood
Johannesburg
SOUTH AFRICA

Tel daytime: (0027) 11 788 4706
Tel evening: (0027) 11 887 0762
Fax: (0027) 11 440 9241

**Hilary G Mackay**
111

Flat 4, Gribton House
Newbridge
Dumfries
DG2 0YJ
UK

Tel: 01387 721125

**Thomas D Mangelsen**
7, 28, 143
(Overall Winner 1994)

Images of Nature
PO Box 2935
2nd Level, Gaslight Alley
Jackson, Wyoming 83001
USA

Tel: (001) 307 733 6179
Fax: (001) 307 733 6184

**Marko Masterl**
75

Rozna ulica 26
61330 Kocevje
SLOVENIA

Tel daytime: (00386) 61 854 313
Tel evening: (00386) 61 851 646
Fax: (00386) 61 854 646

**Chris Mattison**
68

138 Dalewood Road
Sheffield
S8 0EF
UK

Tel: 0114 236 4433
Fax: 0114 236 4433

**Hisaaki Mihara**
65

Kichijoji-Honcho
Musasino City
4-6-6
JAPAN

Tel: (0081) 422 20 3552
Fax: (0081) 422 20 3552

**Florian Möllers**
70

Im Kamp 52
D-49152 Bad Essen
GERMANY

Tel & Fax: (0049) 547 22726

**Steve Morgan**
133

33 Gay Street
Bath
BA1 2NT
UK

Tel daytime: 0860 297513
Tel evening: 01225 840515
Fax: 01225 313553

**William Munoz**
50

PO Box 370
12023 Watson Road
St Iguatuis
Montana 59865
USA

Tel: (001) 406 745 4222
Fax: (001) 406 745 4222

**Amos Nachoum**
86

2000 Broadway
Suite 1204
San Francisco
CA 94115
USA

Tel: (001) 415 923 9865
Fax: (001) 415 776 8489

**Kimio Naito**
89

Chiba Ken
Ichikawa Si Siohama
4-2-45-203
JAPAN

Tel: (0081) 473 99 3544

**Jørn Areklett Omre**
128

Guristuvn 2
0690 Oslo
NORWAY

Tel: (0047) 2 226 1210
Fax: (0047) 2 226 1210

**Nikolai A Orlov**
91

Zoological Institute of RAN
Universitetskaya Nab. 1
Sankt- Petersburg
199034
RUSSIA

Tel: (007812) 567 00 21
Fax: (007812) 218 29 41

**Ben Osborne**
139

Sunningdale
Pontesford
Pontesbury
Shropshire
SY5 0UN
UK

Tel: 01743 790165
Fax: 01743 791982

**Pete Oxford**
78, 132

c/o 130 Fore Street
Barton
Torquay
Devon
TQ2 8DP
UK

Tel: 01803 327037

**Bijal Patel**
142

77 Barrow Street, Apt. 2RW
New York
NY 10014
USA

Tel: (001) 212 727 0928

**Doug Perrine**
25, 36/37, 86

6800 SW 40 ST #499
Miami
FL 33155-3708
USA

Tel: (001) 305 669 0118
Fax: (001) 305 669 9936

### Jörn Pilon
61

*Patrijzenlaan 67*
*3233 BN Oostvoorne*
NETHERLANDS

*Tel:* (0031) 1815 3892

### Linda Pitkin
43

*12 Coningsby Road*
*South Croydon*
CR2 6QP
UK

*Tel:* 0181 668 8168
*Fax:* 0181 668 8168

### Fritz Pölking
16, 20, 62

*Münsterstrasse 71*
*D-48268 Greven*
GERMANY

*Tel daytime:* (0049) 2571 52115
*Tel evening:* (0049) 2571 2864
*Fax:* (0049) 2571 97098

### Jagdeep Rajput
46

*L-5, Hans Apartments*
*East Arjun Nagar*
*CBD Shahdara*
*Delhi*
INDIA 110 032

*Tel daytime:* (0091) 11 462 2939
*Tel evening:* (0091) 11 245 4178

### Tapani Räsänen
92

*Tasalantie 27*
*Joutseno Fin-54100*
FINLAND

*Tel:* (00358) 534 534 929

### Eric Robert & Sylvie Bergerot
111

*57 Rue de Malte*
*Paris 75011*
FRANCE

*Tel daytime:* (0033) 1 4271 9725
*Tel evening:* (0033) 1 4355 9444
*Fax:* (0033) 1 4271 9484

### James H Robinson
31

PO Box 564
*Alamo*
GA 30411
USA

*Tel:* (001) 912 568 7800

### Andy Rouse
110, 133

*Brambles*
*75 Furze Hill Road*
*Headley Down*
*Bordon*
*Hants* GU35 8HB
UK

*Tel:* 01428 712371
*Fax:* 01428 712371

### Jouni Ruuskanen
7 (*Overall winner* 1989)

*Ratakatu 31 As 14*
*87100 Kajaani*
FINLAND

*Tel:* (00358) 86 133026

### Kevin Schafer
12

*2148 Halleck SW*
*Seattle*
WA 98116
USA

*Tel:* (001) 206 933 1668
*Fax:* (001) 206 933 1659

### Heinz Schimpke
84

*Bergheimerstr. 135*
*69115 Heidelberg*
GERMANY

*Tel:* (0049) 6221 26525
*Fax:* (0049) 6221 26525

### Gary Schultz
24, 136

PO Box 81481
*1070 Molly Road*
*Fairbanks*
AK 99708
USA

*Tel daytime:* (001) 907 451 2732
*Tel evening:* (001) 907 455 6988

### Jonathan Scott
7 (*Overall Winner* 1987)

PO Box 24499
*Nairobi*
KENYA

*Agent:*
*Planet Earth Pictures*
*4 Harcourt Street*
*London* W1H 1DS
UK

*Tel:* 0171 262 4427
*Fax:* 0171 706 4042

### Douglas D Seifert
42, 87

*c/o Tiny Bubbles Expeditions*
*1001 Alternate A1A*
*Jupiter*
FL 33477
USA

*Tel daytime:* (001) 407 744 7884
*Tel evening:* (001) 407 746 7896
*Fax:* (001) 407 746 7950

### Anup Shah
21, 48, 49

*c/o 29 Cornfield Road*
*Bushey*
*Herts*
WD2 3TB
UK

*Tel:* 0181 950 8705

*Agent:*
*Planet Earth Pictures*
*4 Harcourt Street*
*London*
W1H 1DS
UK

*Tel:* 0171 262 4427
*Fax:* 0171 706 4042

### Wendy Shattil & Bob Rozinski
7, 96, 120
(*Overall Winners* 1990)

PO Box 37422
*Denver*
*Colorado* 80237
USA

*Tel:* (001) 303 721 1991
*Fax:* (001) 303 721 1116

### Jill Sneesby & Barrie Wilkins
22, 80, 93

*Allied Building*
*93 Main Street*
*Port Elizabeth* 6001
SOUTH AFRICA

*Tel daytime:* (0027) 41 553826
*Tel evening:* (0027) 41 511853
*Fax:* (0027) 41 560727

### Gabriela Staebler
17, 72

*Raldingerstr. 29*
*81377 Munich*
GERMANY

*Tel:* (0049) 89 715780
*Fax:* (0049) 89 715780

### Charles G Summers Jr
7 (*Overall Winner* 1985)

*Wild Images*
*6392 South Yellowstone Way*
*Aurora*
*Colorado* 80016
USA

*Tel:* (001) 303 690 6664
*Fax:* (001) 303 693 4750

### Peter Thomas
94

*4735 Quebec Street*
*Vancouver* BC
V5V 3M2
CANADA

*Tel:* (001) 604 873 2767

### Darryl Torckler
38, 82/83

PO Box 33-693
*Takapuna*
*Auckland* 9
NEW ZEALAND

*Tel:* (0064) 9 480 0832
*Fax:* (0064) 9 480 0832

**Ronno Tramper**
81

PO Box 16
*3984 ZG Odijk*
NETHERLANDS

*Tel daytime:* (0031) 30533484
*Tel evening:* (0031) 340570977

**Roberto Travesi Ydañez**
109

*Ancha de Santo Domingo* N 6
*Granada* 18009
SPAIN

*Tel daytime:* (0034) 585 21164
*Tel evening:* (0034) 958 228455
*Fax:* (0034) 585 21165

**Duncan Usher**
94

*Gut Wissmannshof* 3
*34355 Staufenberg*
GERMANY

*Tel:* (0049) 5543 3450
*Fax:* (0049) 5543 4545

**Philip van den Berg**
79

PO Box 13244
*Cascades*
*Pietermaritzburg* 3202
SOUTH AFRICA

*Tel daytime:* (0027) 331 949121
*Tel evening:* (0027) 331 472728
*Fax:* (0027) 331 427512

**Gus van Dyk**
47

PO Box 777
*Parklands* 2121
SOUTH AFRICA

*Tel:* (0027) 1465 55357
*Fax:* (0027) 1465 55525

**Colin Varndell**
55

*The Happy Return*
*Netherbury*
*Bridport*
*Dorset*
DT6 5NH
UK

*Tel:* 01308 488341

**Tom Walker**
23

PO Box 146
*Denali Park*
AK 99755
USA

**Uwe Walz**
33

*Pommernweg* 11
D-21521 *Wohltorf*
GERMANY

*Tel:* (0049) 4104 3122
*Fax:* (0049) 4104 80412

**Margaret Welby**
50

8 *The Cobbins*
*Waltham Abbey*
*Essex*
EN9 1LH
UK

*Tel daytime:* 01992 712579
*Tel evening:* 01992 710506

**Roger Wilmshurst**
26/27

*Sandhill Farmhouse*
*Washington*
*Pulborough*
*West Sussex*
RH20 4AJ
UK

*Tel:* 01903 892210
*Fax:* 01903 892888

**David Woodfall**
107

14 *Bull Lane*
*Denbigh*
*Clwyd*
LL16 3SW
UK

*Tel:* 01745 815903
*Fax:* 01745 815903

**Konrad Wothe**
29, 35, 102

*Maenherstr.* 27A
D-81375 *München*
GERMANY

*Tel:* (0049) 89 798675
*Fax:* (0049) 89 7914234

*Agent:*
LOOK GMBH
*Fraunhofer Str.*5
80469 *München*
GERMANY

*Tel:* (0049) 89 260 6320
*Fax:* (0049) 89 260 6322

**Martin Wright**
133

180 *Albion Road*
*London*
N16 9JR
UK

*Tel:* 0171 275 7432
*Fax:* 0171 275 7432

**Dr Mamoru Yoshida**
100

4485 *St Andrews Drive*
*Boynton Beach*
FL 33436
USA

*Tel:* (001) 407 734 5559
*Fax:* (001) 407 734 5559

**Solvin Zankl**
104, 140

*Nienbrügger Weg* 163
24107 *Kiel*
GERMANY

*Tel:* (0049) 431 311581
*Fax:* (0049) 431 311581

**Sven Zellner**
147

*Am Trimmelter Hof* 146
D-54296 *Trier*
GERMANY

*Tel:* (0049) 651 10979
*Fax:* (0049) 651 8103 377

**Jean-Pierre Zwaenepoel**
44/45

*Sint-Michiellaam* 57
B-8200 *Brugge*
BELGIUM

*Tel daytime:* (0032) 50 442647
*Tel evening:* (0032) 50 382501
*Fax:* (0032) 50 339463